CLOSE ENCOUNTERS ON CAPITOL HILL

Robert M. Stanley

Providence, Rhode Island

Photographs related to this book are available for free at:
www.unicusmagazine.com

Printed in the United States of America
First printing October, 2006
Revised edition March, 2011

Contents

Acknowledgments

I would like to thank my family for supporting my time-consuming research during the writing of this book. Although we had to sacrifice much of our time together in order for me to complete this book, I believe my investigation of UFOs in Washington, D.C., will eventually benefit humanity.

I would also like to thank the other people that helped make this book possible. They are: Derrel Sims, Robert Dean, Jerry Wills, Nassim Haramein, Philip Krapf, Daniel Sheehan, David Adair, Wendelle Stevens, with special thanks to DC photographer Wilbur Allen.

Finally, I must acknowledge the following sources of public-domain information I accessed to compile a chronological summary of UFO sightings in Washington, D.C., and the surrounding area. Special thanks to: NICAP, NUFORC, BCUFOCC, CAUS, MUFON, HBCCUFO, UFO Database, UFO Info.com, NUFOC, NARCAP, CUFOS, Presidential UFO. com, UFO Casebook, UFO Evidence.org, UFODNA.com, and BibleUFO. com.

Introduction

Over the past 50 years, many people have asked, "If UFOs are real, why don't they just land on the White House lawn?" The aliens would then presumably request that they be taken to our leader. Unfortunately, we don't have one leader on this world, we have many, and most of them can't agree on anything. Furthermore, aliens are not welcome here, so why would they waste their time going to the White House? Obviously they didn't. Instead, they chose to land on Capitol Hill. I am sure many people wonder how an historic event like that could occur without being reported by the media. Well, that's mainly what this book is about.

I became involved in this story quite innocently one morning, in the spring of 2005, after receiving a forwarded e-mail from a professional photographer in Washington, D.C. At the time, I had no idea that this information would change my life. In retrospect, I could have just deleted that e-mail and its photos and dismissed the whole DC UFO story as a mistake or a hoax.

Instead, after careful consideration, I decided to thoroughly investigate all the eye-witness reports and photographic evidence of UFOs on Capitol Hill, in July of 2002. As a result, the deeper I dug into the rich history of UFOs over Washington, D.C., the more I realized it was a huge story that was largely being ignored.

Granted, the alien incursions of July and August in 1952 had made headlines around the world, and there were a couple of clear, night-time photographs of UFOs over the Capitol building from 1952 that I found intriguing. But those events were officially dismissed as reflections from lights on the ground or were blamed on the weather. As a result, the media's interest in UFOs over DC had simply evaporated.

In fact, dramatic and frequent alien incursions continued to occur after the summer of 1952. According to the historic record, the East Coast, specifically the area around Washington, D.C., was clearly a preferred destination for UFOs, but for some reason, this was never reported.

The situation would remain that way until July of 2002 – the 50-year anniversary of the UFO invasion of Washington, D.C., in 1952. During my investigation, I learned that UFOs were photographed or witnessed in DC on July 4, 16, 20, 26, 30 and 31 of 2002.

To their credit, on July 26 and 27, *FOX News* and the *Washington Post* reported that UFOs were seen over DC and that NORAD had scrambled jets to intercept the alien spacecraft. However, in the end, the results were the same as 1952. The UFOs continued to penetrate our controlled airspace and the media and the military officially ignored the fact.

Despite my best efforts, after many months of researching the situation, I had not found a way to get the media and the government to begin a public dialogue about the ongoing, alien incursions of restricted and prohibited airspace around Washington, D.C.

I spent many hours on the telephone and exchanging e-mail with various people that worked in the nation's capital and the media, but they all reacted the same way: paranoid. Although I understood the government's fear and hesitation in addressing this issue, I firmly believed that the public needed to be told that UFOs were routinely violating American airspace, even in DC.

It seemed to me that when the American public was fully informed about what had really been going on in DC for more than 50 years, they would begin to ask intelligent questions of their political and military leaders regarding alien incursions of controlled airspace by UFOs in America.

CHAPTER ONE

Contact at the Capitol

The controversial subject of illegal aliens flooding across America's borders continued to be a heated debate. The issue had clearly polarized public opinion, but I wondered how people would react when they discovered America had a similar problem with UFOs repeatedly violating its prohibited and restricted air space.

As the editor of *UNICUS* magazine, I was dedicated to the exploration of UFO and ET phenomena. I had grown accustom to meeting unique individuals with extraordinary experiences. Yet, I was absolutely amazed when I learned that someone had allegedly photographed UFOs landing on Capitol Hill from 12:30 – 1:00 a.m., on July 16, 2002.

Admittedly, I was skeptical at first and wanted to know all the details regarding the event. When I initially spoke with the photographer, he agreed to share his story and photos only if I promised to publish all of his material. By that time, nearly three years after his ET encounters, he was extremely frustrated by the lack of media interest in his story and photos. He said, "No one will touch this story, but the pictures speak for themselves."

And, there was another catch. The photographer did not want me to reveal his identity. He feared the potential negative publicity that could be directed at him which could jeopardize his credibility as a professional photographer and hurt him financially.

Although I understood his dilemma, I explained that I could not protect his identity forever. Eventually, someone would figure out that he was involved and report that fact. However, I agreed to let the DC photographer remain anonymous while I reported the story. I then wrote an article and conducted an in-depth interview with him regarding his close encounters and photos which were published internationally in *NEXUS* magazine and on the Internet at *UNICUS* magazine.com. Because of the positive response we received from that article and the authentic images, I am now able to reveal the photographer's name is Wilbur Allen.

Strange as it seemed, during a four month period in 2002, Mr. Allen had inadvertently captured images of UFOs three times within a three mile radius of the Washington Monument. I found it highly unlikely that these events were all just a coincidence.

After having dozens of candid telephone conversations and exchanging hundreds of e-mails with Mr. Allen, I got the impression he was sincere about his story and photos. However, I was a bit surprised when he explained that his first close encounter with aliens was 1962, when he was a child. Actually, that information helped explain why almost exactly 40 years later, he was able to capture some of the most incredible DC UFO images ever recorded on film.

The clear, color UFO photos taken at the Capitol made me wonder if our current leaders in Washington, D.C., were aware of those events. After all, part of their job was to be informed. Most of them were briefed daily from a variety of sources. Oddly enough, one such source was Mr. Allen who was a professional cameraman and broadcast engineer that had lived and worked in Washington, D.C., for many years.

He felt it was his patriotic duty to alert the proper authorities and report what had happened. As a result, he went to the Capitol building a few days after the events of July 16, 2002, and met with members of the detective division of the Capitol Police. He then showed them the UFO images he had taken Senate side of the Capitol on July 16 and carefully recalled the night's events.

After a brief consideration of the evidence, Mr. Allen was told that "no crime took place," therefore the detectives would not make a report. Undeterred, he then sent a copy of his photographs and a detailed report to the Office of the President at the White House, but there was no reply. He then contacted officials at the Pentagon. Not surprisingly, there was no official response from the U.S. military either.

Mr. Allen's UFO images were highly controversial and had serious implications for America's national security. I knew that most people would presume he had created the images in a computer, so I encouraged him to have his negatives and slides authenticated, which he eventually did.

When I asked Mr. Allen why he decided to share his controversial photos with the government and the public, he said, "Because they prove that we are not alone in the universe. My photos are evidence of alien incursions of restricted U.S. air space. We are presently focused on the Middle East and other countries where there clearly is trouble, but I think there are much greater problems in Washington, D.C., that need to be looked at."

I then reminded Mr. Allen that the Department of Homeland Security had announced it wanted passenger lists for all flights coming into or even just passing over the U.S. I wondered what his opinion of that was in relation to UFOs violating the prohibited airspace over the nations' capital. He replied that, "It's good to know who is entering our air space on the human side, but I am more interested in the question of who or what is entering our air space on the non-human side. That is a question that we should examine more closely."

I was cynical and reminded Mr. Allen that he wouldn't know if an American intelligence agency was already investigating the matter covertly. After thinking it over for a moment, he replied, "I'm not sure whether this is or isn't being investigated by our government. But one thing I can state with certainty is that when I invited the retired, naval, optical physicist Dr. Bruce Maccabee to assess my images, he initially told me that my images were simply lens flares. That is a level of cover up. There is a level of inconsistency here that is obvious."

However, after spending more time reviewing the data over a few years, Dr. Maccabee did change his opinion about Mr. Allen's images. I learned that Mr. Allen had a growing number of allies regarding his work. After sending his photographic evidence to the retired nuclear physicist, Stanton Friedman, Mr. Allen received an e-mail stating, "I am happy to acknowledge the legitimacy of your photos and the absence of a conventional explanation for them."

I found it incredibly interesting that Mr. Allen had worked for *ABC News* from 1982 to 2000 as a Senior Network Engineer. He worked extensively at the White House and on Air Force One during the Reagan, Bush and Clinton administrations. When asked if he had photographed any UFOs during that time, he said, "That was not a part of my life. It was not something that I set out to do intentionally. The UFOs just happened to be there after I left *ABC*."

I wanted to know why Mr. Allen had walked away from *ABC News* after 18 years of exceptional service. He explained that he wanted to help take care of his father, a Vietnam veteran, who was dying from exposure to the biological weapon called Agent Orange.

One day, while caring for his father, Mr. Allen decided to show him the DC UFO pictures. At that moment, his father grew angry and ordered him not to show the images to anyone. A few weeks later, the Mr. Allen's father passed away. It was a strange twist of fate, but if his father had lived, he would have prevented the DC UFO photographs from ever being released publicly.

Mr. Allen told me that, "My dad served honorably in the Air Force for many years. As a master sergeant, he was involved in advanced warfare in Vietnam. He was a heavyweight scientist for the Precision Measurement Electronics Lab. His work was classified and covert."

As a result, Mr. Allen grew up on military bases around the world attending military school. He recalled that, "I was initially contacted by Extraterrestrial Biological Entities (EBEs) at a base in England called Sculthorpe which is located near another base called Lakenheath. One night, I woke up and saw that there were a whole bunch of EBEs entering my room. That was 1962, and I was five years old.

"At that time, we lived off base in Sherringham, England. It was a farming town. There was no base housing for us to move into then, so we stayed there temporarily. That night, something made me wake up and that's when I saw the alien entities coming into the room. I tried to scream and wake up my older brother, or run, but nothing happened. No screams came out. My brother would not wake up. I was unable to move, and at that point, I just blacked out."

When I asked Mr. Allen if he was sure he was awake during that event, he replied, "That experience is something I can't forget even decades later. In fact, it is the cause of my current sleep disorder. I can't sleep well at night. I can take quite a few *Excedrin P.M.* and still be awake, so I choose to sleep in the day."

I had read of similar cases. No amount of therapy or medication seemed to help certain people that suffered from that level of post-traumatic stress. Mr. Allen told me that, "I suffer from a trauma that shocked the hell out of me. I can't make it go away, and honestly I would rather be awake at night to see what is going on than to be asleep and suddenly wake up to something paranormal."

The second time Mr. Allen encountered EBEs in his bedroom at night was a few years later, in 1967, while living near McGuire Air Force Base, in New Jersey. He was about ten-years old at the time, and it scared him silly.

Base housing was situated directly across the street from a farm pasture, so there was plenty of open area for a UFO to land. One night, he awoke and found there was a single alien entity in his bedroom. He was in an absolute panic and hid under the pillows and covers until morning. For some reason, that particular alien gave him the impression it was female.

More alien encounters occurred in the Mr. Allen's life many years later while living in Washington, D.C. Those events transpired around the time he took the pictures at the U.S. Capitol. When asked to elaborate, he said, "I do a lot of digital recording, both audio and video. I use a program called *Avid*, and mini disks, and all these other portable devices in the digital media. I have electronic equipment that in case of a power failure has a backup power source, so an LED light is always on somewhere.

"One night, I awoke into total darkness which is a physical impossibility in my home, because even during a total power failure you can see ambient city light coming in the windows or from lights on my equipment. But that night, I saw absolutely nothing. There was just total blackness.

"I went back to sleep and didn't think anything of it at the moment. I woke up again shortly afterwards, but this time I was laying on my back, and there were people above me looking down as though I was on an observation platform of some sort; like in a medical school.

"But then, I just went back to sleep. I thought that was a bit odd because I went totally back into blackness. The next time I awoke, I was back home, and the first thing out of my mouth was, 'Oh? They put me back?' I was in my home, in Washington, D.C., that night. That event occurred around the time I took the pictures at the U.S. Capitol."

Clearly, 2002 was an extremely strange year for Mr. Allen. In fact, the odds argued against anyone accidentally photographing UFOs three times in four months. As strange as it seemed, I began considering the possibility that Mr. Allen had been influenced by aliens to provide his photographic services to them.

His first UFO photographs in DC were taken near the Washington Monument on July 4, 2002, during a fireworks show. That night, he was on assignment for the city of Washington, D.C.

The second set of UFO photographs were taken at the U.S. Capitol on the night of July 16, 2002. At that time, UFOs landed on the Capitol building roof, and in the surrounding park. Coincidentally, Mr. Allen was shooting an album cover for a local recording artist that was appropriately named "Bear Witness" at the Capitol.

The third and final time Mr. Allen photographed a UFO that year was on the night of November 11, 2002. That high-resolution image clearly showed a small, spherical UFO hovering over a young, female model's head. The blonde woman was standing on a street in Washington, D.C., totally unaware of the tiny UFO floating over her head. I found it interesting that the metallic sphere reflected the yellow color of her hair indicating it was a highly polished surface.

Unfortunately, one of the DC UFO images came at a price. While Mr. Allen was taking the final exposure of the night at the Capitol, on the 16th of July, he was burned by radiation from a group of UFOs as they accelerated away. That incident occurred Senate side of the U.S. Capitol which really surprised me, because I thought that area had been completely secured after 9/11.

Mr. Allen recalled that, "At the time, I didn't know I had set up my camera equipment underneath all these UFOs. According to my images, a group of four UFOs warped out and left the area. At that time, I captured an image which I believe shows these UFOs in lateral and upward motions just prior to them entering a 'worm hole.' That's when I felt that I was in the thrust of something. Shortly after that event, I noticed I had these very-fine, pinhole-sized burns in my fingernails, and my arms felt like they were charged with some kind of energy."

An infection occurred on his fingers, and Mr. Allen's hair began to fall out rapidly in a small, circular area on the top, rear of his head. The burns on his fingers and the sudden loss of hair in a small area took about a year-and-a-half to heal. He was very self-conscious about the way his hands and head looked and kept them covered most of the time.

However, one day soon after the event at the Capitol, he ran into his neighbor who is a scientist, so he asked her to take a look at the burns on his fingers.

At the time, Dr. Bonette was a cellular biologist that was working toward becoming an assistant professor at Rutgers University. She told me that, "When he showed me his hands, I saw that his nail beds were yellowed and thickened on all ten fingers. All his nails had hardened and were a yellowish color. There were burn marks on his fingertips."

Mr. Allen told me that this condition wasn't painful, but something else very strange had occurred. Tiny green crystals were coming out of his fingernail beds. The green crystals were about the size of grains of salt. He realized this was very strange and decided to save some of the crystals in a small glass test tube which he then hermetically sealed. However, one day, he noticed that the contents of the jar had simply vanished from the sealed container.

I wanted to know more about the process he used to analyze his DC UFO images. Mr. Allen explained that, "I shoot a roll of film which I develop in a dark room and then scan directly from the negative or slide into my computer at 4,000 DPI (dots per inch.) That's super high resolution. For most of my material, I use *Adobe* CS2 software which has a three-dimensional *PhotoShop*. It's extremely sensitive.

"It is state-of-the-art spectral analysis for images. However, the UFO photographs I took in DC are beyond the abilities of *PhotoShop* CS2 which is at the cutting edge of digital technology. Whatever was flying over DC that night was emitting an energy that was beyond the range of current computer-imaging technology.

"There were some colors that my computer system could not analyze. For example, the object that I shot in the water at the reflecting pool at the Capitol; I could analyze some of the spectral data, but not all of it.

"The energy frequencies emitted by the UFOs was too far out there for my computer programs to analyze. I tried to do as many variations as possible for the sake of getting details from these objects. Some of the analysis of these images was most intriguing. It showed that there were other elements included in these things.

"For example, the green objects had a nucleus in them, and some of these nucleuses' were completely different than the objects that were on the ground. There were two sets of green objects sitting side-by-side on the ground that night. They were the same shape and configuration as the objects in the sky except when I analyzed these objects their nuclei were blue. The objects in the sky had a red nucleus."

Mr. Allen told me that he believed those specific images were of the UFOs that extraterrestrial entities had come out of. We had looked at a lot of different photos, so I asked him to be more specific. He said, "I took a series of images of a recording artist sitting in front of the reflecting pool at the Capitol. In one of those photos are three UFOs. Two are in the sky, and one is in the water.

"There is another image that was taken 30 seconds earlier that shows an entity above the Capitol dome; an unidentified entity on the roof and another unidentified entity on the ground. The entity on the ground to the rear of the reflecting pool was the same entity in the very last shot that shows the objects warping out. I do recall these entities coming toward me and surrounding me and then vanishing."

When I asked Mr. Allen if the other two people with him that night had seen any of the UFO activity during the photo shoot, he said, "I saw some anomalies during the shoot, but didn't think that much of it because I was more focused on getting an album cover done. However, I did notice the UFOs in the sky over the Capitol.

"It was approximately 12:30 a.m. There was no one around; not a soul. In fact, as I recall, you could always hear the sound of water splashing around in the reflecting pool, but I heard absolutely nothing during the shoot that night."

His photos indicated that there was no one else in the area at that time. Also, the water on the reflecting pool appeared to be totally calm. But I was still curious about the recording artist and his manager. Had they seen any UFOs that night? Mr. Allen explained that both of the other men saw something strange that night and had a very tough time focusing on the photo shoot.

The recording artist, nick-named "Bear Witnez", was wearing a number 23, *Washington Wizards* basketball jersey. From the photos, the expression on his face indicated he was scared, and his eyes were open very wide.

Since that event, Bear Witnez, who is a big man, has refused to come out at night. According to Mr. Allen, "He's completely spooked, and for some reason he blames me for the event and has disassociated with me."

When I explained to Mr. Allen that fear and ridicule are reoccurring themes regarding UFOs and ETs, he reminded me that when he showed his UFO pictures to his father, he had gotten very angry and insisted that no one should see those photos, ever.

I was curious why he felt that way. After all, these were just photographs. Mr. Allen explained that, "I believe he knew something. Because of the experience I had in England with the EBEs, I knew he had seen something, and in the military they somehow persuade you not to divulge any information at all.

"But he knew something, because my father was involved in nuclear warfare. At the particular Strategic Air Command base where he was stationed, it is a matter of record that there were occasions when UFOs were present."

I was familiar with most of the historic military UFO reports. I understood alien incursions by UFOs were considered a serious threat to all the military establishments on earth. Therefore, it was no surprise when Mr. Allen told me that he never spoke about UFOs with his father. He also told me that he only spoke about it once with his older brother and that he would make no comment either.

Mr. Allen further explained that his father was a senior master sergeant in the Air Force and that his brother was a colonel working at the Pentagon. This made me wonder why he had not joined the military like the rest of his family.

Mr. Allen replied, "I was too rebellious. In fact, I got into trouble on a couple of the bases. For example, after school at Clark Air Force Base, my friends and I were buzzing incoming B-52s with our radio controlled airplanes. That didn't go over too well with the base commander. My dad took some heat for that.

"Had I unintentionally flown my remote controlled plane into the engines of one of the B-52s, it could have crashed quite easily. I got into a lot of trouble for that. Perhaps that's why I chose not to follow my father and brother's path in life."

Mr. Allen told me that during his close encounters with EBEs, he felt as though something was downloaded into his mind. He said, "Afterwards, the thoughts I would have were not what I would consider to be my own. For example, I can't explain how I got the chemical formulations to enhance film to the point where you can see into the dark, in color.

"I never studied that kind of chemistry in school. Another invention involves theories of zero point energy. I created a device that is based on perpetual energies, and I know it works because I have a 3-D model of it working, but I never studied these things. It seems they are just coming out of me. That could be another reason why I didn't join the military."

When I asked Mr. Allen what else the EBEs had taught him, he said, "One of the technical devices that were downloaded into my mind was specifically designed to disintegrate asteroids and other objects traveling in space toward earth.

"This particular device redirects energy from the sun and melts asteroids. It looks somewhat like a space telescope, but it's something more like an organic laser. It amplifies and redirects solar energy captured in space from the sun. There is a tremendous amount of energy flowing around the earth. My device takes that energy and focuses it at a specific point for transmission."

I knew Mr. Allen was referring to the solar wind. Scientists had known for some time that there was a tremendous amount of energy coming from the sun that never reached the earth. Although this was a massive, potential energy source it was difficult to access.

I also knew that if it wasn't used for our defense, it could be used as a deadly offensive weapon. I had read reports that the Nazi's drafted plans for a primitive version of the same type of space weapon. It worked in the same way a child burns an insect using the sun's rays focused through a magnifying glass.

Although Mr. Allen agreed with my analogy, he saw his version of that space-based system being used as an advanced planetary defense from incoming asteroids. He believed that the device would have the power to incinerate anything it was aimed at. That's why he had been very apprehensive about showing it to or discussing the system with anyone in the military other than in very general terms. It was clearly something that had the potential to cause a lot of trouble.

Mr. Allen also told me he had developed a commercial application for his DC UFO images. He said, "I sampled the color patterns from my high-resolution, UFO images and created bit maps that were unlike anything anyone has seen before. I then painted those bit maps into 3-D animation files to generate incredible visual effects.

"The UFO color bit maps I extracted from my UFO images can be applied to 3-D animation in such a way that I can generate effects that no digital studio on earth could possibly create just by using digital paint. I own the copyrights to that.

"George Lucas and Stephen Spielberg do not have real UFO color samples to work with. Even though their effects are great, they are not alien in origin. I am working on the patent for the procedure that I use to create these effects. Again, I did not study advanced chemistry, but the formulations I have to enhance film is unlike anything anyone has ever seen before."

Mr. Allen was clearly an unusual individual that knew a lot about photography. After earning a master's degree in imaging technology engineering, he landed a job working for *ABC News*. He explained that, "It all entailed electronics, and the engineering job at *ABC* was the first to offer me a six-figure salary.

"I was 26-years old making $150,000 a year. They paid me for my expertise. I did my work very well, and I had a 100 percent track record. I never failed at anything, and I did it quickly."

When I asked Mr. Allen what type of camera he used to capture the UFO images on Capitol Hill, and the Washington Monument, he said, "I used a *Nikon* F-5 and a *Nikon* F-100. I only use *Nikon* cameras and lenses. The glass in those lenses is called ED which according to the manufacturer is 100 percent distortion free.

"Therefore, the UFO images I took are not an optical distortion. If that was the case, all the other images I have taken at night over the years would have anomalies in them. This was the only set of images that contained anomalies that could not be identified. For the time exposure image taken in Lower Senate Park, I used a polarized filter over the lens. This changed the attributes of the light and gave me an image that is totally unique."

Early on in my investigation, I explained to Mr. Allen that he really needed to have his images authenticated because skeptics would presume he had created them on a computer. He eventually took my advice.

On January 17, 2006, an independent analysis of Mr. Allen's negatives was performed by a film technician named Mark Rosoff at *Penn Camera* on E Street which is located directly across the street from FBI headquarters, in Washington, D.C. That morning, Mr. Allen entered the film lab and asked the technician to determine if there was any way someone could modify or add enhancements to generate the UFO images on the negatives he had in his possession.

The first piece of film to be analyzed was the three-and-a-half minute exposure from Lower Senate Park taken July 16, 2002. The technician stated that, "On frame 19a of a roll of 800 ISO *Fuji* color film, I see a shot of a building with a set of three groups of four lights in the sky. They appear to have been exposed on the film by the ambient light of the exposure, to the best of my knowledge.

"With any print enlargement it would be fairly easy to detect forgery, because if you add dye after the film has been processed it will fuse into the gelatin a whole other way. As a result, the larger you print the image, the more obvious it would be that you added something after developing the film. I am also enlarging the image with a 4x loop on a light box, but I don't see any tampering here."

Mr. Allen then provided the technician with the other negatives that were taken at the Capitol in 2002. He observed that, "On the next frame of 800 ISO *Fuji* film, I see an object at almost 12 o' clock above the Capitol. I am not sure about anything else, but there is something in the sky far to the right above the tree line. In the next frame, I see an object that appears as a spot in the negative that looks like it has a head and a tail coming up from the trees. There is also a similar looking image in the sky above the Capitol that looks like a flame."

Mr. Allen then asked the technician to examine the object in the water. The technician explained that, "It could be a reflection. There could be another object in the sky that is out of frame casting a reflection on the water. You have to think of all the possibilities. I do see a few unidentifiable objects in this image.

"Keep in mind, most of the images we see that involve retouching or adding something after development are obvious. When someone uses a dye on developed film, it creates a softer image. It is my opinion that these negatives have not been modified. They only show what the camera captured. There appears to be no manipulation after the fact."

The next negative to be analyzed was the photo of the small, spherical UFO over the female model's head. The technician explained that, "On this frame of 400 ISO color film, I see a woman in a dark coat. I see an object that appears as a dot. It is apparently bright yellow in the film. This also looks as if it was part of the original exposure."

The last two UFO images to be analyzed were color slides Mr. Allen had taken on the Fourth of July, in 2002. During his analysis, the technician stated that, "I am looking at two frames of *Kodak* EPT which is a Tungsten transparency film. I see two pairs of bright dots next to the Washington Monument. I see fireworks going off to the right of the Monument, and to the left we have two pairs of lights.

"In the next frame, there are two pairs of symmetrical objects higher up at about one o' clock. I can't say if it is the same two pair of objects, but these are both the same light intensity. Whereas, the objects on the previous frame, the top pair are a little brighter and more distinct than the other lower pair of objects, but that may be due to the haze from the fireworks drifting along. I see frames 28 and 29 showing similar pairs of dots in the film. The color temperature of the light tells me it is very bright.

"These slides do not look as if anything has been added to them. Actually, it would be very difficult to change a slide, which is a positive rather than a negative of the film. You would have to first bleach the film as opposed to adding dye. The bleach physically takes the emulsion away."

When Mr. Allen asked if it appeared that had been done to the slides in question, the technician replied, "Absolutely no way these were physically etched, and for it to have been dye bleached would require a tremendous amount of control to work in that small of an area. These look authentically exposed and have not been altered physically or chemically."

After Mr. Allen had his film authenticated, I asked him if he realized how big this story was. He said, "It is a huge. I have photographic proof of an alien incursion in DC. It's what our military would call an away mission. At that time, alien entities surveyed the U.S. Capitol and then left the same way they came."

Newspapers around the world had reported that in July of 1952, UFOs overflew the DC area twice in one week, but that really wasn't a surprise. During 1952, UFOs were being sighted all over America, and the rest of the planet. However, the UFOs seemed especially interested in Washington, D.C., where they often visited for hours at a time.

No one knew for certain why it happened, but beginning in the year 2000 until the present, there was a dramatic increase in UFO activity again, specifically in Washington, D.C. It seemed odd to me that the media didn't want to report this fact. Perhaps they were afraid to mention it because of the *War on Terror* and the focus on Homeland Security, but the situation really wasn't much different in 1952. America was in the middle of the Cold War, and people were living in fear of a nuclear attack from above.

However, I suppose the *War on Terror* that began in September of 2001 was more intense, in some ways, because we were attacked from the sky and blood had been spilled on American soil. I knew that despite all the government's denials, UFOs routinely traveling through restricted and prohibited air space made the U.S. military very nervous. The truth of the matter was there were many alien incursions over other countries' air space in 2002 as well. Something was clearly going on, but no one wanted to officially address the issue.

During my investigation for this book, I was informed by a DC lawyer, a retired army commander, and a retired naval officer that there had been an effort underway in Washington D.C., toward public disclosure of UFOs by the government. However, after 9/11, that all came to a screeching halt, and no one wanted to debate the issue since then.

Having lived and worked in DC for many years, Mr. Allen knew Bill Clinton's former Chief of Staff, John Podesta, was having no luck obtaining and publicly releasing information regarding UFOs. Mr. Allen told me that, "It seems that no matter what one's political position is, the government is going to remain quiet about the UFO issue. It's strictly hush-hush."

In my opinion this was because the government really didn't have all the answers. Some world leaders felt it would be irresponsible to broadcast UFO events publicly without having any answers to the questions that would logically follow.

I was informed that members of the U.S. government knew this issue not only made them look incompetent, it could potentially lead to anarchy in some segments of the population. It was obvious that our current leaders had not yet figured out a way to responsibly inform the public that alien's had briefly landed on Capitol Hill on July 16, 2002.

Because of the ongoing cover-up, many people still didn't know there was a well-established chronology of close encounters over Washington, D.C., in the past 50 plus years. However, I knew that once people saw the historical time line I had compiled they would understand what was really going on.

Although there had been a lot of UFO activity reported in 1952, it had continued covertly through 2002 and into the present. The bottom line was that ignoring the problem had not made it go away. Moreover, many people didn't recognize this was a very real situation that impacted national security. I was certain that Mr. Allen's photographic evidence would stimulate debate regarding that issue. My job was to help put the data into context, so people could view the events as a whole rather than them being dissected into hundreds of seemingly separate events.

Mr. Allen mentioned that there were two types of people that believed in UFOs; those that thought real UFOs were only saucer shaped and those that knew UFOs came in many shapes and sizes. A UFO could be an energy orb, or a metallic sphere, a long tube, a triangle, or a disc.

In fact, I found there were many decades worth of historical accounts of spherical-shaped UFOs in the public record. During World War II, they were called Foo Fighters. While discussing this fact with Mr. Allen, he suddenly recalled another close encounter he had experienced. He said, "My father was stationed in Colorado for a time at Lowry Air Force Base which is in Denver. One day, he got transferred from Lowry, in Colorado, to Castle Air Base, in California. On the way there, we drove through Arizona. At some point during that night, I looked up in the sky and saw a UFO.

"I told my dad there was a white dot in the sky zigzagging around, and instead of stopping and looking he stepped hard on the gas and sped away. He clearly knew something, but would not give me the pleasure of knowing that he knew something really strange was out there!"

That kind of instinctive reaction really didn't surprise me. It was routine military training; one did not divulge information that could compromise national security. It was potentially hazardous to everyone's well-being.

Mr. Allen had learned this the hard way as a youth attending military school. This was not a military academy for wealthy brats, it was a real military school. Some of the teachers and administrators were civilians, but the majority of the teachers were military officers that worked for NASA, the CIA, etc.

One day, in first grade, Mr. Allen innocently described to his teacher the EBEs he had encountered at night in his bedroom. Soon after that, the school authorities put him in the class for retarded children where he spent the next four years. As a result, he stopped telling anyone that he had seen EBEs. He bitterly recalled that, "I didn't say another thing after that because I knew I was not in the right place to discuss the situation. That was their way of getting back at me."

According to Mr. Allen, "My story and photos illustrate that we are not the only intelligent life form in this Universe. Whatever those objects in the water and air were, they had intelligent entities inside them. It was obvious. At one point, they were stationary. And the next point, they were in motion."

I was beginning to understand that aliens had been covertly interacting with Mr. Allen and a select group of other people in DC. I had often wondered why aliens seemed interested in us, but would only interact covertly with with certain people. When I asked Mr. Allen's opinion about that, he said, "I'm not sure, but I do believe I have been tagged and tracked by them. On the photo I took of the images at the U.S. Capitol, some of the UFOs in the air were discharging smaller, spherical UFOs.

"Four months later, around 11:00 p.m., I took a picture of a small UFO over a woman's head. That UFO was about the size of a quail egg. It was perfectly spherical and had the opalescent qualities of a pearl. The woman was standing on the street corner posing in front of me.

"We were near the corner of 13th and U Street in Washington, D.C. As I took her picture, I saw it. The small sphere was visible, but then it just vanished. After developing the film, I filtered the image, and it showed the object was modulating energy around itself. Each level of analysis showed a different level of energy."

I had read other reports of similar, small, spherical UFOs that I referred to as "mind sweepers." It seemed logical that those types of UFOs were programmed to sweep a specific area for information then return back to base and download their data.

I felt this was possible, because humans were developing a similar form of advanced surveillance technology on Earth. There were reports that the Navy had developed a program called SWARM. It involved artificial swarms of tiny, manmade aerial objects that were programmed to behave like bees. Their sensors were designed to collectively share data gathered from a targeted location.

However, the tiny UFO sphere that Mr. Allen photographed in DC employed a very advanced field propulsion. His digital analysis indicated there were variations of energy on the surface of the sphere that swirled like a whirlpool. The object was clearly modulating highly complex energy fields.

But the image that really surprised both of us involved UFOs warping space over Capitol Hill. According to Mr. Allen, "The three-and-a-half minute time exposure I took at the Capitol showed a set of four UFOs in motion. That image shows four green objects that are in lateral and forwards motion. Somehow, the UFOs created a green trace going up and a blue trace moving laterally in its signature.

"According to the laws of physics, as it applies to light, if a green object moves in a given direction it is going to leave a green trace regardless of the direction it moves. Yet, this object left a blue trace as it moved laterally. This simply goes against the known laws of physics."

Mr. Allen then informed me that he had researched the history of green UFOs and found there were many reported cases of UFOs modulating colors. One historic account noted that as one UFO approached a military aircraft it turned totally green.

He also told me that, "The UFOs over the Capitol were definitely different. I mean, how does a solid object become elastic? This thing essentially stretched like a balloon and then vanished, then reappeared, then vanished?"

Some of the scientists and engineers I had interviewed over the years had told me that they believed UFOs were capable of warping space around their craft. The problem was it required a tremendous amount of energy to warp space even in a small area.

Mr. Allen believed that the formation of UFOs, Senate side of the Capitol, had done just that. He said, "The final photograph of July 16, 2002 showed that a set of four UFOs moving together generated a fractal ring of energy as they vanished. They also left an energy trail in the sky somewhat like a vapor trail from a jet, but this energy trail affected the air all around the UFO. It left the air highly energized by radiation."

The technical term for this is "ionized," and it is a common side effect of plasma engines. Those types of engines generate highly-complex energetic fields that ionize the surrounding air. I was informed by an aerospace engineer that this was what created the many intense variations of brightly colored light around UFOs.

When Mr. Allen told me that a lot of his friendships and relationships had ended because of his close encounters, I was not surprised. Many people I knew or had interviewed regarding close encounters with UFOs experienced the same thing. Politically, personally, and professionally UFOs spelled trouble. As a result, most people didn't want to talk about it.

It seemed to me, that this type of reaction was directly related to one's level of self-confidence. For example, if a person was already feeling insecure in their life and someone began speaking with some credibly about UFOs and ETs, it would create even more insecurity. That was what happened to the recording artist shooting his album cover at the Capitol building. He later blamed Mr. Allen for the fact that UFOs showed up that night.

Mr. Allen confided to me that, "These days, many of the people I know don't want to hang out with me, because they fear a close encounter might happen to them. I feel like I have had to suppress this information since I was five years old. However, I know it was reported in the news that both the Royal Air Force bases at Lakenheath and at Sculthorpe were involved in some very controversial American technologies. And both military bases reported seeing UFOs."

I had read numerous reports regarding UFOs over that area of England. Joint American and British military bases had been visited by UFOs many times over the past 50 years. Despite their best efforts, pilots sent to intercept and or fire on UFOs routinely failed. Clearly, someone or something was flying extremely-powerful, advanced space craft in the Earth's atmosphere with no restriction.

As long as our society in general continued to act as though there was nothing odd going on, it simply enabled UFOs to continue to violate our controlled airspace covertly. Unfortunately, the current policy regarding UFOs had created the perfect cover for highly advanced technology to be operated in plain sight whether it was human or alien in origin. The current policy of denial, dissuasion and deception excused the occupants of UFOs from having any accountability. No matter how I tried, I couldn't understand how that was in humanities' best interest.

There was one specific image of a UFO at the Capitol that I knew would create a lot of controversy in the future. That photo, taken on the night of July 16, 2002, clearly showed a glowing, flying saucer floating above the Senate side of the reflecting pool. Mr. Allen said, "All the images are amazing. They just blow my mind, but that specific image shows a disk-shaped UFO hovering over the water dissipating energy like an ion generator.

"Energy was continually discharged by the UFO around itself. The air around it was completely distorted, and I have the high-definition film to prove it. What I also find amazing is that there was nobody else out there that night."

After doing some research, I confirmed that the ban on commercial flight had been in effect at that time. That area of central DC was designated Prohibited Airspace: P56-A. No flights were legally allowed to come anywhere near a federal building in that area. Despite that fact, Mr. Allen had provided me with a set of exceptionally-clear, high-resolution photos of UFOs penetrating prohibited air space and even landing on the Capitol building roof and surrounding park complex.

I had to admit I was confused when I first laid eyes on those images, especially the one of the UFO sitting on the roof of the Capitol. Many federal regulations were violated that night. I knew that even the Space Shuttle was met by U.S. Customs when it landed, and the crew had to go through a level of decontamination.

Mr. Allen had to have a spotless record to work at the White House and Air Force One. He told me that he believed he was granted a security clearance to work there because he came from a well-respected, military family. However, he felt certain that the government didn't know about his alien encounters. He told me that after what happened to him as a child in England, he didn't talk about it again until July of 2002.

Although I respected Mr. Allen's opinion, I was convinced that at least one military-intelligence group had to have some idea about what was really going on regarding UFOs and ETs. Mr. Allen disagreed, and said, "They officially don't know what's going on. During the event I photographed over the Washington Monument, on the Fourth of July, there was a blue UFO in the sky along with these other things next to the monument.

"That blue UFO showed up again on July 26th, at Waldorf, Maryland. It was chased by two F-16s. It left the F-16s in the dust. That event was reported in the *Washington Post*, but there were no pictures of the object."

The UFO that landed on the roof of the Capitol building was also glowing blue. I found that there were certain consistent descriptions of UFOs that appeared in the historic record. When I put all these events into a time line, a definite pattern emerged. For example, UFOs violated the prohibited airspace of Washington, D.C., on July 4, 16, 20, 26, 30 and 31, in 2002. A similar series of alien incursions had occurred in DC in July of 1952.

In fact, that type of UFO activity had been occurring all over the planet for well over 50 years. However, some areas were considered UFO "hot spots" and Washington, D.C., appeared to be the hottest of them all. When I explained this to Mr. Allen, he said, "You will never catch me going back to the Capitol at night again. It is a hot spot for me. I believe that the aliens are very advanced technically, and if I have pictures of them, they must have taken pictures of me."

My research indicated that many people with a history of close encounters felt drawn to UFO hot spots, but there were always exceptions. Mr. Allen remarked that, "It doesn't make for a very comfortable evening when you have to constantly look up in the sky and make sure there is nothing over your head. Every night I go out, I always look up to make sure the coast is clear. I shouldn't have to do that, but I am still seriously spooked.

"When I was a kid, whenever there was an episode of the *Twilight*

Zone or the *Outer Limits* on TV that dealt with aliens, my dad had to physically kick my ass to bed. I would not go to bed. I fought to stay in a room that was well lit. They had to pick me up and put me to bed. I was afraid to go to sleep. Even as an adult, I don't sleep much at night. When I go out, I feel compelled to take a camera with me wherever I go, just in case, because I'm not sure what's going to happen next?"

Despite the hardships he had endured, I was certain that millions of people would appreciate the opportunity to see his DC UFO images and consider their implications. Mr. Allen informed me that he intended on producing a documentary of his photographic material. I looked forward to seeing those images appear on national television someday.

But, just as his initial production was nearing completion in the summer of 2006, his analysis progressed to another level. The latest scanner technology, which used LEDs rather than a standard bulb, allowed Mr. Allen to extract even greater detail from his negatives.

Because of this, many more UFOs were visible in the images. This included an odd-looking, tiny, black dot in the sky near the Capitol dome. When this very small area was enlarged, an amazing image of another worm hole generated by a UFO appeared. It was one of the strangest photographic images that Mr. Allen or I had ever seen. To view this and other DC UFO images please visit the photography section of *unicusmagazine.com*

CHAPTER TWO

Military Intelligence

In the past 50 years, there had only been a handful of career military officers who dared to speak publicly about the issue of aliens and extraterrestrials. They were brave men like Major Donald Keyhoe, Major Jesse Marcel, Lieutenant Colonel Wendelle Stevens, Colonel Philip Corso, and Command Sergeant Major Robert O. Dean.

In 1963, commander Dean was assigned to Supreme Headquarters Allied Powers, located near Paris, France. At that time, he was advanced to the highest security clearance NATO had (COSMIC) and was assigned to the Supreme Headquarters Operations Center war room.

While stationed in Europe, commander Dean was allowed to read a classified report entitled *Assessment: An Evaluation of a Possible Military Threat to Allied Forces in Europe.* It was a highly detailed NATO report on UFOs and extraterrestrial activity that had been compiled by military representatives from every NATO nation with contributions from the best scientists at Cambridge, Oxford, MIT, and other universities.

Since retiring from the military, commander Dean had dedicated his life to researching and educating audiences around the world about the governments' knowledge of UFOs and ETs. That was how we first met. I really enjoyed his presentation, so I requested an interview. During one of his lectures, he had commented that everyone on Earth had their own agenda. Hearing this made me curious what he thought the world governments and military were doing to prepare to interface with the ET's agenda.

I was not surprised when he told me they were not doing enough and had not started preparing early enough. Specifically, he said, "I don't think they started really addressing the issue until recently. However, I think that the recent surge of UFO subject matter on TV, and in movies, indicates that there is some kind of program underway.

"Someone has decided that they have to get some of this information out. But I fault them for not starting early enough and for not taking the public into their confidence early on. I fault them for trying to lie to all of the people all of the time and frankly, I fault them for underestimating the American people. I think the public can deal with this information if it is presented in the proper way."

Commander Dean had been privately conducting research on this subject for over 30 years and had stated his belief that we were related physically, culturally and spiritually to at least one of the known races of ETs visiting Earth. It was hard to imagine how we could forget such an important link in our evolution.

When I asked commander Dean about this, he said, "The human race is made up of a bunch of damn mavericks. Sometimes we have a tendency to take something that is beautiful and true and screw it up. For example, about 2,000 years ago, a very loving, young man in Galilee [Jesus] had some beautiful stories to tell and some great truths to share. He tried to do that, and look what happened to his message. Not only did they turn it into a religion, which he did not want them to do, they edited and rewrote some of it and turned it into a political structure.

"I am talking about organized Christianity. But I am not just throwing stones at the Catholic Church: I throw stones at all of them. They have taken something very true and very beautiful and misinterpreted it. I am convinced that Jesus was part of this ongoing interplanetary relationship.

"I don't think his life was an accident. I think he was basically what he said he was, and they tried to turn him into something else because we tend to do that. Even in ancient times, in Greece, and Rome, we deified [worshiped] the visitors from space, and they never wanted that."

I agreed with commander Dean and believed that the current perspective we had toward ETs was based, to some degree, on a misunderstanding or miscommunication. For example, in the 1950s the government received a relatively good look at how primitive humans might react to advanced alien technology when they commissioned the Brookings Institute to research the implications of contact with extraterrestrials.

One of the lead scientists involved in the study was the anthropologist Margaret Mead who was apparently a firm believer in angels. She was a key figure on that team of federally-funded researchers. During their investigation, they had traveled to the South Pacific and studied the "Cargo Cult" of New Guinea.

The origins of the cult took place during World War II. At that time, a military pilot flying a cargo plane over the remote, highland, jungle interior of New Guinea suddenly had to perform an emergency landing in a native clearing. Once on the ground, the pilot couldn't directly communicate with the rather primitive people. However, he unloaded his small aircraft full of supplies and gave them away. While he repaired his aircraft, the natives cut a crude runway out of the jungle for him, and he then flew away. Those natives, and their relatives, expected or hoped that this white god named "John from sky" would return one day.

In a way, they were worshiping him and his alien technology. They even built replicas of his aircraft, and its cargo boxes, out of bamboo in hopes that he would come back. That event was used as a model in the Brookings Report.

Commander Dean thought for a moment, and then said, "Granted, there may have been a few aliens along the way who enjoyed being worshipped. But basically, the ET's policy concerning us was that they did not want us to deify them. They wanted to help us grow up by facing the reality that we are not alone. They wanted to help us mature so we could stop beating the hell out of one another. I think this current cycle that we are going through is not a new or unusual cycle, it has probably happened in the Universe hundreds, if not thousands, of times already."

Zecharia Sitchin's writings were in agreement with commander Dean's research. In his series *The Earth Chronicles*, Sitchin had made many well-documented references to the political system of the gods being handed down to mankind. When I asked commander Dean if he thought we were secretly still living under the political influence of these ET gods, he replied, "Yes, to some degree. However, this is a very subtle affair. How do you carefully, gently, lovingly interrelate with a race, to help them grow up, and not rock the boat too much, so they don't go running hysterically into the streets?

"I admire Zecharia. He is one of the few people that has done his homework. When I talked to him in Chicago, I said, 'You know, the whole program is still going on. The ETs are still intimately involved with us.' Then, he gave me a strange grin and told me to read his next book.

"I keep hoping that he will come out some day and tell us the rest of the story. I do believe that they are still here. I think that at some level the ETs have saved our ass a time or two. Apparently, there has been some overt involvement in government with both Russia and the United States. Certain ET individuals have reportedly met with leading officials.

"The story I heard out of the Kremlin was that an ET met with Michael Gorbachev at a Procedium meeting. I also heard from a few independent sources that a certain ET visitor appeared to Presidents Reagan and Gorbachev on a battleship at Malta, during a summit.

"Then, there was an incredible situation that occurred at a missile silo, in South Dakota. The ETs came down in their UFOs and lifted the lid off of one of the silos that weighed 40-to-50 tons. Security personnel responded when the alarms went off and found the silo lid pulled off and set aside like it was a package of butter. After the large UFO left the area, they went into the silo and found that the nuclear warhead had been melted, and the guidance system was so badly scrambled God only knows where it would have gone if it had been launched.

"When we finally had enough courage to share what had happened with the Russians, through other countries intelligence agencies, we discovered that exactly the same kind of incident had occurred in Russia. I think that was when President Reagan finally decided it was time to admit that we knew what they knew. That is what led to some of the public comments made by Reagan and Gorbachev regarding a hypothetical global defense against ETs and how that would affect international affairs."

It was an incredibly interesting insight, but I wanted to know more about a document which the commander suggested I read called *Fire Officer's Guide*. The manual was published by the Federal Emergency Management Agency (FEMA) which he had worked for. Oddly enough, Chapter 13 was entitled: *The UFO Threat – A Fact*. This official fire department manual used a hypothetical situation where a UFO had crashed in a populated area. However, commander Dean told me he believed that portion of the manual was actually based on a real event.

When I asked him to elaborate, he said, "I have been in touch with the Long Island MUFON group about that. Apparently, in November of 1992, a couple of UFOs crashed near the Brookhaven National Laboratory, in Long Island. One of the UFOs went down near a freeway and burned fiercely for hours.

"The other object landed in the middle of a street in a small community and did not burn. The story I was told by witnesses is that these were both extraterrestrial objects, and when the guys from the local fire departments arrived on the scene, the shock of what they were seeing was more than they had ever been prepared to deal with.

"Not only were they dealing with exotic hardware that was totally alien, but they were dealing with alien bodies. Then, the Brookhaven Laboratory's Fire Department showed up, and even some of their guys were having a problem coping with the situation. But they did their best to clean it up and haul away all the wreckage; and then the big political cover-up began. It was that incident, and probably a few others, that led to the publishing of FEMA's UFO emergency manual."

Learning of those events made me wonder whether or not the U.S. military was still in a "shoot on sight" mode regarding UFOs. Commander Dean explained that this was a very-complicated matter. He said, "They revoked the shooting order a number of years ago. However, there was briefly an intercept-and-shoot order issued some time back. They learned real fast, first hand, that this was not a good idea. It is a very-scary subject for the guys in authority.

"You see, we are not just dealing with one group of ETs. Apparently, on an official level, we have established a relationship with at least one of the ET groups visiting earth. There are a couple of other ET groups we have not made any kind of arrangement with and don't necessarily know what their motives are.

"As far as I know, our current policy does not condone shooting at UFOs, but we do try and find out as much as possible about them. Jets will respond and attempt to photograph as much as they can when there have been flyovers and possible UFO landings."

Hearing this made me realize that there had to be lots of classified UFO images in storage somewhere. I began to wonder how many UFO photos the military really needed to make a clear assessment of the situation and why the public could never see them.

I had seen civilian photographs, taken in Puerto Rico, which showed F-14s flying around a hovering UFO. Witnesses claimed that at least one of the military jets disappeared after coming close to the UFO. When I asked commander Dean if the military was shooting more than pictures that day, he said, "As far as I know, the F-14s didn't shoot at that particular UFO. They were just making a few reconnaissance passes. Apparently, the pilots involved in that incident were abducted after getting too close.

Commander Dean explained that, "The U.S. has already lost six F-14s in Puerto Rico. I have their tail numbers, squadron numbers, and the name of the aircraft carrier they were flying off of. That is a pretty sensitive secret, but there have been credible rumors that the pilots are all right. A naval spokesman has said through a number of different people that they know where the pilots are being held and that they are OK."

Apparently the situation was causing some serious problems for the government. I had read reports from various sources that there was a growing political, philosophical, and moral division among the many different federal and military intelligence agencies in America. I wondered if commander Dean knew of a way that all those various agencies could ever become more receptive to having open contact with ETs.

According to commander Dean, "The difference of opinion on this situation has been going on for a number of years. There are two different groups in our government, at different levels, working on this issue. One group wanted to get the information out to the public some time ago.

"The other group not only said no, they said hell no! I think that situation could be resolved with a little firm leadership and solid policy making from the top. A strong President, with a strong Congress behind him, could inform these groups that this is still a democratic form of government and then spell out what we need to do without all the bullshit.

"I think one of the things that has kept me alive, is that I have been trying to help the government at some level to put together a sound, workable, informational and educational program on this issue. They need to start telling the American people what has really been going on regarding the ETs and where we fit into this incredible Universe we live in.

"I think that there is more that can be done. I don't think it is being done fast enough. I don't think they have seriously made up their minds to really do this, and we are running out of time. I don't exactly know what the ET's agenda is, but I have a nagging suspicion that they are becoming a little impatient with us.

"I believe we are ready to address this issue in the open. We need to stand up and acknowledge the existence of extraterrestrial entities. We have known it for a long time. Most of the people I know would like to join the cosmic club. It's time for us to graduate, mature, and evolve. We have got to say openly that we would like to be a part of the bigger picture, but we are not quite ready and just need a little help. I think we need to express and address that issue now, globally.

"The ETs didn't create us, and help us evolve, and genetically work with us over the centuries just to turn us into foolish children, or mere servants. I think they have as much interest in us as we should have in ourselves about growing up and taking our place in the universal community. I am convinced that if our governments, on a global basis, addressed and informed the people on this issue that mankind would obtain more help from the ETs than we ever imagined."

Commander Dean had publicly stated that he believed we were all immortal beings that chose to be here at this time for mankind's next evolutionary leap forward. When I asked him what role he thought spirituality should play in our government, he replied, "That is a damn good question! It should play a role. It does to some degree, however, it doesn't play as big a role as it should. If you are a student of history you know that religious and spiritual factors played a major role in the way the United States of America was founded.

"Our founding fathers knew that that this nation was literally formed under God. We have gotten away from that a little bit over the last couple of hundred years due to this Newtonian, reductionist science we became involved in.

"When I talk about spirituality, I am not talking about religion, I am talking about the human spirit which transcends religion. Every Moslem, every Jew, every Christian, every Buddhist, and every Hindu on this planet has the same spirit; the same spark of God inside him. When people are addressed and dealt with on that level, rather than perceiving them as secular entities, then we really can begin to grow up and become what we should be.

"The human race has got to come to terms with its unity: We are all one. Gandhi, for example, had a world view that transcended Hinduism. He saw the spirit of light on a worldwide basis. When we tap into that spiritual power, our potential is infinite."

I knew commander Dean had spent a tremendous amount of time and energy speaking on TV, radio and at public conferences about the government cover-up regarding UFOs and ETs. When I asked him why this issue was so important to him, he thought for a moment, and then said, "That's a question I have asked myself a few times. In fact, my son recently asked me why I wasn't just sitting back and enjoying my retirement, smoking good cigars, drinking good bourbon, and flirting with pretty young girls.

"Having dug into this issue over the years, and learned a little bit about what is really going on while working inside the military and the Federal Emergency Management Agency, I have concluded that this is literally the most important issue in the history of the human race.

"The fact is simply this: We are not alone and apparently have never been alone. There has been a long-standing, intimate relationship between advanced extraterrestrial intelligence and the people of earth. I think that is the crux of the matter.

"It's not as though the ETs first found us in 1947. That's bull! They have known about us since at least the beginning of recorded history. That's why I take my hat off to Zecharia Sitchin and his incredibly monumental work. I also respect a man in England by the name of Christian O' Brian who is a scholar that has done similar work. There is another man over in Santa Fe, New Mexico, who is a writer, and philosopher, and a researcher that I admire by the name of Neil Freer. He has written a few books on basically the same subject.

"The ETs have been part of our lives since the beginning, but why? I believe the answer is that they had a hand in our being here. However, it appears that in the last few years their agenda, or whatever you wish to call it, has been accelerated.

"I think that as a result of our recent developments in nuclear and other military technologies, we have reached a point where we can literally eliminate ourselves as a species. We can kill ourselves off in many different ways. I think that we have reached a defining moment in time where our species will either make it or it won't. However, I think we've got some type of help out there. I think there are some advanced ET intelligences that not only had a hand in our being here, but I think they are committed to helping us survive as a race."

Despite that possibility, commander Dean and I agreed the ETs couldn't do the work for us. They could only assist us to grow. He then made the analogy of a loving parent who had some adolescent kids that were in trouble with the police, etc. He told me that a truly loving parent would not just give up and walk away when their children were in trouble.

According to commander Dean, "A loving parent or an older brother will offer to help in some way. They will give some guidance. They will encourage subtly, gently instead of moving in and taking over and laying down the law. If they instead show by example and patiently assist and encourage, they will have a positive effect. This is what has happened to us, and it has been going on for quite a while, and that's why I'm interested.

"You see, people on this planet need help facing reality and accepting it. They need to deal with the truth that we are not alone in the Universe and that we have never been alone. I think that this realization on the part of individuals here on this planet will literally lead to an expansion of consciousness on their part. God knows the human race desperately needs to expand its sense of awareness, and its consciousness, because it is critical to our future.

"That is the crux of the matter that will help us make it or not make it. I think that is what will help us begin to expand our awareness, and I'm not just talking about technology. I'm talking about spiritual, and sociological, and psychological awareness. That's why I have worked so hard in this field."

Commander Dean had told me privately that he condemned organized religion for being politically manipulative. Yet, publicly he had stated that we are all immortal, spiritual beings that chose to be here for mankind's next evolutionary leap forward. In my opinion, that was a very-advanced perspective, and I was curious how he came to that realization.

He said, "There is a big difference between religion and spirituality. I'm convinced that the entire series of events that took place in Galilee, about 2,000 years ago, were orchestrated by our brothers and cousins from the cosmos. I believe the entire lifetime of Jesus, who literally was the foundation of the entire Christian Church, was part of that interplanetary program."

Commander Dean's statement reminded me of a book called *Date With the Gods*, by Charles Silva. It had been out of print for decades, but contained a similar message. I knew commander Dean would enjoy reading that story. It offered an alternative explanation as to how and why human ETs had placed the highly-advanced entity we call Jesus on earth.

The story paralleled almost exactly what commander Dean believed to be true. The source of the story was allegedly a female, human extraterrestrial named "Maya" who was living in the Andes Mountains in an underground base.

That area of Peru was a well-known site for UFO activity. According to Mr. Silva, a group of human ETs specifically sought out a human with a pure heart, who would help them get their message to people on Earth that were ready and able to accept the truth about Jesus.

Although it was an obscure book, I was certain many people had enjoyed reading it. It was so interesting that I read it twice. I then wrote to the author and learned that he had been friends with Shirley MacLaine. He told me that he was the fictional character named "David" in her book *Out on a Limb*. However, Mr. Silva was a real person with a fascinating story.

After hearing my summary, commander Dean was not surprised and explained that every major religion on the planet owed its origins to a little bit of information, interference, or encouragement from advanced ET intelligences. He said, "Jesus, a man that I have always felt a loving closeness to, said as much. He said it repeatedly, but people didn't pay any attention. They didn't know what he was talking about. I'm also convinced that the experiences that happened to Mohammed were the same type of event."

Commander Dean and I agreed that this is also what happened to Ezikel, and Moses, and Enoch. They were all charactersinvolved in an interplanetary passion play. I found Enoch especially interesting. He had reportedly been taken up to heaven in a chariot of fire and never returned to earth. Commander Dean insisted that although it was implied that Enoch walked with God, we were really talking about a god with a little g. He told me that there was a big difference between "the gods" and "God." Clearly, there was still a lot of confusion about that.

I knew from my experiences digging through various reference libraries that commander Dean was right. I had spent many hours researching the historic relationships of earthly deities. When I briefly outlined my analysis to commander Dean, he said, "You are an unusual young man. I think you are particularly inspired, and enlightened, and I encourage you to go ahead and do whatever your heart tells you to do. Research, publish; do whatever it takes to get the information out there, because it is in you."

Although I had never thought of myself as enlightened, I did have a sense of urgency. I felt that time was running out. I believed that the human race was about to pass, or fail, an important test, and it was not an exam anyone could cheat on.

Commander Dean agreed. He felt that this was one of the most important issues we could discuss. He said that there were a growing number of people on earth that realized we were running out of time, because the planet was ending a particular cycle: The conclusion of a 26,000-year period known as a galactic year. It literally was the end of an age.

To a measurable degree, our solar system was moving from our current level of energy to a higher level of energy; a fact that was scientifically verifiable. When I was younger, I thought it was nonsense, but I had finally started to understand the cosmic forces involved in this process, and the specific reasons for the powerful energy shifts that were occurring on our planet.

Commander Dean commented that, "I've been doing a lot of research about the astronomical knowledge of the Mayans. I believe that they knew a hell of a lot more than we give them credit for. I really wanted to know why they picked the 23rd of December in the year 2012 to end their calendar. I believe that this 26,000-year cycle, the end of the Picean Age, which is the last sign of the zodiac, is a major part of this process. I call it a transcendent transformation.

"When I spoke in Santa Fe at *the Prophets Conference*, my God was I shocked at the response. They had over 200 people crammed into this room where I gave my little, two-hour presentation and afterwards, I was mobbed! Apparently, what I said triggered something in these people that they either knew before, or just wanted to hear again, so I think you're right. Those of us who have a glimmer of truth are obligated to light a candle and dispel the darkness."

I agreed with the commander, but wanted to switch gears. When I asked him to elaborate on the details of the NATO report on UFOs and ETs he had read, commander Dean said, "By the time I arrived in 1963, everybody had been talking about the study, and I had heard the rumors and had seen the blips on radar, and some of us occasionally talked about the possibilities. But nothing prepared me for what I read late one night, in January of 1964.

"At that time, a controller went into the vault and brought out this huge document and told me to take a look. The title was *Assessment: An Evaluation of a Possible Military Threat to Allied Forces in Europe*. It was stamped *Cosmic Top Secret*. It had eight inches worth of appendices and dozens of photographs. I quickly learned that it was based on a two-and-a-half-year study that was funded by NATO. All the copies were classified and were kept under lock and key.

"Every time I got the chance, while working that post, I would read a section or two of it. It was the most intriguing document I'd ever read. It was put together by military representatives of every NATO nation and included contributions from some of the greatest scientific minds on earth.

"The military knew UFOs were violating all the known laws of physics. The study team had gone to Cambridge, Oxford, the Sorbonne, MIT and other major universities for input on chemistry, physics, atmospheric physics, biology, history, psychology, and even theology. They were all separate appendices.

"I read about theories on Einstein's long sought after unified field theory, the high levels of radiation found at various UFO landing sites, and historic UFO reports that dated back to the Roman era. There were also modern reports that involved our F-105 pilots' UFO sightings and encounters. I had been a skeptic until that time, but the NATO report concluded that this stuff was not science fiction.

"One section I read dealt with close encounters. There was an incident that had taken place in 1963 which involved a UFO that landed on a Danish farm. According to the report, the farmer went aboard with two little alien beings, and inside there were two human-looking, alien men that spoke to him in Danish.

"The report included parts of his interrogation by government authorities and their conclusions that he was telling the truth. In another incident, according to the reports, a UFO landed at an Italian airfield, and the occupants offered to take an Italian sergeant for a ride. He was so scared, he wet his pants. That's what it said. He didn't go up because he was too afraid.

"But the appendix that really got to me was titled *Autopsies*. There were pictures of a 30-meter wide, disc-shaped UFO that had crashed in Timmensdorfer, Germany, near the Baltic Sea, in 1961. According to the report, the British Army got there first and put up a perimeter. The UFO had crash landed in very-soft, loamy soil near the Russian border. It hadn't come apart on impact, and one-third of it was buried in the ground. The Americans and the Russians, who also quickly showed up, had tracked it on radar.

"Inside, there were 12 small, alien bodies that were all dead. There were pictures of the bodies, which looked like the beings known as 'the Grays,' being laid out and then put on stretchers and loaded into jeeps. There were also autopsy photos. The little Grays appeared to be a non-reproductive species.

"According to the report, the autopsy team concluded that the Grays had been popped out of a cookie cutter. They were apparently clones. They did not ingest or process food and had no system for elimination.

"The UFO had been cut up like a pie into six pieces, put on low-boys and hauled off. The scuttlebutt was that it was given to the Americans and flown to Wright-Patterson Air Force base in Ohio. I looked at these pictures and couldn't believe it. My skin got cold, and I thought, 'My God.'

"I had never really believed we were all alone in the universe, but this was hard to swallow. The major conclusions in that NATO report blew me away. It stated that the Earth, and the human race, had been the subject of a detailed survey by several different extraterrestrial civilizations, four of which they had identified in detail.

"One ET race was human and looked almost indistinguishable from us. Another race resembled humans in height, stature, and structure, but had a very grey, pasty skin tone. The third ET race of small clones is now popularly known as the Grays, and the fourth race was described as reptilian, with vertical pupils and lizard-like skin. The report concluded that these alien visitations had been going on for a very long time; hundreds of years or longer.

"The report concluded that the extraterrestrials did not appear hostile. If that were their intention, they would have already demonstrated their malevolence. The military also realized that UFO appearances and disappearances, as well as the flybys over restricted airspace, were designed to demonstrate some of their capabilities. A program or protocol of some sort seemed to be underway since UFO flybys often progressed to landings and eventually contact.

"I wanted so badly to copy that report. I did take a photograph of the cover sheet which wasn't in and of itself classified. But I didn't want to wind up incarcerated at Fort Leavenworth, so I would go to the bathroom and take notes surreptitiously. I was very careful not to get caught.

"I have been through an awful lot in my life, but I've never been able to just walk away from that report. I know that I'm taking a chance by violating my security oaths and speaking out, but this is the most important issue of our times. I can't think of anything more important. The public has been deceived and completely kept in the dark about all of this for decades. It's the biggest scientific, political scandal ever!

"When I read that NATO document, it changed my life. I never really had the time to study it as much as I would have liked to, but the initial reason for the study was a perceived threat from ETs to our allied forces.

"The study concluded that of the various ET groups visiting earth, the aliens that looked human and possessed incredible technology worried the military the most because they could easily infiltrate our society. However, in the final analysis, the report concluded that there was no threat involved."

This was a fascinating revelation. However, if the NATO assessment was accurate, then who was benefiting from all the secrecy, and how could they justify keeping it secret if there was no threat? My question got commander Dean's full attention. "You've touched on a real nerve there," he said with anguish in his voice.

He continued, "This is about the rotten sons-of-bitches, the bastards that act as our illegitimate leaders. I am referring to the guys that are not accountable to anyone. They effectively are the government within our government. Much like the kings of old, they have no oversight. They are spending hundreds of billions of our tax dollars every year. Congress doesn't know shit about what this group is up to. That group has a personal involvement in keeping the lid on the issue of UFOs.

"There are two reasons why. One is that if they can keep us in the dark, they can maintain their control over us. The other reason is greed. There is so much damn profit to be made in some of this technology, if they can ever get a handle on it. A lot of it is the result of recovered alien hardware.

"Not only have there been UFO crashes, and retrievals of alien hardware, but apparently the shadow government has acquired a hell of a lot of advanced technology through reverse engineering. Therefore, I want to know why we are building aircraft like the Aurora and other gas-guzzling vehicles that are based on incredibly loud, enormously expensive, and highly-inefficient technology."

I agreed. It was like using a sledge hammer where a laser beam was required. Although commander Dean had clearly explained that an elite group of humans was in control of ET technology and didn't want to let it go because it represented power and money, I was having a hard time understanding why they couldn't see that by incorporating the advanced ET technology into the world's infrastructure everyone would benefit.

The commander let out a long sigh followed by a moment of silence. I got the distinct impression he thought I was naive. He then carefully explained that the global elite were incredibly greedy, selfish, narrow minded and dangerous. They knew that the minute they did anything beneficial for humanity with the advanced, alien technology there would be a worldwide impact to their profits. They knew the oil industry would literally collapse and that it would be at least 25 years before another energy industry would emerge. The elite could only see this as a costly, traumatic transition that they didn't want to go through.

Then, commander Dean really dropped a bombshell on me. He said the elite group of people that were covertly controlling earth also couldn't handle the current spiritual transformation that was taking place on Earth, because they didn't want to lose control. It appeared that this was a stalemate. Our spiritual and technological enlightenment was eminent, and yet it appeared we couldn't fully evolve due to our corrupt, covert leadership.

When I asked the commander to elaborate, he said, "I have conducted over 30 years of research on this subject and have concluded that the controlling group is multi-national, and they are multi-agency. They are most likely what President Eisenhower tried to tell us just before he left office. He called them the military-industrial complex. But it isn't just a two-part group now. You have to add the military-intelligence community into that. It's a damn nightmare.

"I'm not just talking about the CIA, they're bad enough. I'm talking about the one organization that has more power on earth than God and that's the National Security Agency. The NSA has more power, and has grown so fast, that it has even gotten away from the executive, judicial, and the legislative branches."

I had read about the inner workings of the NSA in a book called *The Puzzle Palace*, by James Bamford. It was a fascinating examination of the covert capabilities and massive black budget of the NSA. There was reason to believe that the NSA had acquired the ability to intercept and decrypt much of the electronic communications between the various ET civilizations visiting our solar system. That information was what gave the NSA the controlling authority over the other intelligence agencies regarding UFOs and ETs.

Years ago, I was informed that the NSA had the ability to listen in on any telephone conversation. According to an anonymous Pentagon employee, as long as a cellular phone had batteries in it (even if the phone was off) the NSA could force it to become active with a microwave signal and use it as a microphone.

I had also read that the NSA's *Project Echelon* was designed to tap into any and all digital communications thus creating a massive keyword search database. The project originally included the electronic surveillance of politicians. That fact ran parallel to what commander Dean had mentioned about the various elected branches of government being totally isolated from the dealings of the shadow government.

He agreed and said, "The shadow government doesn't trust politicians. I'll be honest with you, I have come to the point over the years where I don't trust them much anymore either. They are too easily bought off or black-mailed.

"Most of them are for sale. I think we could probably count the number of good men in the Senate on the fingers of both hands. We could probably count the number of good men in the House on our fingers and toes, and that is a sad state of affairs."

I could feel commander Dean's pain, and it made me sad and angry. I knew he had worked very hard to get Congressional hearings to address the alien agenda on earth. I also knew he had met many insightful, courageous military officers with direct knowledge of UFO and ET affairs.

At one time, commander Dean had worked with CSETI as part of a coalition called "Stargate." Commander Dean had helped bring together astronauts, former intelligence officers, and retired military servicemen that had participated in UFO crash-retrieval operations.

He also helped locate generals, admirals, and even Soviet cosmonauts who were willing to testify to a Congressional committee about what they knew about UFOs, provided they were released from their national security oaths. The videotaped depositions of key witnesses were taken by a Washington, D.C., law firm and stored in its safe while awaiting public hearings.

The activist group had also allegedly acquired crashed UFO metal samples and dead ET tissue samples. The coalition's plan was to take their briefing document, and physical evidence, to world leaders such as the United Nations, scientific academies, and religious leaders for a pre-briefing. The coalition would then make a public disclosure in the following months. CSETI reported that the White House, the Joint Chiefs of Staff, and the United Nations were being enlisted to assist.

On August 17, 1995, commander Dean had announced the beginning of a citizen's campaign to compel Congress to grant immunity to any astronauts, or military, or intelligence personnel that were ready to testify at congressional UFO hearings.

At that time, commander Dean had acquired the services of a political strategist who developed a plan to inject the UFO subject into the 1996 political agenda, including the presidential campaign. The coalition had several Senators, and Congress members, who were in favor of disclosure. The goal of all those efforts was to make UFO and ET information available publicly through televised congressional hearings; however, that never happened due to intense pressure from the shadow government.

When I inquired if there were any more men like Colonel Philip Corso waiting in the wings to go public, commander Dean stated, "There are a great number of them, but they are dying off fast. I knew Phil well, and I miss him terribly. Although it contained some errors, he had only begun to say what he really knew in his first book *The Day After Roswell*. He had a second book that he wrote.

"After Phil died, I talked to his son on the phone. I told him to make copies of that manuscript and put it in a safe deposit box and not to let anyone get access to it. Apparently, they hired an attorney and are planning to publish it. I hope they do, because Phil had a number of amazing things to say that he did not put in his first book.

"I had a long conversation with him in Italy about a year before he died. We were both speaking at a big conference in Rome. I got to know him well, and I really respected the old man. He told me some things that would literally blow your socks off. I was hoping he would have lived long enough to see it in print. I hope his son can get it out."

I was also looking forward to reading Corso's second book. Unfortunately, the next time I asked commander Dean about it, he informed me that the book would never be published. Intense pressure had been put on the colonel's son by members of a powerful, covert group that was named in the book.

Colonel Corso's second book apparently revealed an ongoing, long-standing, covert relationship between a specific group of evil aliens and an elite group of power-hungry humans. That same group reportedly approached Corso's son and instructed him to never publicly release his deceased father's manuscript. They then made him an offer he simply could not refuse. In the process he became a very-wealthy man. As part of the deal, he was told to contact his father's publisher in Italy and threaten him with life imprisonment if he distributed any of the books he had already printed.

However, in September of 2006, I met an individual that had acquired a copy of Corso's second book that was published in Italian. Apparently, some review copies were sent to various UFO researchers before the publisher in Italy was forced to destroy the books he had already printed. It seemed there was a possibility that the details of Corso's second book would leak out someday despite the efforts of that powerful, elite, control group.

When I asked commander Dean to elaborate about this control group and their operations, he said, "There was an article in the New York Times recently about the Australian government. There were some very-strong words spoken in their government. They were damn-well ready to push for not renewing the American lease on the land at Pine Gap.

"They said this was due in part to the fact that American officials would not tell anyone in the Australian government what is going on at the Pine Gap complex. However, over the years, a lot of members in the Parliament had gotten information that something pretty-damn big was going on at the top-secret facility called Pine Gap.

"I don't think they stand a snowball's chance in hell of stopping it, because that's run by the NSA. Other than the one in Yorkshire, England, the one in Pine Gap is probably the largest signals intelligence station in the world. It is so vast, and there is so much going on out there, they will never tell the Australian government what is really happening. Menwith Hill is another NSA facility in Britain, and if our telephone conversation was not being picked up on earlier it sure as hell is now."

I knew he was right. Commander Dean had uttered a "key word." This was one of the most ingenious aspects of *Project Echelon*. Like the Internet, *Echelon* was a massive digital data archive that could be automatically searched by key words. In this way, the system only required a relatively small staff to sift through literally mountains of data that were constantly being accumulated.

Commander Dean agreed with my summary of the global surveillance system, and added that, "I drove around Menwith Hill once, but I was not invited in. That facility is wonderful. It's unbelievable. The NSA runs that one as well."

I had read that there were electronic listening stations placed all over the world and even orbital platforms placed in space that were monitoring all electronic communications on earth. Commander Dean and I agreed that ultimately there was a cosmic conflict being played out on earth between good and evil. Apparently, this battle had been going on since the beginning of life on this world as part of a universal process.

Commander Dean said, "If you read any of our ancient religious records, the core message is clearly laid out that there is an ongoing struggle: dark vs. light. I realize it's a lot more complicated than just that, and I don't want to get into the cosmic aspect of the eternal struggle of our souls, but each of us has to make a choice in our own time."

Clearly so, especially on this planet the struggle seemed to be an integral part of the curriculum. As a dedicated military officer, commander Dean saw life on earth as a battle ground where one made their choices for good or ill. In the process, a soul was either victorious or defeated. It was a planet where one had to play the game of life with conviction in order to win salvation. However, this game was particularly rough at times. Commander Dean told me that he believed this was one of the toughest schools in the universe and that if a soul graduated from planet earth, they deserved a master's degree.

I firmly believed the ETs had played a pivotal role in our evolution and wondered how our government could ever address the issue openly. Commander Dean was lost in thought for a few moments. He then bitterly explained that, "I've just about given up on our government. You know my original idea of pushing Congress to hold open hearings? Well, I learned a few years ago that there isn't a snowball's chance in hell of that happening.

"I spent some time with my son in Washington, D.C., on Capitol Hill. I visited several House and Senate offices, and they all said the same damn thing. They won't touch this subject with a ten-foot pole. Frankly, they're scared."

When I mentioned that this was not real leadership, the commander became really agitated. He said, "They don't know that! They don't want to know that! The Senators and Congressmen won't even get close to addressing this subject!

"I have given up on getting open Congressional hearings. I've given up on any kind of official disclosure. I'm leaving it to my good friends in the heavens above to handle the agenda. As it stands now, only the ETs can create disclosure when they think the time is right."

I understood how truly frustrating the situation was. But statistically speaking, the official disclosure of the existence of ETs would be accepted by a majority of people. For example, *National Geographic* magazine had commissioned a poll to be taken in April, and May of 2005 that asked 1,000 Americans about their perception of UFOs and ETs.

The survey found that 60 percent of people in the United States believed that intelligent life existed on other planets. The survey also found that 90 percent of Americans believed that if extraterrestrials did contact Earth, humans should respond. It was a stunning statistic.

Other findings from the opinion poll were:

Men were more likely to feel excited and hopeful if we officially found life on other planets.

Regular churchgoers were less likely to believe in life on other planets compared to non-churchgoers.

63 percent of college graduates thought there was intelligent life in outer space.

70 percent of Americans thought that intelligent life forms on other planets would be similar to humans.

80 percent of Americans thought it was likely that intelligent life forms on other planets were more advanced than us.

70 percent of Americans thought it was likely that intelligent life forms had developed technology to travel through space.

70 percent of Americans thought that intelligent life forms had developed technology to communicate across deep space.

Of the minority of Americans that did not believe in life on other planets, 66 percent felt that if we should discover life on other worlds we should respond.

Commander Dean and I agreed that a lot more people knew the truth about ETs than the media had reported. However, as a journalist, I had met many people that were hesitant to openly discuss their close encounters. And during my brief experience working in the corporate world, I found it was a big mistake to discuss personal insights regarding ETs and UFOs. I learned the hard way that this subject really upsets some people.

I could just imagine the problems that would come up if a high-level executive or government official began speaking about this topic at work. Over the years, I was informed that some of these key people in society had personally experienced the ET/UFO phenomenon. Perhaps that was why so many people in positions of power were taking psychiatric medication.

In closing, commander Dean told me that some of the government insiders he knew believed we were dealing with hundreds of ET civilizations that were either intergalactic or inter-dimensional travelers. Apparently, NASA had set up a scientific committee years ago which came to the conclusion that there were an estimated 10 billion planets with intelligent life.

Commander Dean was very concerned about that fact. He said, "It's devastating to most of them. The higher they are in the system, the more devastating it is to confront this issue. That's why some of them go over the edge, or live in denial."

CHAPTER THREE

The Alien Hunter

Even though Derrel Sims was a former CIA operative, I didn't hold that against him. He was one of the nicest people I had ever met. One day, in the spring of 2005, Sims forwarded me some UFO photographs taken by Mr. Allen, the professional photographer in Washington, D.C. Clicking on that e-mail made me feel as though I had opened Pandora's Box. I really had no idea what I was getting myself into by investigating this story.

As I analyzed the situation, I learned that although Mr. Sims and Mr. Allen didn't know each other they had something in common. They both had encountered alien beings face-to-face in their bedroom, at night, when they were only four or five years old. Clearly, their ET experiences had deeply affected both of them.

While speaking with Derrel one day, I realized that was why he was adamant about establishing the abduction phenomenon as fact rather than fiction. According to Derrel, his first abduction occurred in 1952: The same year that close encounters with UFOs occurred around the world in great numbers especially in DC. That was the year UFOs repeatedly flew over Washington, D.C., airspace and were photographed directly over the Capitol.

At that time, Derrel really had no reference point to work from. In 1952, there weren't any UFO or alien movies or TV shows that he had seen. He was only four years old at the time. His family lived in Midland, Texas. He had a little bedroom in the back of the house that his dad had added on. Although the room was dark at night, there was a little well house behind his room that had a light about six feet off the ground. The light shone through and dimly lit the room which allowed Derrel to see at night.

The first alien being he encountered had pure-white skin and large, round, black eyes. The alien did not appear to have a nose. There were two tiny holes which Derrel assumed were nostrils. He did not see any external ears; just a slight indentation where the ears should be.

Derrel explained that, "Children remember things differently. The first thing I noticed was that the alien being was white. My memory is that I woke up, and I shouldn't have. I believe that, when the event was over, I wasn't supposed to remember any of this. But I did. The alien being appeared to be as surprised as I was when I opened my eyes. I was suddenly wide awake. I was cognizant immediately which was curious to me, because I had never experienced anything like that before."

It was clearly a good thing that most people didn't see alien creatures creeping around their bedroom at night. But Derrel noticed something else really strange: the being was naked. He explained that, "As I looked at the being, I was shocked to find that it had no belly button and no T.T. That's the way I said penis when I was young.

"I was shocked to see this pure white being with big black eyes, and no nose, and no ears, and no belly button, and no T. T. I couldn't figure out if it was a girl or a boy or what! Looking back on that event as an adult investigator, I realized that this specific type of alien probably does not procreate. It was most likely cloned or manufactured."

Although he has not read it, Derrel's had concluded the same thing as the NATO report: These aliens were clones. I was curious if Derrel had any idea why he was able to remember his close encounter when most people didn't have clear recall of their abduction experiences? He said, "I have thought about that many times. On the night of the first encounter, when I woke up, the being started to move toward me. That's when it did something with his eyes. I don't know what it was, but I instantly became paralyzed. I didn't wake up paralyzed. That didn't happen until the being started moving toward me and did something that seemed to come from his eyes, whatever it was.

"As it moved toward me, the alien being made me focus on its eyes. Although I was paralyzed, I completely freaked out. I pushed so hard against the wall that my bed moved away from the wall. I fell with my little arms wedged between the wall and the bed. My head was laying on the floor with my shoulders still hanging up there on the bed.

"That's when I first realized the alien being had knees and feet. As I was under the bed, the being lifted up the covers on the other side of the bed and then it looked at me with those huge black eyes and tried to change its image. I'm very sure about this part. It didn't physically change its image. It attempted to change my perception of what it was into a circus clown."

This was very strange indeed. Apparently, the alien had attempted to use a form of hypnosis. Without saying a word, the being somehow had the ability to change Derrel's perception of itself from that of an alien into a circus clown. Derrel told me that, while working as an investigator for many years he had met many people with clown phobias who apparently had been abducted. He should know. He ended up with the same phobia from his first alien encounter.

Derrel explained that, "At that point, I was paralyzed in bed. That was when the alien being was on his knees, and I saw his feet, and there were a number of other anomalies I saw. That entire event just stunned me.

"I realized I could control my mind even as a four-year-old child. I wanted to remember whatever this alien thing was as it really was; not as a clown. I discovered that this is one of the things they routinely do. The aliens tell you not to remember a specific event. Or, they will induce a false memory that is so bizarre you wouldn't even believe it yourself. Therefore, you simply dismiss it as a dream. However, I didn't do that. I never did that in any of my events. The alien events in my life lasted for 13 years. They stopped violently when I was 17. But one of my abductions happened during broad daylight while I was hunting in the desert. Abductions do not have to happen in the night. And if they do, that doesn't mean you are simply having night terrors."

Derrel was extremely upset by his first close encounter, but he decided not to tell his parents about the alien in his bedroom. However, as loving parents, they could tell their son was agitated. As a result, the next night, his parents made him sleep between them which had never happened before.

Unfortunately, Derrel didn't get much sleep that night. Even as an adult, he could still clearly recall that while in his parent's bed that night, his mother was sleeping on her back. She wore a little nightgown. Her right arm was laid over her face. His dad was laying on his right side. Derrel was positioned between them. However, both his parents remained sound asleep during his second alien encounter.

Derrel explained that, "I opened my eyes, for some strange reason, and saw the white being from the night before and another one that looked very similar to it, but I could tell it wasn't the same one. I could clearly see both of my parents on either side of me. I was looking for help at that point. So, I took my skinny little elbows and poked my dad in his back, but he just wouldn't wake up. I looked over at my mom, and she was out like a light. They were both totally out. The next morning, when I woke up, I had a strange-looking cut on my leg; what people now refer to as a scoop mark.

"It was weird, because I looked down at my tiny, skinny legs, and I saw the little scoop mark, and what appeared to be a cauterized area, but I couldn't understand what had happened. I kept wondering where the sore was.

"If you cut yourself that deep, there's got to be a sore somewhere, but there wasn't any pain. I kept questioning this, and then the strangest thing happened. I heard a voice in my head that said, 'You fell and hurt yourself.' It seemed like it was programmed. I mean, how many people do you know that speak to themselves in the second person? This was someone else's thinking."

I understood what Derrel was saying, but I wondered if he had ever told anyone about his encounters while he was still a child. He told me he had not and explained that, "I eventually told my dad about it when I was an adult. That happened after he had asked me to speak to my younger brother. This was about 1974, or 1976. In fact, it was shortly after the movie *Close Encounters of the Third Kind* had come out. My little brother was about six-and-a-half, or seven-years old at the time. My father couldn't understand why my brother was so obsessed with UFOs. It was really bothering him.

"My brother was obsessed with UFO sightings. My dad couldn't understand this, because he wouldn't let him watch that sort of thing on TV. He wondered why he was acting that way. One day, he called me in and asked me to talk to my younger brother. After I listened to and questioned my brother, I realized that he was having alien encounters that he had never told any of us about. I was concerned at that point and asked my dad what he would do if the events my brother was relating were true? Clearly that shocked him.

"He said, 'Well they can't be.'

"I replied, 'but mine were.'

"I then proceeded to tell my dad some of the things that had happened to me, and he was just floored. When I finally told my mom, years later, she said, 'Why didn't you tell us when you were younger?'

"I replied, 'You are told by the aliens not to ever tell anybody, or it's like you are betraying them.'"

Over the years, Derrel had become intimately familiar with abductions of humans by aliens. He recalled that, "One of the things we did was to investigate scoop marks. During a medical examination on May 18, 1995, we found that the scoop marks on one of the abductees showed signs of solar elastosis. This is a condition that is brought on by an intense bombardment of ultra-violet radiation, but it was only found in the area of the scoop itself.

"About six years earlier, I had met a lady that drew a picture of herself getting a scoop mark and the little device that was used to do it, and how it scooped out the little area with a buzzing noise. It scooped it quickly. Then, a light seemed to cauterize it.

"We never paid much attention to that until we found out about the other abductee and the evidence that seems to suggest the scoop area had been affected by high levels of ultra violet radiation. What's curious about that is this particular lady has very-white skin. She can't stay out in the sun very long."

I wondered if it was possible that the intense, ultraviolet light would also affect the nerve endings in that area, so people didn't feel any pain from the procedure. Derrel thought that was entirely possible. He explained that the scooped area of skin was very smooth, and shiny, and no hair would grow in the affected area.

Derrel then told me that he reached a turning point in his abduction experiences during his teenage years. He realized there was no one he could go to for help, so he decided to help himself. He explained that, "At the time, I believed I couldn't tell anyone. I was obedient enough to my captors that I never did tell anyone about my experiences until after the last time, when I was 17. My last encounter occurred quite early in the morning; around 3:00 a.m. What was curious about that event was five beings showed up that are not mentioned in any of the literature on ETs.

"I have only met eight other people who have seen this particular type of being. It is so horrific that when I heard these other people describing it, I was just floored. One time, when I was in Los Angeles speaking at a conference, a tall, black man kept walking past my table every so often. I kept asking him if he would like to fill out one of our forms or look at some of our information. He said no and then left very quickly.

"He did that several times. Later, he came back when I was packing everything up after the conference was over, and he said, 'I want to ask you a question.' He then took out a pen and started drawing a picture of a specific type of alien being. When he showed me his sketch, I took the pen out of his hand and finished it for him. All he said was, 'Oh my God! Oh my God... it's real!' and then he ran off with no explanation. That was the last I saw of him. He was one of the eight people that had seen that type of alien being."

When I asked Derrel what was so horrific about that particular type of alien, he replied, "It's not how they look, it's what it wants to do to you." He then told me his sister-in-law had encountered that type of alien being and ended up with grand mal epilepsy.

Derrel said, "Her condition was so severe the doctors said they could not give her more medication, because it might kill her. The only thing we could do for her was pray. I didn't know what else to do. Every person I know that has had an encounter with that type of being, their consciousness has been forever altered."

During Derrel's final alien encounter, he put an end to the contact by literally fighting for his life, or at least that's how he described it. He said, "The day after that encounter, I was perfectly willing to disregard it as just a horrible dream until it started getting dark, and the gut-wrenching fear came back. I had never, ever felt fear like that in my life.

"I was totally conscious. It was 6:30 p.m., and the sun was starting to go down, and I literally ran to my girlfriend's house. She is one of the finest, most honest people I have ever met in my life. That night, I said, 'Rosy you need to listen to me. I need to tell you something that happened to me last night. I need for you to believe what I'm about to tell you.

I know it makes no sense, but I swear it's true.'

"She said, 'I know you would never lie to me.'

"I then proceeded to tell her about my close encounters with the aliens. She just could not figure this out at all. It just didn't fit. Back in those days, around 1965, Betty and Barney Hill's story was about the strangest thing that had been reported. Nobody really knew anything about abductions, and most people didn't believe it anyway.

"My girlfriend saw that I was not going to be deterred, so she took me to see a teacher who was doing studies in scientific anomalies. That's how I actually started my study, with a psychology teacher from high school. Rosy and I went over to his house, and I explained everything to him exactly the way it happened.

"He said, 'Well, you had a terrible dream.'

"I said, 'I already heard that story.'

"He said, 'Well, it can't be true!'

"I said, 'Why can't it be true?'

"He said, 'Because when they come here they are going to land in Washington, D.C., and give the president a big gift and wonderful things.'

"I said, 'I saw that movie and whatever it is we think we know about these alien beings, it's not based on real intelligence. It's not going to happen like that. In fact, it may not happen like anything we understand at all.'

"He said, 'but none of this makes any sense.'

"He was right. In fact, this story still doesn't make any sense to this day. The five beings that showed up in my room during my final encounter didn't match anything that anyone else has ever reported, except those other eight people."

It seemed unusual to me that Derrel was able to fight these alien beings off and somehow protect himself from those same evil ETs in the future. I wanted to know what happened after that. Derrel said, "I felt that I had done something to assist myself there. It really floored me that my event was true. At some point, I realized this was also happening to other people, so I began investigating and working with other abductees and contactees.

"In 1991, I met a contactee and asked her if she would volunteer to help me do a test. This was after doing a three-year study in this field. She wanted to know the details, but I couldn't tell her. However, I did explain that I would install information in her just the way the aliens do; I was going to give her a memory. Since the aliens already knew everything about her, they would know that the implanted memory was not hers. I was testing to see if the information I had was correct. If so, I should get a reaction that proved if the aliens were real and if the abduction event was real.

"I installed the information in the form of a memory. Then, I induced amnesia on both sides of the memory, so that she couldn't remember it herself, and she wouldn't remember where she got it. That way, if the aliens questioned her, they wouldn't be able to get any information. I had no idea if this would work or not.

"After that, she moved to Jacksonville, Florida. That Thanksgiving night, her regular alien handler picked her up, and tagged her, and was walking her toward an area where he wanted her to go. I set the post hypnotic suggestion to go off when she was within 20 inches of the alien.

"When that happened, she literally woke up with her eyes wide open, and was totally coherent, and made a statement that I wish she had never made. She looked at him and said, 'Derrel knows what you are doing.'

"She told me later that for the first time in 30 years the alien had a visible expression on his face: fear. I asked her every question I could think of. After I got all the information, I asked her if there was anything else that I missed.

"She said, 'No, you were very thorough.'

"I said, 'OK. Is there anything else that you are not supposed to tell me?'

"She said, 'Yes' and then proceeded to describe my last abduction at age 17 in detail. Nobody knew the details except me. Yet, she knew it in full detail. How could she know that? She accurately described the five alien beings. She also described a physical object that they left behind. She described everything in a lot more detail than I ever wanted to discuss.

"To this day, she does not know that it is in fact a true story, because I never told her. But when she described my last abduction, I realized that not only might it have been real, I asked her where she got that information she said, 'I heard it onboard the craft.'

"I said, 'What do you mean?'

"She said, 'Sometimes they think you can't hear them.'

"I knew that was true, because I have worked with a number of abductees. I know that abductees can do more than just listen after being switched off by the aliens. I've actually programmed some abductees to get up off the table after the aliens have left the room and go see what's in there, because I wanted to know.

"The aliens have always told their abductees they were going to die if they didn't obey which is totally untrue. But when that woman recalled in detail the events of my final abduction that was what finally convinced me my alien encounters were in fact real.

"She also said, 'I know that they had me move to Florida to get away from you and the other investigators."

"I said, 'Well a lot of us felt the same thing.'

"I guess it worked because soon after that, the same woman and my senior investigator and six other people in two states in several different cities were all picked up during a mass abduction, on December 8, 1992.

"They were all given nasal implants except for one woman that was given an ocular implant. Three nights later, for some reason, they were all abducted again, and their implants were removed, but someone made a mistake with the casing from the ocular implant. It fell out of the lady's eye the next morning.

"Her boss literally forced her to bring it to me. That's the only reason I have it. The curious thing about all this was how my senior investigator found out what was going on. I never told anybody about this woman, and I induced amnesia in her, so she wouldn't remember.

"One day, my senior investigator asked me to look at his fingernails. They were growing so fast they had to be trimmed two or three times a day! This occurred for a brief period right after his abduction. I was sure that something strange had happened to him. When I worked with him, he described the other seven people at this amazing event. I separated all the people and questioned them individually. I learned that every one of them had been taken to the same place and told the same story.

"Two things convinced me that this encounter happened and that my encounters had happened. The first thing that convinced me that the mass abduction had in fact occurred was after my senior investigator told me his story I went to his home and found unbelievable physical evidence. Clearly, something alien had been there. Second, he said that he and the other people had been taken to a space craft that was huge. He estimated it to be about 50-miles tall and 600-miles across!"

That seemed too incredible. Where would anyone hide a craft of that size? Oddly enough, Derrel's lead investigator claimed he knew where it was located, or at least where it had last been seen. He had made a video tape of the TV show *Sightings*. One segment of the show featured an astronomer that had filmed a huge spacecraft moving between the earth, and the moon. The giant UFO was casting a shadow on the moon that was traveling hundreds of thousands of miles per hour. Oddly enough, that event occurred at the exact same time the group of eight people was abducted.

Derrel said, "I couldn't believe it. We had an astronomical sighting as well as eye witnesses. That was something that really interested me about this event."

I then asked Derrel why he hunted aliens. He stated that, "One of the most horrible events I have experienced was when my son was six. Back then, we lived on a large ranch house. One morning, at about 2:30 a.m., I woke up and instantly ran into the living room as fast as I could and saw my little, six-year-old son standing there looking out the window in a deep trance. I watched him for a long time before I asked him what he was looking at.

"He said, 'The little red light.'

"Unfortunately, that's the alien screen saver memory. The abduction event was already over. My son begged me for the next two or three years to work with him, which I finally did. But I didn't want to, and I found his encounter to be very similar to mine. The same entity was involved."

Derrel had brought up a few different encounters with various entities. I wasn't sure which one he was talking about? I need some clarification. He explained that, "I was referring to my final alien encounter with the horrific being. He was involved in my son's abduction as well. It forever changed his way of thinking. It almost ruined his life."

It was still unclear to me how Derrel decided he was going to do something about the situation himself rather than try and find someone to help him. I wanted to better understand why he had decided to hunt aliens on his own.

He told me that his first idea to do something about it was when he was four year old. At that time, Derrel decided he was not going to let the alien make him believe it was just a circus clown. The second time was when Derrel realized what had happened to his son. He knew that there would never be an end to the abductions unless he, and others like him, took action.

Things were finally starting to make sense. The abduction of Derrel's son was the final straw. He explained that, "Like it or not, I hunt aliens. I simply hunt the beings that hunted me and my son. Any hunter knows his prey's habits. He knows everything about them, and he knows how to trap them otherwise he's not a very good hunter.

"They knew everything about me. Now I'm learning all kinds of things about them. An alien was standing next to my bed when I was age four. I don't need any physical proof of that. I know what I saw. I know what was there.

"The aliens hunted me and my son, and they may be hunting you or your family. I am actively pursuing this. For example, if the isotopic ratios of these objects called implants that we extracted from abductees turn out to be extraterrestrial, they should give us a clue as to where the aliens are mining.

"We are then one step closer to knowing where they have been, or where they still are. To me, that's important. I'm happy that everybody's getting on the bandwagon with these different ideas, but I don't need any proof that aliens exist. I already know that for a fact."

Derrel further explained that, "I had some different people get some surgical work done, and I never told them what the purpose was. I already had a number of alien implants in my possession before the first public surgery on August 19, 1995. You see, I discovered the phenomenon of the so-called implantation in 1960.

"At age 12, I was conscious during one of my abductions. I was inside a room, I don't know if it was a UFO or what, but it was a circular room that had a strange light coming from above. Myself and this alien creature were in the room, and someone else was outside the light standing in the dark. The light was very strange because it seemed to have an edge. In other words, if you placed your hand through it, you wouldn't see your hand on the outside of the light.

"I had never seen anything like it before. I still do not understand it at all. But, they didn't know that I could overhear them, and I heard the instructions they were giving to the guy I call my keeper. He made me feel like I was some kind of lab rat. At one point, he took out a large medical tool. It was about a nine-inch, needle-looking thing. I didn't know what it was, but it was a silver-looking, needle type of thing that had a tiny object on the end of it that was very small, like a B.B. only smaller.

"He inserted it into my right nostril, and I felt it go up behind my eye and break the bone as it went through. It was very painful. I still remember the intense physical pain I experienced as he shoved the needle in and brought it out.

"The pain was so intense, I passed out. There's a lot about that abduction, and my final encounter, that I have never told anybody. I may release that information in the future, but I have never publicly described the five beings. That type of alien being is horrific and unforgettable. Once you meet him, he will radically alter your life."

Derrel had obviously been doing his investigative work long enough to formulate an opinion about their intentions toward us. He humbly explained that, "These are not things that I can prove. They are just some things that I have tested. However, I found the alien's reactions to the proactive approach I take as being very suggestive. The amazing thing to me in all of this is that these aliens seem to have such arrogance. Apparently, they believe they cannot be touched.

"It's frustrating, because even if we did know where they are based, we are not going to do anything about it because we don't know what their next move is. Despite that fact, I have continued to be very proactive with my abduction research.

"I think people should understand that I do not believe every story I hear. I have certain criteria that I use to determine whether people are lying or telling the truth. In fact, I'm teaching that technique to the judiciary here in Houston, and it's very effective."

CHAPTER FOUR

Conversation with the Colonel

Another military expert I spoke with about the subject of alien incursions of restricted airspace was retired Air Force Lieutenant Colonel Wendelle Stevens. He was a fighter pilot that had become a UFO investigator after retiring from the military.

Colonel Stevens was born and raised in Minnesota. He enlisted in the Army shortly after high school. Next, he graduated from the Lockheed aircraft maintenance and repair school. He then went on to aviation cadet training and fighter pilot advanced training as a very young second lieutenant in the U.S. Army Air Corps. After that, he attended the first Air Corps Flight Test Pilot School at Kelly Field, where he learned to fly all the aircraft of the Air Corps at the time, as well as a few U.S. Navy aircraft.

During his long career in the military, one of his assignments was to supervise a highly-classified team of technical specialists who were operating hi-tech, data-surveillance equipment aboard B-29s. It was used during *Project Ptarmigon* which involved photographing and mapping every inch of the Arctic land and sea area.

The surveillance equipment was also designed to record and analyze all electromagnetic emissions in the Arctic. The technical team was photographing all anomalous aerial phenomena and recording disturbances in the electrical and engine systems of the aircraft. They were actively looking for external influences caused by UFOs. The data was then delivered by courier nightly to the Pentagon, in Washington, D.C.

Unable to possess any of this information for himself, colonel Stevens began his own UFO research and collection effort; eventually amassing the largest private collection of UFO photographs in the world. He had collected over 4,000 photos during 60 years of research. He began to publish reports on the events and wrote many illustrated articles for UFO publications. He had written and coauthored over 22 books on well documented UFO contact cases. Even in the last years of his life, he continued seeking the elusive answers to the many questions raised by this phenomenon. Colonel Stevens had been a Director of the International UFO Congress since its inception.

During one of my conversations with colonel Stevens, I was shocked when he mentioned that the U.S. Army had confiscated UFO photographs from civilians. I recalled that commander Dean had said the same thing. This type of military action was obviously part of an ongoing cover-up.

I was very interested in finding out what happened to the hundreds of UFO photos that were reportedly taken around the Capitol building in 1952. That year, UFOs were regularly being sighted over Washington, D.C. I wanted to know specifically how he found out that the army was confiscating and classifying these photographs.

Colonel Stevens explained that he was friends with a man named August Roberts who lived in the DC area. Roberts was a studio photographer for a number of news services before he retired. He had told colonel Stevens about the military authorities going around confiscating cameras and photographs. Roberts said they were canvassing houses and interviewing everybody in the area of Washington, D.C., at that time.

It was a historic fact that in 1952, UFOs repeatedly flew over the Capitol building and the surrounding area. Published reports indicated that hundreds of UFO photos were taken as well as movie footage. However, only one or two of these images had ever been seen by the public.

Oddly enough, *Walt Disney* studios broadcast a special TV documentary on UFOs and ETs to select cities in Connecticut, Tennessee, Alabama, Florida and California, without any notice, on the weekend of March 19, 1995. One segment featured a few seconds of historic movie footage showing a number of glowing, spherical UFOs performing wild aerial maneuvers over the Capitol dome at night. During the TV documentary, former Disney Chief Executive Officer, Michael Eisner, made the following statements:

Mankind is in the midst of the most profound event in history; actual contact with intelligent life from other planets.

Intelligent life from distant galaxies is now attempting to make open contact with the human race, and tonight we'll show you the evidence.

From beyond the boundaries of our perceptions, intelligent beings are beckoning mankind to join the galactic community. It's an invitation which is both wondrous and terrifying.

Alien ships seem to arrive in waves, and if the last few years are any indication, planet Earth is experiencing a tsunami of sightings.

As early as 1947, large, alien ships began to arrive; navigated by living creatures. Their advanced physics allowed them to traverse the galaxy and pierce Earth's atmosphere with amazing speed.

More than one alien craft has crashed and was recovered for secret U.S. military research.

Roswell is one site where a crashed, saucer-shaped spacecraft was discovered, along with the bodies of three extraterrestrial missionaries who didn't survive. The debris and the dead were impounded and taken away for top-secret study, while a classified investigative committee was organized by President Truman, and a government cover-up was initiated with a calculated disinformation campaign.

For governments determined to maintain their authority, extraterrestrial contact is pure dynamite.

When Jimmy Carter was president of the United States, his staff attempted to explore the availability of official investigations into alien contact. According to an internal government memo, there are some security secrets outside the jurisdiction of the White House.

In November of 1975, nearly all the Strategic Air Command base in the United States were visited by UFOs.

Indications are that government, military and scientific leaders will soon release nearly a half century of official documentation of on-going alien encounters on earth.

Statistics indicate there is a greater probability that you will experience extraterrestrial contact in the next five years, than the chances that you will win a state lottery.

In the future, most Americans will likely explore outer space aboard crafts of alien origin.

In 1952, Colonel Stevens was stationed in Orlando, Florida. Prior to that, he was stationed in Alaska where he helped coordinate military missions to photograph UFOs. While there, he supervised a special team that had installed tons of classified photographic equipment aboard B-29's. Officially, they flew their missions over the Arctic to spy on Russia.

However, according to the colonel, this team was actually created to collect data on anomalous aerial phenomena. He said, "Some of my superiors, at that time, believed UFOs might be coming from Russia. I insisted that these craft were not made on earth. They were clearly extraterrestrial, but nobody wanted to believe me."

Colonel Stevens had reached this conclusion after learning some of the details regarding data his team was collecting. He told me there was an occasion where one of the B-29's under his command had flown directly over a disk-shaped UFO that was at least 100 feet in diameter. It was just sitting on the polar ice cap, but then it flew away and left nothing on the ground behind it.

He explained that this was significant because, "When we launched an aircraft like a B-29 we needed a lot of equipment and personnel around it. For instance, it required eight oil heaters to fly that plane. There were also people running air compressors that maintained the air pressure in the tires. There were all kinds of people and equipment left behind after an aircraft taxied down the runway and took off.

"But one of my crews performed reconnaissance on a UFO that was bigger than a B-29. It took off from the polar ice cap and left nothing behind! Another time they approached a UFO that was sitting on the water. It then submerged and disappeared into the Arctic Sea. Yet another time, they saw a UFO rise up out of the water and fly away. This clearly was not our kind of aircraft."

I was beginning to understand how the colonel had reached his conclusion that UFOs were not built on earth. Most rational people would conclude the same thing after hearing these various reports coming from trained, military, flight crews.

His opinion was formed step-by-step as these events unfolded from 1947 to 1949, while stationed in Alaska collecting classified data. Apparently, these reconnaissance missions were due to the fact that UFOs were being seen regularly at the North Pole, and someone in Washington, D.C., wanted to know more.

While UFOs were being sighted and photographed flying around Washington, D.C., in 1952, Colonel Stevens was stationed in Orlando, Florida. One day, a test pilot in his squadron was flying an F-100 over the Atlantic Ocean during an engine change test. In that test, he was required to take off with the afterburner on continuously up to 18,000 feet to check all the fuel controls.

As he was reaching the end of his flight, he saw what looked like the *Goodyear* blimp ahead of him at 18,000 feet. He came out of afterburner and realized the UFO was moving away from him. The pilot then went back into afterburner to try and catch up to the UFO, but it zoomed up and away at a steep angle and was soon out of sight. When I asked the colonel if he believed we had any technology that even came close to that of UFOs, he replied, "No. I don't think we did at that time."

It seemed like a strange response. I then asked if he knew of a time in history when we began to develop technology like that. His answer was shocking, he said, "We currently have operational flying saucers. They are being operated by our government right now. One of the later classes of these craft can take off under its own power and go into orbit and return back to base."

I was intrigued and wanted to know, in the colonel's opinion, when this type of advanced aerospace research and development program had started. He explained that in the mid-to-late 1960s, there was a gravity control breakthrough at the super-secret military base called Pine Gap, in Australia. Apparently, the American military built its first operational flying disks there, at that time. At first, there were several prototype versions. These were followed by a series of operational flying discs.

Over time, the technology improved, and the U.S. military had covertly designed and built better versions of the same type of craft. According to the colonel, we currently had operational flying discs in various underground bases. However, this was all strictly military hardware that was classified at the highest levels. When I asked if that technology would ever be declassified for general use, the colonel said, "Probably not for another 10 or 15 years when it has been surpassed by something else."

I wondered if the colonel had any idea why Washington, D.C., was the UFO sightings capital of the world. Although he was aware that there had been a lot of UFO activity over Washington in the past 50 years, he was shocked when I told him that it had the highest number of UFO sightings per square mile in the world.

It was a highly unusual situation. DC was a very busy location. Thousands of tourists visited the nation's capital every week, and there were always lots of media people covering some type of story. It seemed as though someone should have reported the DC UFO connection already.

The colonel agreed and added, "Especially since the airspace over Washington, D.C., is either restricted or prohibited. Nothing is allowed to fly through there without permission. One day, while piloting an aircraft, I cut the corner on a restricted area like that, and I was ordered to land at a nearby military base. They took me in and checked my airplane all over thoroughly.

"They really grilled me for cutting through the corner of that restricted airspace. They knew immediately when I had crossed over the line. They knew exactly which airplane I was and called me on the radio by my tail number and ordered me to land.

"I eventually got out of the $10,000 fine by protesting that I couldn't afford it on my pilot's salary. I told them that the best I could do was $10 a month. After about five months, I got a letter from the Comptroller General stating that is was costing them more to process my check than they were getting, so they told me to cease sending any more checks."

I knew that the restrictions and prohibitions of airspace had become even tighter after 9/11/2001 and grew tighter still after the U.S. invasion of Iraq in 2003. This made me wonder how it was possible that a fleet of UFOs could penetrate an area of prohibited airspace and even land one of their craft on the roof of the Capitol building, in July of 2002. These same unidentified alien craft were also sighted in DC after 2002 and would no doubt continue to appear in the future.

When I mentioned this to the colonel, he said, "That seems a little bit difficult for me to believe, because I know we have active defense systems to shoot down any unidentified aircraft in that prohibited area. Those defense systems are on the ground, and the prohibition is also enforced by squadrons of interceptor fighter jets. They can be over that area in five minutes or less."

The colonel wasn't kidding. I knew that the military was ready to use deadly force against any perceived threat in the sky. However, if they scrambled fighters to intercept, or fired missiles at UFOs every time they showed up over Washington, D.C., people would soon start to wonder what the hell was going on.

Colonel Stevens then told me that he felt the people in charge, in DC, had learned to tolerate much of the UFO activity. Over time, they had learned to recognize which types of UFOs they were not going to catch or communicate with. According to the colonel, "I recall a fighter intercept where two jets were vectored in on a formation of five or six illuminated spheres that were zipping around the skies of the capital area of DC.

"The UFOs evaded the jets every time. They couldn't get close to the UFOs, so the ground crew ordered the jets to try and ram one! However, when one of the pilots went into afterburner, and tried to hit the UFO, it began flying rapidly in circles around the jet which was traveling at close to 1,000 mph. Think about that for a moment, the UFO was circling the speeding jet as if it was standing still!"

I then reminded the colonel that even if the military could lock onto and fire a missile at every UFO over DC, it would cause a major problem because the debris would come down on the capital area. Oddly enough, such an event had reportedly occurred decades ago.

I found a report from 1952 involving a fighter jet that had been sent to intercept a UFO over DC. Officially, that was the first day in history U.S. fighter jets had been authorized to fire on any UFOs in American airspace. At that time, a piece of a UFO was reportedly shot off and fell to earth and was later recovered.

Fortunately, there were no reports of injuries on the ground from the spent bullets and falling debris. The report stated that pieces of the UFO fell into a farmer's field in Virginia. One piece was glowing for a couple of hours afterwards. At first read, that event seemed odd, but then I discovered that it had taken place shortly after the military had issued orders to shoot at any UFOs sighted over the U.S. which made perfect sense.

I was surprised that the colonel had not heard that specific story before. He said, "I was aware of the orders, but I considered them very foolish because someone was assuming that UFOs can't shoot back."

It was a good point. Many years ago, I had read an interesting magazine article by retired Marine Major Donald Keyhoe about that very subject. He claimed that there were credible reports of defensive military action taken by UFOs soon after we adopted the shoot-on-sight policy. Perhaps that was why the military soon rescinded their order.

Colonel Stevens had retired from active duty in 1964, but continued researching UFOs and ETs for the next 42 years. When I asked him if he would have taken the same path in life if he had not been exposed to the subject of UFOs while serving in the military, he thought about it for a moment, and said, "Probably not. I wasn't convinced that such a phenomena really existed until I started collecting the reports for the government and sending them to headquarters at the Pentagon. But I was not allowed to read anything or see any pictures. We weren't allowed to develop pictures in the field.

"Every night, after a UFO event had occurred, all the reports and film were packaged in a metal container and then hand delivered by courier to Washington, D.C. When I came back from Alaska, I went to DC one time and tried to get a look at some of those pictures. They told me I didn't have a high enough security clearance! Keep in mind those photos were in reports I had sent in."

I then asked the colonel if he knew where in Washington, D.C., the reports and photos ended up. He told me that he tried to gain access to them at the Pentagon, but had no luck. He later determined that the real collection and processing area was located in Mount Weather, a secret underground city in the mountains of Virginia.

Colonel Stevens believed that specific underground, government facility was being used as a secure location for the storage and processing of UFO data. Although most people knew about it these days, for decades the facility was classified top secret.

After doing a little research, I learned that construction under Mount Weather had begun in 1936 when the U.S. Bureau of Mines took control of the area and started digging. According to people that had worked at the facility, this was virtually an underground city buried deep inside the earth just 46 miles from Washington, D.C. That specific federal Under Ground Facility (UGF) was reportedly equipped with:

streets and sidewalks

cafeterias and hospitals

its own mass transit system

a TV communication system

private apartments and dormitories

a small lake fed by fresh water from underground springs

a water purification system, power plant and office buildings

However, this was just one of 50 to 100 similar UGF's that had been constructed in the U.S. by the late 1980s. The Department of Defense (DOD) had even proposed the construction of a UGF directly under Washington, D.C. Reportedly, the DOD wanted one underground facility that was close enough to evacuate all essential personnel in 15 minutes. The facility was to be located two-thirds of a mile below the surface of the city of Washington.

Officially, that specific UGF was never built. But, if it actually existed, no one would be allowed to confirm or deny that fact even to this day. The same had been true for the facility at Mount Weather. It was discovered by the media by accident when an aircraft crashed nearby.

According to the colonel, "It's still not a well-known story. They hollowed out a large portion of that mountain and created an underground Capitol with duplicate political figures sitting in positions of power.

"It was designed so that even if an atomic bomb had vaporized the whole DC area, another government was already in power with people there that would keep the country going. However, there was so much anger and infighting over who would hold positions of power that, at some point, they decided to close access to everyone. That's when they put up the barriers. You can't get through now."

A popular term in DC was the acronym "COG," which stood for continuity of government. It played a major role in the federal governments contingency planning. I wanted to know if the colonel knew how long the facility at Mount Weather had been locked down. He estimated it was about 20 years or more.

He said, "I drove out of DC one time heading south toward Raleigh. There is an eight lane highway that comes straight out of Washington towards Virginia, and before it gets to the base of the mountains the highway curves to the south. However, the eight lanes continue straight into the mountain and four lanes turn south in each direction.

"There are striped posts that block progress from continuing on the eight lane section of the highway that lead straight into the mountain. The posts are controlled electronically and will allow someone with the proper clearance to enter the facility, with no traffic, on their own private freeway.

"If you don't have clearance, you can't get through. But the Democrats and Republicans never could agree on who was going to be in charge, so they decided that nobody would go. I think they still have the communications facilities set up to run the entire government from down there, but they don't have trained people in those positions any more. However, I think they took advantage of that expensive temperature and humidity controlled, dust free, secure environment to store the real UFO information."

I was able to confirm that Mount Weather was indeed a highly-secure location near DC that was effectively another Capitol underground. There were rumors that it had been used as recently as 9/11/2001. I also discovered a very strange coincidence. I found a report regarding an amazing event that allegedly occurred in the late 1930s. The report claimed that alien bodies and a dismantled UFO had been stored in the sub-basement under the Capitol building.

The story seemed rather bizarre, but the alleged source of the report was the cousin of then Secretary of State Cordell Hull. Hull was a dedicated public official and an influential, international diplomat that played a key role in creating the United Nations. His cousin, a respected reverend, claimed that Hull had sworn him to secrecy before showing him the alien bodies and artifacts hidden under the Capitol.

When I mentioned this to the colonel, he said, "There could have been a sample located there in a cryogenic case of some type. I know that Wright Patterson Field used to have four alien bodies stored in cryogenic cases in a special room. You could look through the glass at the containers the bodies were in."

In fact, that was the way Hull's cousin had described the situation under the Capitol, more or less. It was not elaborate, but there were reportedly small, alien bodies that had been placed in glass containers filled with some type of liquid. There were also some dismantled pieces and parts of a UFO in the same room.

But this was back in the late 1930s, so I started researching that period in history. I found that there were many people that had not only seen UFOs, but they had encountered aliens, too. This proved that the phenomena had been around long before the 1940s. However, because our perspective of it had changed over the years, it seemed like a new discovery.

Colonel Stevens agreed and added that in the historic annals of Rome there were 28 volumes with reports of soldiers encountering "flying shields" while on military campaigns. It seemed extremely likely that most every civilization on Earth had experienced some type of contact with UFOs and ETs. However, because humans had recently developed technically advanced aerospace craft, and were becoming more aware of UFOs, the public's perception had become much more scientific and less superstitious. Unfortunately, although we were much more aware of UFOs than any time in the past, we were still collectively in denial about the issue.

In the colonels' opinion, our society was still not properly organized or ready to deal with this issue. I had to agree. The federal government had officially washed its hands of any involvement in this issue even when there were clear violations of national security. Airspace was classified restricted or prohibited for a reason. Yet, there were well-documented cases of military, nuclear missile sites that had been intentionally tampered with by UFOs, on more than one occasion, with no retaliatory military action being taken.

Colonel Stevens then stated that, "When we talk about the national government not dealing with UFOs, we are talking about the publicly-elected, federal officials we commonly think of as our government. But they are not in charge, and they do not have control over this kind of information. It is controlled by the ones behind them: the shadow government that we never get to see. They are never elected or voted for by the public."

I knew the colonel was referring to the powerful role that secret societies played. I had read a lot of material related to a shadow government while researching Washington, D.C. In the process, I realized that the occult fit hand and glove with the paranormal and that Washington, D.C., was literally founded on occult knowledge maintained by members of secret societies.

Colonel Stevens agreed and sighted examples such as the Great Seal on the One Dollar Bill, the Presidential Seal and the Seal of the United States as occult symbols. Apparently, some people already knew about the role secret societies played in Washington, D.C. However, it was clear to me that the general public had no idea who was really in charge of DC, and the planet earth.

When I asked the colonel if he thought we would ever see official disclosure, he replied, "Some information will be released, but there will never be a full disclosure because new things are happening all the time.

"A member of the government UFO control group recently died and his replacement has changed the balance of power towards disclosure in that group. What used to be MJ-12 now has more members. It now has a balance of power that leans toward the gradual release of ET information to get the public ready.

"They are just now beginning to release information regarding 12 specially-trained, American, military personnel that were sent to another planet. The US government negotiated an exchange program many decades ago. In the process we got some alien technology. Our team members were scheduled to visit an alien world for 10 years and then return.

"They came back about 15 years ago. They are all deceased now, but the government UFO control group is just now starting to release parts of the 3,000 pages of the debriefing report from the military scientists that lived on that alien world with an alien society for 10 years."

I had been following the gradual release of that information and quickly realized that the final scenes from the movie *Close Encounters of the Third Kind* could have been based on the alleged event. It was fascinating but impossible to verify.

The colonel explained that there would be more information coming. The elite were just testing the waters to see how the public reacted. If we didn't panic, gradually there would be a little bit more, then a little bit more until we had become conditioned to accept such information. However, there would never be a full release because there was always new information developing that they didn't want the public to see.

I was having a hard time understanding the complex situation. I really wanted to know why the elite didn't just release the information publicly and initiate open contact with ETs. Where was the harm in that?

The colonel was clearly frustrated by my question. He sighed and said, "To them, it represents a loss of power. As long as they have the secrets, they maintain a certain amount of power. When they give up the secrets they give up some of their power, and they don't want to do that.

"Nobody wants to give away their power. And as long as they are in control, the information isn't going to just come out. They don't want to give up control. Because of this, there will never be one big public release of information. What they do release will never fully catch up to what is really there. They will always have the ace up their sleeve."

I had always been uncomfortable with the term "they," but the colonel's point was well taken. Due to the government's unofficial covert policy regarding UFOs, it was impossible for humanity to ever have an open relationship with other intelligent beings in the Universe.

The colonel's next comment really shocked me. He said, "I don't know how open it will ever be in this respect; the aliens that visit this planet consider us a primitive species, because we have no plan for an intelligent alien species to come here and interact with us safely and then leave. We have no plan for that to happen. They have to always make contact covertly."

I was surprised by his statement because, according to the colonel, these conditions had been created by humans rather than aliens. Our global leaders, whoever they really were, had effectively imposed a policy of isolation on the human race.

The colonel further explained that, "The ETs have sighted this as an example as to why they don't think we would ever be accepted into their interplanetary community. That age will not come on earth for a long time. We have yet to learn how to become interplanetary citizens. Right now, we are not doing it. We put the rocks in our own shoes before we ran the race!"

I had known for some time there was a serious communication breakdown on this issue. It was very frustrating for me to be dealing with this subject every day on a personal and professional level. Historically, everyone that publicly took a stand on the issue, no matter what their credentials, endured a lot of ridicule. Despite that fact, I knew that something extraordinary was going on with UFOs in DC, and there was no way I was going to simply ignore the story and not report it. The colonel admired my conviction, but cautioned me that no one could ever acquire all the information on this subject, because the shadow government was always trying to keep researchers from gaining access to sensitive UFO data and releasing it to the public.

For some reason, of all the freelance journalists in the world, I was the first to report the DC UFO story and photos from 2002. In fact, I was the only one that really took the time to thoroughly investigate the matter and then report my findings internationally. Ultimately, that was what led me to begin writing *Close Encounters on Capitol Hill* in 2005. At that time, I had no idea that reporting this story was considered a matter of national security. However, my perception changed dramatically on July 6, 2005.

On that day, at approximately 6:00 p.m., I was in my studio writing when a military helicopter entered my neighborhood and began flying circles extremely low over my house. It was so low the entire house started shaking violently! At first, I thought it would just pass over the house and leave. But it kept circling. The engine noise was unbelievable, so after a couple of minutes I went outside to investigate what the hell was going on. That's when I saw the low-flying, black helicopter hovering over my driveway. It was so low I could have hit it with a rock. The crew inside the main cabin was hidden behind tinted windows.

Colonel Stevens became noticeably upset as I recalled my close encounter with the black helicopter. He was well aware of that type of covert activity. He said, "You have got to wonder who finances these projects. Where did they come from? They are not cheap to finance, you know. They don't just grow on trees."

Coincidently, the black helicopter was flying just above the trees around my house. It was flying so low it was scary. The downdraft off the chopper was extremely powerful, and the engine noise was deafening.

The colonel and I both agreed it was illegal to fly like that. The crew had clearly been violating air traffic laws. Living in the city, I had seen helicopter traffic come through my neighborhood occasionally, but I had never experienced anything like that before and hopefully never would again.

After the black helicopter flew tight circles around my house for few minutes and briefly hovered over my driveway, it then headed west for about a mile and was gone for a couple of minutes. Then, it turned around and slowly came back again flying really low. It flew straight down my street no more than 200 feet in the air. My house was located on a quiet residential street, so this was a very-strange sight. However, by then, I was ready with my camera and took a couple of pictures. The images I captured that afternoon proved there were no visual identification markings on the helicopter.

I had no idea what they were trying to achieve during that mission. At least I got a picture to prove it really happened. What else could I do? It was all highly unusual. I had never experienced anything like that before. In fact, although I had researched UFOs for a few decades, I had dismissed many of the black helicopter reports. I presumed that these reports had come from people who were paranoid or had simply witnessed a military exercise. However, after I had experienced and documented the activity for myself, I knew they really did exist. I just couldn't understand their true purpose.

The colonel then told me about a similar case in Charleston, South Carolina. He said that a man named Bill Herman had just finished making a 20-minute audio tape recording of a UFO that emitted a loud buzzing sound. The UFO had just left the area, and Mr. Herman was going back to his car, when a black helicopter flew towards him at tree top level from a nearby swamp.

The military chopper came within a few yards of him and hovered. It was completely black with no identification numbers. It then turned sideways, and a door slid open. Inside was a man sitting on a chair wearing a black suit, black sun glasses, and a black helmet. The man had a big camera mounted on a tripod and was taking pictures of Mr. Herman who stood staring in disbelief at the helicopter.

After taking a few pictures, the man inside slid the door shut, and the helicopter took off rapidly back over the trees at tree top level and disappeared in the same direction it had just come from. I could tell that recalling the event really agitated the colonel. He said, "Who the hell has the money to do that? And how the hell did they know that Bill Herman was there tape recording a UFO?"

It was clear that no one in the government was officially going to admit anything about this clandestine activity. However, I had heard there were government agencies allegedly involved in tracking the movements of UFOs. This had been stated publicly by Ron Rehger. He reported that DSP satellites were secretly being used to tune into a specific energy frequency coming from the UFOs. They could do this because UFOs used an electromagnetic field propulsion system that discharged highly charged plasma which created radio frequencies. Apparently, these electronic signals were fairly easy to tune into if you knew the specific frequency.

Colonel Stevens was clearly angered by this type of well-funded, covert operation. He said, "We have never found a military base where these unmarked black helicopters are sitting on the ground! Why is that? They clearly have a lot of state-of-the-art equipment.

"It reminds me of that incident near Houston, Texas, with that woman named Betty Cash. They were driving down the road when they came upon a diamond-shaped UFO hovering over the highway that discharged some type of energy that burned the road. That UFO had over a dozen black helicopters escorting it."

I recalled that event clearly. It was another example of a close encounter where harmful radioactive effects were involved. The UFO appeared to be damaged and was emitting flames. The road was burned as was one of the witnesses and her car.

But the colonel's point was that no one had any idea where all the black helicopters were stationed. Apparently, only one or two had ever been sighted at any given Air Force base and even those had some identification on them, and they were not really all black. Yet, a dozen of these unmarked black helicopters were witnessed flying as an escort for a damaged UFO, in Texas. The helicopters were clearly surrounding it and attempting to keep control of the situation.

I knew the military helicopter that flew over my house was totally black, and the photographs I had taken proved it had no visible identification. I also knew that no one was legally allowed to fly any aircraft that was not licensed and displayed clear identification markings. All aircraft were supposed to have identification markings just like a license plate on a car.

Colonel Stevens and I agreed that the entire situation was very strange. In part, that was why most people preferred to ignore the subject. The colonel saw this as a reflection of our government which really didn't seem to have control of much of anything. It always seemed to be out of control, at least on the surface.

After many years of research, I had learned this was done by design. The elite were using a process where a covert group not only created a problem they then appeared to solve the same problem. This type of system allowed an elite group to maintain control with the consent of the people. It also created a reliance of the masses on an authority group, but the whole thing was rigged from the beginning. It was a very strange power trip these people were on.

The colonel agreed, and he added, "I don't know if we are going to the bottom of this in our life time. I have devoted 65 years to researching the subject of UFOs, and I don't have any more answers today than when I first started."

It was a startling statement. I had been researching this subject for 33 years and felt like I was just beginning to see the bigger picture: literally. I accidentally came across the radiation connection to UFOs while researching the final UFO photograph taken on by Mr. Allen on July 16, 2002, around 1:00 a.m., at the Capitol, in DC. It was a three-and-a-half minute exposure on film.

While taking that picture, Mr. Allen was slightly burned from some type of radiation coming from the UFOs. I did some research and found that other people had been burned when they got too close to a UFO. A scoutmaster in Florida had been burned pretty badly, and there was a man in Canada that was burned on his chest by a UFO. In fact, the deeper I looked, the more I found reports from all around the world of people, plants, vehicles, and soil that had been burned by the energy emitted from UFOs. However, the most important clue I found was a report written by Air Force Captain Ed Ruppelt in the fall of 1949 detailing how scientists accidentally discovered that UFOs emitted radiation. That was the first time someone noticed that UFOs created a spike of background radiation on *Geiger* counters when they flew over. This clearly indicated that UFOs had extremely-powerful energy at their disposal.

This extraterrestrial energy system represented a clear and present danger. UFOs were incredibly powerful space craft that repeatedly flew over nuclear reactors, and electrical power plants, and cities, and airports, and military bases, and government buildings which posed a direct threat to our national security. If one of those craft were to become unstable, or was shot down with a missile, it could explode with the force of an atomic bomb or worse!

The colonel agreed that this really was a dangerous situation. I then explained how Mr. Allen, the DC photographer, had been burned on his fingertips and the top of his head at the same moment the UFOs created a worm hole in the sky near the Capitol.

According to main-stream science, creating a worm hole required a tremendous amount of energy. Physicists had stated that, hypothetically, someone would have to be able to generate and control an incredible amount of energy to warp space and create a worm hole. Yet, that was exactly what the final photograph taken at the Capitol in July of 2002 showed.

The only reason the worm hole had been captured on film that night was that the photographer, Mr. Allen, made a three-and-a-half minute exposure while using a polarized filter. That technique effectively allowed the 35mm film to capture the UFOs full electromagnetic spectrum of radiation. This gave us a window into what we humans normally saw as a pitch-black, night sky.

From those images, we learned that UFOs emit a lot of energy and even leave a measurable trail of residual energy behind. We also found that where the UFOs created a worm hole near the Capitol, in that part of the sky, it appeared distorted. The energy pattern created a fractal pattern. Although it seemed incredible, the UFOs had literally warped space before they disappeared from DC.

Having spent his life creating the world's largest UFO photograph library, this really got the colonel's attention. I told him that the closer we looked at the time exposed image, the more evident it became that some UFOs were flying out of this worm hole as others were flying in. It acted as a doorway in space and possibly time. When they opened that dimensional doorway, the fabric of space was distorted like a snowflake pattern in that one specific region of the sky. It took my journalism partner, Mr. Allen, and I weeks to understand what we were looking at, because we had never seen anything like that before.

Even after six decades of research, the colonel was still amazed by the powers involved in the UFO phenomenon. I felt the same way. It was clear to me that if ETs wanted to invade our planet there was nothing much we could really do to stop them. According to the colonel, "They would have done it long ago if they wanted to. However, the benevolent ones we are in communication with said that we have nothing they want. There is an entire universe full of resources and other intelligent life forms that are available to them, so why bother with us?"

His statement reminded me that in the bigger picture, our beautiful blue planet was simply a tiny speck of dust in a very large cloud of stars. But I still had one final question for the colonel. He had sent me a copy of a DC UFO photo that looked yellowed with age. I wanted to know how he had acquired that particularly clear image of a group of UFOs passing over the Capitol on July 26, 1952.

Colonel Stevens explained that he had been friends with a man named August Roberts, who was a professional photographer on the East Coast during the 1950s. At the time, Mr. Roberts had the largest photographic collection of UFOs and paranormal phenomena. The formation of spherical UFOs flying over the Capitol was one of them. It was one of the few DC UFO images that had not been confiscated by the government.

As fate would have it, Mr. Roberts received a first generation copy from the news photographer that took it. It was one of the clearest copies I had seen, but it was really frustrating to know that only a few of the 1952 DC UFO photos were ever published. Reportedly, there were hundreds of images captured that year. The colonel and I agreed that it seemed doubtful the public would see those highly-controversial pictures any time soon.

CHAPTER FIVE

Journalist Covers Alien Affairs

Another individual I spoke at length about extraterrestrials with was a retired *Los Angeles Times*, Pulitzer Prize-winning journalist named Philip Krapf. He was the author of *The Contact Has Begun: The True Story of a Journalist's Encounter with Alien Beings*, and *The Challenge of Contact: A Mainstream Journalist's Report on Interplanetary Diplomacy*.

I found it interesting that Mr. Krapf was a complete skeptic regarding UFOs and ETs until reportedly being contacted by human/alien beings and taken aboard their spacecraft, in June of 1997. While onboard their enormous space craft, the aliens requested that he write a straightforward account of his visits with them.

They clearly wanted Mr. Krapf to relay specific intentions that this group of benevolent, interplanetary beings called the Verdants had toward the people of Earth. In his books, Mr. Krapf explained that he and a few other people called deputy envoys had been selected to present this information to humanity at this time.

In 2002, Mr. Krapf revised his book *The Challenge of Contact* due to include important information he had received. According to the Verdants, full public disclosure about ET contact had been scheduled to occur in 2002, but was put on hold because of what took place on September 11, 2001. Coincidentally, 2002 was the year that UFOs were photographed landing on Capitol Hill by Mr. Allen (see Chapter One for details).

The updated edition of *The Challenge of Contact* was extensively revised. It contained new material in a lengthy new chapter and new appendices. However, the story was still based on Mr. Krapf's second visit to the enormous, alien space craft a few years after he had retired from *The Los Angeles Times*.

Before retiring, Mr. Krapf had worked in the field of journalism for

30 years as a photographer, reporter, and as a copy and managing editor. He had spent the last 25 years of his career working at *The Los Angeles Times* on the metro desk where he shared in a Pulitzer Prize as a member of the Metro team that covered the L.A. riots of 1992. Mr. Krapf had been written about in many publications and had appeared on radio and television.

I spoke with Mr. Krapf on the phone one afternoon after receiving his press release. I was interested in learning more about the benefits of contact and the interplanetary cultural and commercial exchange that would potentially ensue.

A lot had happened since his first book, *The Contact Has Begun*, was released in January of 1998. Toward the end of that book, Mr. Krapf had outlined some of the benefits our civilization could expect from having open contact with the Verdants and some of the other 27,000 extraterrestrial species in the Intergalactic Federation. However, Mr. Krapf discovered that when it came to the issue of open contact with the people of earth and alien beings, most people were not motivated to do anything toward this goal unless they saw the benefit from it first.

This placed the challenge of establishing open contact squarely on our shoulders. One of the immediate potential benefits for humans was safe and affordable space travel within our galaxy. Also, a diplomatic embassy would be constructed on earth for the official exchange of interplanetary ideas and information and commerce.

According to Mr. Krapf, "There was a section in my report dealing with the establishment of an intergalactic headquarters here on earth somewhere in the southwest U.S. Supposedly, that is where the talks and protocols would officially take place to establish diplomatic relations.

"This would be a kind of a self-contained city with an international airport and a landing area for alien space craft. There would be people representing various governments on earth who would be briefed, and they would be going through briefing sessions aboard the spacecraft, too, but all of the preliminary talks, and everything else, would be held at this city before things were formalized.

"I'm not a diplomat, I don't know how a diplomatic corps works, but I know that in order to establish diplomatic relations one person decides to talk to another person. Then, if all goes well, they agree that a committee should be created to talk which it does. Then, they take that information to the highest levels of government, and pretty soon they exchange official ambassadors. I am just saying there is a lot of preliminary work that goes into establishing these things."

I was fascinated that the Verdants planned to transform an area of desert into a lush environment somewhere in the southwest U.S. When I asked Mr. Krapf to elaborate, he said, "If I remember right, they said that there would be a 30-mile area in circumference that they would turn into green grassland where a fairly good sized city would be built.

"Some people have tried to hold me to the term, literally, that it would magically become grassland and that it would somehow rise out of the sand overnight, but I don't think the Verdants meant that literally. In other words, in time, it would rise on that chosen area until it was fully developed.

"The grassland or landscaping would appear soon after the city was built. You know, buildings go up so fast these days that sometimes it does almost appear like it happened over night. I'm sure the Verdants didn't mean it in a magical sense."

Something I recalled regarding our pending relationship with the Verdants was that we would have to show some improvement in the way we treated each other. It seemed clear that we would have to prove by our actions that we were responsible enough to receive the benefits that the Verdants and the Galactic Federation had to offer.

Mr. Krapf agreed. He explained that, "We would have to demonstrate that the human species has progressed to the point where it has shown itself to be worthy of inclusion in the intergalactic community of intelligent beings. They are always looking for indications of that, and they have seen some signs of that in our species, but they told me that we are still very savage, and we would probably not be accepted.

"They told me we must remain isolated, because we can't be trusted. But then they saw something in our species that surprised them: our great works of art, and literature, and music, and architecture. Those things demonstrated nobility in our species that the Verdants were not aware of at first, because of all the savagery they had seen on earth. This surprised them, because they had never encountered such a diverse species before.

"Usually, when they come across another species, it is either good or bad, but they don't have the diversity that humans on earth have. There are people with pure evil intent walking around on earth today, and we know who they are, because they are in the news.

"On the other hand, there are people on earth that are very altruistic, and they are concerned and active in improving the human condition and helping other people. This was something strange to the Verdants. When the Cold War ended, they saw that, for the first time in modern history, there was a real chance for world peace. In fact, they have seen much of our history, because they have been watching us for quite awhile. Oddly enough, they know a good deal more about our history than we do.

"They have seen what we can do to each other and how savage and brutal we can be. But then they noticed a more noble side of our spirit. They saw the Cold War ending, and they thought this was probably the first chance in our history that we could achieve world peace. They expected that we would be marching to the beat of a different drummer. We were on the road then, I think, to being accepted into the Federation.

"But then, the 1990s came along. A good example of that decade would be Yugoslavia. For many years, it was under the control of a communist ruler named Tito. That country was a combination of many ethnic and religious groups that were held tightly together by an iron-fisted dictator.

"When Tito's rule ended, and the Cold War was finally ending, you expected people to move towards democracy and kindness towards one another. But what we saw was an explosion of old, ethnic, tribal and religious conflicts.

"That was something that was surprising to the Verdants, and instead of a better society in that region of the world you had tremendous strife. The Verdants saw that, and it troubled them. In other words, it wasn't as smooth a road as they might have expected. The 1990s were very turbulent times."

Clearly, the 21st century had raised a new set of complex issues post 9/11. Mr. Krapf agreed it was a very negative event the Verdants had not anticipated. This was due to the fact that when the Cold War ended in the 1990s, and the Berlin Wall fell, and democracy and freedom were beginning to sweep the world, the Verdants saw that we were moving in the right direction. They did not anticipate that our future was going to be as vicious and as bloody as it had turned out to be.

In Mr. Krapf's second book, *The Challenge of Contact*, the human Verdant he named "Martin" recited a list of things that were obviously wrong with the people of earth. When I asked Mr. Krapf to elaborate on that exchange, he said, "I made the point to Martin that those negative things have been part of our history from the very beginning. He was not telling me anything new. Obviously, the path we were currently on caused the Verdants, and their associates, some concern because there were high-level meetings that were convened to address these concerns. However, I was not included in those hearings.

"This occurred during my second experience on their space ship, and I know they were addressing these concerns, but you would expect problems to arise in any undertaking of this magnitude. That's what management is there for; to solve problems as they arise. Martin was one of those who thought we weren't quite ready. But I believe we are.

"I don't know if pessimistic would be the right term for his point of view. I think the word realistic fits him better. His perspective was that his people were making a mistake regarding their relationship with us. They were obviously not used to dealing with a species of our diversity. Martin just wanted to step back a little bit."

Mr. Krapf had reported that the Verdants forecasting abilities were far more advanced than humans. Apparently, when the Verdants forecast future events they used nearly all potential probabilities. If that was true, given earth's history, the Verdants must have known that there was a very-real possibility that more death and destruction would occur in our future.

According to Mr. Krapf, "That's what the second book was about; these meetings and the fact that the aliens were considering these issues and concerns. After that, in August of 2001, I put out a news release.

"I got word from the Verdants, and I was able to release the news, that they were going to proceed with contact. This was big news for me personally and for the world. It's great news just on the face of it. However, I was the only one who had been contacted and gone public so far. I had put my reputation on the line. I was standing alone.

"I was looking for support, for vindication, because I had been pretty-severely criticized, and perhaps properly so, by the people that wanted proof of my contact with an extraterrestrial race. But, in August of 2001, we were just months away from open contact occurring."

When I inquired if Mr. Krapf was aware that in 2001 there was a serious effort underway in Washington, D.C., for official disclosure of the existence of ETs, he said he had not heard about it. I had interviewed some of the key people involved in that process and knew it was a legitimate goal. I discovered that there was a political will there and a potential mandate on a grassroots level.

Some very-intelligent people had found a way that political pressure could be applied within the current system, with the will of the people and cooperation of their representatives, so that disclosure could have occurred. The project was gaining momentum up until the time that the twin towers at the World Trade Center were destroyed on 9/11. Krapf admitted he was totally unaware that the movement toward disclosure in DC had taken place. Unfortunately, most people remained unaware of it, because much of the process had occurred behind the scenes.

Mr. Krapf said, "I would not be privy to that information anyway. There were people of higher rank than myself that may have known, like some of the ambassadors that had access to confidential information. I was just a deputy envoy who was asked to write a report. I didn't need to be completely briefed on all that is going on. I was essentially just a messenger.

"If they wanted to release some information publicly they might have done so through me, but I am sure there were high-level talks going on. It doesn't surprise me to hear this was going on in our government. I would anticipate it would occur, but I was not privy to that process."

I then asked Mr. Krapf what he thought the most profound and immediate benefits would be from open contact, assuming that someday contact with ETs was officially confirmed and openly accepted by mankind.

Mr. Krapf said, "I'm not sure I can describe that. It's going to be revolutionary. The whole structure of society will change. Our whole culture is going to change. We will be engaged in interplanetary commerce and culture. It's going to be such a revolutionary series of events. I would anticipate that the standard of living of the average person in the world would improve tremendously. I don't see how a society can really be successful and move into a utopian mode and still have some people that are living incredibly wretched lives."

I knew what Mr. Krapf was referring to: the human condition on earth. In my life, I had traveled to more than 50 countries and had witnessed the harsh reality that many people on our planet did not have access to adequate water, food, a telephone, or a car. It was shocking. These were things that most people in America, like me, tended to take for granted.

Mr. Krapf agreed. He said, "More people die each year from contaminated water than any other cause in the world. I mean, there's such a discrepancy in the standard of living between the haves and the have-nots. I see a new balance coming into play, because we desperately need it. All people should have a basic, decent standard of living where they don't go to bed hungry, and they have access to health care. In other words, they will be sharing in the wealth of the planet which belongs to everybody."

Mr. Krapf had reported that the Verdants found 20 percent of the people here on earth to be evil at heart. They were the ones that didn't share in a utopian world view. When I asked him to elaborate, he said, "I was naive about this at first. But let's say you are a Texas billionaire that is getting obscenely rich from oil and gas energy reserves. You fly in your private jet to Las Vegas, then take a limousine to the casinos, and stay in a $10,000 a night room, and have the prettiest women in the world at your side because you are a high roller living that life style.

"Then, one day, the news reports that someone has discovered a source of cheap, clean energy for the world. This is not good news for you because it means that your kingdom will soon become penniless as oil loses its value as the primary source of energy. Well, if wealthy people in a position of power, and privilege, are not willing to personally kill to save their empire, they would be perfectly willing to hire someone to murder the competition for them.

"I sincerely believe that people in that type of position are so selfish they would actually take human lives to save their own empire. We saw examples of this recently in the looting of large corporations by their executive officers. They were only motivated by greed and didn't care at all about the thousands of other people that were hurt in the process."

I was painfully aware of the dark side of humanity. It made me wonder if the majority of earth's people would ever realize that only a small minority of humans were preventing everyone from having open contact and commerce with the intergalactic federation. However, I was optimistic that once the good people of earth fully understood the situation, they would be motivated to really clean house and effectively deal with the bad guys who were making life difficult for everyone else.

Mr. Krapf told me he believed that ideally we were headed for a system where everyone was included more equitably in society; sharing the earth's resources. However, if we didn't achieve this in the future we would not be accepted into the intergalactic federation of worlds.

Apparently, the Verdants, and their associates, would insist on that because it was how their societies worked. Everyone was held in the same regard and shared everything equally. Their societies were altruistic and cared about everyone's well being.

When I asked Mr. Krapf if he had any idea how we could effectively deal with the 20 percent of the evil people that were making life difficult for the rest of mankind, he didn't have an answer. Granted, it was no small problem.

According to Mr. Krapf, "The paradox is that it's ours for the taking, because we are the majority. However, as long as you keep people in ignorance and poverty, they are powerless. They can easily be manipulated. Whereas, when people become more educated, and are no longer ignorant, they are not as easily manipulated.

"In our democratic government, we have the opportunity for a majority of citizens to vote the right people into office, however, the elite minority of people that control the money and the power are somehow able to influence the majority at times to endorse their agendas. Many people behave like sheep. I have seen up to a dozen people whose lives revolve around one powerful person."

Having grown up living next door to the rich and famous in Malibu, California, I had seen that type of behavior all too often. I believed it was another factor that the Verdants, and their associates, had carefully considered when it came to dealing with the people of Earth. If the Verdants, or any other group did too much to assist us, some people on Earth would quickly become dependent on the ETs, or simply idolize them.

Mr. Krapf considered my statement for a moment, then said, "I don't think there is any danger in that, because I never got any indication that they are here to hand us our future on a silver platter. They have repeatedly stressed that earth's destiny is in our hands. I personally believe that if we did self-destruct with a nuclear war or somehow managed to blow up our little planet, I don't think it would really matter that much on the cosmic scale. It is just one little sparkling speck of dust in a vast ocean.

"If we annihilated ourselves, the Federation would just move on to the next planet. However, I do think they care about us. I think they are generous, and I think they really hope we make it, but they are not here as our saviors. That's what some people misunderstand. They want the Verdants to come to earth as our saviors and fix all the problems we created for ourselves, and that's just not the way it works."

As if that wasn't bad enough, Mr. Krapf and I agreed that there were some people in power that would like to use the extraterrestrial presence as a scapegoat for deploying our military in space. Since many of us didn't want to take responsibility for our actions, it would be easy to make the aliens out to be the next big enemy.

Mr. Krapf said, "This was another area I was very naive about. When I was first told there were people on earth that opposed contact, I thought, 'This is such a magnificent event, who would oppose such a thing?' Then, I found out that there are those in the military who oppose contact, so they can stay in power. In essence, the power, prestige and privilege of it are what motivate the forces of opposition to maintain the cover-up.

"I also learned that there are those people who know the aliens are here, but they want nothing to do with them, because they are frightened. I call them planetary isolationists. They simply want nothing to do with the ETs. Then, there are those who think we may or may not be able to trust the ETs. They believe we should be very careful and keep the ETs at arm's length for a while.

"Then, there are those that oppose the ETs for religious reasons. After going public with my report, I got letters from people stating their religion and quoting their dogma to me regarding man's place in creation. They believe that because aliens are not mentioned in their bibles, they simply cannot exist. But if extraterrestrials really do exist, that means these people would have to rethink their entire religious belief system. When you ask someone to question the religious beliefs that have guided them all their life, I guarantee you most people would strongly resist doing that."

In my life, I had studied all the various religions of earth. Recently, I had seen a television documentary on Islam and the teachings of the prophet Mohammed. What really struck me about him was that prior to becoming a powerful religious leader, he was actually hated by many of his peers and had to flee for his life.

Their anger toward him, in part, was based in part on an extraordinary experience Mohammed reportedly had while in Mecca. He claimed that one night he was visited by the Archangel Gabriel who transported him through the heavens. Mohammed was very observant in his trip and counted seven layers as he traveled up into the heavens on his journey to Jerusalem.

Upon arriving there, he claimed to have met with other prophets from the past, at the Dome of the Rock, before being returned home through the air, to Mecca, by the Archangel. When Mohammed later described his close encounter to some of his friends and family they thought he had gone crazy and got very upset with him. In time, that experience became the basis for a new religion.

Most people would agree that angels, by their very definition, were from the heavens. They were alien to this world. In other words, they lived in an area we now referred to as outer space. What I found a bit hypocritical was that when an angel was encountered by someone in a religious context, it was considered acceptable to people of faith. However, if the same being had been identified as an alien in a secular environment it was suddenly perceived as a threat or something evil.

Mr. Krapf and I agreed that all religions to some degree started out as cult followings of a visionary leader. In time, if that same cult acquired enough members, it became respectable to the other religious groups. Despite that fact, I still considered myself an optimist. Mr. Krapf felt the same way. He said, "I find myself tending to believe that as dangerous as the world is right now that somehow we are going to stumble through and prevail. At times, I get a little down, when I see the opportunities that were missed and how close we came to doing something really magnificent, but I really am optimistic. I believe that we are going to get through the tough times without destroying ourselves and our planet. It's a long, hard, tough road, but you have to keep things in perspective.

"Ever since humans have been walking on this world, we have been beating each other over the head. I have a theory about our civilization. We know that humans lived in tribes for most of history and that most of those tribes were rather small in numbers.

"There was very little conflict within the tribes, because each person had a role to play. There were those that had to make tools. There were others that knew how to hunt and others who could clean the carcass; one who could take care of the children; another could weave blankets or stitch animal skins into clothing.

"In those days, when the tribes were small, everyone was important like a family. And when you lost someone from your tribe, the entire tribe lost an asset. It was very hard to train someone else to replace that person. As some of the tribes grew larger than say 100 people, you suddenly had two or three people that did the same job.

"That particular tribe could actually survive if there was a hostile conflict and people were killed, because it had excess people. As these tribes grew larger and larger, individuals became less and less vital to the survival of the tribe."

Mr. Krapf's point was painfully clear. In the process, people had become expendable. Every individual person that died in our civilization didn't make that much difference to the survival of the species. However, if we lived in a tribe of 50 people or less, each one of us would serve a very important function. A single loss of life would be difficult on everyone's survival. It made perfect sense.

Mr. Krapf had talked a lot about the Earth's moon in his books. He stated that the Verdant's huge space craft was located on the far side of the moon: the side we never see. I was deeply moved by his description of the view of outer space from the observation deck of their craft. Seeing the immensity and complexity of the Universe first hand was clearly a humbling and formative experience for him.

During our conversation, he mentioned to me that the moon had always held various symbolic meanings to the many cultures of earth; particularly when mankind first set foot there. A collective transition of consciousness had taken place at that time; due in large part to the televised images of the earth as seen from the moon. It truly was a giant leap for mankind. It allowed us to view ourselves as one species living on the same planet.

Even though the moon landing was made possible by the Cold War, that one ethereal image of earth, spinning in the vast darkness of space, was a chance for humanity to collectively look in the mirror.

I believed that there were similar transformational events that would occur in the future. I knew there was a greater potential yet to be achieved on this planet by its people. I felt that even though we were constantly in a state of war, there were still opportunities for us as a species to come to a greater awareness of our unity and true potential.

According to Mr. Krapf, "It's a tough problem, but I see the solution as education. I am not religious and do not have a reason to be intolerant of other people's beliefs. I have noticed that the more educated a person is the more open minded toward other people's views they usually are.

"I believe the whole world needs to come around to that way of thinking some day. Religion should not interfere with anyone's rights. For example, look at Afghanistan where everyone has a gun, but they don't have enough food or medicine. That's crazy! Those guns and ammunition are expensive. If all that money was used for schools and other things, it would be a better society."

It was a logical observation, but I knew there were millions of people who remained fanatical in their beliefs and were fundamentally afraid of others. They tended to always take a defensive position. However, I was optimistic that there was a way to educate that portion of humanity and give them an opportunity to catch a glimpse of how wonderful the world could be someday once we had learned how to live together in peace.

I knew it wouldn't be easy. Our collective track record for human rights abuse was appalling. For example, we had wasted an incredible amount of time, energy, resources, and lives on warfare in just the 20th century. Whereas, if humanity had focused all its combined time, energy, resources and talent into a manned space program, people could have colonized and terra formed the moon and Mars years ago. However, some evolutionary progress was still being made during the Cold War era. Out of a military communications need, the Internet was born and quickly proliferated across the planet at an exponential rate. In a relatively short time, even in the poorest countries, people all over the world were able to communicate with each other.

I believed that, in time, this new digital medium would transcend all language and cultural barriers. Powerful teaching tools like that made me think it was possible to someday move past our immediate problems. I saw a day coming when a multimedia presentation would be shown around the world that demonstrated mankind's potentially rich future in outer space.

Mr. Krapf agreed and noted that higher education often lead to a freer exchange of ideas and wisdom and tolerance. It was important to be tolerant of other people that were non-violent. We both acknowledged that this was a precursor to mankind becoming a member of the intergalactic family.

Although I was optimistic, I knew that in time we would either learn to make better use of our resources or become extinct. It was a cruel paradox that while the surface of the earth was mostly covered with water, the vast majority of it was unusable for drinking or agriculture. It was very time consuming and expensive to desalinate ocean water and the millions of tons of fresh water located at the polar ice caps of our planet, particularly Antarctica, were simply unavailable to us.

It was a little-known fact, but there was actually a severe shortage of fresh water on earth. It had been reported that 70 percent of our fresh water reserves are used for agriculture. This made me wonder why we were not using hydroponics in green houses to grow our food. That way, most of the water would be efficiently contained instead of being lost to evaporation. For example, of the water we used for irrigation of crops 50 percent of that simply evaporated into the air.

In a more-perfect world, futuristic greenhouses would create a controlled environment year round. They would be highly productive and keep pests out without using harmful petrochemical insecticides. And, more importantly, they would recapture most of the evaporated water and recycle it back to the crops.

After years of researching this problem, I learned that the answer to this problem is a very-simple process called condensation. In fact, this process can be artificially controlled with machines called dehumidifiers which are commercially available now. An average commercial dehumidifier can capture approximately one gallon of water an hour out of the air in most regions on earth.

At some point, we will have to employ this type of system to help insure our survival. Obviously the air is polluted and any water captured by artificial condensation would have to be filtered, but it beats the alternative. Most of the ground water on earth is incredibly polluted as are the rivers and the oceans; especially near the coast lines. Although it would require a huge commitment for our civilization to change the way it manages its water resources, it would be worth the effort.

Mr. Krapf agreed, but pointed out that a major change like that would require a lot of money, because everything on earth used money to operate. Although that was true, this new water-capturing system was a proven, viable, commercial venture. I liked to think of it as creating rain in a box. Another important aspect of the system would be to collect water in inflatable storage containers that were mobile, so that the operation could easily be moved from one location to another as needed.

This was not rocket science. The technology and materials were already available. Mr. Krapf then pointed out that wealthy industrialists would not make a move to this more efficient type of system unless they saw a profit in it. Until then, it would only be done by idealists on a small scale who were promoting it. In other words, someone that was rich and powerful had to fund it.

I agreed, but it was a fact that most farmers were losing huge amounts of money using the current method of irrigation, because it was highly inefficient. The only way most of them could stay in business was through government subsidies. In other words, everyone was paying extra money for this inefficient process.

Mr. Krapf said, "Absolutely, and as long as the 20 percent of the bad people on earth continue to control the government and government subsidies, things will not change for the better."

Although I was glad to get Mr. Krapf's opinion on this subject, he felt no one in the media would listen. I disagreed. I knew there was always an audience for any message; good or bad. I also knew that even though the main-stream media was intentionally ignoring these types of inno-vative ideas, it really didn't matter. Information flowed freely these days through public venues like the Internet and talk radio. As a result, there were many ways to get the word out.

I reminded Mr. Krapf that when communications satellites were first launched into orbit around the earth, in the 1950s, Marshall McLuhan coined the phrase, "The Global Village." At that time, our electronic village was still in its infancy.

By the beginning of the 21st century our village was in its teen-age years and was still acting immaturely with its new found ability to communicate ideas and information digitally. However, I knew there were transformational, social events that would occur in the future that would accelerate our society into a more mature phase.

When Mr. Krapf asked me to explain, I told him that people would continue debating the existence of extraterrestrial beings on earth and their future relationship to us. And, at some point, all the people of earth would have the opportunity to vote on a crucial issue: Should ETs be wel-come to peacefully visit Earth? Yes, or no?

A real-time total of the electronic votes would be displayed on a secure web site. In my opinion, such an event would mark a turning point for the people of earth. I had been informed that a global, democratic vote on the issue was a key preliminary step that needed to take place before open contact with ETs could occur on Earth.

As part of this process, a rally needed to take place in Wash-ington, D.C., to raise awareness of alien life. The event would include a multimedia presentation where people from all walks of life on this planet would learn that even though we had not invited extraterrestrial beings to visit earth, they were still coming here covertly. The rally in DC would help humanity realize that if a simple majority of people from this world (51%) were to vote yes and welcome open contact and commerce with peaceful ETs, it would allow them to visit us legally. This, in turn, would pry open the doors to the final frontier for earthlings: outer space.

CHAPTER SIX

Legal Eagle

One day, it occurred to me that the only way I could successfully navigate the political swamp of Washington, D.C., was to consult a lawyer. I found that the District of Columbia had more lawyers per square inch than any other city on earth. But where could I find a lawyer in DC that really understood the politics of contact with UFOs and extraterrestrials?

Eventually, I discovered the law office of Daniel Sheehan; a social activist who had served as a legal counsel on the Karen Silkwood case, the Iran Contra case, the Pentagon Papers case, the Watergate Burglary case, and the American Sanctuary Movement case.

He had established the Christic Institute in Washington, D.C., which for nearly two decades was America's preeminent public-interest law firm. I was surprised to learn that Mr. Sheehan had a unique history of investigating the issue of extraterrestrial intelligence and the UFO phenomenon.

In 1994, Mr. Sheehan had defended Dr. John Mack from an investigatory panel of the Harvard Medical School after Dr. Mack's courageous publication of a book dealing with alien abductions. However, this was not Sheehan's first encounter with the issue of UFOs, alien beings and American law.

In 1977, while acting as General Counsel to the United States Jesuit Office of Social Ministry in Washington, D.C., he had served as a special consultant to the United States Library of Congress Congressional Research Office Project on Extraterrestrial Intelligence ordered by President Jimmy Carter.

In that capacity, Mr. Sheehan had been given access not only to the classified portions of the Air Force's infamous *Blue Book* special report files, but he had also read the confidential report prepared for the Science

& Technology Committee of the United States Congress by the Library of Congress Congressional Research Office pursuant to that presidential assignment.

When I spoke with him in 2005, Mr. Sheehan was acting director of The Strategic Initiative to Identify the New Paradigm. In that organization, Mr. Sheehan shared the responsibility for the formulation of a new world view. He advocated a view that extraterrestrial intelligence existed in our Universe and that the representatives of one or more of those extraterrestrial civilizations were presently visiting our planet and interacting with select members of our species. It was a view I shared.

I wanted to know, from Mr. Sheehan's perspective, how well he thought the "Disclosure Project" in Washington, D.C., had gone. He said, "For me, it began when I was retained by Dr. John Mack at the Harvard Clinical Department of Psychology. I represented him in front of the Harvard faculty after he wrote *Abductions: Human Encounters with Extraterrestrials*. Because of that, I got to meet a substantial number of people that worked in the field of UFOs sightings, close encounters, alien abductions, etc.

"That was how I met Dr. Steven Greer and a number of people in the government's higher echelon that had reported UFO sightings and alien contact. When I was preparing to present to the Harvard faculty committee the best evidence regarding alien abductions that Dr. Mack was talking about in his book, I argued it was a perfectly sound and important public policy issue to be addressing.

"In the process, I encountered a number of high-ranking officials such as the chief investigator for the Federal Aviation Agency. There was also a colonel in the Air Force, a general in the Army, and others.

"After we finished with that, I met Dr. Greer. He had been saying for some time that he thought the U.S. government would be coming forward with some type of official disclosure about them having made contact or establishing a relationship with an extraterrestrial civilization"

Even though I wanted to see official disclosure on this issue some day, I sincerely doubted it would occur in my life time. Mr. Sheehan felt that the U.S. government should at least admit to having recovered a vehicle from an extraterrestrial civilization.

He said, "It is known by the U.S. executive department, at least by the various military and other intelligence agencies, that UFOs are a real phenomena. From 1994 through 1998, I had a number of conversations with Dr. Greer where he insisted that disclosure was going to happen soon. But, I consistently maintained that I didn't believe that was likely to happen in the foreseeable future because of my experiences with the national security bureaucracy of the U.S. government.

"I had been involved in various cases ranging all the way from my legal representation of the *New York Times* in the Pentagon Papers case, in 1971, to the Iran Contra case, from 1986 to 1992. As a result, although I established a relationship with Dr. Greer, he perceived me as being someone that was not confident that disclosure was going to happen.

"However, in time, I saw that Dr. Greer became more and more convinced that disclosure by a government agency was not likely to happen. That's when he decided he wanted to create a public process by which many of the people we had been talking to over the years regarding government disclosure could come forward and divulge information as a private citizen. Thus, he formed a group to deliver that revelation to the public."

Sheehan was referring to what came to be known as the Disclosure Project. He told me that the plan had been drafted by Dr. Greer and others including people working at the *USA Network*. They were trying to produce some responsible documentaries about issues involving sightings of UFOs and contact with or abduction by ETs.

Apparently there were a number of people working with Dr. Greer, including Commander Robert Dean and rocket scientist David Adair, that were trying to assemble some type of private presentation of the available information in as an official context as possible.

Mr. Sheehan said, "We all got together to have a presentation in Washington, D.C., at the *National Press Club*. A number of staff people from various Congressional Committee's and Congress person's offices were invited so that there would be an official presentation made to actual members of the U.S. government."

Mr. Sheehan had initially been contacted by Dr. Greer at the recommendation of a number of different people that thought it was a good idea to have legal counsel for the project. Clearly, there were legitimate legal concerns for many of the potential disclosers due to the fact that they were active or retired U.S. government employees and agents with sensitive information. These people did not want to be viewed by the federal government as intentionally violating their loyalty and secrecy oaths if they revealed classified information. There were fines and prison time that could be imposed for such an act.

Mr. Sheehan explained that, "I met with the people that were planning the disclosure presentation and began to develop legal information about this. Then, I met with each of the 21 people that had been interviewed in depth by Dr. Greer and a number of other people.

"There were probably 50 or more candidates for the top slots. After they finally honed it down to about 21 people, I then met with each person individually, on an attorney-client basis, in a confidential setting. We discussed what security oaths they had taken and what legal context they had experienced the ET/UFO information they had acquired. I advised them as to what I thought would be legally appropriate to communicate publicly, and in that context we went forward and presented these peoples stories in Washington, D.C."

I could only imagine what Pentagon and White House officials were thinking at that time. They clearly did not want to address the issue officially in Congress. Understandably, it was a very tense time on Capitol Hill.

According to Mr. Sheehan, there were large numbers of international and national media people that attended the disclosure presentation. At that time, the media was also provided with videotaped copies of detailed comments that some of the witnesses had made in their interviews prior to the public presentation.

When I asked Mr. Sheehan who had attended the presentation on official business, he told me that there were a number of congressional staffers that attended, but not in any official capacity. They were just there to listen to the presentation and receive videos of the complete interviews.

After the presentation, while acting as legal counsel for a number of the disclosers, Mr. Sheehan went with some of the Congressional staff people to the respective offices of their United States Congress person. In some cases, he met directly with the Congress person and presented the UFO disclosure information to them. He then asked them to take the material into consideration and urged them to try and develop hearings in the United States Congress to publicly air the UFO/ET information on Capitol Hill.

He said, "That was my involvement in the process. After we completed the actual disclosure process, Dr. Greer went around the country on a public speaking tour. He presented a video tape of the actual disclosure presentation in Washington, D.C.

"He gave public speeches about the project and sold the video tape to interested people that attended these public events around the country. He was communicating to the people of America on a grass-roots level, but that was the end of my involvement in the project."

I wondered if Mr. Sheehan had ever mentioned to Dr. Greer, or anyone else in the disclosure project, the classified UFO pictures he had seen in the Library of Congress. If so, why didn't anyone try to get permission to show that material at the disclosure presentation at the National Press Club?

Mr. Sheehan said, "Yes, I made it known to the disclosure group, but we could not use it publicly, because *that material remains classified.* The material I was allowed to see was a series of pictures on microfiche. That's a little can of film you put into a viewer and crank by hand.

"That particular file of classified information was made available to me in the context of a major study that was being conducted by the Congressional Research Service, Science and Technology Division at the request of the Science and Technology Committee of the House of Representatives.

"They had made their request in response to a directive given to them by President Carter. In the end, I don't know what the official status of that classified information was. However, as a result of that congressional study, I was allowed to view classified sections of *Project Blue Book.* The understanding at that time was the Library of Congress Science and Technology services would file a request with the U.S. Air Force to have that material de-classified, so that they could determine if they could use any of it in the two reports they were preparing to send to the House of Representatives.

"They sent it to the Science and Technology Committee back in

1977, or 1978, but I don't know what the final status of that report ever was. I do know for certain that two reports were prepared and sent to Congress. Then Congress was to make a decision as to whether or not they were going to de-classify those reports and make them available to the public."

It was an interesting bit of U.S. history I had obviously missed in school due to government censorship. I wanted to know more about the Air Force's classified UFO report and why certain members of Congress and President Carter were so interested in it.

When I asked Mr. Sheehan to elaborate, he said, "I know that the Congressional Research Office based their conclusions regarding the probabilities of extraterrestrial intelligence in our galaxy upon a mathematical model. The politicians did it that way rather than state that they placed absolute confidence in any particular UFO photograph, or document, or verbal account from a specific witness.

"In so doing, they were able to avoid the controversy surrounding the credibility of one source or another. In any case, they concluded that there was a very-high probability that there were from two to six technologically-advanced, highly-intelligent civilizations within our galaxy in addition to our own."

Although that made sense, Mr. Sheehan and I agreed that there was still a very important threshold for our civilization to cross. In order for America to make any real progress on this issue, someday a government agency would have to file an official report with the U.S. Congress stating that we were in fact not alone in the Universe.

When I asked Mr. Sheehan if the Congressional Research Offices reports were ever made public, he said it seemed unlikely. However, he knew for certain their findings had been sent to the House of Representatives and to the Science and Technology Committee.

I then asked Mr. Sheehan about the classified, Air Force photographs he had seen in the Library of Congress. I wanted to know if he could estimate what year the pictures of the crashed UFO were taken based on visual clues alone. From what he had already told me, I knew the photos could not have been related to the Roswell event.

Mr. Sheehan said, "It was clearly not the Roswell site. It was in the winter time, and there were U.S. Air Force personnel stationed all around the UFO. The military were dressed in winter gear with heavy parkas and fur hoods. I saw name tags on their outer garments. There was a camera man taking still photographs. He was in a couple of other photographs, so there had to be more than one photographer.

"I also recall there was a person that looked like he was taking a movie of the site. The technology of the camera indicated that this was not a video camera. It looked like a little, 35mm, reel-to-reel type of film camera, so I would put it somewhere in the 1960s. At least that was my sense of it, from what I briefly saw.

"I could clearly see it was a snowy area and, because there were a number of photographs, it appeared that the extraterrestrial vehicle had hit a flat field and skidded across an open area before crashing into an embankment. The space craft had actually dug into the embankment to some extent. It was kind of pitched up at a slight angle into the edge of the embankment."

Mr. Sheehan told me he still had a copy in his files of the alien hieroglyphs he had seen in one of the photographs. He said that although he was not allowed to take any notes he had decided to quickly trace the alien images anyway.

He aimed the overhead projector down on to the cardboard backing of a yellow legal pad he had placed on the desk. He then physically traced the image in order to create an accurate copy. It was a risky but courageous move.

Based on all his legal experience in Washington, D.C., I wanted to know what he thought the political implications were of having open contact with extraterrestrial civilizations. Mr. Sheehan said, "Well, open contact is a major issue. I mean, if there was direct and open contact with a representative of an extraterrestrial civilization, it would have absolutely enormous social and political implications. But even if it were established that covert contacts had taken place between the U.S. government's executive branch and representatives of an extraterrestrial civilization, it would have substantial implications on us officially and politically. You would have the significant problem associated with the administrations current official policy on this issue that denies any of this is true.

"I think, in that scenario, there would be a significant percentage of the population that would just be puzzled by the whole thing and wouldn't know what to conclude. That is because a majority of people in America have been conditioned to believe that nothing is true until an official authority says so. But to answer your question as to what the political and social implications would be for open contact, I would say they are absolutely marvelous."

Mr. Sheehan and I agreed that it sounded like a good idea that would be difficult to implement. He explained that, "If the appropriate federal authorities and political institutions were to decide that they were ready to make a public acknowledgment of such contact, it would imply that they had realized there was a way that extraterrestrial contact could be adequately integrated into the human culture without having negative consequences.

"Open, official contact with representatives of an ET civilization really has gargantuan implications, because it would then be accepted by a majority of the people. It would be understood that this was not a threat to our society and our culture. That would be an absolutely astonishingly important line for our civilization to cross.

"It would be equivalent to one of the species altering steps that have occurred in the physical evolution of the human family, such as between Australopithecus and Homo Erectus. Something of that magnitude would undoubtedly have an impact on society. Every field of human knowledge would be transformed by this type of event."

Mr. Sheehan told me that as a young man in 1963, he planned to go into the Air Force Academy, in Colorado Springs. He had planned to join the Air Force to become an astronaut in the hopes of some day meeting an ET.

His statement made me wonder that if he had taken that route in life, and become an astronaut, if he would have been allowed to know more about the ETs than he currently did. After thinking it over for a few moments, Mr. Sheehan said, "It is an interesting question that I had not considered before. I would preface my response with a truism that was told to me by Bob Fink. He was the Chief Investigator for the House Subcommittee on individual rights, and he had participated in the Pike Commission Investigations. They were the House side of the Investigations of the Church Committee on the Senate Select Committee on Intelligence Abuse. After working for many years in Washington, D.C., Bob had come to the conclusion that one would be a fool to ever take a security oath or a secrecy oath, because it was absolutely unnecessary.

"The reality was, if you were adequately professional about it, you could find out virtually anything that you wanted to know in Washington, D.C., and not be restricted under legal sanctions from making it public. Based on my 35 years of experience, I do believe this is true. However, if I had gone into the Air Force's astronaut program, and had risen through the ranks as a graduate of their academy program, odds are I would have become an officer. If that had happened, and I had access to the highest levels of policy-making, I would have advocated that we develop a much more aggressive astronaut program.

"As you know, there are some rather puzzling features about the U.S. manned space program. For example, why would there have been such a huge, national program that allowed us to place men on the moon repeatedly and then we just suddenly stopped?

"After all our success with the *Apollo Program*, we went to a geared-down process of trying to put up pieces of the Space Station which they are still working on. At the time, I would have entered the manned space program, back in the 1960s, realistic projections for my graduating class would have taken us to 2001. By then, we were scheduled to have a fully operational space platform.

"It would have served as the staging area for manned missions to the Moon and Mars and other places. All of that would have worked directly with the Hubble Telescope program which should have been used to ascertain years ago that there were clearly planets orbiting nearby star systems.

"But to answer your question, despite Bob Fink's truism, I believe that as an Air Force officer I would have been in a position to access high-ly-classified information that had been obtained by a much more agres-sive manned space exploration program than we have today. Therefore, I would have been able to find out whatever was known publicly and pri-vately in the field of extraterrestrial intelligence. As for intelligence regard-ing the potential ET contacts now, I don't know, because the civilian UFO research community hasn't gotten itself organized to any degree yet. I'm still hopeful that it will, but so far it hasn't gotten itself organized to a level where by it could put together an adequate investigative fund for a full-scale investigation.

"A project like that would be effectively undertaken the way we did in the Karen Silkwood case, and like we did in the Iran Contra case, and the way that we have handled other cases like that. However, those types of investigations cost millions of dollars. It takes lots of money to hire lawyers and conduct professional-caliber investigations with people that are retired from various branches of the military and federal intelligence agencies.

"There would need to be personal contacts at the highest levels of these agencies, and you would need to have funding to be able to do that in a sound and completely responsible manner. That has not yet occurred, but I am still hopeful it will happen in my life time. There is still time to accomplish that. It is one of my major intentions."

I was cautiously optimistic that the problem could be legally addressed some day. However, it had become clear to me that the people who currently held positions of power on planet earth were opposed to having an open relationship with ET civilizations or officially acknowledging their existence.

When I mentioned to Mr. Sheehan that this position had created a potential conflict of interest, he said, "I would assume so. But I'm not sure they would oppose having any contact at all. You see, no matter which world view you embrace, when one looks at the entire spectrum of various world views, none of these paradigms would actually oppose having any potential contact with ETs.

"They may well oppose establishing any type of treaties with them. They may also take the position that we should not trust them. This is because the first world paradigm contains people that are obsessed with maintaining security, and they basically don't trust people from this planet or any other planet for that matter. They simply don't trust the Universe. Therefore, they would clearly not support establishing any type of trusting relationship with an extraterrestrial civilization.

"The second world paradigm contains people that derive their entire sense of value on identifying some ultimate other. They are engaging in a fundamental, dialectical struggle and competition with the ETs. These people would advocate having nothing more than a simple, arms-length, dialectical, adversarial relationship with the ETs. Even to the point of recommending a massive, covert, military system that would ostensibly be capable of fielding forces in outer space to combat and defeat an ET civilization.

"I have talked about that on a number of occasions. It's quite clear that the second world paradigm dialecticians, that hold positions of power in the entire U.S. military intelligence community, clearly advocate doing just exactly that.

"As you work your way across the spectrum of world views, you find differing perspectives on this issue, but I don't believe that any of them would actually oppose having any kind of contact whatsoever with ETs. At least, I have never encountered anyone actually advocating that."

I knew it was not something anyone in power would ever admit officially. If they were to advocate that type of isolationist policy, it would imply that the issue had credibility. In my opinion, that was why the official policy regarding this issue was still based on denial, dissuasion and deception.

Mr. Sheehan and I agreed it was a rather unfortunate situation. He added that, "It is not just being applied to the UFO or ET intelligence issue. It's a general principle that prominent people in the first and second world view paradigm take with regard to the public. They really do not believe that the public can be, or should be, trusted with anything involving national security information."

I could see Mr. Sheehan's point, but it was clear that what we were discussing here transcended the security of nations. This was an interplanetary level of politics that we were not adequately prepared to participate in. We had yet to officially create a political process that dealt specifically with interplanetary affairs.

Mr. Sheehan agreed and added, "Now, the question that arises is if in fact there has been covert contact with either extraterrestrial representatives themselves, or even their technology, it would prove conclusively that extraterrestrial vehicles are here on Earth. If that is true, then I have no doubt whatsoever that there has been some progress made with regard to establishing some type of international organization to deal with this situation on a formal or informal basis. It would be contrary to any of the current political processes not to take steps to address that issue."

It seemed logical, but I wanted to know what Mr. Sheehan thought of the photographs, and radar returns, and eye witness accounts of UFOs repeatedly flying over Washington, D.C. I was specifically interested in his reaction to the photographs from July 16, 2002, and the implications of alien space craft violating our controlled airspace and actually landing on Capitol Hill.

His response shocked me. He said, "Based on everything I have seen and researched, it's clear that those people currently acting as responsible representatives of this world have come to a confidential [covert] conclusion that there is one or more extraterrestrial civilization existing in our galaxy which are highly developed. Therefore, they either have or very likely will have in the foreseeable future the technological means by which they can establish contact with people here on earth.

"That is why I believe it is highly probable there is some type of formal or informal system and organization that exists on earth in which the leaders of the major nation states, such as the U.S., and Russia, and France, and England and others, have established specific scenarios that would allow their representatives to respond to extraterrestrials attempting to make contact.

"I am 98 percent confident that such a completely-classified structure already exists on earth, based upon the available data. Contrary to a lot of people's opinion, our leaders are not stupid just because they have a different world view. Just because they have a different mode of ethical reasoning does not mean they are stupid or else they wouldn't be in those positions of power. Of course, there are stupid people in every world view. But they don't usually rise to very high levels of responsible positions."

If I understood correctly, contact with ETs was occurring unofficially. However, officially, the subject of UFOs and ETs was still off limits. Apparently, on this issue, our world leaders preferred to publicly assume the position of scared Ostriches which made them appear ignorant and vulnerable.

Sheehan explained that, "There is an old adage: one would much prefer to appear as a fool rather than a nave. In other words, rather than have people perceive them as detestable and despicable leaders that have information they are hiding from everyone, most of them would rather publicly appear as silly or ignorant."

It took a moment for me to realize that Mr. Sheehan was saying that our leaders were just playing dumb to some degree, but there was a paradox. They couldn't just restrict the air space over Washington, D.C., for everything except UFOs. Or could they?

According to Mr. Sheehan, "Restricted and prohibited airspace not only applies to military bases, but everywhere else as you well know. We allegedly have instituted highly restricted or prohibited air space over some of our most sensitive bases, and yet there have been numerous reports of UFOs actually penetrating and landing at these sites.

"The veracity of those accounts is beyond any reasonable challenge. The events were witnessed by colonels in charge of missile bases that have testified to this under oath. They have filed official reports on this."

During my research, I had read many of those cases, and it really was quite shocking. Perhaps that was why, although skeptical, I initially thought it was possible for UFOs to have landed on Capitol Hill. However, I learned that many people believe landing a UFO in DC was impossible because after 9/11, and the *War on Terror*, the level of security in the air, and on the ground, had become extremely tight. Despite that fact, FAA records showed there had been over 3,000 aerial anomalies that appeared on radar in restricted and prohibited air space around the DC area from 2003 to 2005.

Clearly, all the radar anomalies were not UFOs, but according to the photographs and eye-witness accounts I had compiled, alien spacecraft continued to violate U.S. air space at will; especially in DC. Was it possible they had someone's permission to do this?

According to Mr. Sheehan, "In my opinion, There is an entire category that has been set aside by all of the major intelligence agencies of the U.S. government that would have authority over any circumstances of an encounter with this particular phenomenon. There is a whole special category that they have for these things."

Mr. Sheehan's mater-of-fact statement took a moment to sink in. Was he implying that there was a covert protocol that existed to deal with this? When I asked him to elaborate, he said, "For example, they either don't talk about that or if it rises above a certain level of contact, there is nothing they can do about it anyway, so they just put it in a special box. However, based on all my experience as a professional investigator, and lawyer in these areas, it doesn't necessarily follow that there is some kind of unofficial protocol or sub-rosa arrangement that has been worked out with ETs. It doesn't mean they are being permitted to do this through some concession and some exchange of things of value.

"I want to be very clear about this. My understanding is that there has historically been this category of paranormal phenomena on our planet, and when the data is confirmed to have come from an ET event the people in power just place it in the special box they created just for that. They think there is nothing we can do about this, so they just put it in that box and then they give each other a wink and a nod and agree not to talk about it.

"I believe that is a very real phenomenon at the highest levels of all the different U.S. government agencies and departments that would have any realistic opportunity to encounter these particular phenomena.

"That is a significant range of agencies such as the FAA, all the military branches, the intelligence community and even National Park rangers. This would include virtually anyone in the government that had jurisdiction over any of the locations where ET activity may occur. They have a special black box into which they place that data."

It was an interesting revelation, but even if there was no official protocol, or an intricate covert reporting network for UFO intelligence, the official goal was apparently to contain the information whenever possible. It seemed like paranoid behavior to me.

Mr. Sheehan added that, "One can go into some analysis of what type of mind set that thinking represents. Before he died, I had many discussions about that with Dr. Mack who was the head of the clinical psychiatry at Harvard Medical School. He was attempting to figure out what this all meant.

"He was researching this strange, abhorrent type of behavior on the part of allegedly intelligent and responsible people and wanted to know how they could possibly be in such denial? He wanted to understand how they could set up a black box for something that they just won't deal with? In fact, there were all kinds of data that proved people engaged in that type of behavior all the time.

"Generally speaking, when one is presented with new information that is completely incompatible with their world view, most people will just stare silently for a moment and then move on to the next subject.

"People do that all the time. It has been clinically established that there is this collective category that some humans have created for themselves; a mental black box where they keep putting things into it. It's where the old saying, 'out of sight, out of mind' comes from.

"At the present time, that is where the issue of ET and UFO phenomenon has been placed for some people. Fortunately, it is an increasingly smaller segment of the population that engages in this type of thinking. The media has yet to accurately report this, but it is really a minority of people that maintain this black box of denial.

"There is a significant majority of people in the Baby Boom generation, born between November of 1942 and November of 1963, and a substantial majority of the new millennial children, born in the last 21 years, that are completely confidant that the UFO phenomenon is absolutely true.

"They know that extraterrestrial civilizations exist and that there has been contact here on earth and that there have been thousands of UFO sightings that are verified and that the government agencies know about this. An overwhelming majority of us already know this and accept it.

"The fact is, as pointed out by Dr. Thomas Kuhn in his major treatise on the way scientific theories evolve, he said, you really don't succeed in changing the fundamental paradigm of a generation with regard to a given issue; the old leaders simply die.

"A new paradigm is then adhered to by a younger generation based upon their being more open-minded about things and having no major practical reasons to deny something that is true. When that generation rises into maturity, and they become the leaders of the culture, the paradigm simply shifts. That's what's going to happen. It's what's happening right now with regard to the UFO issue.

"When the remnants of the World War II generation and then the Korean War generation pass away from leadership roles, virtually all those leadership roles will be taken by members of the Baby Boom generation. When the majority of the millennial generation reaches adulthood and are active voting members of society, we are going to see the paradigm shift further, and everyone will start saying that the existence of ETs was always known."

It almost sounded too simple. Mr. Sheehan was saying that regardless of all our efforts toward getting official disclosure to occur, it was just a matter of time before it happened as a natural progression anyway. Unfortunately, I was growing impatient and wanted to know how much longer he thought this cultural, evolutionary process was going to take.

He said, "In our lifetime, it will simply become a majority view which then becomes the rule of law. That's what will happen with the issue of ET and UFO phenomenon. My guess is that we are going to probably cross this line around 2012, ironically enough. We will then move through a major transition right up to 2020. And in that eight-year period, you are going to see the World War II generation falling completely from the scene.

"Even the members of the Korean War generation are going to become so antiquated that they start retiring from major positions of power, and the Baby Boomer generation will rise into its full ascendancy. By that time, a majority of the 75 million members of the millennial generation will have entered adulthood and will be active members of the community. In my view, that is a very special eight-year period where this group will take charge of the operative paradigm."

It was a fascinating forecast of dramatic changes in political power on planet earth. At the time we spoke, Mr. Sheehan was busy writing his new book *Paradigm Politics: The Clash of World Views and the Remaking of the American Political Order at the end of the Cold War*. He told me that, "In order to understand what the implications of the eighth world view are, you really need to understand in detail what the other world views positions really are and how they are clearly delineated from each other.

"It is important to recognize what the basic categories of belief are that go into making up our world view vertically. You also have to know how the world views relate to each other horizontally. Then, you place them next to each other on a spectrum for comparative analysis.

"That's what we really need to do in order to create an educational tool, so people can look at a graphic chart and see relatively where the different world views are and what the comparative beliefs are in each of the world views. For example, in regards to how the entire universe came into being. There are fundamentally different conclusions people have about that subject. In essence, that's what my book is about."

It sounded like a road map of ideas. The graphic presentation he was creating would allow us to see where we had been and where we were headed as a society. Specifically, it showed where some people were located in the spectrum of ideas and where others stood on a wide range of key issues. I realized this was an important step forward, because everyone was clearly not on the same page.

From my perspective, the next evolutionary step on earth was going to affect every aspect of life. It was not going to just change one area like physics for example. It would change everything. Mr. Sheehan agreed and added that, "This next evolutionary phase we are going through is affecting the whole mode of reasoning we engage in. It's changing our philosophy, our political views, our theories of human psychology, and our modes of spiritual expression. Our entire social environment is being impacted by this."

Indeed, we were living in difficult, transitional times. It reminded me of the old saying, "It's always darkest before the dawn." It seemed to me, that was what the *War on Terror* was really all about. We were currently experiencing the darkest days before a brighter age of enlightenment.

Mr. Sheehan agreed, and he added, "It's a major last gasp effort on the part of the adherents of the second world view paradigm who are in some degree allies with what remains of the first world view paradigm adherents. They are paranoid isolationists that fear the cosmos. This latest war is a last-gasp effort to try to militarize and establish a global, national security state control, because they are afraid that their reality is going to dissolve right in front of their eyes."

Mr. Sheehan's insight really struck a nerve. Recently, I had realized the real reason global oil industries were gouging everyone at the gas pumps was due to the fact that they knew more efficient energy sources and technologies would become available in the very near future.

During the 1990s, I had spent years writing reports on upcoming technologies for a Japanese auto manufacturer. That company, like all others, invested millions of dollars and thousands of man hours every year forecasting future scenarios.

One day, it occurred to me that the oil industry was doing this type of future research too and could see what was coming, more or less. The forecasts I had worked on made it clear that transportation, and other energy related industries, would not rely exclusively on oil in the future.

Mr. Sheehan said, "That's absolutely right. Some people might say that these companies are taking advantage of the last days of an old paradigm. It's likely that they are attempting to build up a huge amount of capital to fund, and invest in, and in some cases buy out the new technology to retain their monopoly, more or less, of energy."

When I mentioned to Mr. Sheehan that this type of behavior seemed a bit neurotic, he said, "Not really. From their narrow point of view, they have established an artificial structure known as transnational corporations. Unfortunately, there is no legal or financial responsibility on the part of any of the owners of the company, the stock holders, or on the part of the management, or on the part of any of the Board of Directors for anything they do wrong.

"They have created this artificial entity called a corporation that can be liable to no degree beyond its own capital resources that it actually has in that corporation, so they have no conscience. There is absolutely no conscience whatsoever, so in a certain sense they don't suffer from the type of guilt that is the normal, human, built-in restraint on one's personal conduct.

"Rather, they conduct themselves in a way that is designed to solely and simply maximize the immediate, short-term financial interests of the owners of the corporation. They behave in a way that is not technically psychotic or even neurotic it's just abhorrent to the rest of us, but that is their mode of ethical reasoning."

I stood corrected. But in my opinion, that type of behavior was not human. My comment clearly struck a nerve with Mr. Sheehan. He said, "Oh, it isn't human! That's the entire point! That's why one would have to disagree so profoundly with William Rehnquist. He was the Chief Justice who wrote the major Supreme Court decision which stated that corporations were people and that they were endowed with all the same unalienable, fundamental, natural-law rights as any living human being. That is just profoundly incorrect."

Although I was not a lawyer, it seemed obvious that this situation was undermining the whole rule of law. Mr. Sheehan agreed and added that, "It's undermining the entire human civilization, and it needs to be one of the major premises of even a moderate politics in the future. That social structure has to be amended. It has only been in place since about 1868, and it needs to be undone.

"If people want to do business that's fine, the new paradigm people are not opposed to that. They are not opposed to the entrepreneurial spirit. They are not opposed to people getting a fair return for their investment and their time. However, they do believe everyone has to be responsible for the things that they do."

I appreciated the way Mr. Sheehan had articulated the lack of ethics involved in corporation's verses the rest of the human race. That system seemed to encourage criminal behavior. However, in my opinion, this was more than just corruption. In some cases it was simply insane behavior. The level of greed, corruption and cruelty involved just to maintain power indicated these people were mentally unstable.

For example, how could any public official swear an oath to uphold the constitutional laws of the U.S. and then decide to violate their oath because they believed that by doing so they were actually helping the country? That type of contorted logic seemed crazy to me.

Mr. Sheehan knew I was referring to the *Iran Contra Affair*. He sighed deeply and said, "It's not technically crazy. It's just pursuant to a particular world view. For example, the political platform of the first paradigm world view is Machiavellian. Machiavelli actually said it clearly in his book *The Prince*. When he wrote it, at that time, one's actual loyalty was only to one's self not to any common wheel or any larger community. This was of course the lower manifestation of the first paradigm world view."

It was an interesting point, but I firmly believed that type of thinking divorced one from the human family. Mr. Sheehan agreed that many people from the first world paradigm had lost their humanity. But if that was true, then what had they become?

Mr. Sheehan said, "You are asking an important question. They believe they exist somehow separate from the rest of the universe. They experience themselves as a nodule of consciousness residing up behind their eyeballs somewhere. They live in constant fear. They have no trust of the universe. They have no trust of the physical environment or the planet. They have no trust of the human family. They have no trust of any other individual. They are constantly engaged in a quest of vanquishing, and conquering, and dominating, and attempting to obtain more power and more material wealth to fill in the gaping hole at the center of their spirit. They are attempting to make themselves feel secure, but it is completely antithetical [diametrical opposition] because you can never in fact fill that empty space with those things."

I agreed, but to me, that type of thinking seemed like a form of insanity that needed to be addressed. Mr. Sheehan calmly replied, "I had many hours of conversations regarding this subject with Dr. John Mack who was the head of the Department of Clinical Psychiatry at Harvard Medical School. He started out thinking as you do that it was some form of clinical insanity.

"He deeply probed this and analyzed it. Eventually, before his death, he came to a realization that led to his confrontation with the Harvard University faculty. It became clear to him that this was just a different world view. He realized that people who are adherents to a consistent set of beliefs that make up an integrated world view are not, In fact, insane."

I was beginning to understand what Mr. Sheehan was saying; there was no internal conflict of interest in these individuals. He agreed and added, "They conduct themselves in a completely consistent manner that has integrity. It is just that you and I disagree with it. But they are not certifiably nuts. They are not delusional. They are not psychotic. They are not anything like that. They, in fact, conduct themselves in a completely consistent manner, and they do so with complete equilibrium."

Although Mr. Sheehan's statement made perfect sense, I knew there really was something alien about the current field of mental health care. According to the dictionary, the legal term for a psychiatrist was an "alienist." As an attorney, Mr. Sheehan recognized the term and was aware that an alienist had the legal authority to declare if a person was sane or not in a court of law.

My point was this, the term "alienist" related specifically to the power a court of law had to place *a lien* on one's property or person; (Lien is a French word meaning "knot or binding"). This was an extremely important correlation. It seemed clear to me that there was a connection between placing a lien on a person and being abducted by an alien.

But there was more. I discovered that over time the science of alienism (psychiatry) had, in fact, alienated a large percentage of humanity. The reason for this was simple. According to the *Encyclopedia of Psychiatry*, if a person had a paranormal experience, it was considered technically invalid because scientists could not replicate and study it in a laboratory using their methodology.

This really was rather ironic considering the quantum nature of the universe; specifically as it related to the UFO/ET phenomena. Most people had no idea this could happen, but if someone had a paranormal experience with an ET or a UFO and openly talked about it, an alienist had the legal authority to invalidate their claim. Furthermore, if an alienist chose to do so, they could order a person they had diagnosed as delusional into treatment. In other words, they could commit someone that had experienced the paranormal to the mental ward.

It was a strange paradox, because according to the *Encyclopedia of Parapsychology*, humans, in their current physical form, could not understand the divine nature of God until they had personally experienced a paranormal event.

Whether intentional or not, alienists had divided modern civilization into two groups. Everyone was placed on one side or the other of the psychological fence which did not serve us well, in my opinion.

As we continued our conversation, I realized that Mr. Sheehan was reshaping my view of the world, but this wasn't the first time. About 20 years earlier, I had followed his legal work on the Iran Contra Affair. At that time, I was stunned to learn about the drug trafficking, illegal arms sales, and money laundering by groups within our military and government. It was a very-traumatic period in my young-adult life. I realized there was an air of unaccountability by those that held positions of power. At some point, to preserve my sanity, I completely turned away from politics. However, the Iran Contra affair surfaced again in the 1990s when President Clinton was being impeached. Various conservative radio talk show hosts reported that both presidents Bush and Clinton were involved in the military drug trafficking in Arkansas, at the Mena Airport.

Mr. Sheehan could relate to my frustration with the situation. He said, "To give you some solace, the reports of that were actually quite distorted. My law firm in Washington, D.C., was responsible for discovering the illegal activity at Mena, Arkansas. When Terry Anderson contacted us and sent us the data regarding how he worked at Mena and explained all the other illegal activity that was going on, we sent in one of our investigators named Gene Wheaton. He was a former OSI operative for the Air Force.

"We sent him to Mena, and he essentially found out everything that was going on there. We then brought that information to the local District Attorney and the Attorney General and sat down with then Governor Clinton to discuss it. It was perfectly evident that Governor Clinton was not involved in this stuff in the beginning. He didn't even know about it.

"The fact of the matter is that the entire base was being run by Barry Seal with Richard Seacort. They were key players in the Iran Contra affair. That's a completely different group than the Clinton people. But what happened was, when Clinton got access to all that information, like every other political animal in Washington, D.C., he figured out a way to transform it into a tool for increasing his own political power.

"It wasn't that he became involved in a corrupt manner in the actual endorsement of the drug smuggling or anything like that. What he did do was simply let it be known in the circles of leadership around the country that he knew about this, and like everything else it is just another thing that you can play like a poker chip.

"But you have to play at the table in order to increase your personal power, and that is exactly what Clinton did. Of course, when he ended up coming into power by being elected president, he was almost immediately attacked by Henry Hide and Dick McColumn, from the Fifth District out of Florida, who had been intimately involved in working directly with colonel Oliver North and that whole 'off the shelf enterprise' crowd that held private meetings with the liaison from colonel North's office

"They went after President Clinton and tried to impeach him on any conceivable thing they could. They went after him in a very-intense way, because they couldn't stand the fact that he had somehow processed the dark secrets of the Iran Contra operations and had simply brokered that knowledge to help get himself into the presidency."

It was a sobering insight that Mr. Sheehan offered. Clearly, he was well informed on the inner workings of Washington, D.C. I recalled that President Clinton had expressed an interest in UFOs. He had asked his Chief of Staff, John Podesta, to investigate the matter. But, from what I understood, like the Carter administration, they didn't get very far with their investigation.

According to Mr. Sheehan, "Clinton also had Webster Hubbell investigating it. He was the only person who was indicted for the White Water scandal. Clinton had assigned him the responsibility for finding out about the UFO issue. Clinton also had direct conversations with Lawrence Rockefeller. I know, because Lawrence told me about that."

I found that information very interesting because Mr. Rockefeller had funded the *UFO Disclosure Project* with Dr. Greer. According to Sheehan, "Lawrence had also offered to fund our entire investigation, to present the data to defend Dr. Mack against the Harvard faculty, to show that abductions were indeed true.

"It really was a great loss to the UFO/ET research community that, before he died, Rockefeller did not decide to dedicate a significant portion of his estate to further finance major operations like this."

According to what I had learned during my conversation with Mr. Sheehan, the truth was going to come out in time; with or without well funded investigations. How long that process would take was open to speculation, but it was clear that the collective realization that we were not the only intelligent being in the universe was unavoidable.

CHAPTER SEVEN

Alien Engine at Area 51

Late one night in June of 1997, an inventor named David Adair was visiting his friend, actor John Vernon, who lived in a million-dollar mansion located in the Santa Monica Mountains. That night, Mr. Vernon listened intently as David spoke for hours on the phone with talk show host Art Bell giving many amazing, intimate details of his extremely unusual life story.

While broadcasting to millions of Americans that night, Mr. Adair looked out over the twinkling city lights of the San Fernando Valley and hoped that someone in the vast, radio audience would hear his story and one day help him produce another working fusion reactor.

I was one of the people listening to the show that night. Although I had never heard of Mr. Adair, I was fascinated when he described how he had engineered the world's first fusion rocket prior to graduating from high school. That work ultimately led him to a brief tour of the infamous Area 51, in Nevada.

As I listened to Mr. Adair on the radio, dozens of questions raced through my mind. That night, I could not sleep at all. At the time, I was employed by a Japanese corporation to write a comprehensive, technical report on mobile, "flight-weight" fusion reactors. It was a highly specialized subject. As a result, I became determined to find Mr. Adair and ask him how he had generated stable reactor containment fields. At the time, I had no idea that he was only living about 30 miles from my home.

Unfortunately, I found that Mr. Adair was extremely difficult to locate, and after a few months I gave up trying to contact him. However, as fate would have it, while attending a Hollywood, Halloween party a few years later, I discovered that one of my friends knew Mr. Adair. After I got over my initial shock, I insisted that my friend introduce me to Mr. Adair as soon as possible.

About six months later, I had my first of many long and incredibly interesting telephone conversations with Mr. Adair. As a result, we decided to meet. A few weeks after the tragic events of 9/11/2001, he invited me to his home. Although he had spoken to many large audiences across the country, I found that Mr. Adair was actually a very-private person. I was fortunate to be shown his private collection of news clippings and other personal items of interest from NASA and the Navy.

I began by asking Mr. Adair about the government disclosure letter he and his associates had been circulating. He told me that the letter was based on a series of events that occurred when he testified for Dr. Steven Greer in Washington, D.C., in 1997.

According to Mr. Adair, "Dr. Greer is a highly intelligent and very arrogant person. Despite the fact that he sequestered me for quite a few hours, I still like the man. However, I think he finally met up with the real covert world. People in the UFO community talk about it a lot. You can talk about it all you want, but I guarantee you if you ever met a real covert operative you would flip out, because they are very serious. They are lethal, and there is no negotiating. For example, about five weeks after I testified, Dr. Greer's assistant died."

It was shocking, but true. I recalled reading that she had contracted an unusual form of melanoma. It was a fast-acting cancer. Mr. Adair explained that, "Once they reach a diagnosis for that, you are lucky if you have six weeks. She was an extremely aggressive female. She really disliked anyone that could challenge Dr. Greer's leadership position.

"I heard that they went to a meeting at the Pentagon, and she started telling these career military officers how, why, and when they should proceed with disclosure. After that, they decided she was expendable. They set an example by killing her.

"Dr. Greer has four daughters, so he is totally vulnerable to blackmail. That's how he was brought in and turned into an unwilling spokesperson for them. They are controlling the speed and content of disclosure. At the rate they are going, we will all be old and grey before they release everything. However, I think it's happening that way because the disclosure timetable is not really in human hands."

When I asked Mr. Adair if he was implying that the extraterrestrials were in charge to some degree, he replied, "Exactly. It's all about when they are ready, and until they are ready, there is nothing anyone can do to make it happen."

I then asked if he had any idea when the ETs were going to come out of the cosmic closet. He thought for a moment, "Perhaps they don't even know when that will be. I think they are just monitoring the course of events as they unfold on earth. Because of what happened with the terror attacks on 9/11, everything has changed dramatically.

"As a matter of fact, every item regarding UFO disclosure that we were talking about prior to 9/11 officially doesn't exist anymore. The media doesn't cover anything other than the *War on Terror*. Someone has completely eliminated the media's spotlight from focusing on anything regarding UFOs or ETs.

"I have a lot of friends in Congress that owe me favors, and I have never asked them to do me a favor in the past, but I recently did. They basically said this really was not a good time to be asking them for favors. However, I had requested that they give Dr. Greer his hearing on disclosure. You see, after five years of working towards disclosure, the doors are all slamming in his face.

"The congressional and senatorial leaders I spoke with told me that the reason Greer is not making progress is because his method falls outside the political system, therefore, he doesn't have the clout required to make disclosure happen.

"He failed to find a political process that the politicians would respond to. It's called the 'what's in it for me deal?' However, I came up with a formula on how that might work. The men in power that I talked with were willing to advance the disclosure project only if it was dealt with inside the current political power structure. It had to be a process they could accept."

Mr. Adair's plan was simple, but powerful. It required getting a mandate from the people. He explained that the person that brought that bill to the floors of the House and the Senate would have to be firmly set in their career. They would be near the end of their career and actively seeking a legacy.

He said, "This was the formula that hit a nerve. This was the method we agreed upon to move the agenda forward. Basically this process has been in the works for a few months, and that is where the form letter on my web site comes in. It has picked up thousands of requests from American citizens that I will eventually turn over to these politicians who will then use them as a starting point.

"What we want is very simple: a congressional hearing that will grant covert operatives total immunity from their national security oath. I'm tired of Dr. Greer telling us that he has hundreds of witnesses. I know he is not blowing smoke regarding this issue, because in 1971 I personally saw dozens of people working on these things at Area 51.

"I saw them underground working on all these different crafts and back engineering lots of stuff. I believe there are lots of people that have spent 30 years or more working on these types of projects. Imagine what they could tell us? But more importantly, they would be able to tell us who signed their pay checks."

When I asked Mr. Adair if this was why he was pushing so hard for public hearings, he said, "Absolutely. This event should be immediately broadcast on *CSPAN* or some other media company. I really want the whole world to hear what these hard-core engineers have to say.

"I know that during the short time I was at Area 51, I was taken through offices that were off to the side of the hangers and labs. They took me to a room and locked me in it. I saw a lot of people working down there as we were walking past these offices."

When I asked Mr. Adair to explain how he ended up at Area 51, he told me it began when he started building rockets in the late 1960s. This got the attention of a local Congressman who funded Adair's second-generation, fusion rocket. People began talking, and the local Mount Vernon newspapers got wind of the story. According to Mr. Adair, it was the fastest vehicle ever built on Earth.

He then showed me a newspaper clipping regarding one of his rockets. In his portfolio, there were lots of newspaper stories that he had saved. Probably the most outrageous thing Mr. Adair told me was that he had been funded by a Congressman named John Ashbrook. Anticipating my disbelief, Mr. Adair handed me an old photo and said, "Here's a picture of me with Congressman Ashbrook. I am giving him a working miniature model of a Saturn 5 rocket as a present.

"He was a very powerful Congressman from Ohio. He was chairman of the Internal Security Committee of Congress. That's a pretty powerful place to be. He was also on the Education and Labor Committee which is how he funded my work through the Department of Education. They gave me a grant. All these letters here are from Congressman Ashbrook.

"See how old these newspapers are. This one is dated July 8, 1970. When the Air Force showed up to inspect my second rocket, they were totally gung ho for all the formulas and the prototype I built from scratch.

"They knew I was onto something, so they funded me through the *National Science Foundation*. Then, my mother got concerned because the government people were really getting involved in our lives, so she went and talked to General Curtis LeMay. He really liked my mother a lot, and he had seen the newspaper stories, so he came over to talk with me. Later he talked with Congressman Ashbrook.

"The next thing I knew, LeMay told me he was going to be my buddy; that he was going to be my project manager. Actually, that was the greatest thing that could have happened to me. I found out much later that it was LeMay that saved my ass."

That was some powerful protection. According to the history books, the leaders of the Soviet Union were terrified of general LeMay. Mr. Adair then said, "A private investigator pulled the records for Congressman Ashbrook from the Library of Congress and found all this documentation. The investigator was shocked to learn that I was telling the truth.

"In one letter, I told the Air Force that without the right electronics, and the right formulas to compress and scale down the fusion engine I was building, I could not complete my work. I would need a really-big vehicle to put the engine in, and it was going to be a damn big engine!

"Eventually, I found an ICBM, Titan 3 that had been pulled out of mothballs and had been given to the *Center for Science and Industry*, in Ohio. They had recently drained all the fuel out of it and parked this thing in a storage area. It was flight ready. I would have had to reconfigure the entire engine, but everything in the electronic housing was perfect, so I told the Congressman I need the Titan 3.

"Look for yourself. Here is the letter stating, 'We are working with them in regards to obtaining the old Titan rocket on your behalf.' Now, I have a question for you. What is a congressional letter regarding the securing of a Titan 3 rocket for a 17-year-old civilian doing in my files? Don't you find this a little odd?"

Actually, I found it more than a little odd, but I urged Mr. Adair to continue. He said, "Here are the signatures of all the politicians involved. All these letters I have from Congress are due to the special project I was working on. After a while, I got the Titan rocket. During that time, I had more information-based dreams and from that I eventually reconfigured the fusion engine down to a workable size.

"Everybody loved that, because hauling a Titan rocket around is pretty tough to do: its 30-stories tall! After I told them I could compress this thing down to an engine that would fit in a 12-foot tall rocket housing, I had to build everything from scratch which is what all this is."

Mr. Adair then pointed to old images of technical diagrams and explained that one of his first rockets had been equipped with an electronic stealth device that he had created. This was decades before the U.S. military built a similar system. He explained that as a cover story, he built one rocket specifically to show the local people. He said, "The Air Force guys came over to my house every day. They took their uniforms off and walked around in T-shirts and shorts, so the locals would think they were just average people helping me with all the rockets I was building.

"When the town folks came by, they thought, 'Man he's building a big one this time!' But we really had two rockets in production. I used one of them to win science fairs with, but here is a picture of the design we used to move past the prototype stage with. The fact was, we had an operation in the front and another in the back, and it worked well. That was my introduction to covert activities."

It was clear to me that Mr. Adair was deeply involved with the military. We met at his home a few weeks after 9/11, and he was nervously waiting for a phone call from the government telling him whether or not he would be called back to active duty.

When I asked him about that aspect of his life, he said, "I am a patriot, but I hope I'm not called back. I have always been a double-edged sword with every agency I worked with. I have this really bad habit of telling the truth in front of everybody, and that doesn't go over well with the covert operatives.

"It also makes me a real management problem. The military found that out in a hurry. I've always walked a fine edge with them. They know I will work with them, but they also know they have to be careful what projects they put me on and what they expose me to. People often ask why I haven't been killed. The simple answer is; I'm still useful. I know something, so they won't just destroy me, because I still cooperate, and that makes me valuable."

Apparently, Mr. Adair also had some unseen forces protecting him. When I asked him to elaborate about that, he said, "There were so many times I should have been killed in crashes and explosions, yet I was the only one walking away; sometimes without even being injured. However, I am human and I have been hurt in the past while serving in the military and ended up in the hospital for a long stay, but I'm still alive."

I wanted to get back to Area 51 and the *Disclosure Project*. I was curious what his role was. Mr. Adair explained that, "All this documentation that I am showing you here, I brought with me to Congress. When we first started this project, Dr. Greer told me that he had 125 hardware contact people which sounded right to me, because I had seen a lot of people working at Area 51. I knew that most of them worked there full time.

"Greer wanted me to testify on April 9, 1997, in Washington D.C. I didn't want to do it, because I was really treading a fine line regarding my national security oath. However, I was able to tell my Area 51 story, because I was only 17 years old when those events happened. According to Constitutional Law, the federal government is prohibited from signing a minor to a national security oath.

"That's why Strom Thurmand once told me I was the biggest loose cannon on the deck. He said that because they had shown me all that alien hardware before I signed an oath. Anyway, prior to briefing Congress, Greer and his people had me tell my story.

"Getting me to DC was a problem. I didn't want to go, but Dr. Greer just kept calling me every day until finally, two days before the hearings, I agreed to go. I changed my mind after he asked me how I would feel if all those people testified at a closed door hearing without me. I would have missed out on a unique opportunity."

"When we arrived, I went to the prescreening room, and there were only 11 witnesses! I immediately wondered where the rest of the 125 people were. I knew my story would be nothing compared to the other people that had worked decades on these projects. I believed that being one guy among 125 would be relatively safe.

"As I recall, 11 of us were asked to tell our stories, and nine of the eleven had only seen lights and blips on radar or in the sky! I remember thinking this was not good. The tenth guy was an attorney from Nashville. He said he was in the basement of the Pentagon in 1960 working as an encryption officer.

"His commander walked in one day and threw a piece of metal about one foot long on the table and told the men it was debris from an alien spacecraft. He ordered his men to try and decode the alien symbols. Greer said that there was no way they could decode that at the Pentagon. I was glad that there was at least one other guy in there besides me that had seen a piece of alien hardware."

I could just imagine how intense the meeting in Washington, D.C., must have been for Mr. Adair. I was curious if he still recalled what he told the disclosure committee about himself. He laughed and said, "Hi. I'm the guy that built the fastest rocket on earth. It was powered by the world's first electromagnetic fusion containment engine.

"When I flew my second prototype, it landed in one of the world's most top secret Air Force bases in history: Area 51. My life changed forever when they took me underground and showed me that alien engine. The damn thing was still alive! It was a symbiotic engine: an intelligent machine that could interface with biological entities, humans or alien. It worked very similar to the Soviet heads up display technology featured in the fictional movie *FIREFOX*.

"Theoretically, when the pilot would think 'lock and fire', the fighter jet would respond. It was a symbiotic relationship. I wonder where they got the idea for that. Well, I know for a fact that the alien engine/power plant I saw had that capability."

That type of technology almost seemed too incredible to be true, but in May of 2006, the Advanced Telecommunications Research Institute and Honda Research Institute announced they had developed a "brain-machine interface." The new technology enabled the decoding of natural brain activity for the near real-time operation of a robot without having to implant sensors in the head and brain. The technological breakthrough offered amazing possibilities for the control of machines by human brain waves alone simply by wearing a highly-advanced helmet.

Mr. Adair explained that the alien brain/machine interface he saw in the early 1970s allowed the pilot and the engine's artificial intelligence to become symbiotic. He believed it was a perfect way to travel through space. The space craft and the pilot were essentially one.

Although that was an amazing technology, I wanted to know what had happened after his fusion rocket landed at Area 51. According to Mr. Adair, "To make a long story short, I managed to sabotage my rocket soon after I arrived, because I realized they were going to use it as a weapon.

"I rigged it to explode when I got permission to inspect it. They had no idea what I was up to, so they assigned me a driver to take me to the landing site. The reactor was still intact, so I put a foreign material in the core and then turned it on. A few minutes later, it exploded into a million pieces. Although I got in serious trouble for that, the military still showed me the alien engine in the underground base. That's when I realized why they were so interested in my engine.

"There was nothing on earth like my electromagnetic fusion containment engines, because they were so fast. We used Inconel/Carb-Nte with deuterium for fuel in the reactor. My fusion engine, compared to liquid fuel or solid propellant engines, would be like comparing a Model-T Ford to a Lamborghini. My rocket took off so fast it went from zero mph to 8,754 mph in about four and half seconds."

Although it sounded impossible, Mr. Adair claimed his rocket flew so fast from a standing start that no one saw it leave. He said it would be like trying to watch a bullet leave a rifle barrel. As a result, everyone at the launch site, other than himself, initially thought it had blown up.

He explained that, "I built it mostly of out of titanium. We had every kind of known material for lightness and strength incorporated in that rocket. However, because of the extreme G-force of the launch, everything inside was just warped."

Despite that, the engine was still intact when the rocket landed at Area 51, because it had come down on a parachute. According to Mr. Adair, "That is when it got weird, because there were a lot of characters involved. There was one man that was really on my case. He was a person that Dr. Werner Von Braun had warned me about. I met Von Braun as a child, because I was doing all this work with rockets in the early 1970s when we were landing men on the moon.

"Because I was in that kind of environment, I got to attend parties where all the original *Apollo* 7 astronauts would show up and Dr. Von Braun was there. That's how we all crossed paths, and I started interfacing with him. Von Braun warned me that if, during my rocket work, I encountered a man named Dr. Arthur Rudolph, I should be extremely careful, because he was a really dangerous individual.

"He was the chief architect of the Saturn-5 engines of our *Apollo* moon rocket. Dr. Rudolph came into the U.S. with Von Braun and other German scientists under *Operation Paperclip*. Dr. Rudolph had been a full colonel in the Gestapo. He had ordered hundreds of thousands of Jews, and other people, to be killed during the building of the V-2 rockets at Peenemunde, in Germany.

"If someone made a mistake, he would put a cable around their neck and slowly lift them up until they were strangled. Then, he would disembowel the body and leave it hanging there for everyone to see. There were rotted corpses hanging all over the place. They would also feed people sawdust and water. This would take the hunger out of their stomach until they fell over dead. They would then replace them with more fresh people."

It was a bizarre situation. The man was clearly evil, yet he was the winner of the highest award NASA could bestow. Mr. Adair's tone was deadly serious when he said, "If you think I am making this up, look at this. Here is a copy of the *Atlanta Weekly* with pictures of people who were hung. And here is an American passport being handed to Dr. Rudolph.

"The Mossad finally caught up with Dr. Rudolph. On May 25, 1984, he was deported from Los Angeles to Munich, Germany, by the OSI (Office of Special Investigations) due to war crimes. I wonder why the national press corps didn't tell us about that. NASA doesn't want to acknowledge any of this. Here is a picture of Dr. Arthur Rudolph. He looks like a kindly, little-old grandfather, but here is some of his handiwork. See all the dead people."

The news photos were horrific. Mr. Adair then explained that General LeMay had sent him from Mount Vernon, Ohio, to Wright Patterson Air Technical Intelligence Center, in Dayton, Ohio. From there, Adair, his rocket, and some colonels got onboard a C-141 transport and flew to White Sands Missile Range, in New Mexico.

Soon after they arrived at White Sands, a black jet showed up. According to Mr. Adair, "General LeMay had warned me that if a black, DC-9 jet showed up, it would represent a real problem for me. Sure enough, out of that jet stepped these guys wearing black suits and mirrored sunglasses. Among them was one little guy wearing a khaki uniform. I knew that was Dr. Rudolph, because Dr. Von Braun had shown me his picture."

I was really curious if Mr. Adair knew who Dr. Rudolph was officially working for. He said, "I'm not really sure. I think it was one of those alphabet soup intelligence agencies, but he was officially working for NASA. As soon as he got off the jet, he asked to see my rocket. When I asked him who he was, he claimed he was just a guy that inspected rockets for the government. But when I asked him if he was from NASA, he said he had never worked there.

"Then, we walked over to my rocket, and I opened up an access panel. He leaned over to look at the engine and began mumbling to himself. He seemed really upset. I think it was due to the fact that I had built something he thought was impossible to do.

"I took that opportunity to lean over and whisper in his ear. I said, 'Did you know that proportionally this engine has 10,000 times the thrust of the F-1, Saturn-5 engines Dr. Rudolph?' He stood up and was furious. He wanted to know who I was and how I knew so much. I told him I was just a kid that launched rockets in the cow fields of Ohio.

"Actually, I had friends around me that were Air Force colonels that general LeMay had assigned to take care of me. I was doing my best to cooperate with the military, but I got really upset when Dr. Rudolph told me he wanted to change the landing coordinates on my rocket. I still recall how nasty he was about it.

"The navigation system I was using was off-the-shelf technology. Back in those days, it was all analog. I had my system programmed so that the rocket would come back down within a two-mile radius of the launch site, at White Sands, in New Mexico. But Dr. Rudolph had me reprogram the coordinates so that my rocket would land 476 miles northwest of White Sands in an area called Groom Lake, in Nevada.

"Well, I immediately pulled out my national survey maps, and I looked at Groom Lake and wondered why in God's name we were launching up to a dry lake bed in Nevada. It was so far away. That's when Dr. Rudolph yelled, 'Just do it!' He was really hostile. I had been warned many times by Von Braun and LeMay that if I ran into Dr. Rudolph not to push his buttons.

"With that in mind, I reset the coordinates on the guidance system, and we launched my rocket, and it took off perfectly. Sure enough, it landed right on target. Oddly enough, it wasn't until they made the movie *Independence Day* that I ever heard the term Area 51.

"I always knew it as Groom Lake. It was the only name I had ever heard for that place, but as we were getting ready to board the jet to go and recover my rocket, I said, 'Hey, do you see these rubber tires on this plane? Would you please tell me how you are going to land this thing on a dry lake bed? This thing is going to plow into the ground and never leave.' Someone yelled at me to shut up and get in the plane, and after a while we arrived in Nevada.

"As we flew over the landing site, I looked down at these twin 10,000-foot runways, and I realized there was a huge base down there. Soon after we landed at this military base, that didn't exist on any map, I started getting really concerned. I was trying to locate any Air Force emblems, Navy emblems or any kind of logos or emblems that would identify who the commanding authority was, but there were none anywhere on any of the buildings.

"Normally, the standard pattern painted on water towers at an airstrip is an orange and white checkerboard pattern. But at this base, everything was painted either solid white or solid black. They were not conforming to any code.

"After we debarked from the plane, we got on this go-cart-looking vehicle. It looked kind of like the electric carts that you see at airports. Then, we drove from the landing strip to a series of hangers and headed into the center one. It was really cool they way this place was built.

"There were all these really-big lights at the top that had louvers on them, so the light would shine down. When I got close to the buildings, they looked old and ratty, but underneath it was a metal alloy unlike any I had ever seen. It was an incredible-looking stainless steel type of metal which I thought was really unusual to use for buildings that size.

"When we got inside the hanger, we went down to the basement area. Actually, we drove into the hanger, and there were little yellow lights flashing and big hanger doors. Then, out of the ground came all these little pipes with chains attached that blocked off all the doorways. Then, the whole floor, about the size of a football field, slowly dropped down. The entire hanger floor was an open air elevator."

I could clearly visualize what Mr. Adair was describing. The system was designed to lift some very-large, very-heavy equipment. The floor was made of concrete on a steel frame. The whole thing went up and down on giant worm screws which made it a lot more stable than a hydraulic system.

Mr. Adair explained that, "Nothing can take a heavy load like a worm screw; however, these screws were the size of Sequoia trees, and there were at least 12 of them lifting the floor! We went down at least 200 feet until we rested flush with the floor of an underground hanger that was huge!

"It had a really-high, arched ceiling that went so far in either direction you couldn't see the end of it. It just went on forever. You could park a hundred 747s in there, and they wouldn't even be in the way.

"At that point, I asked someone what in God's name they did with all the dirt. They just looked at me really strange and didn't answer. I guess they didn't expect me to try and figure things like that out. I never saw any dirt because everything had concrete over it or was covered with some type of ceramic material. The walls were at least 30-feet high and all along them were different workshops and laboratories and periodically there were huge work bays. We drove past all kinds of aircraft that I had never seen. Some of them I had seen before, but even those were really exotic.

"The most interesting thing about this to me still is how well lit that underground area was. There were no shadows anywhere, and I didn't see any light fixtures. I was wondering how they generated that much light. It didn't look like the walls were glowing or the floor or the ceilings. I know it sounds strange, but every square inch of this place was perfectly lit and yet there was no visible source of light.

"After we had been driving for a while, and we had passed a lot of different aircraft, we took a road to the left that led away from most of the other activities. I saw a lot of people working on stuff. All those aircraft appeared to be operational, but some of them I had never seen before or since. They were shaped like a reverse teardrop. There were others that looked similar to the flying wing. One aircraft, the XB-70, was a Delta Wing bomber built in 1959."

When I asked Mr. Adair if he recalled the exact date he was at Area 51, he calmly replied, "June 20, 1971. And when we arrived at this one big room, it was just amazing. We drove up beside these large steel doors, and then one of the officers got out and put his hand on a scanner type thing. Then, it flashed a light at him. At the time, I thought it had taken his picture.

"In hindsight, I would have to guess that it was actually a retinal scanning device. After the officer was electronically scanned, the door opened up. That's when I realized it was a security system of some kind.

"You need to understand that this was 1971. At that time, we had no laptops, no modems, no FAX, no VCR, and no cell phones. We didn't even have handheld calculators. *Texas Instruments* developed those about five years later, so where in the hell did these guys at Area 51 get all that technology?

"As soon as we went into the room, I immediately noticed the temperature dropped. It was warm in the big open areas we had just come from, but it was very cool in this room. It was so cold you could almost see your breath. As we entered the room, the lights, wherever they were coming from, came on. Again, there were no shadows being cast anywhere.

"Then, someone threw a switch and activated a hoist attached to some cables that were attached to a big tarp. The tarp was lifted straight up and sitting on this huge steel platform was a giant, electromagnetic fusion containment engine.

"I immediately recognized it because its configuration was similar to mine, but it was the size of a *Greyhound* bus. Mine was only about the size of a large watermelon.

"You can recognize engines that are comparable. If I had an internal combustion engine taken out of a *Model-A Ford* and had it sitting on the ground, and you pulled an engine out of a *Dodge Viper*, today, and placed them side by side, you would recognize that they operate on the same principle of internal combustion. But the difference in performance between the two is unbelievable.

"It was the same situation with my little engine and this giant thing they had locked up underground. They both ran on the same principle, the same configuration, but the level of sophistication was like that of the Model-A compared to the Viper engine. The engine they had in their possession must have been incredibly powerful. But there were many design features that I didn't recognize, for reasons that soon became clear."

I could hear the stress building in Mr. Adair's voice as he began recalling the emotional events. At this point, he was just looking at the engine at Area 51 and wondering where the rest of the space craft was. He explained, "That's where the argument started. They asked me if I liked what I saw. I said, 'Yeah, but I'm confused. I thought I was the first one to build one of these engines. That was when things really started getting odd.

"The colonel that was with Dr. Rudolph said, 'Son, we want you to help us with this design here since yours is very similar to it. You do want to help your country don't you?'

"Well, growing up I listened to Anita Bryant's records before bed and slept with an American flag blanket. I was very patriotic even in the '70s, so at first I agreed with the colonel that I wanted to help. However, I was very curious and wanted to know where all the people were that built this engine.

"He thought for a moment, and then said, 'Well, they are on vacation right now. You're off on summer vacation right?'

"And I said, 'OK, did they leave any notes on their work that I can look at?'

"Then he said, 'Well, they took them with them as homework. You get homework, right?'

"I was thinking this was really condescending. I was 17-years old and they were treating me like a child. But that's how they treated 17 year olds back then, so I figured I would play along with this asshole. I agreed to help, and that's when I told them I needed to get a closer look at the engine. They agreed, at which point I walked up and got up onto the platform it was resting on.

"The closer I got to that engine, the more I realized that these people had no idea what that thing really was. They were still trying to figure it out. It clearly didn't belong to us. When I was about three feet away, the first thing I noticed was a perfect shadow of myself on the engine.

"If you recall, earlier I told you there were no shadows anywhere, so how was my shadow showing up on this thing? Stranger still was the fact that the shadow moved about a half a second behind me, and that really got my attention!

"I got the impression it was a heat-sensitive, recognition alloy. Then, I realized we didn't have any material that could do that. I looked up at the engine, and I asked for permission to climb to the top, because I wanted to see the damaged area. The exterior had a hole about four feet in diameter on one side. That was the area that most interested me. It was located right in the middle of the reactor. When it comes to the plasma flow in the reactor core of a fusion engine, think of a figure eight, and right where the two circles cross each other it's like the eye of a hurricane.

"That's where the damage was located on this engine. Knowing my own engine, I was sure that this thing had experienced some kind of breech in the electromagnetic flux field that acted as the containment field and harnessed the power of the reactor.

"These engines basically function like a magnetic bottle or self-contained sphere. As long as the containment field is stable, you have the power of a star or a hydrogen-bomb continuously detonating.

"It's not impossible to figure out how this works. We know it occurs out in space all the time. All stars have extremely powerful magnetic fields that act as a containment field for their hydrogen plasma.

"We also know that black holes can suck an entire galaxy full of stars into their point of singularity. Obviously a black hole has no problem containing that fusion energy. That's why I mathematically figured out a way to artificially create a black hole.

"There was one major difference; I based the design of my containment field on a figure eight. That way, once it had become stabilized, it would always implode and consume itself without pulling everything around itself in; like a black hole.

"It appeared to me that the alien engine I saw at Area 51 had somehow lost its stabilization in the figure eight area of the containment field causing serious damage. That's why I was so curious about the hole.

"The way that engine was built was amazing. There wasn't a single screw or rivet or any weld seams anywhere on this entire device from end to end. It looked like it was grown rather than assembled. I realized that whoever built it had some really incredible manufacturing techniques.

"Years later, I was able to replicate this process, to some extent, in an experiment that I built. It flew onboard one of the 1993 Space Shuttle missions. It was part of the 'Get Away Special' program. That's where you rent space in a 55-gallon drum for your project.

"There was always a question if it was possible to shape liquid metals in a weightless environment. But on that experiment I melted metals together in a micro gravity. As they floated in space, I then spun and shaped them into any type of dimension I wanted because I had figured out a novel way to control this process."

Mr. Adair then explained that the control mechanism was a real phenomenon. With it, he had discovered a way to make a form without using a physical mold. He could take a fluid glob floating in a weightless environment and control it.

When I pressed Mr. Adair for more details, he explained that, "For every geometric shape and dimension there is a corresponding sound wave. Knowing this, I created a machine that was attached to a Moog synthesizer. It acted as the control that allowed me to replicate any shape I wanted simply by playing notes.

"The synthesizer generated interlocking, standing sound waves that would vibrate, even in space. That system allowed me to sonically shape the liquid metal. It proved to me what I had suspected when I first saw the engine at Area 51 in 1971. Whoever built that engine used a similar process. This raised an even larger question in my mind, one that I have never discussed publicly. I still wonder who could have built an engine that size in space."

It was a very important question. Mr. Adair was certain that the engine he saw at Area 51 had been engineered in a weightless environment in outer space. Specifically, he believed it would have been manufactured in deep, intergalactic space away from any planets or stars' gravitational fields.

He explained that, "The less gravity the better, because of something called gravity convections. You don't want any gravity convection currents to show up in the alloy-shaping process, because it creates tiny flaws that weaken whatever you are manufacturing.

"But back at Area 51, when I placed my hands on the engine to pull myself up, I began climbing up the exterior of the engine, which was designed with an exoskeletal structure. The best example I have found of this are the designs of H.R. Geiger. He is the designer that created all the sets of the *Alien* movies. He was the first person I know of on earth to depict that organic technology; where the ribbing of the ship looks like vertebrae. The engine I saw looked exactly that way."

I knew what Mr. Adair was referring to. It made sense that the most-advanced level of transportation design would mimic nature. He then told me that when he first saw the movie *Alien*, his friends thought he was having a seizure. He was shocked because it was the same design he had seen when he crawled into the entrance of the big alien engine at Area 51.

When I asked him if he had ever drawn a sketch of that engine he said, "Yes. It is on a video called the *UFO Uncoverup*. It's not correctly done, but it's a good start. I still have to finish the details. Anyway, it was easy crawling up the outside of the thing because of the exoskeletal structure."

I was curious about what it felt like when he touched it. Mr. Adair explained that the engine was warm which didn't make any sense at all. It was so cold in that hanger he could almost see his breath. He looked around on the floor, but saw no power lines. At that point, he asked himself how in the world that this alloy could be staying warm.

Mr. Adair recalled that the metal was really hard. It was the hardest material he had ever touched. It didn't give anywhere and strangely the surface tension on it felt more like a baby's skin. It was supple, but hard and warm? He thought it was very strange for metal to behave like that.

At that point, he wondered what the heck was really going on. He recalled that, "As I was crawling up the engine, wherever I touched it, the surface reacted. I knew that was strange, and when I turned around and looked at the Air Force guys all their mouths were hanging open. I assumed that the reaction they were seeing hadn't happened for them.

"Wherever I touched it, there were these really amazing blue-and-white swirls moving down through the hull of this thing; like wavelengths that you see on an oscilloscope. When I pulled my hands off, it stopped.

"I said to myself, 'Wow! This thing is reacting?' I continued to climb up until I reached the center area, and it had these vertebrae that branched off with cascading fibers. They looked almost like fiber optic cables filled with some kind of fluid. They were very-small tubes the size of angel hair pasta. There were millions of these things cascading over the hull of this engine, and I thought that the patterns looked very familiar. Then it dawned on me. They looked like neural synaptic firing patterns.

"There were millions of them going out everywhere on this thing, so I thought maybe the engine was designed with an exoskeletal brain. At that point, I reached out and grabbed some of the fibers and found they were really tough and that there was fluid in them.

"Wherever I touched that engine there was a reaction like a tremor of lights. As I walked down into the damaged area, I got to enter the interior of this thing. When I finally came out of the engine again, I said to the Air Force guys, 'You know this thing is more than a propulsion system. It is a power plant. It obviously came out of a big craft of some kind. Where is it located?'

"At this point they were already not happy with me, but I continued. I said, 'A craft like this must have had a crew. What did you do with those people? This is clearly not American or Soviet technology. This is some kind of extraterrestrial entity. How old is it? Did you dig it up? Is it millions of years old or did you guys shoot it down?'

"Man, they got really upset with me then. They told the MPs to take me down off the engine. When I came down, I was really pissed off. I had seen enough to know what was up. I knew that engine was from somewhere other than earth. What I didn't know was where it came from or how long the military had it in their possession. But it was obvious that my whole world was coming apart at that moment.

"You see, I grew up in a world where the government would never lie. We had landed on the moon about a year before and here the Air Force had this alien technology, and they weren't saying anything which made me furious."

I could see the anger flashing across Mr. Adair's face as he recalled the events, but I continued to politely press him for information.

He had told me something in an earlier conversation that I found really fascinating. I wanted him to describe how he was able to see the interior of the reactor. I was especially interested in the strange crystals he had seen.

He explained that before he made his military escort angry, he had asked for permission to inspect the inside of the engine where it had been blown open. He wanted to know what specifically had happened in the damaged area.

He said, "They hesitated on that request. They agreed to let me go, but before I went inside the engine they told me to make it brief. I then went down into the main area, and there was some incredible looking technology up and down that engine!

"I didn't get more than three feet into it before I came up to a wall. This wall looked like the shutter on a camera lens. It had lots of interlocking fans that would contract or expand. I noticed there was this round, little pod-thing there, so I put my hand on it and when I did, the wall shuttered open in front of me. It made a slight noise as it opened."

After the lens-like door opened, Mr. Adair was suddenly in the central area of the reactor/engine. Once inside, he was able to look deeper into the engine. He said, "What I saw in there was fascinating. It was such a trip being in there, because when I worked on my fusion engines everything was so small. Some of the parts were so small I had to machine them under a microscope. Yet, here was a larger version of my basic engine design that was big enough to walk through!

"It was like being a microbe crawling inside my own engine. That thing was simply incredible. Where I had manufactured a part to achieve a certain function in my engine, this thing would have something else in its place. It was stuff I couldn't even begin to recognize. There were these crystals that were facing each other. They were fabulous-looking crystals that were integrated into this plasma duct type thing.

"In my engine, I had such a hard time getting a cyclotron to curve the blast waves I needed for propulsion. This thing had some kind of venting system that allowed them to flush their plasma out through an area that looked the gills of a shark.

"The whole thing was so organic looking. It looked like a living machine; both organic and inorganic incorporated together. It was an oxymoron. How do you explain something like that? I got to see a lot of stuff in there that I couldn't believe."

I then asked him how many minutes he thought he spent in the control room of the engine alone. He recalled it was no more than five minutes, but it felt like a week. Mr. Adair had mentioned earlier that he had a photographic memory. I knew that he must have captured lots of images in his mind's eye at that moment. He said, "I was just absorbing it all. When I left, I didn't touch the pod, but as soon as I passed that area, the door closed behind me. I never told the Air Force guys that I went into that part of the engine"

That fact was really interesting to me. Mr. Adair didn't think the military knew there was another compartment in the interior that they could enter. Furthermore, he believed the artificial intelligence in the engine would not grant them access. He insisted there was "a presence about the engine" like that of a person or an entity. He sensed it had its own intelligence. That's why he was so angry when he came out of the engine. He knew there was no way humans could have built it.

He said, "That engine used some kind of crystal containment field power that we can't even imagine. I would have to work on it for a long time to figure out how they were doing the fractions. Where I was using the plasma in a linear mode, this thing was designed to go any direction it wanted with its plasma flows. That's impossible to do with a rocket, but this thing was amazing. I really wondered who in the hell had built it!

"As I started coming down the outside of the engine, that's when we got into a big argument, and I noticed that now, wherever I touched the engine, it was no longer reacting with the nice blue and white swirls of energy. The swirls had changed to reddish-orange, flame-looking patterns. As I calmed down to try and figure out what that was, the swirls changed back to a bluish white more tranquil-looking pattern.

"That's when I realized that the engine was not just heat sensitive, it reacted to brain waves. I know it sounds strange, but it was symbiotic and could lock on to how you think and feel. It was aware and was capable of total interface. It knew I was there and, at that point, I knew that it knew I was there."

I wanted Mr. Adair to explain the connection of all this to the photograph I had given him of a complex, fractal, energy pattern in a crop circle from England. The picture had been taken near the Chilbolton Radio Telescope.

He said, "I don't follow any of this crop circle stuff, but there is a connection here in the energy patterns involved. The first time I looked at that image, I noticed that there are three circles. The way they are interlocking in this pattern refers to the figure-eight, energy pattern I mentioned earlier.

"If you look at the axioms of the smaller circles that move outward from the bigger circles, it indicates the energy fields are stabilizing. This is critical to sustaining the electromagnetic containment fusion reaction. When you first sent me that image, I immediately recognized it as the same image I saw mentally in 1966 when I started working with it mathematically on paper.

"At that time, I had reoccurring dreams of this image and began building electromagnetic fields based on that, but I still needed to work out the math that would allow me to stabilize the equations. I was surprised when I looked closely at that specific crop circle image and saw the two little curves on the outside of the bigger arcs.

"That is how you build a replicating echo effect in these fields which allows you to build a second field on top of a first field. The reason that would be so convenient is because you could have one field that is containing the engine/reactor and the other containing the ship.

"The other neat thing about that crop circle image is, I built a three-dimensional model of that in 1966. If you imagine a stack of donuts; the engine and the craft are located inside the hole of the donuts. As these fields begin to stabilize around the engine, the echo effect occurs. It is like a stack of donuts encased in the secondary field.

"It is somewhat of a paradox, but you can solve an immensely powerful equation with this power plant. It tells us how we can travel millions of times faster than the speed of light without breaking the laws of physics."

I had never considered that was possible, but Mr. Adair quickly demonstrated the concept with a plain piece of paper. He said, "Just take a sheet like this and fold one side to the other. Traditionally, we think the shortest distance between these two points is a straight line, but there is a quicker way to get there. Imagine that this piece of paper is 200 million light years across. Well, even with a spacecraft traveling at the speed of light, it would still take 200 million years.

"But what happens with a warp drive is the secondary field starts shaping space. With enough power output this field begins curving space/time. Like all black holes, they bend light and space around themselves.

"Space begins wrapping itself around the craft when the engine fields stabilize and the space surrounding them begins to roll up like a scroll. Then, when you are ready, you turn on your engines and move in a linear fashion, but you only need to travel the thickness of the paper.

"After a couple of minutes, you shut your engines off and now you are 200 million light years across space. You just went millions of times faster than the speed of light without breaking the laws of physics."

It was an amazing concept. A spacecraft using a system like that would only have to travel a fraction of one percent of the distance! When I asked him if he thought this type of transportation would adversely affect the fabric of space, he said, "No, because the fabric as we know it is elastic, so this can be done without affecting all the time/matter systems inside of space. We are talking about a trans-dimensional jump. It's not necessarily a blast thorough linear space, but a journey through transspace.

"That's why you can do this type of flying with these kinds of engines, in these kinds of crafts, and still be on a relevant scale. The writers for *Star Trek* never wanted to address this issue."

I had often wondered what the *Enterprise's* fictional engines were supposed to be warping. Mr. Adair explained that they were designed to warp the square root of space, which is 1,500 times the speed of light. They fictionally warped space using things we clearly didn't have at our disposal: antimatter and dilithium crystals. When I asked him to explain how it theoretically worked, he said, "The engine was a matter/antimatter reactor. The energy from the engine was fed to the dilithium crystals. They would then emit a resonant energy field.

"The big cells that ran down the sides of the engine room were the matter/antimatter charging units that contained the annihilation reaction. In real life, that would be extremely difficult to do because the explosive power from a total annihilation would generate an incredible amount of energy.

"That fictional energy was then channeled through the crystals that were able to keep the energy field resonating at a uniform frequency. You can just imagine how much power there would be from a matter/antimatter annihilation reactor that was running through and around the ship."

I wanted to know if there was anything else Mr. Adair could tell me about generating such highly complex energy fields. He said that what we were discussing was not a jet propulsion rocket engine that spewed fuel out a nozzle that would then give a vehicle forward momentum. Instead, we were talking about real, interstellar star ships that used most of their engines power to warp space. He carefully explained that, "The types of engines we are using today have liquid and solid fuel propellants. Those engines don't really give all the power we would really like to have. We need a different form of power, and that's where I think the electromagnetic fusion containment engines would fit in well.

"I'm not the only one who is doing studies on these things. NASA began its research along these lines parallel to the time I was doing my research. If you look up on the NASA web site at Marshall Space Flight Center in Huntsville, Alabama, you will see in their long-range planning departments there are 77 engines listed. These are all designs that would get you off earth and yet, publicly, they are only using two of those designs right now. There are 75 engines that the public hasn't even seen yet. My engine is listed in there as an Electromagnetic Fusion Containment System. The only difference between my design and theirs was how to stabilize the containment field."

When I told Mr. Adair it was my understanding that sustained stabilization had not officially been achieved in a fusion reactor yet, he said, "That's correct, and that's how the whole math problem began for me. I couldn't hold the fields together long enough either. I finally got some help and was able to sustain the field for about four-and-a-half seconds which may not sound like much, but I believe NASA's version only lasted about .0089 seconds."

I knew from my research that he was right, and it made me wonder if humans would ever build a practical fusion engine in the future. One thing was clear; if we had such an engine, we could then generate a stabilized echo field. With that ability, we could then warp space and travel from one point in the galaxy to another in a matter of seconds. It really was a fascinating concept.

According to Mr. Adair, "*Star Trek* never really addressed the fact that at warp nine they could not have received radio transmissions, and when they returned to base everyone they knew would have died long ago. They didn't want to talk about that paradox, because they couldn't; it's just too damn complex. At those speeds, they would be moving faster than the lights on their own ship.

"They didn't want to talk about those types of very-complex problems. But it was crucial that I addressed issues associated with that type of physics for the engines I was building. It really was a trip to be working on that fusion engine design, because it was not just a rocket engine. Even though it will work that way it's not really achieving its true potential. You see, by keeping the reactor contained, it becomes a power plant."

I knew exactly what he was referring to. The engine's energy would feed back into itself instead of opening one end of the reactor. He explained that, "In my first two rockets, I would literally let the fusion plasma spew out as it regenerated and let the containment fields modify their shape. I know it will function that way. The problem is that everything is so complex, at the math end of it, I have not been able to figure out how to sustain the reaction in a steady field."

I then reminded Mr. Adair that based on the energy pattern that appeared in the wheat field at Chilbolton it seemed that someone already knew the answer to the problem. He had mentioned earlier that the pattern looked like the same thing he had envisioned as a blueprint for a fusion containment and warp drive system. However, he cautioned me that, "It could just be a message. What's on there is more like a general diagram. There's nothing specific in the details that would help me figure it all out. The containment fields are so hard to do. That's the problem with fusion reactors. They are extremely hard to contain, particularly where the actual figure eight makes a closed loop and is running at infinity. I just can't seem to sustain that. The problem is you have to build mathematical models that allow you to see the algorithmic pattern these things run in."

I then suggested he use the *Complexity Theory* as a model to create software that would generate the required fractal energy fields. He agreed with my suggestion, but explained that he would also need an incredibly-powerful computer to do the calculations.

He said, "Computer processors all have the same problem. Stephen Hawking and I came to the same dead end on speed. We had 1 GHz processors and what we needed was at least 85 GHz. You have to be able to extend these algorithms out to where you see the fractal patterns emerge."

Based on *Moore's Law*, I knew that it was just a matter of time before humans made computer processors powerful enough to do this. I also knew that the software involved would need to generate fluid, fractal energy fields that could adapt to changes in the environment. It was the only way the system could remain stable in the chaotic energy of the Universe.

Mr. Adair agreed. He said, "You have to counter for that as a mathematical equation, because if I'm off a little right here, when I get over there, I'm way off. Because of the immense width of the Universe, it's really hard to do this work without the right computational speed."

At the time of our interview, I had only been researching "flight-weight" fusion reactors for about six years, but I clearly understood what he was saying. This was not rocket science. It was light years beyond that.

Many people, including Mr. Adair, believed that fusion energy would be the power source of the future. However, the ongoing research and development of sustained, stable fusion reactors was proving to be very difficult.

Although there had been a lot of progress, scientist and engineers were still attempting to reach the break-even point. In the process, they had created a large body of engineering and scientific knowledge showing that it could be made practical once they perfected the magnetic containment field.

Mr. Adair explained that fusion power would radically change our lives. However, if UFO disclosure ever occurred, we could begin quickly integrating some of the more advanced alien technologies into our infrastructure. In his opinion, it would be a difficult, but beneficial transition.

I found that Mr. Adair's claim about NASA researching various types of fusion engines was true. According to a principal research scientist, named Dr. Thio, from the Propulsion Research Center at NASA/Marshall, "The challenge is to adapt fusion for space propulsion. Magnetized Target Fusion (MTF) is one of the major approaches that we are studying. MTF tries to operate in an intermediate regime between the conventional magnetic fusion and inertial confinement using a laser."

It had been reported that NASA was working with Los Alamos National Laboratory and the Air Force Research Laboratory to adapt MTF for propulsion. The problem with conventional magnetic confinement was that it operated at a very low energy density. To achieve sufficient power, the fusion reactor needed to be very large which made it more expensive.

On the other hand, inertial confinement fusion only used a tiny amount of plasma with an energy density that was 1,000 trillion times greater than a magnetic confinement reactor. However, it required a driver to heat and compress the target in a short time which increased the cost.

According to Dr. Thio, "MTF tries to operate at not too low or too high an energy density and achieve a reasonable rate of fusion activity with a density 10,000 to 100,000 times higher than magnetic confinement, and 10,000 to 100,000 times lower than laser fusion."

The NASA team found it was more economical to use powerful capacitor banks that drove electromagnetic implosion process. In that system, a magnetic field confined the target plasma and insulated the inertial wall that imploded to cause the fusion.

The bottom line was this; even if sustained fusion was achieved under current methods, the MTF reactors were too large and heavy to use in space ships. According to Professor Kammash of the University of Michigan, "The size is quite prohibitive. We want to make the physics work without using very large magnets. The mirror magnets for a fusion rocket would weigh about 401 tons. The heat radiators would add 240 tons."

Kammash also reported that his students were experimenting with a droplet radiator design that used liquid lithium as a coolant that could reduce the radiator mass to 57 tons. They had successfully flown a test model of this system aboard NASA's KC-135 low-gravity aircraft.

I found it interesting that, over the years, NASA had discovered that a rotating magnetic containment field would force the plasma into behaving as if it was in a conventional magnetic mirror system. That was exactly what Mr. Adair had done years earlier. However, his system worked much better. It employed two cyclotrons that generated twin, rotating, magnetic fields.

By using that type of reactor, the size, weight, and cost of a fusion powered spacecraft would be dramatically reduced. While researching this subject, I learned that one of the earliest compact fusion reactor design concepts was developed in the 1950s by Philo Farnsworth. He had pioneered most of the fundamental technologies for television during the 1920s and 1930s.

It was reported that a scientist named Dr. Nadler had received a research grant from NASA and was working at the University of Illinois to fully develop the technology that Farnsworth had first developed in 1950: fusion in a small bottle. Dr. Nadler reported that, "You can use the energy it generates to power electric propulsion, or simply use the plasma for thrust." Oddly enough, that was the way Mr. Adair had described his electromagnetic fusion containment engine.

Most scientists referred to the technique as Inertial Electrostatic Confinement or IEC. It was a system that didn't require the use of massive magnets and lasers. Instead, the IEC device used a hollow cathode, and the natural charges of electrons and ions, to form virtual electrodes that helped confine ions in a small spherical region at the center of the two-foot diameter IEC vacuum chamber.

By the end of the 20th century, the IEC had achieved a pulsed current of 17 amps at 40,000 volts. The IEC had also gone from producing one neutron, released by deuterium+deuterium fusion in every 10 cycles, to more than 100 neutrons per cycle. Dr. Nadler proudly stated that, "NASA funding has allowed us to make some historic advances. I'm happy to report that everything is looking good for increased reactivity."

In time, it was discovered that IEC fusion created an "energy well" in the middle of a conventional magnetic field and in the IEC chamber where fusion was induced. Thus, it was far more self-contained than other fusion reactors. But there was still one piece of the puzzle that didn't seem to fit. Mr. Adair had mentioned seeing crystals (like the fictional *Star Trek* technology) in the alien fusion engine at Area 51. I wondered what they were actually used for.

While conducting further research on this subject, I was surprised to find a report that claimed "double-crystal fusion" could pave the way for a new type of portable energy device. The technical report stated that scientists at Rensselaer Polytechnic Institute had developed a tabletop accelerator that produced nuclear fusion at room temperature. The device used two opposing crystals to generate a powerful electric field. The inventors believed it could potentially lead to a portable, battery operated, neutron generator for a variety of applications.

According to Yaron Danon, associate professor of mechanical, aerospace, and nuclear engineering at Rensselaer, "Our study shows that crystal fusion is a mature technology with considerable commercial potential. This new device is simpler and less expensive than the previous version, and it has the potential to produce even more neutrons."

The device was essentially a tabletop particle accelerator. At its heart were two opposing "pyro-electric" crystals that created a strong electric field when heated or cooled with deuterium gas. According to professor Danon, "The electric field rips electrons from the gas, creating deuterium ions and accelerating them into a deuterium target on one of the crystals. When the particles smashed into the target, neutrons were emitted; a clear sign that nuclear fusion had occurred."

A research team led by UCLA physics professor Seth Putterman had built a similar apparatus in 2005, and although it used two crystals instead of one, which doubled the acceleration potential, it did not require cooling the crystals to cryogenic temperatures. This was an important step that reduced both the complexity and the cost of the equipment.

The new study also verified the fundamental physics behind the original experiment. This suggested that pyro-electric crystals were a viable means of producing (or amplifying the energy from) nuclear fusion. It also meant that commercial applications may be closer than originally thought.

According to professor Danon, "Nuclear fusion has been explored as a potential source of energy for cities and factories, but the most immediate application may come in the form of a battery operated, portable, neutron generator. Our most recent device is capable of producing about 200,000 electron volts."

It was no secret that new versions of small, powerful and relatively in-expensive fusion reactors were being designed and developed around the world. In fact, if our species ever wanted to travel through interstellar space we would have to harnesses the power of fusion or something even greater. I knew there was one man that could help make that dream come true: David Adair.

CHAPTER EIGHT

UFO Tech Talk

While conducting research for this book, I was fortunate to have a candid conversation with an aerospace insider. However, that individual didn't want his name to be directly associated with UFOs and requested to remain anonymous. Therefore, I must refer to this person as Mr. X.

It was too bad that the subject of UFOs still caused fear and ridicule; however, things were beginning to change. According to a recent *McDonald Douglas* memo, they were actively seeking to exploit UFO technology to use in future aerospace design and development.

I began my conversation with Mr. X by asking him if he could comment on the work of John Searl who had given a public demonstration of his electric-powered, aerospace technology in May of 2005. Mr. X replied, "I am vaguely aware of it. I know of his claims and what they are about, but I'm not an expert on it."

Although I did not consider myself an expert either, I knew a lot more than most people about Searl's work. It involved a cascading electron generator that, at full power, would create a powerful, rotating, electromagnetic field of energy.

Searl lived in England and had been working very hard on his projects for quite some time. He had privately started his research and development decades ago. He based his technology on re-occurring dreams that he had in his youth; much like David Adair.

Throughout his life, he remained passionate for the instructions he had received in his dreams and felt they were too important to ignore. Even though Searl didn't have a formal background in electronics, after a lot of trial and error, he finally designed and engineered a working field-propulsion generator.

He eventually mounted his experimental generators in small, saucer-shaped craft. However, he unintentionally lost all the early prototypes. Reportedly, when one of his generators would reach the point of over unity (more energy coming out than going in) it became super conductive.

The generator would then break away from the workbench and shoot up through the roof of his barn into space at great speed. This happened to all of his saucer-shaped craft. When I mentioned this, Mr. X suddenly recalled reading accounts of what had reportedly occurred in Searl's private lab. It was quite bizarre, but intriguing.

Searl admitted that he didn't know how to control his early prototypes. It was only through trial and error that he began to understand how he could begin to control the device once it had reached a critical state of power.

According to Searl, one day, as a Canadian television crew was filming one of his saucer prototypes that was hovering in the air near his lab, he noticed that for the first time his saucer remained stationary after becoming super conductive. However, when the broadcast-quality TV camera was turned off, the saucer instantly shot straight up into space and was never seen again. Later, Searl realized that the frequency of the energy waves coming from the camera had been interacting and remotely controlling the electromagnetic energy waves of the saucer.

In the mid 1990s, while working at a Japanese corporation writing technical reports, I had the opportunity to read the technical details of Searl's experiments. It was clear Searl had a lot of setbacks. Sometime in the 1970s, he had loaned a working model of his electric-powered saucer to the U.S. military. Reportedly, the design and development group that worked with the saucer couldn't get the funding to finish the project because it was too complicated, and it turned too fast to be flown by human pilots (an incorrect assumption on their part).

The saucer really needed to be semi or fully automated, but computers at that time were not small enough and smart enough to assist pilots to control an advanced aerospace craft. More importantly, the military couldn't understand how field propulsion would eliminate inertia inside a vehicle.

Mr. X then asked, "Is there anything that you have read that tells you categorically that what this man claims actually happened?"

It was a simple question that required a complex answer. I explained that more than 10 years earlier, I had interviewed a man named John Thomas who owned a workshop on the East Coast of the U.S. He had been privately researching and developing prototypes based on Searl's work. Mr. Thomas sponsored the web site www.searleffect.com, and he was dedicated to making that new technology commercially available to everyone in the future.

Apparently, Searl had run into some legal trouble after he connected one of his generators to the electrical panel in his laboratory, and the meter started running backwards. Because no one understood how his generators worked, he was subsequently accused of stealing electricity from the power company.

It was an expensive legal mess, and Searl was a poor man. As a result, he went to prison for a while, and during that time his workshop was burned to the ground. That was when his wife got really upset and destroyed the rest of his work. It had been a real up-hill battle. I knew Searl's work was not easily validated and did not merit the same attention of the global aerospace corporations and military groups that Mr. X worked with.

Mr. X said, "I really shouldn't have ignored his work. But I did feel that there was too much noise to signal ratio with John Searl. Part of it too was not having the time to research his claims, but it certainly is something I should do."

I wondered if Mr. X had read a book entitled *Japan's Secret War*, by retired Army intelligence officer Robert Wilcox. The book revealed the covert Japanese development of an atomic weapon during World War II. Apparently they had received some help from the Nazis.

After thinking for a moment, Mr. X told me that he had read that book. It was an amazing bit of military history few people were aware of. The information in that book made me realize there were many advanced scientific developments that had taken place covertly during World War II, especially by the Germans and Japanese. Some of that technology, like warping space with rotating electro-magnetic energy fields, was still being kept a secret. I knew the work had continued covertly, and it seemed a shame that the general population was not allowed to learn more about this technology and share in the benefits.

Apparently, that would never happen on this planet as long as we were being controlled by a covert, elite group. And, unfortunately, we couldn't put the newest technology genie back in its bottle. To me, the situation seemed dangerous because nuclear power was one level of energy that humans had been using for good or ill. However, the levels of energy involved in a torsional, space-warping, scalar technology was something far greater than that. It tapped into the zero point field of universal energy.

Mr. X agreed and cautioned that this power source was greater in its initial phase and much more unpredictable, because we didn't really understand the fundamental physics at work. He said, "We have a broad sense of what the physics are. But in the case of the nuclear breakthrough, there was a much more refined understanding of the processes at work which led to nuclear fission and fusion to some extent.

"In the case of zero-point energy, there seems to me to be a less-defined understanding of the physical processes at work, and that makes the scientific community very uncomfortable.

"From an experimental stand point it makes this science rather dangerous, because you don't know what direction it's going to head off in. You could get energy from it. You could get propulsion from it, but you could also get a bomb from it, and all of these things are up for grabs at the moment. It's a potentially dangerous place to be in.

"I still think that the possible rewards, just from an environmental stand point, are remarkable. I think this is the answer for our future survival. This type of zero-point technology is not appearing now by accident. It's emerging because we need it. What has to happen next, for the processes to work, the science underpinning this needs to be fully understood so the technology can be controlled."

Searl had said the very same thing back in the 1960s. Part of his vision/dream/message involved something he called the "Law of the Squares." This formula was an energy schematic that allowed one to interface and begin to gain control of chaotic, zero point energy fields.

People referred to these torsional energy fields as "scalar waves," "zero-point energy," or a "singularity." It was related to black holes, but a stable access point would theoretically be a worm hole or stargate; what scientists called an Einstein/Rosen bridge. Although it was very difficult to generate and stabilize, a "singularity" appeared to be the most effective way to gain access to other dimensions of space/time/energy.

Searl had always maintained that the cosmos was very temperamental and incredibly dynamic. However, the *Law of the Squares* essentially allowed one to calibrate a chaotic energy system so that a relatively balanced control system could be achieved.

Even so, Searl had a very-hard time working with it. What he lacked was a supercomputer running his *Law of the Squares* algorithm as software. The next step would be to link that digital control system to a working field propulsion generator's hardware.

It was astonishing to me that a man like Searl, with such an elementary education, could create a mathematical model that was so fundamentally brilliant. It made me feel that perhaps there was a cosmic mind involved in our evolution that was sending us a message through a savant.

Searl stated that part of the dream/vision he was given was quite clear. A cataclysmic event would occur in mankind's future. It would hit us like a giant steamroller if we didn't act now. He felt that the information he was given was not just for him; it was for humanity because we were in great peril. He insisted that without this knowledge, that granted us access to the higher laws of nature, we would not survive. It all seemed rather visionary, but plausible.

Mr. X commented that, "I do believe, based on my years of involvement and study in this area, that there may be some relationship to consciousness and the way a singularity in a quantum vacuum works and the effects stemming from it seem to behave.

"I really believe one's consciousness has an influence on the universe. It's quite unscientific on my part, but in terms of the bigger picture, the fact is we are now getting a surge of interest in this zero-point field. There seems to be an accelerating activity in gravity-related research and quantum vacuum energy experimentation and exploitation. This tells me that collectively our consciousness is being led to this next level of innovation.

"The world is crying out for some kind of change. Our planetary resources are dwindling. Not just from the standpoint of natural energy resources, but also in the field of aerospace and defense. I'm seeing a marked decrease in the level of innovation that is going into the product."

When I asked Mr. X to elaborate, he replied, "In the 1940s, 1950s, and 1960s you had an explosion of technical innovation in the aerospace arena. Barriers were being broken all the time. People were going from Mach 1, to Mach 2, to Mach 3, and in the last couple of decades there have been some significant military breakthroughs. Stealth was one of them. However, in terms of pure aerospace innovation, getting from point A to point B faster and more efficiently, there has only been incremental change. There has been no significant breakthrough in the aerospace field since the invention of the jet engine and radar in the 1940s.

"For example, to get even modest increments in performance increases, say from the *Boeing* 747 to the *Boeing* 787, *Boeing* and the U.S. government had to spend billions of dollars. That tells me we are reaching the end of the innovation cycle. The aerospace industry really needs that next quantum leap to take mankind to the next stage of evolution. I do believe that field propulsion is the direction that this breakthrough will come from."

I knew what Mr. X was referring to. Field propulsion was a process that everyone on Earth was experiencing. This field was the reason they didn't feel any inertial motion of the planet despite the fact that our Solar System was orbiting the galaxy at approximately 5,000 miles per second. Additionally, the earth orbited the sun at approximately 200 miles per second in a slightly different direction. Despite that fact, the rotating, electromagnetic field propulsion of the planet gave us the effect of zero inertia.

Although some scientists questioned how any physical being could possibly survive the high rates of speed and acrobatic aerial maneuvers of UFOs, field propulsion was the best explanation. With UFOs, the energy from a field propulsion system was being applied equally to the entire craft rather than just one specific area of the craft, the way a rocket or jet engine would. Mr. X agreed with my explanation.

I then expressed my belief that the problem of controlling field propulsion was not just technological. We also had to contend with our limited understanding of the physics that operate our Universe. It was going to be a huge challenge for certain people to let go of their old teachings and embrace a new model of physics.

Mr. X then told me that this difficult process had been going on quietly behind the scenes for decades. Some of the players were in the U.S. and some of the greatest innovators were located in Russia. Unfortunately, a lot of what they developed came about during the Cold War era when there was ample funding for such truly-advanced, covert projects.

I knew what Mr. X was referring to. I had read about some really-amazing discoveries involving consciousness in Russia. During their experiments, the Russians had accidentally found that there was a connection between consciousness and rotational/torsional energy fields. The findings were very bizarre and contradicted the *Standard Model* of physics, so they had been largely ignored by scientists in the Western world.

I then asked Mr. X about the work of Townsend Brown. He had been an early leader in the use of rotating, electrostatic devices. These devices apparently reduced the effects of gravity in a small area. I wanted to know if Mr. X knew anything about the extent to which the aerospace industries had actually employed Brown's work.

Mr. X explained that, in recent years, there had been an increased interest in Brown's work by the U.S. military and NASA. These agencies had conducted scientific studies of Brown's B-field effects. He said, "I think it was Jonathan Campbell, at NASA, that has been quite controversial because his patent application was approved for a Brown, electrostatic device.

"Of course the whole electrostatic, 'lifter device' has developed recently. It is based on Brown and his work, but it is still highly controversial. It has divided the antigravity community as to whether this is a true antigravity effect or whether it is an ion wind.

"For me, the 'lifter effect' is on the edge of being weirdly unquantifiable and relatively mundane. If this is an ion-wind effect, then that's something we can explain away. If it's not, if the lift component is stemming from the interaction of electrostatic fields, with say the quantum vacuum singularity fields, that would clearly be a more interesting development."

I then told Mr. X that in the case of "lifter" technology I believed its electro statically generated energy field was directly affected by the earth's naturally occurring electromagnetic field propulsion system.

Mr. X replied that, "The really interesting thing is that there are such a huge variety of opinions and beliefs as to what is going on with the Brown effect. It never ceases to amaze me that this particular debate has not really been resolved yet."

For most people this was true. But I knew that the "lifter" engineers were missing a critical step for generating an operational field propulsion system. Like most people, the "lifter" design engineers remained unaware of the value of rotating electrostatic fields.

That was the core problem with electrostatic lifters; their energy fields were too static. Those energy fields needed to be more kinetic, but not in a linear sense. Those fields needed to be rotated and in the process become torsional in order to propagate an amplified energy field. Then, to create propulsion, that field must be modulated and rotated at the proper speed. The greater speeds one rotated the field, the greater the effects one created for propulsion.

Mr. X said, "I had not considered that in regards to lifter technology, but you are absolutely correct. Rotation plays a major role and seems to be the underpinning link between all of the reported effects from Russian rotating superconductors to the German resonance-chamber experiments."

Actually, I was very curious if the Germans, or whoever was secretly developing that type of rotating energy field to warp space, could warp time as well. Mr. X believed it was potentially possible. As far as we knew, space and time were connected. It made me wonder if some of the UFOs that had been sighted and photographed over the past 50 plus years were actually aerospace craft from the future moving back through time?

While processing my question, Mr. X was silent for a few moments. He then explained that, "I don't research UFOs, but given what we are seeing, I think it's entirely possible. Based on what little I have investigated into the arcane properties of rotation and electromagnetism, and the alleged effects that were apparently generated by German scientists, there appears to be this kind of torsional effect on space time in a very localized way.

"If you can scale that up, I have no doubt that you can introduce even more interesting effects in the fabric of space and time. I have seen enough UFO data to know that there really is something going on. It's not just people making things up or something that is wholly dreamed up out of thin air. There does appear to be an underlying phenomenon there.

"Clearly these craft are breaking the light-speed barrier in some way. If UFOs really are space craft from other planets, other solar systems, or other galaxies, whoever designed and built them must have found a way to manipulate space/time.

"Or, it could be some iteration of us in the future doing exactly the same thing. However, I think that is entirely consistent with the data I have seen especially in terms of what the Germans were doing covertly decades ago."

Mr. X's statement stunned me. I really did not expect such a candid response from this well-connected, aerospace insider. To be sure I heard him correctly, I asked him if he really thought UFOs could be space craft from our future or our past or both?

Without hesitating, he replied, "Yes. Potentially it is all true."

During our conversation, I was a bit shocked when I realized that not only could UFOs potentially travel through time/space, they wouldn't need fueling stations! Unlike a rocket, these advanced time/space craft were tapping into the primordial energy field of the cosmos. It existed in the past and it clearly existed in the present and the future; it was everywhere at all times.

Mr. X agreed and added that, "It's always been there, and with this system you've got a propulsion device that needs no fuel as we know it. It never runs out of energy, so it's the perfect vehicle, but in a way that we can't quite control yet.

"The thing I found terribly inconvenient, with people like John Searl is that they would always say that the moment they turned the cameras on, the device stopped performing. But it does in a funny kind of way mirror the kind of interaction of energy and consciousness you get when people are present in these experiments."

I explained to X that in Searl's case it wasn't just any kind of camera. It was a television-broadcast camera that emitted a specific radio frequency. Apparently the radio waves from the camera had interacted with the electromagnetic waves emitted by the *Searl Effect Generator* which was superconductive and generating millions of volts of electricity at the time.

I then asked Mr. X if he thought that quantum vacuum, zero point energy fields could ever be harnessed safely for useful applications? I specifically wanted to know if it could happen in our lifetime.

He replied, "If you mean a stable, singularity energy field, I not only believe it can be safely contained, I know people that are doing it. I do know them. However, for the moment I am limited in what I can say, because those people have requested anonymity. But the short answer to your question is yes. I am satisfied with my interaction with these people, and seeing what they have done, that extraction of useful energy is not only possible, it is already happening.

"It is grounded in legitimate science. Clearly, lots of people have stated publicly that they have built singularity generators of some type. The problem has always been getting adequate verification of the processes at work. I'm kind of skeptical by nature. However, in order for the aerospace industry to make the next quantum leap forward, the technology has got to come from somewhere else. It has got to come from another community which will cross fertilize the field of aerospace science. I think that is what is happening here, and I think the bridges are being built by a lot of people who want to see this project completed."

I agreed, but I knew that part of the problem was that this subject had remained covert for too long. In order to be accessible to mankind, it needed to be released from the control of the elite. Mr. X commented that, "It was intentionally buried away. But we all knew about antigravity on some level. It was the stuff of science fiction. We have seen it in so many movies, and it has long been associated with UFO reports. However, we now know that there is real science underpinning this stuff which has created a trend. People, who were previously scared to discuss this subject, because it was taboo, are becoming less and less afraid to speak about this subject in public.

"It's there for people to see, and it's important for people like them to see that others have come forward and are discussing it too. The societal barriers, in that sense, have really broken down. If nothing else, I am glad that this subject can now be discussed without people feeling as though they need to go off and snicker about it in the other room."

I then commented to Mr. X that Viktor Shauberger was another

European inventor I had researched while working for the Japanese. This made Mr. X curious why the Japanese were researching the work of John Searl and Viktor Shauberger.

I explained that there was only one group in America doing that type of research that I knew of. During my time at that company, I had researched and reported on the technical advancements being made in mobile, "flight-weight" nuclear reactors. However, I never got an explanation regarding what was being done with that data.

My first assignment was to track down rumors of a working, flight-weight, aneutronic (no neutrons) fusion reactor and report my findings. My report was initially based on a research paper written by an eccentric, European physicist named Bogdan Maglich who had been employed at one of the universities in Southern California. The paper outlined the future of fusion based on a self-colliding reactor design called a Migma.

Following clues provided by Maglich, I interviewed scientists and engineers from the university system, and the military industrial complex, trying to verify his technical details. All my research material was then sent directly to a lab in Japan. Oddly enough, while conducting research on nuclear power, I accidentally came across the book *Japan's Secret War*. That experience was still fresh in my mind. The day I learned the Japanese had secretly developed a nuclear bomb program in WWII, it really floored me.

Mr. X wanted to know where the research lab I had worked at was located. I explained it was in the Los Angeles area, but it merely served as an American extension of the home offices in Japan. I found it interesting that the Japanese government agency MITI was highly effective at interfacing with all the heavy industries in Japan. There appeared to be a much higher level of cooperation between private and public agencies in Japan. They shared information more openly with each other compared to American agencies. However, I learned that when the Japanese interfaced with foreigners, they were very secretive. They were focused more on getting information and sending it home. They clearly didn't like to share information. Once I realized that, I became apprehensive about the research I was doing for them.

Mr. X commented that, "It doesn't surprise me, on one level. On another level, it does surprise me that there is an interest in advanced technology and science that is quietly being exploited by the Japanese."

I had found that the Japanese were, by their societal nature, very quiet; especially when it came to outsiders. I felt fortunate to have been allowed to learn more about Asian cultures than most Caucasians. It was both a difficult and educational experience.

I was also lucky to have had access to lots of exotic research material. In the process, I learned a lot about the work of Viktor Shauberger. He was considered the father of implosion technology; a process that was diametrically opposed to the explosive technologies that we relied on today.

According to his records, the principle of implosion had to do with a self sustaining, rotating flow of liquid or gaseous plasma which had a self-containing effect that also decreased the temperature of the plasma in the generator. The implosion-based plasma generators attributed to Shauberger operated in a way that appeared impossible based on our current understanding of the *Law of Thermodynamics*.

I then asked Mr. X if he knew the location of the original drawings, or had found any evidence, of working devices being manufactured based on Shauberger's design. He explained that, "I made copies directly from the Shauberger Archive, in Austria, which is run by his grandson. It's clear that the drawings had been signed off by the SS, in Mathausen concentration camp. Initially, this was all Nazi-funded research.

"But what's really interesting to me about the Shauberger story is that I was able to find, by piecing together the rather cryptic kinds of clues that he left in the archive in his letters and notes, that he was clearly engaged by the Germans during the war. Unfortunately, what I cannot do is marry that data about Shauberger's movements, and the people and the companies that he worked with at the time, with physical evidence that the technology works.

"I can only presume it works. However, I don't see why the German's would have invested so much time, effort, and money into Schuberger and his processes if they didn't work. There are Shauberger turbines out there, but I know of none that have worked. I wish someone would come forward and tell me that built one in their back yard, to his designs and instructions, and it worked fine. Over the years, one or two people have told me that, but they were never able to furnish the proof."

I knew there was a reason for that, but I wasn't sure if I should discuss it with Mr. X or not. After a few moments of contemplation, I decided to tell Mr. X I had met someone with limited access to the next generation of Schauberger's aerospace disc.

Mr. X was clearly shocked by my statement, and I hesitated to continue or conversation. It was such a bizarre story, I didn't think anyone would believe it had really happened. After a few more moments of silence, I explained to Mr. X that in 1991, my wife and I had been introduced to a human being that claimed to be an alien.

I knew that part of his claim was factual because his family was Dutch; therefore, he was a resident alien in the U.S. However, years later I found that commander Robert O. Dean had read a NATO report regarding a UFO landing on a Danish farm in 1964. Two of the alien occupants were human looking and spoke perfect Dutch.

In my case, one night we were invited to our human/alien host's house in the Los Angeles area. He then showed us home videos he had taken of some highly-advanced, flying discs. We were told that these craft had been manufactured here on earth by his race. He also claimed that these space craft were capable of time travel which I found extremely hard to believe.

The home video showed people boarding the craft. We could clearly see the interior of the circular craft which was rather mundane. The craft then took off, and in the next scene we saw a formation of three disc-shaped craft flying somewhere over the Pacific Ocean.

Mr. X remained silent as I explained that the video was phenomenal. I didn't see how anyone could have edited special effects of this nature into a home video tape. It was just amazing. On another occasion, our host had shown me a Polaroid photograph of one their smaller, disc-shaped space craft that had landed in the Mojave Desert during the day.

Mr. X then questioned if the video and photos were any good. I explained that the Polaroid image was quite clear and looked genuine. As for the video, we had seen people moving around the interior of the craft. At one point, our host told us to watch carefully as the energy shields were lowered on one of the other, nearby space craft. The camera was aimed out the viewing screen at one of the other alien craft flying in formation. Suddenly, the exterior of that craft appeared to burst into flames all over.

Something had dramatically changed in the energy field surrounding the craft. Our host explained that the pilots of the other craft had lowered their energy shield. Apparently that shield allowed their craft to move in relative silence. Without it, their plasma powered space craft were too loud and could be seen for miles in all directions, especially at night.

That part of the video was simply amazing. At that moment, there were flames leaping off the skin of the nearby space craft, but this was not like the exhaust from a rocket engine. I could see that the energy from the space craft's field propulsion system was reacting with the atmosphere of the earth. It looked as if the ionized air around the craft was catching fire. It was the most bizarre thing I had ever seen on video.

I wanted to tell Mr. X more, but I remained cautious. I knew that our human/alien host was extremely paranoid and manipulative. In retrospect, I believed that he showed us that UFO video as part of an elaborate cover story. I suspected that these terrestrial-built, exotic, aerospace craft were being controlled by powerful groups outside of the government. However, I was told that these covert groups had influence over key individuals within the government. They also had connections to people serving in the military. It was my understanding that these elite groups were only motivated by the acquisition and maintenance of power.

I hesitated to even mention it, but I knew that the secret societies in Austria and Germany had played an instrumental role in the research and development and applications of advanced "alien" technologies. But it didn't stop there.

They had developed all kinds of exotic technologies over the past 50 years. Many of those devices had not been made available to the public, as yet. Perhaps there was a good reason for not introducing those technologies into the current market place, but the devices clearly did exist.

Mr. X remained skeptically silent. I knew this was a strange story, but I was confident that the plasma propulsion systems onboard the space craft I saw on video, and in person, were based on Shauberger's work.

I believed this because I often asked our human/alien host about the engine design on the space craft his race had built. He was extremely secretive and refused to give me any technical details. However, I was determined to learn how they were powered.

As I got to know him better, he had bragged about the efficiency of the engines, so I tried to follow up on that angle. He told me that the engines didn't use any fossil fuel for energy; they ran on water. This really didn't make any sense to me, technically, at the time. He explained that starting the engine only required a small amount of energy from standard batteries to initiate the cycle and get the engine up and running. Once that occurred, it would run indefinitely.

In retrospect, everything he told me then sounded like the Shauberger turbine/generator system that I learned about later. However, at the time, I didn't know who Shauberger was and had not seen his engine designs. About four years later, I went to work for that Japanese corporation and laid eyes on the complete works of Shauberger and Searl for the first time.

That information changed my opinion about some of the UFOs that were being sighted regularly on Earth. I realized that most of the UFOs built covertly here on earth lead back to Shauberger's prototypes. Although he didn't have the time and money to take it to the next level, someone else clearly did. In our candid conversation, Colonel Stevens was adamant about this secret gravity-control breakthrough.

Mr. X commented that, "It's entirely possible. I know from his diaries that he was running all around the area of Austria, Czechoslovakia, Southern Poland and parts of Germany doing something very secret, but he never said what it was, so who knows?"

I realized that Mr. X was still skeptical about my story and rightfully so. Unfortunately, I was not in a position to prove my story without any hard evidence. However, I knew that even our human/alien host was only granted limited access to that advanced space craft and technology, wherever it came from.

One day, I confronted our host and told him that he and his race needed to go public with hard evidence of their existence. He became extremely upset and broke contact with me. He clearly felt threatened by the fact that I had even suggested going public. It seemed really strange to me, because my wife and I were publishing a magazine about extraterrestrials at the time. Our host was fine with allowing us to publish some of his information as long as we referred to him as an alien.

He claimed he was part of a race of human's covertly visiting earth. He said they were from a binary star system and that they were only about 100 years ahead of us technologically. In every other way, we were identical.

I insisted that he go public with the whole story, including the technology they possessed. Even though there was still a lot of fear and secrecy surrounding this issue, I wanted to see full disclosure. Mr. X sighed deeply and then commented that, "It has obviously taken you years to become familiar with this territory. It took me a decade to become familiar with it, so we have had plenty of time to adjust to this information. But if one is not educated in this field, and were a regular nuts and bolts technologist that was suddenly confronted with all this new information, it can be pretty scary. It flies in the face of all your training, and background, and discipline. Therefore, a lot of people just can't accept it."

I thanked Mr. X for being so understanding and agreed that this type of information was difficult to digest or believe. I then asked him if he had been able to track down the specific German technology that ended up in Russian hands at the end of World War II.

He replied, "According to Podklentov, a lot of materiel went indirectly to the Russians. He told me that his father had been employed by a part of the Soviet government/establishment that was assigned to evaluate Shauberger's work.

"Given the quantity of research that was going on in different areas, claimed by the Soviet Union during the Cold War, I can only imagine that a fair amount of German, advanced technology ended up in Soviet hands, but precisely what is hard to say."

That made sense, but I couldn't help wonder if the German's advanced research and development program moved to another location. Mr. X could not provide any details, but assured me that the research was ongoing. He said, "There has been some information that recently came to light that is corroborative, but the basic story still stands; the Germans were trying to manipulate the fabric of space and time. The question is: what for?

"It seems to have been a multidisciplinary experiment. It was nothing more than that. It wasn't a test run of a device that was about to go into production or even advanced development. I don't think it was that advanced, but it was an experiment into a very fundamental property of the nature of the universe.

"I think that there were avenues stemming from that research that the German's wanted to exploit. I can't say much more about it right now, but there were multiple applications. There were propulsion applications, I think there were energy applications, and I think there were weapons applications."

I was glad Mr. X had confided with me on this sensitive issue. I had no doubt that what he said was true. However, I believed that the origin for this exotic research was probably based on arcane knowledge gleaned from ancient artifacts and manuscripts.

I knew most people remained skeptical about this, but the research I had conducted over many years indicated there were advanced levels of technology achieved by some of our ancient ancestors. Some of that technology and science was very advanced even by our standard. I knew there was a mountain of evidence to argue in favor of this position, and Mr. X agreed.

During my years of research, I had learned it was actually a coalition of secret societies that were in charge of developing ancient technology they had acquired. These secret societies clearly influenced the Nazis and helped fund their world-wide expeditions to locate and recover these artifacts which would give whoever unlocked these ancient secrets an advantage.

Mr. X was well aware of this and knew that some of these expeditions reportedly went to India and Egypt. In fact, fascinating artifacts were discovered there and elsewhere on earth. Mr. X commented that, "I know where you are coming from, and I think that there is some supporting evidence for that position. I wouldn't disagree with it at all."

Before ending our candid conversation, I informed Mr. X that in January of 2006, a fascinating article regarding the future of aerospace had been published by *New Scientist* magazine. It featured the extraordinary developmental breakthrough of a "hyper-space" engine that could potentially allow humans to one day travel through interstellar space travel and possibly even into other dimensions. Reportedly, the device was being investigated by the U.S. government.

The hypothetical engine was based on a controversial theory. Hypothetically, it worked by creating an intense magnetic field that, according to ideas first developed by the late German scientist Burkhard Heim in the 1950s, would produce a gravitational field that resulted in thrust for a spacecraft; like a warp-drive system.

Also, if large enough magnetic fields were created, the craft could slip into a different dimension allowing incredible speeds to be reached. Switching off the magnetic field would result in the engine/spacecraft reappearing in our current dimension.

Perhaps that was why the U.S. Air Force had expressed an interest in the idea. I had read reports that scientists working for the Department of Energy had a device known as the Z-pinch machine. They believed that they could generate the kind of magnetic fields required to drive the hyper-space engine with the Z-pinch technology and were interested in running further tests.

Some of the scientists who put forward the idea believed that if everything went well, a working engine could be tested in about five years. Other physicists cautioned it was based on a highly-controversial theory that would require a significant change in the current views regarding the laws of physics. However, if it became operational, it would be amazing. The benefits would be almost unlimited.

There were quite a few physicists who had a different opinion, but if the theory was correct, then this was not science fiction, it was a scientific fact that would dramatically impact our future. That type of space-warping engine would enable the next generation of space craft to travel to different solar systems and perhaps even other Universes, or other times.

CHAPTER NINE

Earthbound Extraterrestrials

Strange as it may seem, one of the people that I interviewed about the subject of earthbound extraterrestrials claimed he was an ET. He was clearly an unusual individual who had caused quite a bit of controversy during his 1995 national television interview on an *NBC* talk show *The Other Side*. That's where we first met.

Jerry Wills was originally invited to come on the television show because he wanted to deliver a message that had reportedly been given to him by ETs he met while in Peru. That afternoon, at the *NBC* studios, in beautiful downtown Burbank, Jerry was introduced to the television audience as, "the man who believes he's from another world." But Jerry was quite serious about his origins, his purpose, and his quest in life. I overheard some people in the audience that sarcastically questioned if he was a real-life superman with superpowers.

I was also interviewed on television that afternoon and was highly skeptical of Jerry's story, because, to me, he looked like just another earthling. He stood six foot eight inches tall, had blonde hair and blue eyes. At the time, he was married with children and owned a successful, electronic equipment repair business.

But after the show, I was curious and wanted to know more about him, so we exchanged phone numbers. And as I got to know him better, I could see he had some compelling reasons to believe that he was not originally from earth. Although I could neither confirm nor deny his information, he honestly believed what he said. I also knew that the truth was often stranger than fiction especially when it came to the subject of extraterrestrials.

According to Jerry, his initial contacts with human-looking ETs began when he was 12-years old while living in a remote, wooded region of central Kentucky. The ETs would signal him through a high-pitched, beeping noise and mentally show him the meeting place. These ETs told Jerry that they were from Tau Ceti.

During one of these meetings, Jerry was deeply upset by domestic problems and was considering running away from home. The ETs offered to let Jerry come with them, but he was concerned about worrying his mother who was the only person on earth he felt close to. It was then that the ETs told Jerry that he was adopted. Not sure if the ETs were lying to him, he confronted his mother with this information. She became very defensive and proceeded to show him a birth certificate and then walked away in tears.

It wasn't until one night in November of 1991 that he received more information about his true origin. At that time, a blue ball of light flew into Jerry's bedroom and transformed into a radiant human being or possibly a hologram of a human ET. In any case, the individual in the light said he was sent to deliver a message; Jerry's mother was going to pass away in one month's time and would soon let him know the real circumstances of his adoption.

The enigmatic, glowing being also told Jerry his biological parents did not live on earth and that he had been selected before birth to come to this world. However, he was not the only child brought here. Before the being of light departed, he explained that part of the reason why Jerry needed to learn the truth was because it was time to bring others into the awareness of who they really were and why they were here: To help with the great changes ahead on earth.

As predicted, Jerry's adoptive mother passed away one month later. However, prior to her death, she admitted to Jerry that his birth certificate had been falsified. After those events occurred, Jerry realized that both his adoptive parents had known of his extraterrestrial origins and why he was so fascinated with other worlds in the Universe.

When I asked Jerry to tell me about the human-looking ETs he had met with in Peru, he said, "They are members of a society. Their society is a very-large group of individuals, and groups on different worlds, that are cooperating and working together. It's what people here call the Federation. There are other names for it, but the ETs I talked to say that they are members of a very-large society."

When I asked him what the ETs form of government was like, he explained that, "They have an exceptionally clear way of communicating with each other. All the different members and groups of that society are very powerful telepathically compared to humans on earth.

"It's like a United Nations, but much larger, and all these different people communicate very easily. As a result, there aren't any hidden agendas. Therefore, they have a greater understanding for a given issue. They all know what the truth of an agenda is, so it's easier for them to solve problems."

This made me wonder what type of problems the ETs had. Jerry explained that, "A majority of the problems for governments here on earth come from the fact that nearly all people in positions of power are working within their own agendas and are bound by their egos. The political system on earth seems to revolve around people's hidden agendas. The ETs I met aren't limited by hidden agendas and their egos."

Hearing Jerry's statement reminded me that commander Dean had said essentially the same thing about our leaders. When I asked Jerry if he was aware that Robert Dean had publicly stated that he saw classified military documents, while at NATO, regarding a group of ETs that looked exactly like us, he said, "I know commander Dean. I would say that his information is accurate. I know it is true, because the ETs told me the same thing."

As mentioned in Chapter 2 of this book, commander Dean had reported that by the early 1960's, the military powers on earth were deeply concerned that human-looking ETs could easily infiltrate our society and government. However, the military analysts eventually concluded that this did not pose an immediate threat.

When I asked Jerry why there were human ETs that felt a need to live among earthlings covertly, he replied, "There is a need for them to be involved. Much of what I am telling you is drawn from contacts I had with the ETs from 13 to 18 years of age. At that time, I didn't fully understand the depth of what they were telling me, but apparently there is more than one group of ETs living on earth, at this time.

"Something happened between the governments of earth, and this other group of little, grey-skinned beings who don't have the earth's best interest in mind. There are four other extraterrestrial races based on earth as well as the group called 'the Grays.' They came into the picture because they are extraordinarily powerful telepathically; at least as far as most earth people are concerned.

"This allows them to enter our earth, often unseen, using a type of hypnosis. These other groups are here with the Grays, and they each have their own agenda, but the Grays are pretty much in control. They are control freaks. Any situation they feel a need to, they will try and control. They came to earth with a couple of different agendas. One is that this planet is very rich in resources. There is a lot of stuff here that they don't have, such as people.

"The Grays are not physically capable of doing things that humans can do. We adapt easily to adverse situations and climates. We are strong enough, and smart enough, to be trained, and we are easily manipulated. As a result of that, we are a valuable resource to them.

"They also need to have planets they can use as a base of operations, because they are a long way from their home world. Earth is in close proximity to other planets they frequent. Those other worlds are inhabited by people who have been genetically altered. They are the offspring of people from earth and of people like those on earth.

"These people are acting as the laborers on their home worlds. But they don't see themselves as laborers like we would here because they don't have anything to compare it to. In their minds, they are simply serving the Creator by what they do.

"That is their indoctrination from infancy, to be caretakers of their planets, and this is pretty much the way we started out here on earth. But as those people evolve and gain consciousness, eventually they will become more independent like us. They will have problems, but by that time things will have changed on the other worlds and the Grays will have expanded their territory."

When Jerry told me that the Grays were in control of the situation I had to ask him if there was anything anyone here on earth could do to stop them. He said, "No."

I then asked if that was why the benevolent, human-looking ETs had infiltrated and were living secretly on earth, he said, "That is exactly right. Earth, and its people, are about to go through an enormous evolutionary change. It's already started.

"As a result of that, we're gaining higher degrees of consciousness and are becoming less and less affected by what the Grays can do to us to some extent. However, if we're not careful we're going to go the opposite direction, to the dark side, and that's what the Grays want.

"In order for them to remain in control we can't evolve, and certain measures have been taken to insure that we don't evolve. They are trying to keep the knowledge of our true potential a secret. They are also helping to break down the various governments into either a one world organization, that is being directly manipulated by the Grays, or no government whatsoever; anarchy."

Clearly, this was not a good situation. I wanted to know what Jerry thought the good ETs were doing to help keep us on a constructive, evolutionary course. He said, "They are doing a number of things. They are starting to make contact through various people to help them achieve a higher awareness. In turn, what they expect is that these inspired people will contact others in our society and essentially do the same thing exponentially to create a mass increase of awareness.

"That doesn't guarantee it will happen, but it is what they are trying to achieve. The good human ETs are living here and have gone into key positions of our society. They work in government, and corporations and different cultural centers. They are quite good at what they do with their telepathy.

"They mentally implant thoughts that inspire people to look in new directions. They do not take positions of major authority; they don't want that at all. But they are in a position to direct the motives of other key people around them in a helpful way.

"For example, the ETs I met in Peru told me that they wanted people to establish a community there where they would be free to interact peacefully with people. They would like to see this happen someday. It was tried before and there were some problems. I was being realistic about the prospect of people from other countries coming to Peru, buying land, and living there to interact safely with ETs. I wanted to know what the government of Peru was going to think about this.

"The ETs I met told me not to worry about it; that they already had people working in all the governments of the world. We wouldn't have any problems getting through the political red tape, so I put it to a test. With just a few phone calls, it became clear to me that it would in fact be easy to do. There were networks already available to me, where I would talk to a person who referred me to the person who could help. It wasn't a problem, and I was pleasantly surprised by that."

When Jerry appeared on national television in America and was introduced as an earthbound extraterrestrial, he mentioned that the US government had been involved in creating a fake birth certificate for the family that adopted him.

When I asked him to elaborate, he said, "I don't have any absolute proof of that, but what I have been told, and what I found to be true, is that the ETs delivered me to Fort Knox as an infant. I was only there for a short time before they took me somewhere and started running tests on me. After a couple of days, I was entrusted to my adopted parents. A birth certificate had been prepared, and given to them, and they took me home with them, to Denver.

"Every few years, I had to go to a place in Florida that was only accessible by an air-boat. I remember going there at least twice as a little boy. We lived in Colorado, so going to Florida was a big deal.

"We went deep into this swamp, and there was this huge fence with barbed wire around the top and soldiers wearing fatigues with guns. We went into the compound, and there were doctors who kept me for two or three days. My adopted mom and dad would be there, too."

I wanted to know what Jerry's adoptive parent's connection was to the U.S. government. Although he could not find any records, he knew that his adopted father was in a branch of Army Intelligence. However, he passed away when Jerry was just seven-years old.

I then asked Jerry where he first met his adoptive parents. He said, "I was told that my adoptive parents were instructed to go to a particular cabin in the woods to retrieve me when I was just an infant. My biological parents are out in space somewhere or are living on another planet."

When I asked Jerry if he was part of a positive ET intervention, he said, "Yes. There are many ET children that have been seeded into the earth's population. It is my understanding that in order for the Grays to keep the good ETs away from earth they had to make an agreement with some of the earth's governments. To circumvent that situation, the good, human-looking ETs seeded the earth with children of their choosing.

"As these children grew up to be adults they would be taught, to some extent, by the ETs secretly. They also would quickly adapt to the native culture and would therefore blend in as far as their appearance. They wanted us to blend in, so that we would be here on the planet in the event that they could not."

I then asked Jerry if he thought that was what the global defense shield known as *Star Wars* was really for. He said, "Yes. This is primarily the work of the Grays. I know there is a space-based defense shield which helps to insure that no one comes to earth uninvited. I have known about this for years. When the good ETs gave me the crystal ball, in 1983, that was one of the things they mentioned. They were concerned about the earth's defense shield.

"The crystal ball the ETs gave me serves as a symbol of all things united unto the Creator; it is also a facilitator for people and helps them achieve higher awareness more easily. Some of the people who hold this crystal ball may even be one of the children who were brought here like me. We don't know each other."

When I asked Jerry why he was the first of the group to go public, he said, "There is a lot of disinformation out there. I wanted to give some correct information at least as I knew it. Also, it takes a lot of nerve to stand up and speak out about this subject. It scares some people really bad, but I'm not afraid to say it. I was also thinking that if I'm not afraid to say it then some of the others would be inspired to tell who they really are.

"But it's kind of complicated. There are some people on earth who think they are ETs who aren't. On the other hand, there are some who think they aren't, but actually are. I didn't think that was going to be the case, but I've received a lot of phone calls and letters from people who tell me how great it is that I said what I believe to be true and that it's about time. Most of the ETs living here secretly don't have the nerve, or simply don't feel the need, to reveal their true identity. Actually, I think it's much more important that we come to terms with what lies ahead for us as a society here on earth.

"We are getting ready to experience a new beginning, another potential step in the process of evolution that will forever change the way things are on earth. In order for this change to be facilitated, people need to come to terms with the fact that they are part of the process of creation. We can make things better or worse. Our intention, determination, and sense of direction are what make the difference. We all need to take responsibility for the future. If we don't, someone else will."

In time, I became friends with Jerry, and I was surprised to learn that he actually did have a superpower. This special ability was not fully activated until he was a young adult when he fell from a very-high scaffolding and was badly injured. One of the paramedics that treated him said that he could help him recover quickly by transferring energy from his body to Jerry's. He explained that it was similar to the way one jump starts a dead car battery with a good battery.

Jerry agreed to let the medic heal him with bio-energy and was soon feeling better. The paramedic then told Jerry that he had the same ability to heal people. He explained that if he chose to, Jerry could learn to heal people by accessing powerful, universal energy fields and direct them compassionately to the sick or injured.

This was in fact what eventually happened. But there were more amazing adventures ahead for Jerry. He was compelled to continue traveling to the mountains and jungles of South America despite the many risks involved.

One day, I spoke with Jerry right after he had returned from one of his trips into the most remote, rugged, dangerous jungles on the planet. I always enjoyed hearing about his latest discoveries. When I asked him about his plans to document some of the ancient ruins he had located in the Andes, he said, "I'm definitely going to go back. I'm trying to enlist the aid of some people in Peru to get us into some of the other areas that are located in out-of-the-way places where no one ever goes.

"Some government officials warned us against trying to do it. The National Institute of Antiquities and Culture is in charge of these things. There's another group called PROM that tries to promote Peru.

"But the more I looked into this, I found there were many subdivisions of the government that had their hands out or felt they needed to exert some authority or power. Everybody there wants to sell you a permit with their seal of approval, and at some point it gets kind of ridiculous.

"I believe the whole idea is to keep track of who's going in there, and if anything of value is found the government wants to know how much they can take for themselves. When we went into the remote jungle the first time, we were just going for a hike and stumbled on some things. We later made the determination that the only way we could go back in there was with a helicopter and some assistance in order to locate the biggest city of this ancient metropolis.

"The government was very ho hum about it all. They wanted to know how much money we would give them. I told them that I wasn't doing this as a philanthropist. I was doing this because it is interesting. I wanted to know if they were interested in getting at what we found, but they wanted money up front. I told them I was not going to pay them to do this. It was their country, not mine. They didn't like that very much, and that meeting was basically a big waste of time.

"The main man for this sort of thing in Peru is named Mr. Fuhita, but I don't think they want these cities found for two reasons. One, they want their own people, from within the country, to find these things. Yet, there really isn't anyone in Peru who is interested, or has the resources, to go and do what we did. Most everyone down there is struggling just to make ends meet.

"The second reason is there are very few people who have what it takes physically and mentally to go where we went. The people who are capable of going into that terrain and coming out alive are not wimps. It's extremely rugged terrain. That is still God's country. It is not like anything I've ever seen. It is absolutely the wildest, roughest most phenomenal countryside on earth."

From the way Jerry described the lost cities, they were clearly connected by ancient roads. The area he visited was part of an empire. Jerry and I agreed that the citizens of those cities must have tamed the land long ago. I then asked him why he thought the cities had been abandoned.

He believed that the indigenous citizens had simply migrated to other parts of South America. According to Jerry, "It is hard to imagine this while living in America, because if you were to go 50 miles in any direction here you would see lots of telephone poles, roads, cars and cities. However, if you go 50 miles in any direction from one of these lost cities in the Andes, you are still going to be in the middle of the largest wilderness on the planet. If the citizens of these lost cities decided to move 50 miles away, who was going to know?

"These cities are all situated about one-day's journey by foot which is not even 50 miles apart and yet, finding the next city is like looking for a needle in a hay stack. The Amazon Basin is about 50 million square miles of mostly untamed wilderness."

Jerry then described the ancient road system and showed me pictures of ancient stone walls that were very-well built. It seemed to me as though the cities were all connected to a central civilization. Jerry said, "Yes, they were, but to what degree I can't say. I don't know how far the roads extended, but they definitely led in and out of these cities. In older, published reports there were bridges and great throughways that someone had carefully constructed. But over the course of 4,000 years or longer, these things are no longer functional."

I knew that historically, newer cities were often built on the ruins of older cities or temple sites. Jerry recognized I had a valid point, but doubted that this was the case with the ruins he explored. He also mentioned there was an abundance of gold in the area. I wondered if the people that once lived there had mined the precious metal. Jerry said, "Well, gold apparently didn't have the same value to them that our society places on it. We look at gold today mainly as a precious resource for jewelry. But the ancient Amazonians saw gold as a metal that was both pretty and useful.

"I don't think they had to mine the Earth to acquire gold. There's enough of it just in the rivers to pick up. I found a 20-kilogram nugget of gold just lying on the hillside in the mud. If I had scratched around, I might have found the piece that it broke off of. It's everywhere.

"However, it's incredibly dense forest, so you never know when you might happen upon a big piece of gold. Traveling four or five days, you will most likely find something. If you really started clearing things away, there is no telling what you would find.

"At this one city, they used rocks that contain gold veins to build with. These same rocks have pyrite and some white quartz crystal with spider veins of gold in them. But for the most part, there were black rocks with big chunks of gold. The black rock looked like shale. I'm not an expert on what the ideal gold-bearing stone is for pure gold nuggets, but it's not rare up there in the Andes."

When I asked Jerry if he thought that was why the government of Peru didn't really want anyone going up there, he said, "It could be. There is one Canadian company somewhere up there in the Andes that has permission to acquire gold using a commercial extraction technique, but there really isn't any mining involved. You just need to hose the mud off the hillside and look at the rocks."

I wondered what Jerry wanted to ultimately see happen with the lost cities he had been exploring. He explained that, "We want all the pictures and information made available to the world. All interested people should be able to go to the Internet, or TV, and sit down and explore these cities on video or in a virtual reality type of atmosphere. I am completely prepared to go there and take massive amounts of film of the entire site so everyone can see this.

"Currently, it is too dangerous for just anyone to go in there because of the drug cartels and the terrorists. I rode right through some of the strongholds of the terrorists, but they had already been told that we were coming and what our purpose was.

"In the past 20 to 30 years, things have gotten pretty rough up there. Before then, there were not many people living in that area; except for the farmers who were spread far and wide in the area. Until recently, no one really had a clue that there was anything significant up there."

I had read some rather interesting books that indicated British and German explorers knew quite a bit about that area. Apparently, they had a very strong interest in that area. Jerry said, "I understand various explorers may have known that there was an ancient city in a specific location somewhere, but I'm telling you that to get into those jungles requires an act of God. It is not the sort of thing that is done by ordinary people. Honestly, this is the most unbelievably difficult terrain to navigate I've ever seen in my life!"

I knew Jerry was telling the truth. There were many reports of people exploring that region that had disappeared for whatever reason. Many of them had been trying for a long time to find the legendary lost cities of gold and the treasures they held.

According to Jerry, "There is a good reason why people disappear down there. There are various types of snakes whose bite will kill you in 15 minutes or less. There is one snake that is just as green as the jungle, and it lives in the trees.

"There is a red snake that lives on the ground, and in the bushes. There is no anti-venom for any of these snakes. There is a very real fatality factor to consider when you go into this area. There are also highly-aggressive, black bears in the area that are an average of six-and-a-half feet tall. I have a picture on my web site of the skin of one of those bears."

I had seen many amazing photographs that Jerry had taken while in the jungle. It was intriguing. When I asked him if he still planned to go live in South America and set up a community there to communicate with ETs, he said, "Yes, but our focus has changed somewhat. We are going to Peru to set up a research community. It is going to be geared toward botanical studies. We want to learn how to use the medicinal plants from the Shamans.

"But the ongoing study into the lost cities is a real fascination for me. I am very interested in the possibility that there are ancient records located in one or more of these cities that we can read which could make a difference for us now.

"You see, one of the things I haven't told anyone about is that there is a place somewhere up there, and it may be like this in each city, but there is a place where they stored information. I believe it was a place where they kept their historical records."

I was fascinated by the fact that Jerry had seen indications of intact archives at one of the ancient cities. He had seen some hieroglyphs around the ruins. Historically, that was what advanced cultures of every age had done in their cities; create a library.

Jerry also mentioned there was one particular mountain in the area that had a lot of UFO sightings. He explained that, "One of our guides was up on that mountain filming with a video camera, one afternoon, when a UFO swooped down into the valley and just hovered there for quite some time. The guide got some really good footage of that UFO. Unfortunately, soon after that, the video camera and the videotape were stolen."

I then asked Jerry if he thought there was a connection between the lost cities and ETs. He said, "I think that these cities are places that the ETs are quite familiar with and have used in the past. They were probably just used as a place to land, and get water, and shelter, but I think they found the jungle cities were quite interesting as well. You see, It's not that bad on top of the mountain: there aren't as many bushes and trees. In fact, at one site on a mountain there is an ancient city that is completely intact."

When I asked Jerry why all the ancient cities were not built on the areas located above the jungle floor, he said, "The really ancient ones are. The ones that were built later were built further down the mountains because there was more agriculture down there. But for the cities located on top of the mountains, no agriculture was possible.

"The local people I have spoken with say the ancient ones were trading with other groups down the mountain or living in one area and visiting another. I think what might have happened was that they were hunters; not farmers. They would go out to hunt and bring the food back home. In one of the buildings I was in, there was a large room. Keep in mind this building was constructed of carved stone blocks. The walls and ceilings were made of cut stone.

"It was built with carved blocks of stone that were set without mortar just like Machu Piccu and so many other sites in South America. Even the floors were paved with stones. At the end of this one large room, there was a big chair made of stone, and above that large chair hung deer antlers."

When I asked Jerry how long it had been since anyone last lived in that city, he estimated it had been thousands of years. This made no sense to me because if it was such a good place to live, and the city was so well built, then why did they abandon the area?

Jerry said, "I think the answer to that would be determined by what they were living off of. For example, if they were hunters then perhaps a huge earthquake scared off all the animals. Or possibly they regularly migrated. If they were migrating, then they would seasonally return to these stone cities."

It seemed like a reasonable explanation, but it would have taken massive amounts of food to sustain enough people to build just one of these stone cities. They would have had to be very-well organized to feed that many people. Clearly, it took a lot of work to build one of these cities.

Jerry agreed. However, he thought that there would have been enough food to support the entire civilization even without agriculture. He said, "It's a very lush jungle. It's full of things to eat. I don't think there is as much animal life there now as there was maybe a thousand years ago or more. I am sure that the place was absolutely overrun with animals, but there are more people living throughout the valley now, so many wild animals have left the area."

I wondered if Jerry had seen anything like a graveyard in the ancient city. He told me that his team found a site that had some pretty unusual burials. They were nothing like what he had expected to find. They were circular stone containers built down into the ground that were covered with stones. There were thousands of these types of burial pits.

Jerry had no idea how deep they were because he didn't do any excavations, but they were usually about three-and-a-half feet across. According to Jerry, "I was told by an archaeologist that the people who lived there would dig the hole down deep then, over time, they would fill it up with a bunch of bodies. Each one of these circular burials most likely represented an entire family.

"That was their burial site. The first person to die was placed at the bottom and so on with a layer of stones separating each body. As time went by, I think the ones near the top would have the most intact artifacts, but none of these have been excavated. At least not the ones I saw."

I was confused. If Jerry had discussed this with a local archaeologist, did that mean they were actively investigating these ruins? He then explained that the government really didn't have the money to do proper excavations, and it was simply too dangerous to go in there. Another factor was, until recently, the ancient cities had only been a rumor based on hear say.

I realized that other people must have been to these ruins before Jerry. I wanted to know how he had learned the location of the ancient ruins. He explained that, "The people who first found these sites are local farmers who live deep in the mountains and periodically have to go looking for stray cattle. There have been occasions where the cattle were trying to scrape parasites off their hides and were rubbing against an ancient stone wall and accidentally exposed it.

"This sparked the interest of the farmer who then discovered a building. The fellow who found that one city on top of a mountain only went up there to find some of his cattle. When he arrived in the city, he couldn't tell if his cattle were in there or not because the site was so big. It was getting dark, so he decided to camp out.

"The next morning, the cattle had found him. He then chased the cattle through the city to see if any bears came out after them. When he was sure the area was safe from bears, he went and looked around a little bit. But he got freaked out because it looked like someone was still living there. He left in a hurry and would not go back until we coerced him."

According to Jerry, the farmer thought someone still lived there because all the people's belongings were still inside their houses. It was like a ghost town. The people were just gone. The farmer said the place was 'full of demons' and that he didn't want to go back in there. He was truly afraid. However, over the next few years, he found five cities that were located on the eastern slope of the Andes in the region of San Martin which is south and west of Iquitos.

I then asked Jerry if he thought these cities were originally connected to some larger Amazonian empire. He said, "Yes, but it appears this specific empire stretched down the eastern slopes of the Andes much like the Incas who were living along the western slopes. I don't think the Incas and this other group of people got along very well.

"Even though the Andes mountain range helped separate the two groups, the Incas went in there, but they didn't like dealing with these people. This other group of people were tall, with white skin. They had auburn or red or blonde hair and green or blue eyes. The Incas said that these people were the most ferocious warriors they had ever witnessed."

When I asked Jerry if these people had developed metal weapons, he said, "They had all kinds of weapons. They were quite masterful with a bow and arrow and spears. They had other things that the Incas had never seen before. I have only been told about this, but they apparently had slings.

"It's an odd weapon, but some of these are still being used in the Lake Titicaca area. I bought one down there and the local kids showed me how to use it. You know, like in the book *Clan of the Cave Bear*? The one woman used a sling."

I then told Jerry that historically, Vikings were not known for fine masonry. He then reminded me about the Celts. They had apparently migrated in seagoing boats from Africa to the British Isles. With those types of boats, some of them could have also migrated to South America or wherever they wanted.

According to Jerry, "Some of the people in South America apparently still worship the Norse god Odin and speak Gaelic which I found to be extraordinary. But if you take a look at some of the masonry work of the Celts, like Stonehenge, these were sophisticated people.

"There is also a connection to the Great Flood. It was on some of the stone art we found. Up on the side of a mountain we found a huge stone that was partially uncovered. On the surface of that stone was a line drawing etched into stone of the flood, and it really made me wonder. There are records of a time on earth when there were apparently no rainbows. In the images on the rock, at one end, shows a woman whose face is in terror. Her hair is curled up on the ends. In another area, past the other different figures, one of which looks like an angel to me, there is a rainbow. Under the rainbow is a sun with rays of light coming off of it, and in this sun disk is the face of a woman with a rather solemn expression. Above the rainbow there is a line with a circle at the end of it. That would represent the moon.

"I have come to believe that there was a time when there was no moon. In Zechariah Sitchin's research of Sumerian text, he described a time when a planet passed near the earth and big changes started happening. I have also read some Chinese text describing how the sun stood still in the sky for three days. How is that possible?

"What I think happened was that the ETs in that era who wanted to wipe out life on earth brought the moon in which slowed the rotation of the earth down and forced it to start turning the other direction. Instead of the sun rising in the west, it began rising in the east.

"I also believe the axis of the earth was not the same as it is today. The poles of the planet were actually located near where the equatorial zone is currently. If that is true, then what you end up with is a total different arrangement of ocean to land mass. However, as soon as you change these things, water will leave the ocean and begin racing over everything, and the next thing that happens is massive rain and floods. So, under those conditions, 40 days and 40 nights of rainfall are not out of the question."

It was a sobering thought. If true, perhaps that was why humanity suffered from a collective amnesia about its true historical past. However, the memory of a global flood was one of the most universal themes in all of the ancient legends on earth.

A few years later, I spoke with Jerry after he had returned from another very-intense, two-month trip to Peru. His team was trying to reach a very-remote location, deep in the jungle, where many strange stone statues had been reportedly discovered. However, shortly before his team arrived to set up base camp, a group of people were murdered in that area. As a result, his team went on to explore another location which he described as "heaven on earth."

I listened intently to Jerry's latest adventures, but I was also eager to tell him about the strange events I had been investigating regarding UFOs in Washington, D.C. I also mentioned that I had found graphic evidence of a historic, covert relationship between ETs and Masons. I then speculated that there may be a current connection to ETs and secret societies in Washington, D.C.

After hearing this, Jerry was silent for a few moments. Something I had said caused him to suddenly have total recall of a childhood memory that shocked the Hell out of both of us. He proceeded to rapidly describe secret rituals he had participated in with Masons when he was quite young.

After we both calmed down a bit, Jerry described the chronology of events for me in greater detail. He said that the Masonic rituals began for him around the age of three. During that time in his life, after a certain hour at night, Jerry's father (a Mason and ranking military officer) would take him to the Masonic Lodge in Denver.

After arriving, they would descend into the lowest level of the building. Jerry was then instructed to completely disrobe and put on a skin-tight, one-piece type of garment. He was then lead to an area he described as a stage. A bright spotlight was then focused on him while the rest of the room remained totally dark. He was instructed to stand in a specific location and respond to the questions asked of him.

Jerry could tell by the sounds of the different voices of the men that there were many Masons in the room. They would chant words to him that he didn't understand. He was very intimidated by this experience and cried the first few times, but soon became acclimated to the ritual. It was a regular practice that continued for about four years until his father passed away when Jerry was seven years old.

Soon after Jerry's father died, some Masons came to his house and tried to take him away from his mother. She refused to give him up and threatened to call the police. Jerry clearly recalled that after the Masons left the house, his mom quickly packed some things and took him to stay with her sister. However, his mom soon decided it wasn't safe to remain in Colorado, so she put Jerry in her car and they drove non-stop to Kentucky.

Jerry and his mother ended up staying in a chicken coop behind someone's farm house for a couple of days until they found a place to live. Eventually his mom remarried. Jerry spent the next decade growing up, more or less, like the other children his age. However, when he was 18-years old, he was approached on three separate occasions by Masons and invited to become a member. He was approached once by a Senator and once by a Congressman. The third and final time he was approached by the son of one of the Masonic politicians. The son offered to give Jerry a large gold ring if he became a member. On all three occasions Jerry declined their offer.

CHAPTER TEN

Inter-dimensional Intelligence

As a journalist investigating reports of UFOs and ETs, I had interviewed many interesting people. One day, in 1997, I was contacted by a man named Nassim Haramein. Although he appeared to be an ordinary human being, he had discovered some extraordinary information about the cosmos. I found that his theories about the universal forces of creation were reminiscent of other enlightened souls such as Buckminster Fuller, Viktor Shauberger, Nikola Tesla, and John Searl.

After carefully reviewing his work, I realized that Mr. Haramein's information could be the catalyst needed to unleash mankind's true potential. But what fascinated me most was how he had acquired the inspiration for his research: contact with ETs.

Mr. Haramein's first close encounters with extraterrestrials occurred in 1969, when he was seven years old. At that time, he was living in Montreal, Canada. According to Mr. Haramein, "At that time, I had encounters with alien beings that came into my room. They visited me a few times within one month. In fact, I think it happened every night during that month. My mom never said anything about it to me at the time, but she eventually admitted that she had seen them one night."

When I asked him why he thought ETs wanted to visit him, he said, "I really don't know. I had conscious memories of my visitations after they occurred. This is not information that I recalled later under hypnosis. But I remember very little of what happened between the times that they took me out of my bed and when they brought me back to my room. The only thing I remember clearly while being with them was driving their spaceship."

Although Mr. Haramein was just seven-years old at the time, I really wanted to know what he recalled about flying a UFO. He said, "I was given the helm. I remember tapping into the central nervous system of the ship. They gave me control and my consciousness became one with the gravitational field of the ship. You see, gravity is a point of singularity, and it is the same thing as a living soul. You are a point of singularity creating a gravitational field of experience."

Hearing this reminded me what David Adair had said about his experience with the alien engine at Area 51. It had the ability to connect with his consciousness and react to his brain waves. According to Mr. Haramein, "The ETs technology links directly to your DNA structure which is your cellular consciousness. That's how I was able to drive their star ship. At the time, I didn't understand this information. It came to me later as I matured and began to do research on this subject. But I clearly remember controlling the spaceship with my consciousness and that it was very unstable at first. Eventually, I was able to control it a little better."

As an adult, Mr. Haramein became a professional skier and a scuba diving instructor. He also taught rock climbing and mountaineering. As exciting as these activities were, he felt a need to research the mysterious origins of life in the universe. At age 11, he began meditating. This inspired him to begin collecting data for what was to become his life's work.

When asked to elaborate on his research, he said, "When I started meditating, there was a big change in my life. That was when I first learned of the link between atomic structures and consciousness. When I was 26 years of age, after meditating for many years, I had another experience that inspired my research.

"I had been badly injured while skiing. My back was really damaged, and I had been in bed for about a month-and-a-half. That particular night, for some reason, I was feeling better. My back felt very good, so I started to meditate. Moments later, I saw a huge ball of light, appear in my room. As I stared at this beautiful, strange ball of light, I felt it pulling me outside my bedroom. Soon, I was outside the earth's atmosphere. Then, I was taken past the moon and beyond.

"Eventually, I left this solar system and was passing other solar systems until I arrived at a massive ball of light at the center of the galaxy. As soon I saw it, I began to enter it. I was traveling incredibly fast, but as soon as I entered that area everything stopped. It felt like I was floating in a ball of liquid light.

"There was a humming sound that was really incredible. I was filled with many powerful emotions of love, and joy, and happiness, and I could feel that there was a lot of information that was downloaded into my being. At one point, I was so overwhelmed, I said, 'This is too much.' As soon as I had that thought, I was suddenly back in my room sitting up in my bed and sweating! I was in shock. But I felt an incredible, peaceful feeling. I felt like a lot of things had changed in my head. I could feel physical, electrical patterns changing in me for the rest of the night, and I couldn't sleep."

I wondered how that experience affected Mr. Haramein's back injury. He said, "My injury was basically over, from that moment on. The next day, I started walking without a cane for the first time in almost two months. The doctor's that had been treating me thought I was probably not going to be able to continue my professional skiing career. Yet, I was skiing that season after my meditation experience. It was very powerful.

"But I thought it was strange that the morning after the event, I went to my desk and began to write, which is not something I would normally do. That morning, I went to my desk, and I felt inspired to write. I was guided to draw a double star tetrahedron with a series of mathematics surrounding it. It just came out of me, and all the mathematics started to correlate together toward a specific arrangement. That was the start of the physical, mathematical concepts of my research.

"I remember looking at the drawing and not knowing what I was actually doing. But in my subconscious, I already had a memory from school that helped me to interpret what was coming through.

"I began to think about the image and the numbers, and I realized I was being shown the geometry for the foundation of existence. It is how hyperspace moves time and space to create the sphere using the double star tetrahedron. Although I started to work with that information, I went back to skiing and other things professionally."

I was curious where Mr. Haramein's research led him next. He said, "For the next few years, I put the research aside, but I kept on learning. I did a lot of traveling. I visited the pyramids in Mexico and so on. What re-ignited my interest was a research paper by an American engineer named Hugh Harleston Jr. He had spent 15 years measuring and studying the ancient city of Teotihuacan, in Mexico, near Mexico City.

"This was very exciting information for me to see. Mr. Harleston's conclusions relating to the mathematical layout of Teotihuacan was striking. For instance, he found that the city was laid out exactly like the solar system. It showed the elliptical courses of each of the planets including Neptune and Pluto which were not discovered by European cultures until the 1900s.

"But what was really incredible was that Harleston's conclusions about the mathematics of the city seemed to indicate that the Aztec's had knowledge of the geometry of a tetrahedron within a sphere. That information was crucial to my research, because it re-ignited the flame within me to follow up on that information. But I could hardly believe what I was seeing on paper, because it was so similar to what I had drawn after meditating and having that illuminating experience with the spheres of light.

"During that experience, I had a vision of numbers relating to the frequency of the light spectrum. I saw how each light wave also related to a sound wave. These light and sound waves connect to energy centers of the body which is our link to consciousness. Harleston found that the long, straight, Avenue of the Dead, in the ancient ruins of Teotihuacan, had precise mathematical references to show each frequency of the light spectrum and the related sound wave octaves as well. Harleston's conclusions were that the embedded message of the city's architecture was that the Universe is infinitely big to infinitely small within a specific geometry which is related to the tetrahedron within the sphere; like the carbon atom."

I then asked Mr. Haramein if he thought this provided a code that allowed us access or control of the Universe through resonant harmonics. He said, "That is correct. Resonant harmonics are the key to all universal power, and they are directly related to light and sound waves. That was really exciting to me that Harleston found that entire complex at Teotihuacan, when averaged mathematically, had a numerical constant of 1.059.

"This is very close to the constant that Buckminster Fuller found within the isotropic vector matrix at 1.06066. It is one part in one thousandths away from being an exact match which is easily accounted for by Harleston's own margin of error. Harleston said that there might be a connection to the 'four frequency isotropic vector matrix,' so I started to look deeper at that relationship."

I wasn't familiar with this information and asked Mr. Haramein to elaborate. He explained that, "It is a 20 tetrahedral vector matrix in which the tetrahedra are stacked together to form one large tetrahedron. Mr. Fuller believed this matrix is the basic mathematical blueprint of the universe. When I really began to study this, I found that there were some anomalies within the matrix. I noticed that the matrix was not polarized. I realized that there needed to be a polarity in the tetrahedral grid in order to represent known universal forces, so I added another matrix to the system.

"I found that there are cavities between the 20 tetrahedrons that take the shape of octahedrons. This is contained within the matrix and it is shaped like a double pyramid: one pointing up and the other pointing down. I thought of these as the resonance cavities in space/time, pulsing subatomic particles in and out of the vacuum structure. Incredibly, when we look at a single matrix, there are four tetrahedron spaces in the middle that are reversed (pointing downward) and rotated 180 degrees.

"The reason they are there, and positioned that way, is to accept the reverse matrix and generate a perfect, polarized structure. It all fits perfectly when you put the 20 tetrahedrons of the matrix into another one and push them together. In the process you make a three dimensional representation of the Star of David. The geometry you get in the middle of that space is a cube octahedron or vector equilibrium, as Bucky called it, because it is the only geometry in perfect equilibrium in all vectoral possibilities. Actually, one matrix alone has the geometric potential to accept the other and is incomplete without it."

I then asked Mr. Haramein if the second missing matrix acted like a catalyst or amplifier to unlock the full potential of the first matrix. He said, "Correct. And as soon as you have created a vector equilibrium you end up with a point of singularity in the middle.

"As I mentioned earlier, this is the point of gravitational collapse or the point of absolute stillness. You see, movement needs stillness to balance itself, like an axle on a wheel. This is the axis that is nonlinear because it moves inward. It is light moving in. We understand radiation as an expansion, but we don't yet understand the source of radiation as a contraction."

I recalled reading that Viktor Schauberger had done quite a lot of research about the powerful, centripetal (contracting) forces of implosion in nature. He had dedicated his life to finding a way that mankind could learn to apply this knowledge to our modern technology. It seemed so simple: contractions were the opposite polarity of expansions.

According to Mr. Haramein, "It is simple, but profound. This was a whole new page in my research. I found that the matrix eventually develops into 64 tetrahedrons to create the full matrix potential. I included this information in my first book, *The Harmonic Sphere: The End of a Cycle*."

I was curious at what point in his research Mr. Haramein realized that people like Stan Tenen of the *Meru Foundation* and Richard C. Hoagland of the *Enterprise Mission* were developing similar conclusions from their research. Mr. Haramein said, "I was already years into my research. I had been researching the connection to ancient civilizations and finding things I had only theorized about, but were physically demonstrated in ancient cultures. So, I kept looking in that direction and finding all sorts of incredible information linking the geometry and the mathematics of the 64-tetrahedron matrix to ancient text and calendars.

"The sacred Mayan calendar, the Tzolkin, gives the exact mathematics of the tetrahedral grid that I had conceptualized. For instance, the lobe structure produced by the spheres around each tetrahedron, which resemble electron orbitals, added up to 84. When you take the numerical matrix from the Tzolkin calendar and add up each row, they all produce the number 84. Furthermore, you can actually average all the numbers in that system, and they become a seven. Seven is the number of the symmetrical axes of rotation of a tetrahedron, and I found many more relationships throughout the years. All this was rather incredible."

That was an understatement. John Searl's "Law of the Squares" worked on a similar principle. Again, it seemed as though a universal mind was at work constantly helping us to evolve through certain receptive individuals. A few years after his journey within "a sphere of light", Mr. Haramein finished the mathematical structure that he had started. He said, "At one point, while working on my discovery, I went into a trance state for three days, and all the numbers came out. That's how I finished my original equations. The reason I was being pushed to finish this work is because I was looking for the constant within the system: a numerical code that would represent the entire system.

"When I finished the mathematics, I ended up with 12 x 7 = 84 plus the rotational value of my equation which was 8 + 8 = 16. 16 + 84 = 100. This represented 100 percent. However, I had to divide that number by the vertices of the tetrahedron intersecting the sphere plus the singularity at the center. So, I divided 100 by 9, and when I entered this equation into my calculator it read 11.11 to infinity. This was striking to me, because that number had been following me throughout my life.

"Entire books have been written about that specific number's meaning as a gateway or path to spiritual ascension. So, my gravitational collapse, or my center of the equation, had a value of 11.11, and when I added in the geometry of the Tzolkin grid, I ended up with exactly 11 rows on each side of the matrix. This proved to me that there was much more about the Mayan calendar's mathematics that fit perfectly into the knowledge of the geometry of a 64-tetrahedron grid space/time structure."

I wondered if Mr. Haramein thought that the Maya and other ancient cultures had acquired their advanced physics data from their encounters with ETs, in part, like he did. He felt that this was possible, but not critical because it was part of our very essence waiting to be discovered.

I agreed that this information was timeless and felt it was a universal key that allowed anyone to unlock the forces of creation and learn how to operate them. Mr. Haramein said, "Yes. It is teaching us how to operate creation. That's very true. I'm not sure if the ancient people got their information exactly the same way I did. It is clear that the geometry of the crystal grid was known to the ancients at some point in time. For example, it is found in the architecture of the early Egyptians. Much of that evidence is still physically there in those immense rocks that were somehow moved over vast distances.

"There is no way that these megalithic stones were moved by the methods that archaeologists have proposed. It could not have been done with sheer, brute strength alone. There are some stone obelisks in Egypt that weigh in excess of 1,000 tons. That is far more than anything that we could lift even today. And it has been proven that these stones were cut hundreds of miles away from where they were found.

"Obviously, there is evidence that some advanced technology was used in Egypt, at some time. There is also evidence that there were 'sun gods' or some kind of alien visitors that apparently brought some advanced information to these ancient civilizations. I think that some of our ancestors did have this information, and they had some idea how to operate it.

"At the same time, I think that even if those visitations had never occurred, any evolving civilization's consciousness would grow over time to reflect these basic principles because it is encoded into everything including our atomic structure: our DNA. So, these geometric codes will find a way to come out of us. All you really have to do is look back and see the patterns repeating in generations of ancient knowledge."

I wanted to know what sort of technology this information could be applied to in our future. Mr. Haramein thought about it for a moment, then said, "I believe that in the near future we are going to experience events that will have crucial repercussions to our survival capability, and that would be the time that we need this technology the most in order to be able to move onward and upward to a higher level of knowledge: a higher state of being. In fact, the concepts of ascension may not only be spiritual but literal. As a society better understands the true structure of space/time and learns to control gravity, they evolve on many levels."

When I asked him what type of life-changing events he was referring to, he said, "There is evidence that the magnetic field of the Earth and Shuman resonance is rapidly changing. Data now shows that the equator of our planet is getting fatter and the poles flatter which means that our gravitational poles have already shifted by 90 degrees.[1]

"This may be directly related to the earth's magnetic field and may be a precursor to a field reversal. You see, there is a lot of evidence that indicates that the universe actually creates itself in pulsed rings, even in the atomic structure. The model for this would be two vortices intersecting and creating a point of extreme gravitational collapse: a powerful point of singularity which emanates rings at its equator. The reason that scientists like to describe creation as a 'big bang' is because they are only looking at the past. When we look into outer space with a telescope, we are looking thousands of years behind us to the moment when our universe emerged from the center of a massive black hole. But that event could in fact be only one of multiple rings of creation.

"We cannot see the ring that came before, or the one that comes after, because that is not on our time continuum. We can only see into the immediate past. The ring that would have emerged just after we did would not be visible from our perspective, and the ring that emerged just before we did would not be visible either. Curiously, scientists are finding that there are stars in our universe that seem to be older than our known Universe. It is possible that our new-born, expanding ring would eventually catch up to the older one and cause an overlap, and in that overlap you would find some stars that were older than ours.

"If that model is correct, and there is actually nothing in physics to prevent this from occurring, the vortices and ring structure dynamics that produce a double torus, with rings at the equator, would apply to all scales and would explain the structure of our planetary system where planets are in orbit, more or less, around the equator of the Sun. This applies to galaxies as well where galactic discs form around immense polar vortices, meaning the central black hole of a galaxy.

"Scientists' still don't quite understand the mechanism of this yet because they cannot find 96 percent of the mass necessary for these observable dynamics to occur. And so, this is saying that the rings of creation, just like we see in the fractal designs of some crop circles, are fundamental and complementary to universal design.

"We are just about to move from one ring to another in our galactic disc. This event should result in an increase in solar activity and encourage the reversal of the earth's poles in our near future. It will also increase the temperature of the Sun and our Earth will experience an accelerated melting of its glaciers at the polar ice caps."

Although these revelations were fascinating, I really wanted to know how we could use this tetrahedral, geometric information to protect our modern civilization. Mr. Haramein comments were shocking. He said, "I think that this technology was used to maintain the earth's magnetic field the last time a reversal occurred about 15,000 years ago which ended the last ice age.

"The magnetic field was maintained last time by beings from outer space that came to help. I believe that is why the pyramids, and other megalithic structures, were built all over our planet as part of this crystal grid technology. You could consider it a gift from the gods.

"It was put in place to maintain the magnetic field during the time of spin reversal. I believe that these beings from space left all the information that we need to reproduce that same technology in the future. They did that so that we could maintain the magnetic field ourselves during the next spin reversal which I believe is scheduled to occur around the year 2011.

"I think that is why some people are talking about the coming of a 'photon belt.' This so-called belt is actually the end of one ring and the beginning of another with a dark area in between. That is my theory. There is evidence found in some crop circles that is indicative of this technology as it relates to space and time.

"There was one formation that showed two circles intersecting, creating the petals of the *Flower of Life*. In the middle it had the *Eye of Horus*. A few months earlier, there was a lot of talk about a picture taken by NASA of a star that had gone supernova.

"That image showed two rings intersecting and creating the shape known as the *Flower of Life*. I found it extremely interesting that we were seeing the same geometry of time and space on a picture of an event in the middle of outer space and in a field in England. The rings emanating from that explosion in outer space are hundreds of thousands of light years across. They are immense. The energy created by that supernova literally lit up the geometric grid of time and space in that area making the matrix visible to us for a while.

"The current theories about supernovas tell us that this exploded star would eventually become a pulsar, but this is not what was found. After the two rings dissipated, we found nothing. And now, the top astronomers are saying that what was really left was a black hole. So, all of a sudden, we have a black hole at the center of what was a star.

"This evidence is supportive of the concept which states that there is a black hole at the center of everything. A star has a small black hole living at its center fueling its dynamic rotational and radiating patterns which we call the ergosphere. It is the dynamic, plasma layers surrounding a black hole event horizon which makes it appear to us as a star. Some subatomic, theoretical models also predict that the centers of atoms are actually mini black holes.

"In 1996, we first discovered a planet orbiting around another solar system. That planet was found to be orbiting around a pulsar which is thought to be the harshest possible environment. If, at the end of its life, a star explodes into a pulsar how could there be planets orbiting around it? That is physically impossible. If our sun, which is 99 percent of the mass of our solar system, exploded there would be no planets left. So, what are we seeing when we look at a pulsar?

"Incredibly, what we are seeing are two very powerful vortices touching at the equator. They are energetic rings that emanate outward in very regular pulses. Scientists can calculate when the next ring is going to pulse down to the last nanosecond. That is how precise the energy dynamics are. I believe that this is the basic geometrical and systematic organization of the universe creating itself.

"A supernova is actually a solar system being created as the ergosphere of a star explodes due to an imbalance between the rotational force of the black hole at its center and the mass of the ergosphere of plasma surrounding it. The plasma released Into the solar system then self organizes rapidly into a planetary system, because of the intense magnetic and rotational dynamics such as Coriolis forces. And that is why we see planets orbiting there.

"There are many physical observations that help confirm my theory. For instance, the north pole of Saturn has a hexagonal shape. It is a two-dimensional, vector equilibrium that you get at the middle of the three-dimensional matrix that I mentioned earlier. The reason that this is showing up on the north pole of Saturn is because the structure of space/time influences the Coriolis plasma dynamics of gaseous planets. This is true throughout creation for any planetary body. For instance, we know for a fact that all the material found in our solar system comes from our sun. Thus, our own solar system could have been created by a smaller bang of our local star: the sun."

When I asked Mr. Haramein why the rings of Saturn were composed of lots of ice even though there is no water on that planet, he said, "The particles of the ring are mostly ice because that's what the universe does, it creates water molecules. In fact, recent studies have shown that water is prominent everywhere in our universe. It is found even emerging from sun spots on our sun or floating in immense clouds in intergalactic space. Water's matrix is also tetrahedral. It is a liquid crystal. This is the vehicle for information to move through the structure of the vacuum to the energy grid of organic systems and consciousness. When the human cell develops it does so in the water within a woman's womb.

"The first cell of gestation divides into two then four, and yet it always arranges itself as a tetrahedron. There are three cells on the bottom, and one on the top. When those four cells multiply to make eight, the four new cells arrange themselves in the shape of a reverse tetrahedron.

"When merged together, this forms the three dimensional *Star of David* inside the womb. From that pattern of 8, it grows to 16, 32, 64, and so on, to the 100 trillion cells that comprise the complete human body. This growth is all based on the specific geometrical pattern of the double-star tetrahedron and the cube octahedron which is also known as the vector equilibrium."

I was beginning to see why he thought this inter-dimensional information was the foundation of all physical manifestation, and I wanted to know more. According to Mr. Haramein, "It is the basic geometric pattern that creates life at all levels. That is why, when you reproduce the tetrahedral crystal grid and rotate a magnetic field appropriately in plasma, you can actually tap into that geometry of time and space. It will form a hyper space that will recreate specific boundaries with the universal forces.

"This has been called the *Akashic Records* by some, because all information in the universe is available at that point of entry. This is why the applications for this knowledge are so profound. You can also regenerate cells with this technology.

"When you look at the story of *Genisis*, the people that lived before the flood had incredible long life spans. Most of them lived at least 600 years. The story insists on giving the specific age of everybody at that time. Long ago, during the 'age of the gods,' in Egypt, Isis revived Osiris in the Osirion temple at Abydos. She is said to have achieved this miracle through her 'magic' which was actually an ancient technology.

"We also find in the Osirion temple an image of the so-called *Flower of Life* that was somehow burned into the 100-ton, pink, granite pillars in a way that the atomic structure was altered to produce the design. When we look at the construction of the image, and apply the crystal grid of the 64 tetrahedron to the geometry of the symbol, it is a perfect fit. Each tetrahedron is contained within the sphere.

"There is evidence that this technology was used to regenerate cell tissue. When you approach the system, it will come into full contact with your DNA structure which is made up of 64 codons of amino acids. There is data indicating this ancient technology may have later become the so-called 'Ark of the Covenant.' When people tried to approach the Ark, they were either struck dead or were made sick by its energy. Only certain people could approach it and live. According to these legends, depending on a person's intentions, the Ark could become destructive to them or heal them of some of the most tremendous illnesses.

"There is a link to the Chinese culture, too. The *I Ching* is made of 64 hexagrams, and each hexagram is arranged in six lines. If you take six lines, and place them in a three dimensional space, the only geometry you can obtain is a tetrahedron. So, when you follow the code of the *I Ching*, which shows the opposite between each number, you can reverse the tetrahedron and get the exact same grid again."

When I asked Mr. Haramein if this reversed tetrahedron acted as the opposite polarity needed to complete the equation, he said, "Exactly, and the *I Ching* is directly related to this universal knowledge. In China, they have found over 200 mummified bodies in the high desert of the Gobi. These are a white-skinned people with blond hair and blue eyes.

"They are over 5,000 years old, and it is still unclear where they came from originally. But there are ancient Chinese legends about how some of their earliest knowledge originated from people that came from elsewhere, like the sun gods of Egypt and the sky gods of the Maya. Chinese history maintains that these white-skinned visitors built pyramids in the Gobi desert and elsewhere in China."

I knew there were confirmed reports of ancient pyramids in China that had not been investigated. Only recently were Westerners allowed in to examine the ruins of some of the pyramids found there. One of them has a base diameter almost as large as the great pyramid in Egypt. I found it interesting that an aerial picture of these pyramids indicated that they aligned with the stars much like the pyramids at Giza which mirrored the constellation of Orion.

When I asked Mr. Haramein if he was aware that pyramids had recently been found in the Pyrenees Mountains, in France, he said, "Yes.

They are linked to the Masonic and Rosicrucian orders. They have a lot of information on that, but it is very difficult to retrieve because of the hierarchy within those groups. Actually, Edgar Casey mentioned that the Atlanteans went to the Pyrenees Mountains and built pyramids there. So far, he has been very accurate in his information about Atlantis."

I then informed him that ancient pyramids had also been discovered in Japan. Unfortunately, these were also not being excavated and researched. Mr. Haramein believed there was also at least one ancient pyramid in Australia. He said, "It is located near Brisbane, about an hour-and-a-half inland from the coast. Nobody knows about it yet. But when I saw it, I thought it was amazing how much that mountain looked like a pyramid.

"I wanted to see it up close, but it is on privately owned land, and I was not able to get permission to go and investigate. However, I was able to obtain a topographical map of the area, and the faces of the pyramid-shaped mountain are aligned perfectly to magnetic north. The chances of it being an artificial creation are very high, and I would love to go and investigate it someday. It is currently covered with dirt and jungle growth. There are lots of ancient ruins like that around the world. But I think this coming shift of polarity on our planet is going to usher in major changes in our consciousness."

If that was true, humanity needed to prepare itself to receive this new information and the potential it would activate in us. According to Mr. Haramein, the development of resonant harmonic technology would bring us to a new level of understanding and appreciation of universal forces. I felt that it would also increase our level of responsibility to use it wisely. We needed to work with it or be destroyed by it.

Mr. Haramein agreed and added that, "It is important to prepare ourselves to become synchronized with this new system. Much of the old system is going to fall apart, so this technology will not be applied to negative or militant applications."

When I asked Mr. Haramein if he was familiar with gamma-ray bursts, he said that he had studied them. Scientists had reported that these amazing, high-energy events occurred randomly throughout the universe releasing massive amounts of energy in all directions. But astrophysicists were still not certain how or why these events happened. There were many theories, but none had been accepted as conclusive. It was one of the biggest mysteries in modern astronomy. I wanted to know how gamma-ray bursts fit into Mr. Haramein's research.

He said, "This is exactly what I am working toward. Again, this relates to the energy emitted from a black hole. You see, this is why our sun is burning. The black hole at the center of our sun is generating this tremendous fusion reaction. But if we were at the middle of the sun we would experience it as zero Kelvin, because it is a full contraction of time/ space. The center is a singularity that is at absolute zero degrees and that is also what is at the center of the earth."

His comments regarding black holes and fusion really got my attention. One of the main-stream, scientific theories I had read regarding the future of fusion reactors involved freezing the fuel down to absolute zero. In that state, known as a *Bose-Einstein* condensate, the molecules changed from particles in a wave form to wavicles: particle/waves that were packed much closer together. Thus, it would take much less energy to fuse the atoms. This would hopefully lead to a stabilized fusion reaction from the frozen fuel.

Mr. Haramein and I agreed this information had great implications for our future. He said, "I am so excited, I get the chills just thinking about this. It is time for us to learn that creation is a constant loop; that the universe is not in a state of entropy. It is a constant loop from infinitely large to infinitely small. The reason that most scientists favor the entropy theory is because they don't yet understand that absolute cold and absolute heat are simply opposite polarities of the same energy loop.

"If you are seeing the emanation of light moving outward, you perceive that as heat. But if you are seeing that same emanation of light moving inward you perceive that as cold. Currently, we are very familiar with the universal energies as an emanation moving outward, but the contraction of light is very much misunderstood.

"The reason for that is we still don't understand that everything is moving at the speed of light in all directions because of Universal contraction and expansion. Our planet rotates around the sun which is moving at 5,000 miles per second through the galaxy, and the planets are following in a spiral pattern around the sun. As the sun moves around the galaxy, it creates another spiral. And our galaxy is moving around the center of the universe creating another spiral."

I could see what Mr. Haramein was saying; there were an infinite number of vortices contracting or expanding in creation that needed to find their equilibrium or they would simply dissipate back into the matrix. He said, "That is correct. And the moment we understand that this is all a fractal system, from infinitely big to infinitely small, we can start to accurately compute the true speeds of all these interstellar bodies, relative to our scale of observation, in the fractal structure of space/time. Every point is divisible to infinity making every atom a mini black hole.

"That is why the atom is not subject to entropy. And that is why we had to come up with the quantum physics and quantum mechanics theories to explain away the problems with our classical theories of physics that said the electron was always going to collapse into the nucleus.

"It was thought that the electron would radiate all its energy and then crash into the nucleus. So, they had to find a new formula, but it just went around the problem without explaining the true reason why this was not happening. If we understand that the atom is compressed light, which is still moving at the speed of light in a vortex, within a matrix of vortices in all directions, each point contains the whole: it is a hologram.

"Each point is a gravitational collapse of time and space. That is why our theories in physics, and in mathematics, brought us to the point where we can understand that there are in fact infinite interconnections in time and space; what some people are calling 'wormholes.'

"These points are all connected to all other points because the matrix of creation is moving in all directions at the same time, and movement is related to consciousness. Depending on where you are at that point you will see movement relative to yourself. For example, when you are traveling in a car moving at the speed of light, and there are no windows, you cannot see how fast you are going. The only movement you will see is in your immediate environment inside the car. It is relative only to you and the other passengers in your car. But, in fact, you are moving at the speed of light.

"This is exactly what we are experiencing every moment of every day on this planet. It is important for us to know that we are light in motion as a contraction and an expansion at the same time. We are connected to the entire creation even though we only experience a small part of it and its movement.

"We are somewhat restricted in our understanding, and perception, and our technology, because we do not take into account these facts. What we see in the night sky is stars radiating light into space: tiny expansions of energy. Everything else in the darkness of space is a contraction of light and is cold. But that is why there really is no empty space. All of creation is full of the energy matrix forcing everything to spin within the continuous wheel works of nature. Understanding these dynamics is the key to our evolutionary growth to both a new level of consciousness and a new level of technology."

This insightful information was helping me see why some UFOs could move between dimensions and how they were able to become invisible. These advanced craft were obviously contracting space/time in such a way as to disappear from our sight, or by reversing the drive, their craft could glow as bright as a star.

Mr. Haramein said, "That's right. The ETs can reverse the polarity of light at will. That's why they were called the 'sun gods.' Not because people were worshipping the sun, but because the visitors' technology radiated just as much energy as the sun; just as the Ark of the Covenant has been described. There is evidence that the Ark, as described in *The Bible*, was just a container for a highly-advanced technology that was originally placed at the center of the Great Pyramid at Giza."

Hearing this really got my attention. I had visited the Great Pyramid in the mid 1970s. I walked into the King's Chamber, located in the middle of the pyramid, just as a tour guide struck the so-called sarcophagus (a rectangular stone box) with a wooden mallet, and it rang like a bell. But the sound waves emanating from that ancient stone box were unlike anything I had ever heard or felt in my life.

The spiraling, sonic resonance gradually filled the polished, granite room before slowly dissipating like water draining out of the room. But, for one surreal moment, the energy in that stone room shifted in a very-strange way. Afterwards, I noticed that the lid for the stone box was nowhere to be found. Also, one corner of the box appeared to be melted as if there had been a powerful accident. From that experience, I concluded that the theory that the Great Pyramid was built for burial purposes was wrong. In fact, no mummy was every found there. To me, it appeared to be the largest machine on earth using resonance technology, but it was broken.

Mr. Haramein said, "Yes. There was a crystal matrix generator, within a plasma field, located in the center of the Great Pyramid. It was later placed in a special container that we now call the Ark of the Covenant. The resonant harmonic device was about one foot in diameter. It was used to create an energy vortex at the top of the Ark; what they called the Seat of God or the Throne of the Lord. It was also called a Merkaba, but this vortex is described in *The Bible* as God appearing in a bright pillar of cloud.

"It was a vortex, or pillar of light, that appeared between the two cherubim. It was a beam of energy emitted from the device in the Ark. There is a drawing of this event that was rendered by the Rosicrucians. That is one of the things that led me to believe that the Ark was based on a resonant harmonic technology.

"It also had all these unusual properties such as reversing the flow of water which is an anti-gravity force, and it was seen to move on its own at times. What is even more fascinating is that I looked at the word God and found that in the preface of *The Bible* it tells you how the words were translated.

"The word God in *The Bible* is a translation of the Greek Tetragrammaton which is represented by the four Hebrew letters that make up the name YHWH. But the root of the word can be interpreted as tetra (for tetrahedron) and grammaton (for gram) which is a measurement of weight or gravity. So, all of a sudden, I had found another significant link.

"Even the Star of David, for some reason, kept changing names throughout history as it follows the Ark of the Covenant. The double-star tetrahedron, or the Star of David, in earlier days was called the Seal of Solomon. Evidently, Solomon had possession of the Ark and that is why he had ordered the building of the Temple of Solomon to house the Ark of the Covenant. That is in *The Bible,* and it is very specific.

"The prayers of those people associated with the Judaic faith were supposed to be directed toward that temple. I find this to be very significant as well as the *Star of David* symbol which became the *Star of Zion.* Sure enough, the Ark of the Covenant was located at Mount Zion for a very-long time. And so, this name change seemed to correlate with where the Ark was or who was in possession of it. The fact that this specific geometry is associated with the Ark is surprising to me."

I then asked Mr. Haramein if anyone had shown interest in building a commercial, resonant-harmonic crystal-plasma generator. He said, "No. I have only recently gone public with this information. Before that, I worked on my own. For nearly three years, I worked in the desert with very little contact with the outside world. However, I am currently looking to collaborate with others and to finish my research. I have been writing a new book called *Crossing the Event Horizon*. It will include detailed graphics of all this information."

I later learned that Mr. Haramein was able to find like-minded people he could work with to help enlighten humanity. Together, they created the *Resonance Project Foundation*. It was a clearinghouse for highly-advanced knowledge that could be accessed at www.theresonanceproject. org. I looked forward to seeing what new technologies emerged from this collaborative effort based on Mr. Haramein's inter-dimensional research.

1) *Science Magazine*, Geophysics, Redistributing Earth's Mass, and Detection of a Large-Scale Mass Redistribution in the Terrestrial System Since 1998, Anny Cazenave and R. Steven Nerem, Christopher M. Cox and Benjamin F. Chao.

CHAPTER ELEVEN

UFOs Photographed
Landing on Capitol Hill

It seemed very odd to think that alien incursions of restricted airspace in America would continue to occur post 9/11. It made me wonder what other strange events were yet to come over the prohibited airspace around Washington, D.C. However, based on the historic record, it was a certainty that close encounters in DC would continue to occur in the future.

I was amazed when I first learned that UFO statistician Larry Hatch had discovered a little known fact: Washington, D.C., held the record for the highest ratio of UFO sightings per square mile in the world. Although it is a relatively small area, statistically DC has had hundreds of times more UFO activity per square mile than any other city on earth. It is significant that Mr. Hatch also found 10 neighboring East Coast states were runners-up to Washington, D.C., for the most UFO sightings in the following order:

Massachusetts

Rhode Island

Connecticut

New Jersey

Delaware

New Hampshire

Maryland

Pennsylvania

New York

West Virginia

The statistical data indicated that UFOs were interested in a specific location of the U.S. East Coast: the same location that wealthy Europeans had first arrived and began creating and maintaining the enterprise known as America.

Although I suspected there were probably more, over the course of a year, I was able to locate more than 200 eye-witness accounts of alien incursions by UFOs over Washington, D.C., from 1850 to 2006. I found it interesting that the number of alien incursions in DC had fluctuated dramatically over the past 60 years.

For example, during the period from 2000 to 2006, UFOs were sighted in DC at an average rate of 10 times per year. From 1960 to 1999 there were only sighted at an average rate of once a year. However, from 1950 to 1959 they were sighted at an average rate of nine times per year in DC. Prior to that, from 1850 to 1950, they were sighted less than once a year.

In my research, I learned that the first photograph of a UFO passing over Washington, D.C., was accidentally taken from an airplane that was flying over the newly constructed Pentagon in 1942. I also found that the first time the U.S. military had attempted to intercept a UFO over DC was 1948. And, despite the military's best efforts, the prohibited/restricted airspace over DC was dominated by UFOs during most of 1952. It was this level of alien incursions which ultimately led to UFOs being photographed landing on Capitol Hill exactly 50 years later, in July of 2002.

However, this was an ongoing affair. On September 4, 2006, *FOX News* in Washington, D.C., aired a few seconds of live video of the Capitol on their 10:00 p.m. newscast. Inadvertently included in the footage that night was a UFO hovering over the Senate side of the Capitol, just above the dome. The UFO cast an eerie, green glow over the area.

But, that's not all. While searching the Internet for images of the Capitol building, I discovered a UFO photograph that had been accidentally taken by an eighth-grade student. The picture was posted at an unknown date in 2006 with a series of other images related to the student's school field trip to Washington, D.C. Judging from the position of the sun and moon, the UFO photo was taken in the late afternoon.

The picture clearly showed the moon just to the right and slightly above the Capitol dome. On the left side of the dome were at least five white, spherical UFOs that looked identical to the UFOs photographed at night over the Capitol in 1952 and then again in 2002.

Unfortunately, no one appeared to be ready, willing or able to deal with the problem. For example, on July 24, 2006, at around 8:45 a.m., another alien incursion took place in Washington, D.C. That morning, at least one local resident witnessed a UFO hovering in the restricted airspace of the capital. According to the witness, "I was sitting outside a cafe drinking my coffee. I was just off K Street. The sky was clear blue with no haze. While looking straight up, I saw a small, white UFO about the same size of a very-bright Venus. It seemed to be hovering or had a slightly-discernible motion. Most of the time, it was stationary. It was not an aircraft or a helicopter. It was utterly incomprehensible."

Fifteen days earlier, on July 9, 2006, at approximately 10:30 p.m., another alien incursion transpired in Washington, D.C. That night, some local residents were enjoying a fireworks display. After the show, one of the residents witnessed six whitish-yellow, disc-shaped UFOs passing silently overhead in a formation. The fleet of UFOs moved from one horizon to the other in less than 30 seconds.

Two months earlier, on May 26, 2006, at approximately 11:10 p.m., another alien incursion occurred in Washington, D.C. At that time, the DC photographer, Mr. Allen, looked out a window in his home. In the sky, he observed a small, red, spherical UFO moving at a phenomenal rate of speed in the direction of the Capitol building at a low altitude. According to Mr. Allen, the object was moving so fast and was so silent he felt a rush of adrenaline while watching it.

A week earlier, on May 17, 2006, at about 12:20 a.m., another alien incursion took place in Washington, D.C. That morning, while driving home from work in the heart of DC, a motorist was headed south on Interstate 295. As he passed Bolling Air Force Base and the Naval Research Lab, he sighted a Stealth aircraft flying over the freeway that was headed toward the air base.

On the other side of the freeway, he saw a black, triangular-shaped UFO with three red, circular lights on each corner. In his opinion, the stealth military jet appeared to be escorting the UFO which was slowly descending for a landing in an area with very-large trees. That densely forested area is located across the river from the Naval Research Lab. There is a fence that surrounds the entire area.

Two weeks earlier, on May 4, 2006, around 10:00 p.m., another alien incursion occurred in Washington, D.C. That night, while leaving class, a college student looked up and witnessed four white, illuminated UFOs circling in the sky. They kept circling and coming together then spreading out. After a few minutes, the UFOs grouped together and disappeared. The witness had never seen anything like it before.

The previous month, in April of 2006, around 11:00 p.m., another alien incursion occurred in Washington, D.C. That night, three friends went outside to smoke cigarettes. While looking up, they witnessed some fast-moving, red, flashing UFOs darting around the sky. After about 10 minutes, the UFOs disappeared. Then, helicopters with searchlights patrolled the area for about 30 minutes before leaving.

That same month, on April 15, 2006, at 10:37 p.m., another alien incursion transpired in Washington, D.C. That night, a local resident was outside looking up and noticed a strange, bright-red UFO heading in his direction. The UFO ended up passing almost directly overhead. It had a single red light located in the center on the bottom.

The witness estimated that the UFO was about 1,500 feet across. He noted that it blocked out the stars as it flew silently through the sky. After the UFO passed over the witness, it traveled another mile or so. It was clearly visible, and very bright, until it got over the heart of DC and then vanished.

According to the witness, "The light on the UFO was pulsating when I first noticed it, and then it was steady for about two minutes. Then, it shut off for about five seconds. It then turned back on and remained that way until it passed over the capital area. I'm not sure if it vanished when it got over the National Mall region or just turned its red light off, or perhaps it was pointing in a direction I could not see.

"The red light was hard to explain. It looked like a light being shined into your eyes from a distance, such as catching a glimpse of a laser pointer that someone is aiming in your general direction.

"I have no idea what the UFOs actual shape was because the body of the craft was dark and blended perfectly with the sky. However, I estimated its size to be about 1,500 feet by the amount of stars it was blocking out."

That same month, in April of 2006, another alien incursion occurred around 10:00 p.m., near the Pentagon. At that time, a local resident was surprised to see a brilliant, green and gold UFO moving very fast and low in the sky. It looked as if it would crash into Fort Myer which is located near the Pentagon.

Early that same month, on April 5, 2006, at approximately 9:00 p.m., another alien incursion took place in Washington, D.C. As a local resident was preparing for bed, he casually glanced out the window and witnessed a large, oval-shaped UFO with flashing green and red lights that flew slowly in front of the moon. As a result, the moon was covered up completely for about a minute and a half. The astonished witness noted that it looked as though an eclipse had occurred.

The previous month, on March 15, 2006, around noon, another alien incursion took place in Washington, D.C. That day, at least one person witnessed a flash of bright light in the sky and then saw a UFO. The strange craft was in the area for approximately 30 seconds before it left.

One month earlier, on February 15, 2006, around 4:15 a.m., another alien incursion occurred in Washington, D.C. Early that morning, a local resident walked out onto their balcony to have a cigarette and witnessed two dim, yellow-white UFOs pass overhead. At first glance, the witness thought they might be military jets. But after the first two UFOs had passed by, he noticed a string of about a dozen similar, dim UFOs that moved across the sky in a loose V-shaped formation. He also noted that they glowed through the cloud cover as they flew away.

The previous month, on January 25, 2006, at approximately 6:00 a.m., another alien incursion transpired in Woodbridge, Virginia. While driving that morning, a local motorist witnessed a bright-white, slightly-flickering light in the sky that wobbled slightly, but very rapidly, and was too bright and too big for a star or planet. The UFO hovered in the sky and was visible to the driver all the way into Washington, D.C. Two days later, at the same time, on the same route, the UFO appeared in the sky again. Occasionally, it seemed to move up, down, and side to side, very slightly, and very rapidly with a slight wobble. It was not seen again subsequently by the witness.

Earlier that month, on January 1, 2006, strange as it may seem a Washington, D.C., resident was reportedly abducted shortly after midnight. At that time, a local school teacher had stepped out of his apartment onto the sidewalk to smoke a cigarette when he was suddenly enveloped by a powerful beam of light that he described as feeling like "pink bubble gum" all over his body. The strange light somehow paralyzed and transported him into a spherical UFO that then took him to an undisclosed location.

Some time later that night, the same UFO returned the teacher to the sidewalk outside his apartment where he collapsed. He could not move for a few minutes, but was still conscious. He noticed that three Washington, D.C., police cars drove by at high speed with their lights on and did not stop to assist him as he lay helpless on the sidewalk.

About six weeks later, the teacher was working a second job at night, as a chauffeur, when he inadvertently met the DC photographer, Mr. Allen, at his home. While viewing Mr. Allen's photographic portfolio, the school teacher was also shown some of the night-time, 2002 UFO photographs taken at the Capitol. Upon viewing those images, the teacher suddenly began reliving his alien abduction experience. Although he was a very-large, strong man, the teacher suffered a nervous breakdown.

He began acting as though he could not move and was sobbing hysterically while repeatedly saying something about "pink bubble gum" as he desperately tried to break free of an invisible restraint. Mr. Allen quickly turned off the UFO images and tried to calm the teacher down. Later, the teacher apologized for his bizarre behavior and briefly recalled his abduction experience to Mr. Allen.

The previous month, on December 6, 2005, at approximately 8:40 p.m., another alien incursion took place in Washington, D.C. That night, while standing on the balcony of his apartment, a local resident witnessed a group of UFOs moving across the sky in a "worm-like, wiggling formation" toward the National Mall.

The witness noted that there were up to 12 glowing UFOs moving in a straight trajectory together, but they snaked through the sky. The odd formation of glowing UFOs was well within the earth's atmosphere, and they made no sound.

The astonished witness wanted to believe that because this event occurred in the prohibited airspace over Washington, D.C., it must have involved some type of experimental military craft. But because the UFOs made no sound and snaked through the sky as they flew it made him doubtful that these were earth-built aircraft.

About one month earlier, on October 26, 2005, at approximately 6:50 p.m., another alien incursion took place over Washington, D.C. That evening, a pilot with more than 12 years of flying experience was driving his car south on the outer loop of the Washington, D.C., beltway on Interstate 495 heading towards the I-95 south. After passing the exit for US-50, a strange light configuration in the sky came into view on the right side of the highway and caught the pilot's attention.

He could clearly make out the lights of a helicopter. To the left of it were two white lights that were too far away from the helicopter to be attached to it. They seemed to be keeping pace with it and remained in perfect formation with it. As he got closer to the helicopter, it crossed over the highway above him. He noted that it appeared to be a *Black Hawk* helicopter, but he was extremely focused on the two unidentified white lights next to it. He couldn't make any sense of what they were.

As the helicopter flew over, he saw that the two white lights were not part of an aircraft or the helicopter, but instead seemed to be just floating in the sky next to the helicopter in perfect formation. He then lost visual contact with the helicopter, and the unidentified white lights.

He quickly put the event out of his mind and focused his full attention on driving again. However, a few minutes later, another bright-white UFO appeared in the sky, to the right of his position on the road and immediately began to drop straight down. Having just seen a helicopter in the area, he immediately thought they were dropping flares. But, he changed his mind when the UFO dropped straight down for five-to-seven seconds at an increasingly fast rate of speed. It then suddenly stopped on a dime and became stationary in the sky.

Even though the pilot had 12 years of aviation experience, he couldn't explain how the UFO could have instantly stopped in mid air after accelerating straight down vertically and then remain stationary for quite some time.

What he found utterly amazing was the fact that this UFO was visible in the sky the entire time, yet apparently no one else was looking at it. At that moment, the pilot realized that there really could be amazing UFO activity over DC and most people wouldn't even notice!

During the summer of 2005, the self-avowed, reincarnated extraterrestrial entity commonly known as "Tom Cruise" spearheaded the media campaign for Steven Spielberg's reproduction of the classic sci-fi movie *War of the Worlds*. Ironically, as that fictional 1938 UFO invasion of the East Coast of America was returning to movie theaters everywhere, the real-life, wide-spread fear from a UFO invasion was occurring in the skies over Mexico.

The bizarre events south of the border were largely ignored by the world media at the time, but this really was not a new story. Since the total solar eclipse in 1990, thousands of people had witnessed and photographed massive "fleets" of UFO as they swarmed through Mexican airspace.

What I found more disturbing was that none of the world's media seemed interested in the fact that an ongoing UFO invasion was also occurring over the East Coast of America and was focused specifically on Washington, D.C. It seemed slightly ironic that this was allegedly the most secure airspace in the nation. If that was true, then why were there so many UFOs still violating that prohibited airspace?

For example, on July 27, 2005, at approximately 6:30 a.m., another alien incursion occurred in Washington, D.C. That morning, a local resident witnessed a disk-shaped UFO that was flashing multiple colors against the dark sky. The UFO was seen hovering for a few minutes before landing on retractable legs for about 10 minutes. The legs then retracted and the UFO rose vertically and disappeared almost immediately. The witness noted that one motorist was frightened by the event.

Thirteen days earlier, on July 14, 2005, about 2:45 p.m., another alien incursion occurred in Washington, D.C. While at the Washington

Monument sightseeing, a tourist noticed three military helicopters flying by, so he took a picture. Later, when he downloaded the image into his computer, he noticed there was a UFO passing low over the area.

One month earlier, on June 14, 2005, around 3:00 a.m., another alien incursion was captured on film in Washington, D.C. The images were taken by Mr. Allen; the professional photographer that served as the catalyst for my DC UFO investigation. That night, Mr. Allen took a series of high-resolution, color photographs of a group of UFOs over his home in Washington, D.C., near the White House. These objects were clearly in violation of prohibited air space.

Mr. Allen was awake that night when he noticed some strange lights in the sky. He decided to take his professional-grade tripod and camera outside to see what would happen. As a result, images of a glowing-blue craft and some white spheres in a triangular formation were captured that night over a period of many minutes. The event potentially indicated an ongoing level of cooperation between the photographer and his alien subject.

About one month earlier, on May 22, 2005, around 10:00 p.m., a glowing, pale-blue UFO was seen circling a group of houses in DC before quickly leaving the restricted airspace of the capital. According to one of the witnesses, "At first we thought that it was a raid light or a government light, but it seemed to be staying over just a few houses."

Earlier that month, on May 2, 2005, around 8:45 p.m., another alien incursion occurred in Washington, D.C. At that time, a neighbor of Mr. Allen witnessed an incredible alien incursion of restricted airspace when a large, V-shaped swarm of UFOs flew swiftly and undeterred over the nation's capital.

When I spoke with the witness on the phone, about 24 hours after the incident, he was still in shock. I found the man to be highly intelligent and very credible. At the time, he was earning his Ph.D. in anthropology at a Catholic university.

On the night of the UFO sighting, he was in his apartment on U Street, N.W. looking out the window when he saw a police helicopter flying at approximately 400 feet over S street. According to the witness, this was a normal sight. However, the helicopter caught his attention because its searchlight was on which usually meant the police were looking for bad guys on the ground.

At that time, the searchlight of the helicopter went directly over what appeared to be a very-large swarm of bees. The witness thought this was very strange, not only to see such a swarm at that altitude, but he realized that these objects must have been a lot larger than bees to see them that distinctly from about an eighth of a mile away and approximately 400 feet up at night!

The witness noted that the police helicopter then flew off as though it did not see anything unusual. That was when he began looking more closely at the strange swarm of objects that was cloud-like, but seemed to have the distinct shape of a very-large triangle. It was about the size of a football field and was much larger than any aircraft.

He estimated that the triangular formation of small, spherical UFOs was easily as large as two city blocks. It also emitted a faint light which could have been city light reflecting off of it, but it seemed to be generating a very-faint light almost like it was shimmering or creating a weird phasing of light; like that of a heat wave coming off of hot asphalt.

The huge swarm of UFOs flew against the wind at a rapid, steady speed. It flew over Logan Circle to Capitol Hill, across the National Mall toward the Lincoln Memorial, and then over the Pentagon within a matter of minutes. The sighting left the witness wondering what the Hell he had just seen flying through the prohibited airspace of DC.

Historically, the official response to that question was:

Temperature Inversion Layers
Weather Balloons
Ball Lightning
Swamp Gas
Lens Flares
Gremlins
Meteors
Birds
Stars

Regardless of what the official explanations were, on April 27, 2005, another incursion of controlled airspace caused quite a commotion in the heart of Washington, D.C. The event illustrated just how serious any violation of American airspace was for the government; especially in DC. News video taken at the White House during the event showed Secret Service agents armed with shotguns running through the area preparing for some sort of ground assault. None of them were looking upwards and watching the sky which made me wonder what the Secret Service really thought the threat was. Afterwards, their spokespeople claimed it was simply clouds and birds.

That explanation was simply ridiculous. Did they really expect people to believe they needed to evacuate the White House every time there were clouds or birds in the sky? The one true official statement regarding the event was that incursions of prohibited/restricted airspace happened very frequently in DC.

According to the *Associated Press*, an over flight of the White House by a possible UFO resulted in security agencies evacuating President George W. Bush from the executive mansion. It seemed highly unlikely that an unidentified blip on a radar screen, allegedly caused by a cloud or a flock of birds, would force security agencies to evacuate President Bush and Vice President Cheney from the White House.

The press reported that the alert had been triggered that morning when government radar around Washington, D.C., registered a return that was mistaken for an airplane flying with no transponder or radio. When first seen on radar, the unidentified object was about 30 miles south of Washington, D.C., flying slowly towards the capital.

The unidentified object simply disappeared after about 10 minutes. The FAA spokesperson said they believed it was not an aircraft, but was probably a cloud or several birds which frequently showed up on radar. A Homeland Security spokesperson reported that military helicopters were on patrol around the capital and quickly determined that an airplane had not flown into restricted airspace.

Despite that fact, armed Secret Service agents surrounded the White House compound. At that time, President Bush was taken from the Oval Office to a bunker underneath the building. He remained in the Presidential Emergency Operations Center for only a very short time. Vice President Dick Cheney was taken to a secure location that was not disclosed. It was later rumored he had gone to the massive underground federal facility at Mount Weather, Virginia.

About one month earlier, on the night of February 23, 2005, another alien incursion occurred in Washington, D.C. At that time, a man and woman were driving south on Interstate 495 when they noticed two distinct, triangular bright lights ahead. They continued driving and passed directly underneath the large UFO. They looked up and saw that there were actually four triangular lights.

The witnesses noted there were sets of lights that were directly opposite each other. On one end of the UFO, there was a small red light, and on the other end was a very-small, blue-green light. The UFO remained stationary during the sighting and was between 1,000 to 1,500 feet in the sky. It was a very-long, very-large, dark craft.

Eleven days earlier, on February 12, 2005, at approximately 3:00 a.m., another alien incursion transpired in Washington, D.C. At that time, a man was driving through the capital. Looking up, he noticed a huge UFO passing overhead. He could immediately see this was not a normal aircraft. He observed the UFO for about a minute. He could see it was a disc-shaped craft that was slowly passing through controlled airspace. He estimated that the alien craft was the size of five commercial jets combined.

Two days earlier, on February 10, a National Parks web cam photo was taken at 3:15 a.m. that showed a very-large, unidentified object flying across the Potomac River near the Pentagon.

A month earlier, in December of 2004, people again reported seeing something strange in the sky above the nation's capital. Pilots, crew members and passengers on a flight from Las Vegas, to Washington, D.C., witnessed flashing green lights hovering in the clouds above Dulles Airport, even though nothing showed up on radar.

That same month, on December 9, 2004, at approximately 3:00 a.m., an alien being was reportedly sighted in Washington, D.C. That night, a security guard was working in the nation's capital when he noticed a strange being that was about seven-and-a-half feet tall. The being appeared to be very thin, was grey to dark black in appearance, with large, glowing eyes, and a larger than normal head.

According to the security guard, the alien's eyes looked as if they were small lights. It had long arms that were folded up across its body as it stood motionless in the shadows of the alley. The alien gave the security guard the impression that while standing still nobody would see it. The creature stayed in the shadows and moved silently as if it were floating. The bewildered security guard was about 40 feet from the alien; watching from inside his car with the lights off. The event ended when the creature turned and suddenly vanished into thin air without a trace as though it had optical stealth technology.

The security guard recalled that the northern capital region had been downgraded to a lesser security alert a few days earlier. The area was well traveled both day and night, and it was a high crime district, but the alien creature could appear as a shadow. Someone could walk right past it at night and not see it unless they knew what they were looking at.

He did not report his close encounter because he was worried people would laugh at him, or call him crazy, or fire him. However, he could never forget the eyes of the alien being and the shadow-like appearance it had so he posted the information on the Internet anonymously.

The previous night, December 8, 2004, another alien incursion took place in Washington, D.C. At that time, a dark, flat, V-shaped UFO was witnessed passing about 20 feet above the tree line. It made no sound at all as it flew across the sky for about four to five seconds over the neighborhood of Friendship Heights, in Washington, D.C.

The previous night, December 7, 2004, another alien incursion occurred in Washington, D.C. At that time, a photojournalist was on the National Mall, standing in the Ellipse, taking pictures of the recently lit Menorah. When the photographer went home, she was surprised to find she had unintentionally captured three images of two blue UFOs ascending in the sky. Coincidently, the Ellipse was where a fictional UFO had landed in the 1951 sci-fi classic movie *The Day The Earth Stood Still*.

Seven days earlier, on the evening of November 30, 2004, another alien incursion occurred in Washington, D.C. At that time, a local resident had just sat down to check her e-mail when she looked out the kitchen window at the moon and noticed a strange, bright star that suddenly began to move away.

The witness was looking toward the Pentagon and Reagan National Airport when the UFO ascended slowly from its original position. It then decreased in size as it moved off and vanished from the sky. Commercial aircraft were on their flight path below this and could be seen flying over the Potomac River.

The witness also reported that this was the second UFO sighting she had experienced at her DC residence in 2004. Earlier that summer, she had seen an identical UFO while looking over the Potomac toward the Pentagon and Reagan National Airport.

Halloween is a scary time of year in America, as it should be, but it sometimes gets a little-extra spooky in Washington, D.C., especially on the National Mall. That night, on October 31, 2004, at approximately 8:00 p.m., three friends, ages 17 to 22, went to the World War II Memorial, located next to the Washington Monument, which marks the center of P56-A (prohibited) airspace.

One of the witnesses recalled that while he and his friends were looking up at the stars, they sighted something that looked like a star moving across the sky at an incredible speed. Moments later, they sighted two or three more star-like objects which quickly joined the first object. The UFOs glowed bright white and were flying circles around one another while changing direction and speeds in ways that were completely impossible for any known aircraft.

The witnesses watched in amazement as the UFOs would hover and then accelerate across the sky in an instant. It was incredible! The UFOs were able to reverse course and fly backwards with no turning radius. They could stop on a dime and fly backwards and loop the loop. The witnesses noted that at one point, the UFOs moved in geometric formations and in a figure-eight type of design.

After a while, the UFOs disappeared behind some very-high clouds. All the UFOs were dim and very far away. According to one of the witnesses, it would have been extremely hard to see the event if a person was not directly watching the sky that night. Later, when speaking with some friends, the witnesses heard there were similar UFO sightings that had occurred over Washington, D.C.

A month earlier, on September 29, 2004, at approximately 2:30 a.m., another alien incursion occurred in Washington, D.C. The event caused some motorists to have a most unusual drive in the nation's capital. That night, one of the witnesses was sitting in his car at a stoplight when he first noticed a very-bright light, about two miles away, near Reagan National Airport.

At first, the witness thought it was a plane coming in for landing. But as he drove closer, he realized the light was stationary. As he drove to the entrance of the airport, he saw a huge, disc-shaped, silver UFO with beams of light directed down toward Andrews Air Force Base which was visible on the other side of the Potomac.

The UFO hovered about 100 feet off the ground for a few moments. It was at a slight tilt, and its lights were only coming from the lower half of the disk. By this time, the astonished witness had slowed his car to a crawl to watch the hovering UFO. It then suddenly jumped to a position above the 14th Street Bridge.

This was done so effortlessly and quickly that he did not actually see it move across the sky. It just somehow reappeared above the 14th Street Bridge. As the witness continued driving through DC, he could see the UFO in his rear view mirror. He also noted there were at least two other cars on the Parkway, and a few more on the bridge, that could have sighted the UFO.

One night earlier, on September 28, 2004, at approximately 1:45 a.m., another alien incursion transpired in Washington, D.C. At that time, a local resident was driving through the capital and witnessed a very-large, round or disc-shaped UFO that had a very-bright, white light surrounding one side with other small flashing lights. The alien craft was estimated to be the size of four commercial jets combined. The UFO was observed hovering over some buildings. The amazed witness followed the UFO in his car for about five miles before it moved out of sight.

The previous month, on August 31, 2004, at 3:39 p.m., another alien incursion occurred in Washington, D.C. That afternoon, two sisters were standing on the balcony of their sixth-floor apartment located in the prohibited airspace of Washington, D.C. According to one of the sisters, it was a perfectly-clear day. The two sisters were looking up in the sky when they saw a large UFO appear out of a cloud.

They looked at it for a second or two and realized that the craft did not have any features that they would normally recognize as a plane. The sisters watched it for a few seconds before it disappeared back into a cloud.

They reported that the diameter of the UFO was slightly larger than a full moon. It had no lights. It was flying in a south-easterly direction and ascending slightly. It made no noise. The object was not shiny and appeared to have a texture. It was a metallic color closer to gold than silver.

The UFO was within the no-fly zone and was off the normal commercial flight paths that the two sisters regularly observed from their residence. They noted that the UFO was flying at an altitude normally used by helicopters, but was traveling at about the speed of a jet. However, the sisters quickly realized it was not a jet. It had no wings or markings other than what appeared to be a dark band about one third of the length from the back end.

Although it was difficult to accurately judge the UFOs size, the sisters could tell it was extremely large. They estimated that the UFO was at least twice the size of a commercial airliner and moved very smoothly and silently. There were no visible lights on the craft.

About two weeks earlier, on July 17, 2004, around 6:00 p.m., another alien incursion occurred in Washington, D.C., While driving south on 13th Street NW, at least one motorist saw an amazing flash of white light silently explode off the ground from the horizon upwards into the air and disappear.

The witness recalled that the event only lasted less than a second, but he was certain he saw something strange in the sky. He had no idea what it was. The size of the flash was quite narrow and was approximately 10 miles away from where the witness was driving. It appeared to be another example of alien, space-warping technology being observed in the area.

That same month, in July of 2004, a UFO political action group was busy lobbying in Washington, D.C. At that time, copies of The *Sci-Fi Channel's* UFO documentary *Out of the Blue* were hand delivered to 435 members of Congress. The goal was to inform U.S. leaders about the national security implications of the UFO phenomenon.

This political lobbying was part of the "Advocacy Initiative" which was a privately-funded effort to release classified documents through the Freedom of Information Act. The group was urging the government to disclose what it knew about UFOs. The effort was spearheaded by the *Sci-Fi Channel* and President Clinton's former Chief of Staff, John Podesta.

Two months earlier, in May of 2004, another alien incursion took place in Washington, D.C. Early that morning, a federal employee was walking to work from the Smithsonian Metro. He approached a crosswalk and stopped to wait for the light to change. While looking up in the cloudy grey sky, he noticed some bright-white lights that were motionless in the distance. At first, he thought it was an elevated bank of lights similar to those found at a ball park or a construction site. Then, he thought it was a plane because the area was not far from Reagan National Airport, but the unidentified lights remained motionless.

He could not get a closer look because he was stuck at the intersection. At that time, the UFO started to move away and drifted slowly behind the trees. He knew a plane could not hover like that. Helicopters hover and then move. This was clearly no helicopter, and it had multiple, bright-white lights. The UFO was last sighted over Maine Avenue, not far from the Pentagon, near a bridge over the Potomac River.

That same month, on May 21, 2004, around 10:30 p.m., another alien incursion occurred in Washington, D.C. That night, a local resident was watching television in bed when a thunder storm moved into the neighborhood. Suddenly, there were two strong bursts of static on the television about a minute apart.

The witness had just climbed into bed and was looking out the large windows in her bedroom. That was when she noticed some strange lights moving in the sky. The witness then got out of bed and looked out a window that faced Rock Creek Park. At that time, she saw four individual balls of light that were moving rapidly in a circular, counterclockwise pattern.

The witness was shocked at first, but quickly went next door to get her roommate. Together the two women stood at the window and watched the bizarre light show for approximately 10 minutes. Towards the end of the sighting, the strange balls of light seemed to simply fade away through the heavy cloud cover until there was only one UFO left. That single ball of light eventually faded as well.

The women noted that the cloud cover was heavy and that the balls of light appeared to be circling one particular cloud. The lightning was intense that night and lit up the entire sky several times as the women watched the UFOs.

The previous month, on April 15, 2004, at 4:44 p.m., another alien incursion took place in the Washington, D.C., area. That afternoon, a businessman flying out of DC was observing air traffic out his window when he suddenly noticed elevated contrail activity.

At that time, while searching the sky, he spotted a strange, bright light. The businessman then realized that the brightly glowing UFO was flying at an altitude of approximately 50,000 to 60,000 feet. He noted that it was either stationary or was moving very slowly.

He recalled that the UFO was a bright-bluish orb that seemed reflective but was much brighter than the surrounding sky. The businessman was able to take one picture, but chose not to make it available to the public. The same type of object was photographed landing on the roof of the US Capitol a couple of years earlier.

The previous month, on March 13, 2004, just before dusk, another alien incursion occurred in Washington D.C. At that time, a married couple witnessed a UFO while driving their car in DC. The wife saw the UFO for approximately eight seconds. She estimated the disc-shaped craft was about three city blocks in diameter, and it flew at a very-low altitude. She also noted that there were many flashing lights of different colors on the underside of the strange craft.

That same month, March of 2004, another alien incursion transpired in Washington, D.C. At that time, a local resident was driving on Interstate 95 when he witnessed a metallic, shiny, oval-shaped UFO in the sky. The craft was only visible for about six seconds before it disappeared into a cloud.

That same month, in March of 2004, another alien incursion took place at night in Washington, D.C. At that time, a husband and wife were sitting outside on their patio. Suddenly, their attention was drawn to look upward at approximately 20 dim lights that were about the size of large stars. However, these lights could not have been stars because they were moving slowly across the night sky.

The wife realized that these were separate objects and noted that, from time to time, several of the UFOs would quickly fly away from the formation of other UFOs and dart sideways and forward. However, the formation of UFOs generally moved together as a large cluster. The astonished husband and wife watched the UFOs passing over DC for about a minute before they silently flew out of sight.

About three months earlier, on December 13, 2003, around 2:00 a.m., another oval-shaped UFO was sighted over the Pentagon for about six seconds. The UFO was traveling fast and low. According to one witness, "It started as a yellow-white, thick circle with a faded sort of bluish aura/haze, traveling above Interstate 66. The UFO was not too high and not too low. It flew extremely fast and changed shapes from a circle to an oval and changed to a white color. Then, it sort of zigzagged and then jumped as if penetrating into the sky as each end of the oval crossed into one another and disappeared."

About one month earlier, on November 30, 2003, around 4:00 p.m., another UFO was sighted by local residents over Washington, D.C. The UFO was very bright and was stationary at times before moving out of the area. According to one witness, the light from the UFO grew smaller as it moved away over a 10 second period until it vanished.

Ten days earlier, on November 20 of 2003, *FOX News* reported that Air Force fighter jets were once again scrambled and that the White House was briefly evacuated after "birds" or possibly "disturbances in the atmosphere" tripped radar that monitored the restricted and prohibited airspace around Washington, D.C.

Federal Aviation Administration spokesman, William Shumann, said, "It's a false radar target. When NORAD (North American Aerospace Defense) fighters got to the location of the alleged violation, they found nothing."

Shumann explained how, "Flocks of birds or atmospheric disturbances might have caused the false radar reading, which was initially thought to be a small plane flying within five miles of restricted airspace around the White House. It's one of those electronic gremlins that pop-up, but there was no aircraft there."

About four months earlier, on July 22, 2003, just before 9:30 p.m., another alien incursion occurred in Washington, D.C. That night, a local resident had just turned off the lights in their apartment. The witness then looked out a window and was startled to see what appeared to be a large passenger jet flying low over the apartment building! However, this was prohibited airspace in the middle of Washington, D.C. The witness knew that passenger jets never flew over the building, so he raced to the window and pulled out the screen to take a closer look.

At that time, he sighted a UFO that was shaped like a giant boomerang. It had several flashing lights around its edge and was flying low, slow, and silently toward the west. When the UFO reached the Potomac River, it turned south and continued on its way until it was out of sight.

A month and a half earlier, on June 1, 2003, at 10:34 p.m., local residents witnessed two UFOs over the Pentagon. According to one witness, "There were two dimly-glowing, cigar-shaped, UFOs that travelled parallel with each other. Then, one UFO shot up into the sky. They seemed to be stable at first, and then the object on top seemed to shoot up into the sky very rapidly while the object below travelled in a straight line until they both disappeared. However, they were visible for about 15 seconds."

About three months earlier, on March 8, 2003, around 8:15 p.m., another alien incursion took place in Washington, D.C. That night, a husband and wife witnessed a strange, V-shaped UFO passing almost directly overhead. The married couple noted that the UFO was totally silent. They reported that the alien craft had a bright, continuously-white, round light on the tip of each end.

The white spherical lights had a very sharp edge and were quite different from the lights on ordinary aircraft and were of a much purer-white color. A much-smaller, pure-red light was located in the middle of the UFO. The red light would grow brighter then dimmer. The body of the spacecraft was quite strange. Although its silhouette was visible by the back lighting in the cloud, it was rather vague because there was a subtle light around it that seemed to vibrate or flicker around the edges.

According to the husband, "It was flying very low and was neither climbing nor descending. The most striking thing of all was the absolute silence! As it passed over us and left the area, there was a bizarre silence, stillness, and smoothness that is hard to put into words.

"Later, at 10:46 p.m., I heard a roar in the sky that vaguely resembled a loud jet, but was distinctly different somehow. Then, after a maybe four-to-five second duration, that roar suddenly subsided. I rushed downstairs and onto the front porch where I was surprised to see an identical

UFO on exactly the same course! As with the earlier UFO, I watched it pass almost directly overhead as it moved in an eerie silence across the sky to the same spot on the horizon where the first UFO had headed and disappeared.

"During our first observation, the sky above the UFO was overcast, but during the second sighting it was totally clear with stars and planets visible. However, I could see no body on the object; just the wing. This time, the wing of the UFO seemed to shimmer in a light-distorting way that made it much-less clear and no sound was heard!

"I found that really a bit spooky because both UFOs were clearly moving under their own power, steadily, along precisely the same course. It was as if both had traveled upon the very same invisible track in the sky! I suspect these UFOs are some type of stealthy, black-project aircraft that is somehow propelled silently. But I question the wisdom of operating such a vehicle over a highly populated area within the prohibited airspace of Washington, D.C."

About two months earlier, on the night of January 27, 2003, another alien incursion occurred over Washington, D.C. At that time, while looking out their bedroom window, a local resident saw a strange, flashing UFO that was hovering about five miles high in the sky. The witness noted that the UFO flashed and changed color frequently sometimes making jerking erratic moves. Occasionally, brief, smaller flashes of light popped up around it. The flashes of light from the body of the UFO were white and sometimes yellow.

It's important to note that during the 15 months following the aerial terrorist attacks on 9/11, military forces had responded to more than 600 incursions of the restricted and prohibited airspace around the heart of DC. However, only a few of those violations involved small aircraft flying off course.

For example, on December 17, 2002, *ABC News* reported that two fighter jets had been scrambled, to intercept a small plane over the nation's capital. The plane had flown into restricted airspace over Washington, D.C., but officials determined it posed no threat and called off the intercept.

Yet, on December 16, 2002, *CNN* had reported that Air Force F-16 fighters were sent to intercept an unidentified target at 10:30 a.m., after radar detected a potential violation of the 15 mile prohibited flight zone around the nation's capital (P56-A). Officials speculated that either a flock of birds or an anomaly caused by high winds resulted in the radar reading which indicated a possible violation of restricted airspace 18 miles north-west of Reagan National Airport.

We know that F-16s were sent to intercept any intruders and maintain a combat air patrol over Washington, D.C., for at least one hour that night, and air traffic was briefly halted at that time. The U.S. military allegedly found nothing (again); however, an eye-witness account by a local resident dispelled the theory that all the unidentified radar returns were simply birds or clouds or high winds, or electronic gremlins.

The witness reported that at around 10:50 a.m., on December 16, 2002, a UFO was sighted over the northeast corner of Washington, D.C. That morning, she heard two fighter jets passing overhead which caused her to look up in the clear blue sky. The witness had lived on Air Force bases for many years and was familiar with the sounds of jet engines. She thought the military jets were escorting someone out of the restricted airspace.

But when she looked up, she witnessed a UFO that was visually about the size of the full moon. The UFO flew very fast and had a bouncing motion. It was much larger than any airplane. It flew in from the north at a speed comparable to that of a fast fighter jet. According to the witness, the UFO sighting only lasted about five seconds. She estimated the UFO was about three miles from her position near the Lincoln Memorial (P56-A). It flew slightly higher than a helicopter, was oval shaped, made no sound and left no exhaust.

Its bouncing flight pattern reminded her of the pulse reading on a heart monitor. She noted that the UFO was made of a silvery metal that reflected the sunlight. The bottom half of the UFO was darker due to its own shadow. As it left the area, it traveled low in the sky over a rooftop. The witness reported that if the military jets were looking for the UFO, they had just missed it.

I doubt the military did not see the UFO. Keep in mind, the above alien incursion occurred exactly six months after UFOs were photographed landing on Capitol Hill and NORAD scrambled jets to intercept ten days later. The military was well aware of and probably very frustrated by the ongoing UFO activity in the controlled airspace of the capital area.

Eight days earlier, on December 8, 2002, at approximately 5:00 p.m., another alien incursion took place in Washington, D.C. At that time, a disk-shaped UFO was seen violating restricted airspace. The witness was so scared by their experience they chose not to make a complete statement. It made me wonder how many other people had sighted UFOs in DC but were simply too frightened to report it.

The previous month, on the night of November 19, 2002, another alien incursion took place in Washington, D.C. At that time, a family was outside observing the Leonid meteor shower in the clear, dark sky. According to the father, his family witnessed three orange, triangular lights fly overhead in a very-tight formation. At first, the family considered that these were just F-16s that were on patrol over Washington, D.C. But they quickly realized there was no engine sound as was typical from F-16 over flights.

Suddenly, the orange lights merged and then spread apart. The left lead light flew off at almost a 90-degree angle before the other orange lights zipped quickly to the western horizon and were obscured by the full moon.

Eight days earlier, on the night of November 11, 2002, another alien incursion was captured on film in Washington, D.C. At that time, professional DC photographer Wilbur Allen inadvertently took an amazing nighttime photograph of a very-unusual UFO. It was a small, metallic sphere about the size of a large gum ball that defied gravity. It silently floated over the head of a beautiful, blonde model for a moment before swiftly flying off.

The previous month, on October 25, 2002, *WIRED* magazine reported that a group of Washington, D.C., insiders were involved in an effort to officially disclose the existence of UFOs. A former Capitol Hill staffer had reportedly called on the government to release secret evidence from UFO crash sites.

According to the article, the *Coalition for Freedom of Information* was funded by the *SciFi Channel* and directed by Washington, D.C., lobbyist Edwin Rothschild. The group hoped to acquire government documents and crashed UFO debris for scientific analysis.

Rothschild said neither he nor former Clinton Chief of Staff, John

Podesta, had heard any new rumors about UFOs from the Oval Office or Capitol Hill. Apparently Rothschild and Podesta were unaware of the fact that UFOs had been photographed landing on Capitol Hill a few months earlier, in July of 2002.

According to Rothschild, people and pilots around the world had seen things that shouldn't be there. He wanted to encourage a sustained, scientific study of UFO materials. He claimed that some people in the government wouldn't listen unless a lawsuit was filed against them. Rothschild also said that hard-core skeptics, especially in the media, were killing the UFO debate. He felt that he and Podesta, and others in DC, were working against a big ridicule factor that was blocking disclosure.

About one month earlier, on September 8, 2002, at approximately 8:00 p.m., another alien incursion occurred in Washington, D.C. That night, a local resident witnessed a thin, metallic, rectangular UFO that floated silently across the skyline above the Potomac River and the Key Bridge. The UFO was visible for 30 minutes. It glowed red, white, and green and tilted rhythmically while moving horizontally.

During that same month of September 2002, around 9:00 p.m., another alien incursion transpired in Washington, D.C. That night, five friends were visiting the Capitol building. One of the individuals walked over to some Capitol Police officers and asked if she could take a picture. Later, when she and her friends returned home and viewed the photos in a computer, they noticed a glowing-white, disc-shaped UFO hovering over the Capitol.

According to the photographer's husband, who is a minister, "As we were viewing the photos, we noticed this round, saucer-like object right above the Capitol. As we zoomed in, there was no mistake about it, it was a UFO. The photo is unbelievable! I am reluctant to send it to anyone. It may be worth some money since the UFO was right above the Capitol."

Unfortunately, that photo has not been published yet.

The previous month on August 20, 2002, between 12:30 and 1:30 p.m., an unmarked black helicopter was sighted over Washington, D.C. According to one witness, "While out at lunch today, my date and I saw a very-shiny, black, Huey (UH-1D) helicopter hovering above the buildings between K Street N.W. and Dupont Circle, and then between 17th and

20th Streets N.W., about three miles north of the White House.

"I first saw it when I was walking to lunch. Then, my date and I saw it hovering near Dupont Circle. It was lacquer black and had no markings. It was a Huey similar to the Vietnam-era, Air Cavalry transports. The doors were shut, and there didn't seem to be anything different about it except that there was no Federal Aviation Administration, or military, or police identification."

Four days earlier, on August 16, 2002, at approximately 2:00 p.m., another alien incursion transpired in Washington, D.C. At that time, a young tourist was standing in a field by the Washington Monument taking photographs when he accidentally captured two images of a UFO. He estimated that the disc-shaped craft was 10 to 50 feet wide and 8 to 20 feet tall.

According to the photographer, "It was in the early to mid afternoon on a very-windy day that these pictures were taken. The photographs were meant to be of the Washington Monument, but after being developed, you can clearly make out the UFO. On the first picture, you can see a helicopter flying far below the UFO, so it gives you an idea of how high up this thing might have been. I would say it was between the upper troposphere and the lower stratosphere. In the second picture it seems that the UFO is much lower, although it is harder to judge the height.

"It is too high to be a kite or bird in the first picture, and too low to be a plane in the second picture. It is not a blimp or an airplane, and it is too elongated to be a weather balloon. As I see it, there is no reasonable explanation."

It is important to note that these images were captured exactly one month after UFOs were photographed landing on Capitol Hill.

The previous month, on July 31, 2002, between 4:45 and 5:00 p.m., another alien incursion took place in Washington, D.C. That afternoon, a local resident was walking across the bridge to Roosevelt Island when she saw a red UFO hovering in the sky over DC. The UFO appeared to be stationary or moving very slowly at 1,000 to 2,000 feet elevation.

The UFO was visible to the witness for approximately five to six seconds. The UFO was initially solid and blocky in appearance, but in the final seconds of the sighting it turned on end and reflected the sunlight like a shield. The UFO then seemed to change shape as it shimmered like a flag in the breeze and then disappeared from view. It was most likely another example of optical-stealth technology.

One day earlier, on July 30, 2002, another alien incursion took place over Washington, D.C. At that time, a pilot working for a large airline company witnessed a UFO being chased by some military jets. However, nothing was reported on the news.

Four days earlier, on July 26, 2002, at approximately 1:00 a.m., another incredible alien incursion took place in the nation's capital. That night, UFOs once again violated the restricted/prohibited airspace of Washington, D.C., putting the military on high alert.

Two fighter jets were scrambled to intercept a UFO that had appeared on the radar screens monitoring restricted air space. A witness on the ground saw the jets chase a "blue light" that flew off so fast it simply disappeared. At the same time, it also disappeared from radar.

The F-16's were seen and heard being dispatched from Andrews Air Force Base. Local residents reported seeing a bright-blue UFO in the sky being chased by the military jets. Other witnesses called in to a local radio station, confirming that Andrews Air Force Base had scrambled some jets and that NORAD was investigating. However, this time the UFO was glowing orange.

One of the eye witnesses to the enigmatic events that evening was a 30-year resident of southern Maryland named Gary Dillman. He was a retired policeman with the Washington, D.C., Police Department who had 15-years experience as a private investigator. He was working security at a large sand-and-gravel operation the night of the UFO incursion and attempted military intercept.

He had worked security at that site for the past five years and was very familiar with Air Force activity in the area. That night, Dillman was stationed in Brandywine, Maryland, which is about 10 miles southeast of Andrews Air Force Base.

Around 1:00 a.m., while sitting in his truck with the driver's window partially down, Dillman heard fighter jets being scrambled from the general direction of Andrews Air Force Base. He could tell they were flying very fast on a southeast course fairly low in the sky.

Dillman noted that some of the jets used their after burners. He then witnessed three of four jets that would disappear in the east and then reappear and circle the Washington, D.C., area, before flying southeast again.

From 1:00 a.m., to about 1:30 a.m., the military jets kept returning

Dillman could see that some of the jets were making very-tight, banked turns and were flying in circles. One jet was observed banking hard to the right, then hard to the left and then back to the right again as though it was closely following something.

From 1:00 a.m., to about 1:30 a.m., the military jets kept returning to the area of Andrew's Air Force base, but did not land. These jets were not flying in formation, but were banking left and right and flying in a circle several times as if chasing or looking for something.

Dillman decided to call a local radio station in Washington, D.C., to alert them that something unusual was happening. After making the phone call, Dillman was standing outside his truck and observing the jets when he suddenly saw an unidentified, orange ball of light appear in the sky.

As the UFO came out of the sky toward the earth, Dillman thought it was a meteor. However, as it descended, it appeared somewhat brighter and larger than a meteor. When a fighter jet made a deliberate banked turn toward the UFO, it suddenly changed course and flew off.

Ten minutes later, the jets were still flying in the area and the orange UFO appeared again about 15 miles from Dillman's vantage point. He could see that the UFO was being followed closely by a jet. He watched in amazement as the jet and the UFO both flew south for a moment and then banked into the southeast again until disappearing in the clouds.

Dillman called the radio station again and reported what he had just seen. He described the UFO as being perfectly spherical. From his perspective, it visually appeared slightly smaller than a golf ball held at arm's length, and it made no noise.

The next day, *FOX News* correspondent Shepard Smith reported that, "On July 26, the nighttime skies over the nation's capital came alive with blue and orange lights streaking across the sky. So say a lot of panicked people who called in to a local radio station. No joke here. American fighter jets were in hot pursuit.

"NORAD confirmed to *FOX News* that two F-16's did scramble, but found nothing! A mystery in the sky above Andrews Air Force Base;

that's the one the President uses."

FOX's DC correspondent Brian Wilson continued the story. "It's fair to say Shepard that there are a lot more questions than answers at this point, but something strange was going on in the Maryland night sky last night.

"Here is what we know. At 1:00 a.m., the folks at NORAD saw something they couldn't identify in Maryland airspace, not far from the restricted airspace of the nation's capital.

"The track the UFO was taking caused them some concern, so they scrambled two DC Air National Guard jets to check things out. They confirmed that two F-16s from the 113th Wing were vectored to intercept whatever it was that NORAD was worried about.

"However, when the pilots got where they were supposed to be, they said they didn't see anything. NORAD would not provide details about the exact location, direction or speed of the object they were tracking [but allegedly did not see].

"Independently, a number of folks who live in Waldorf, Maryland, which is not far from Andrews Air Force Base, and not far from the nation's capital, called local radio station WTOP to say that about the same time, they witnessed a fast-moving, bright-blue light in the sky.

"They claimed that the unidentified light was being chased by military jets. One witness told the radio station that the jets were right on its tail, 'As the thing would move, a jet was right behind it.'

"An investigation is underway, but National Guard spokesman, Captain Sheldon Smith said, 'We don't have any information about funny lights.' By the way, this just happens to be the 50th anniversary of a series of still unexplained UFO sightings over the nation's capital, a story that made banner headline news in 1952."

Unfortunately, NORAD and the National Guard lied about not seeing the UFOs that they were chasing that night. They did this because the current, official, U.S. government policy regarding UFOs prevents any federal or state agencies from telling the public the truth.

Meanwhile, that same night, around 1:15 a.m., a father and son who live near the Pentagon had gone outside to get their cat off a ledge on the second-floor window. They were both looking up at the side of the house, wondering how to get their cat down, when two spherical, white

UFOs flew overhead. They estimated the UFOs were visually about the size of a baseball held at arm's length. The UFOs were visible for about two minutes before moving away, but they soon came back.

This time, both UFOs flew very close to the witnesses. That's when the father and son realized the spherical UFOs were actually rather small. Both UFOs stopped for a moment, and then one of them flew away at a right angle to its previous flight path. The other UFO remained motionless for approximately five seconds before continuing, more or less, in its original direction. These were two separate UFOs that were flying in tandem at first and then separately. They were clearly under intelligent control and were silent.

Six days earlier, on the night of July 20, 2002, another alien incursion occurred in Washington, D.C. At that time, a local resident witnessed a UFO shooting across the sky. According to the witnesses, it looked almost like a green flare, but strangely different. It was the second time in the past few months the DC resident had seen that type of UFO flying over his neighborhood. As stated in the next report, these same green spheres were photographed at the Capitol.

Four days earlier, on July 16, 2002, between 12:30 p.m., and 1:00 a.m., an unprecedented alien incursion of prohibited airspace occurred over Washington, D.C. It was a Tuesday night when professional DC photographer Wilbur Allen went to shoot an album cover for a local recording artist, and his manager, using the Reflecting Pool and Capitol building as a background. Based on the images that were taken, there were no other people seen on the Capitol grounds at that time. However, in the first two photographs, there were at least a dozen UFOs that had penetrated the prohibited air space at that location. A few of these vehicles landed for a brief period. One of them actually landed on the roof of the Capitol! As that was occurring, one of the other UFOs entered the Reflecting Pool and submerged itself while another UFO hovered nearby over the water emitting an eerie looking energy field that reflected light beneath it.

That night, all of Mr. Allen's photos were captured with a *Nikon* F-100 camera which was equipped with a distortion-free, *Nikor*, ED, 200mm, F 2.8 lens mounted on a professional tripod. The exposure time was 1/15th of a second on high-speed film: ISO 800. However, the ISO meter on the camera was set at 1280 to slightly overexpose the film and increase the overall density of the image.

After taking a series of pictures in front of the Capitol building, the recording artist and his manager left the area. Mr. Allen then moved his professional camera equipment nearby to the edge of the Capitol building's Lower Senate Park. He estimated that 20 minutes elapsed before taking that final shot of the evening, which meant the time was approximately 1:00 a.m.

That image had an exposure time of three-and-a-half minutes. Incredible as it seems, in that image, hovering in the sky over the Carpenters Union building is a very odd-looking formation of four UFOs. And in the distance, a large swarm of tiny spheres were grouped together in a triangular formation.

Near the ground, there were two emerald-green UFOs. However, floating in the air in front of Mr. Allen were two oval-shaped, semi-transparent spheres of energy that he believed were UFOs equipped with some type of advanced, optical-stealth device.

As if that wasn't strange enough, the formation of four UFOs over the Carpenters Union building emitted a powerful energy pattern. The highly-complex signature of their energy fields was captured on the film due to the long exposure time and their close proximity to the camera. The image indicated that just prior to leaving the area, the UFOs managed to create a "Star Gate" or "worm hole" in the sky over Capitol Hill.

Unfortunately, that final photograph came at a price. Mr. Allen's fingers, and the top of his head, were slightly burned by the radiation from the UFOs and took about a year-and-a-half to heal. His neighbor is a cellular biologist who had witnessed the burns on Mr. Allen's hands. She later confirmed to me that his fingers were indeed burned by some type of intense energy.

Mr. Allen told me he was unintentionally positioned underneath the UFOs that night. According to the time-elapsed photograph, the formation of UFOs had literally warped space in the sky above him. Upon further analysis of the image, it was clear that the group of four UFOs had somehow moved both up and sideways at the same time before entering the "Star Gate."

At that moment, Mr. Allen had been caught in the thrust of the UFOs warp drive. He said it felt as though he had been hit by a strong breeze with a fine mist, but there wasn't any moisture. Soon after that, he noticed there were very-fine, pinhole-sized burns in his fingernails, and his arms felt like they were charged with some kind of energy.

But there was more to this bizarre story. Just 12 days earlier, on July 4, 2002, Mr. Allen had been on a commercial assignment for the city of Washington, D.C. That night, he was taking high-resolution, color-slide photographs of the city skyline and fireworks near the Washington Monument. Only later, when he developed the film, did he notice the UFOs. Mr. Allen was using a *Nikon* F5S camera with a distortion-free, *Nikor*, AF-ED, 600mm lens mounted on a professional tripod. He was using *Fujichrome* tungsten film with a 160 ISO rating. However, the meter on the camera was set at 1280 ISO to slightly overexpose the film and increase the overall density of the image.

That event marked the beginning of Mr. Allen's strange series of UFO photos sessions in DC. He had no idea that during a New Year's Eve celebration in DC two-and-a-half years earlier, at the same location, many other people had witnessed the same type of fireworks and UFO activity on the National Mall which is P56-A prohibited airspace.

The previous month, on June 6, 2002, at 7:00 p.m., a yellow-glowing, spinning UFO was seen outside a White House window, behind President Bush's head, during a televised speech.

Five months earlier, on January 7, 2002, around 5:45 p.m., near the Pentagon, a bright-green light was seen through cloud cover which lasted only a second or two with no sound or sonic boom. According to one witness, "It looked as though it was a meteor entering the atmosphere, but it was made no noise and was seen through the clouds. It was heading south on a parallel flight path to Reagan National airport. It disappeared over the horizon.

About one month earlier, on December 14, 2001, at approximately 11:30 p.m., another alien incursion occurred in Washington, D.C. That night, some local residents were watching a meteor shower when they sighted two illuminated UFOs that changed directions in flight. The brighter of the two UFOs was actually three lights in a triangular formation.

The smaller UFO followed the triangular formation of UFOs back and forth across the sky. The UFOs moved together slowly across the sky at an altitude of 5,000 to 10,000 feet. After a few minutes, the triangular formation of UFOs vanished, and the other UFO turned in the opposite direction and flew off towards the horizon.

One month earlier, in November of 2001, another alien incursion occurred in DC. That night, something strange in the sky was inadvertently televised by the *BBC* during their coverage of the U.S. presidential elections. The *BBC* had switched to a Washington, D.C., studio for a live interview with their election correspondent.

A viewer later commented that while conducting an interview, the *BBC* correspondent was seated in front of a window through which a backdrop of night-time Washington, D.C., was clearly visible. At that time, a UFO slowly drifted in from the top left corner of the window and hovered for the rest of the interview. The object was disc-shaped with a soft blue glow. Oddly enough, that was the same color as the UFO that would be photographed landing on the Capitol building in the summer of 2002.

About two months earlier, on September 11, 2001, another possible close encounter took place in Washington, D.C. While reviewing a video taken at the Pentagon during the attack on 9/11, a UFO researcher noticed that, "A small, mini helicopter flew by and a guy pointed at it. Then, a few seconds later, you can see a pair of small orbs passing each other in perfect synchronization. The motion is perfect. The small UFOs circle the area two times about three or four feet off the ground. This little movie shows how our technology compares to whomever or whatever they are."

As incredible as it seemed, about two weeks after the terrorist attacks on 9/11, around 11:00 a.m., another alien incursion occurred in Washington, D.C. One of the witnesses reported that she and her friend sighted a fast-moving UFO that moved in a low, straight trajectory. At the time, on a sunny day, with a clear sky, the witnesses were standing on 16th street looking south toward the White House.

The UFO was first seen passing just above the building tops as though it was landing. It looked like a silver-white, opaque, sphere. It was visually a little larger than a tennis ball held at arm's length. The witnesses lived in the area and had heard of other sightings in DC, but chose not to elaborate.

About two months earlier, on July 23, 2001, around 6:20 p.m., another close encounter occurred in Washington, D.C. According to a DC resident, "This is no joke. This evening, *Delta* flight 434, and a couple of other aircraft, reported to Washington Center that they sighted a large, flaming, falling object. The first report stated that an object that looked like a large ball of flame was noted passing by the aircraft at their 10 o'clock position. After the unidentified object passed by, one pilot reported there was a large, visible contrail along the UFOs downward path."

About two months earlier, on the evening of May 12, 2001, another alien incursion occurred in Washington, D.C. At that time, UFOs were sighted by people in their cars. One of the witnesses reported that while driving with a friend, she looked up at the sky and saw an orange light approaching but thought it was an airplane. As the light grew closer, she thought it had to be a helicopter but realized it was just too big and low, and there was something moving inside the orange-glowing UFO.

The closer she looked at it, the more she realized it wasn't normal. The UFO was shaped like a cigar, and there was something inside moving side to side very rapidly. She noticed there was an orange glow around the UFO, but not under or on top of it. She was amazed how close the UFO felt and how fast it was moving without making any noise. She could not comprehend how it just suddenly moved from one point to the other in fractions of seconds and then disappeared.

The previous day, on May 11, 2001, at approximately 2:55 p.m., another alien incursion took place in Washington, D.C. At that time, three local residents witnessed a large, round, metallic, silver-colored UFO passing slowly over the area in an easterly direction until it became hard to see. Coincidentally, this was the same day that the UFO *Disclosure Project* was occurring in DC.

The previous day, on May 10, 2001, the *BBC's* Washington, D.C., correspondent Rob Watson had reported on the efforts for official disclosure on the issue of UFOs and ETs. Regarding the goal of the *Disclosure Project* attempting to get open hearings on Capitol Hill, Watson prophetically ended his article by stating that, "Despite the impressive military credentials and undoubted sincerity of the witnesses, Congress is unlikely to move on their request for an open hearing unless a space ship landed on or at least within sight of Capitol Hill."

Oddly enough, 14 months later, UFOs would be photographed landing on Capitol Hill as suggested. Yet, the Congress and the media would remain silent on the subject. I wrote to Mr. Watson in the summer of 2005 and cautioned that one really must be careful what they wish for; they might just get it. He did not reply.

Two months earlier, on March 14, 2001, at approximately 2:10 a.m., another alien incursion transpired eight miles west of the Washington Monument in prohibited airspace. At that time, a government agent observed two incredibly-fast, dimly-lit UFOs moving across the sky under 1,000 feet. The witness noted that each UFO had at least 15 white lights.

Although the UFOs moved together most of the time, the UFO on one side would suddenly change its altitude 100 feet without any sign of acceleration. It would then jump back and follow the general flight path of the other UFO. Both UFOs appeared to move effortlessly and silently. However, the witness noted that when the UFOs were almost directly overhead he heard a slight "whooshing noise."

Nine months earlier, on November 19, 2000, around 10:00 p.m., another alien incursion occurred near the Pentagon. At that time, local residents observed a UFO flying across a commercial flight path to the Reagan National Airport, in Washington, D.C. That night, the witnesses looked up and observed blinking lights that were unlike any aircraft they had ever seen. As the UFOs flew silently across the sky, they alternated from white to red then white again.

The strange lights then changed position and formed a well-defined, circular pattern. The witnesses noted that the formation of UFOs seemed to move in a pattern of front and back and then side to side while moving forward almost as if they were silently floating rather than flying.

The lead witness then pointed out this unusual sight to their daughter and her friend who were both honor students at George Washington University, the same school where the lead witness worked.

All the witnesses watched in amazement as the UFOs flew towards them and then passed over their house. The alien craft continued to move through the sky with a very-exacting movement and blinking light pattern when suddenly, they were met by another UFO. Moments later, all of the UFOs disappeared.

What puzzled the lead witness most about the sighting was how alien craft like that could fly over a heavily-populated area, across a commercial flight path in controlled airspace, and then continue toward the direction of the Pentagon. The witness believed that pilots and or radar operators would have had to pick something like that up. In spite of this, no military action was taken and nothing was reported on the local news.

About two months earlier, on September 29, 2000, during the daytime, another alien incursion was witnessed in Washington, D.C. At that time, a local resident was lying on the grass at the National Mall, across the street from the Washington Monument, facing the Capitol building. The witness was staring up at the clear-blue sky when he noticed what appeared to be an airplane. However, he soon realized it was, in fact, a metallic UFO that was reflecting sun light. It was flying extremely high in a straight line and looked like a little ball.

The witness then noticed another UFO, the same size and appearance, which was flying towards the first object. At one point, he thought they were going to have a head-on collision, but just as they were going to hit, they very quickly spun off in opposite directions. The UFOs then flew around each other in circles occasionally disappearing and then reappearing.

The witness also noted that when an airplane passed through the area flying at a lower altitude, the UFOs suddenly disappeared. About a minute later, after the plane had left the area, one of the UFOs reappeared and began to fly around and then another UFO appeared.

Ten days earlier, on September 19, 2000, a disc-shaped object with revolving red and white lights was sighted hovering for 10 minutes over the Pentagon.

One of the reports I found of close encounters with aliens in DC was so strange that I initially decided not to include it. However, after considering the bizarre nature of my investigation, I changed my mind. The following, dramatic close encounter on Capitol Hill allegedly occurred sometime in the year 2000. While sitting in a park near the U.S. Capitol, a DC resident witnessed a man in an expensive, three-piece suit walk by. The next day, the witness saw the same man in the same suit walk by again. Then, the day after that, the witness saw the same man wearing the suit walk by again, so the witness decided to follow him.

At that time, the witness followed the man in the suit into a public bathroom about two miles from Capitol Hill. The witness noticed that right after the man in the suit had entered a stall the most awful, pungent odor filled the air. Curious, the witness quickly went to the stall next to the man in the suit and peeked (a very strange thing to do).

That was when the witness realized that the man in the suit wasn't really going to the bathroom. He (It) was actually an alien taking off its human costume. The witness was shocked when he saw that the man in the suit was really a tall, grey humanoid alien. When the alien suddenly noticed that someone was watching, the witness ran out of the bathroom with the alien in a human suit chasing after him.

The witness then ran to the nearest police station and told them what he had just seen, but they accused him of being hysterical and hallucinating. When the witness walked out of the police station, the grey alien in his human disguise looked straight at him and reportedly said, "Nothing you do will ever make them believe [I exist] and there is nothing you can do to stop us from the invasion of your planet."

The witness then passed out and woke up in a hospital two-and-a-half hours later with the same alien in a human suit sitting in a chair next to his bed staring at him. When the witness asked the alien why it was acting like a Congressman, it said, "So I can have control of your government."

When the witness asked the alien where it was from, it took out a piece of paper and drew some star maps that were way beyond the witnesses' comprehension. Unfortunately, he didn't save those pieces of paper (not that this would constitute proof).

The next evening, the witness was at his home trying to understand what had happened when he heard a knock at the door. After he opened the door, two men dressed in black suits asked him his name. Just as he began to tell them, he was hit across the head and blacked out. He then woke up in an insane asylum. A doctor came into his room and told him that everything he had seen the past few days was a delusion and that he had been declared legally insane.

He was allegedly held against his will in that facility the next four years before being released. Soon after, he left the United States. He said that he had reported his experience to alert the public that the governments of the world knew about the aliens. He claimed that the U.S. government had a treaty with at least one group of ETs that could not be trusted.

That same year, on March 25, 2000, at approximately 3:30 a.m., another alien incursion took place in Washington, D.C. That afternoon, a local resident was standing in their backyard with a friend when they heard what sounded like a low humming coming from the sky. When they looked up toward the sound, they were amazed to see a gigantic UFO that looked like a flying green city with a spot light that was projecting toward the ground.

The strange UFO had red and green lights circling the bottom area of the craft. It hovered in the same position for about 30 seconds before it slowly drifted out of sight. The witnesses reported that the size of the UFO was simply immense. They described is as looking like something straight out of the movie *Close Encounters of the Third Kind*.

A few weeks earlier, on March 3, 2000, around 10:05 p.m., another alien incursion occurred in Washington, D.C. That night, a federal employee was standing in Constitution Gardens, near the Lincoln Memorial, when she sighted what at first looked like a shooting star. However, she noticed that the light did not fade away the way falling stars usually do. She then realized that there were actually two glowing UFOs which were flying parallel to each other in silence at great speed.

She recalled that the bright UFOs were small and white with a pale greenish glow. They were flying too fast to be an airplane. She watched in astonishment as the two UFOs merged into one and then changed again so that one appeared to be following or chasing the other. She noted that the UFOs disappeared into the lights of the city after about 10 seconds. She immediately went back to her office, at an undisclosed federal building, and wrote everything down because it seemed like such a strange event.

Two months earlier, on January 1, 2000, around 1:00 a.m., another alien incursion occurred in Washington, D.C. That night, two friends were attending America's millennium celebration on the National Mall. After watching the New Year's Eve fireworks and laser lights, they decided to go home.

As they walked through downtown DC, the sound of multiple explosions made them jump. They soon realized it was just more fireworks being launched from a barge in the Potomac River behind the Lincoln

Memorial.

From their position, they could see flashes from the fireworks reflecting in the office windows from nearby buildings. After a few minutes of fireworks, one of the friends noticed what appeared to be a shooting star near the horizon. He recalled thinking that the timing for shooting stars during the fireworks was great. However, as he continued to look at the sky, he saw more shooting stars only this time he got a better look at what they really were. He soon realized that they could not be shooting stars, because they didn't burn up in the atmosphere.

He then witnessed a pair of dimly-lit, round UFOs flying in formation, passing almost directly overhead. They were definitely not meteors. They looked identical. Although they moved at high speed, he was able to see them well enough, while they were in sight, to realize they were not shooting stars.

Less than a minute later, three large, identical, cigar-shaped UFOs passed overhead while moving at about the same speed. It was one New Year's Eve celebration the young man would never forget. The incident was very similar to what Mr. Allen captured on film, at the same location, during a fireworks display on July 4, 2002.

CHAPTER TWELVE

Forty Years of SNAFU with UFOs

The 20th century was a very-active time for UFOs to penetrate America's airspace. During that period in history, there was often little or no effort made by the government to intercept most of the unidentified flying objects in the controlled airspace of Washington, D.C.

For example, on November 16, 1999, another UFO was sighted over Washington, D.C. It was described as a large, fireball-type object that appeared to be falling from the sky. However, as some of the astonished witnesses later recalled, at one point the "fireball" began accelerating upward.

About two months earlier, on September 10, 1999, at 9:41 p.m., another UFO was sighted near the Pentagon. According to one witness, "I was sitting on the couch watching TV when I saw a strange light out my window. It looked like a large, falling star entering from the west heading earthward."

One month earlier, on August 14, 1999, at approximately 8:00 p.m., another alien incursion took place in Washington, D.C. That evening, a local resident was walking along a busy sidewalk near Dupont Circle. She looked up in the partly-cloudy sky and was surprised to see a black, stationary, disk-shaped UFO that remained motionless for approximately two minutes before it disappeared.

The previous month, on July 11, 1999, around 5:30 p.m., more UFOs were sighted over the Pentagon. According to one witness, "There were four glowing, oval-shaped objects that did not look like balloons or airplanes. They were in the area for 15 minutes.

"My friend and I were outside at her pool. I could see the Pentagon from the balcony. At some point, I opened my eyes and looked into the sky. It was sunny and the sky was clear blue with scattered clouds.

"I could easily see jets passing at 30,000 feet and birds flying through the clouds. Visibility was pretty good. While gazing into the sky, I saw what appeared to be four bright, shiny-colored objects that were elongated oval in shape. They appeared to be way up there.

"They were traveling north to south as a group and were moving slowly and smoothly at speeds that varied with each other. The prevailing wind was pushing clouds in an east-west direction. These objects did not appear to be high altitude balloons.

"Throughout my life, from time to time, I have observed helium balloons in flight until they disappeared. These objects did not look like balloons. One would slowly catch up with the other and another would seem to slow down. Over the course of 15 minutes my friend and I watched the objects continue to move across the sky until they finally disappeared."

. The previous month, on June 6, 1999, another alien incursion took place at approximately 10:00 p.m., in Washington, D.C. That night, a local motorist witnessed a glowing, cigar-shaped UFO hovering over the city.

Five days earlier, on June 1, 1999, another UFO was sighted over Washington, D.C. One witness described the object as slowly falling across the sky and then moving in an instant at times. It had a green glow around itself. It looked like a large, bright fireball or ball of lightning.

Less than two months earlier, on April 22, 1999, around 11:00 a.m., another UFO was sighted over Washington, D.C. According to a retired U.S. Capitol employee, "A U.S. Capitol police officer and I were working on the west steps of the Capitol when we noticed something strange flying straight up at about 15,000 feet. It was moving from north to south over the Capitol dome.

"The object was a bright, silver disc. It was moving relatively slow and would stop on occasion. There was a bright-white flash emitting from it about every minute or so. We couldn't tell if it was from the object or a reflection coming off of it.

"The object was flying in a rather-odd pattern. It would stop for many seconds, make a sharp left or right movement, then start moving straight again. At times, it looked like it was moving in a zigzag pattern and then it would make right angle turns. We couldn't figure out what this was because the area it was flying in was prohibited air space.

"The police officer notified his superior about the object, but I don't know what they did from there. The object was literally straight up above the Capitol dome and was also seen by the tourist that noticed us looking at it.

"We watched the object for about 20 minutes until it went out of sight toward Virginia. Sorry it took me so long to report this. I recently ran into the Capitol Police officer who witnessed this sighting with me, so I decided to finally report it."

Eight days earlier, on April 14, 1999, at approximately 8:30 p.m., another alien incursion occurred in Washington, D.C. One witness reported that while driving along the Capitol Beltway with the sunroof of his car open, he noticed an extremely-fast, bright-green, spherical UFO in the sky. He was astonished by the UFO as it passed rapidly overhead on its way into the heart of Washington, D.C., and then turned in the direction of Andrews Air Force base.

The witness estimated that the UFO was flying at tens of thousands of miles per hour. He had never seen anything like it. He could not judge the altitude, but noted that the UFO was incredibly bright and had a slight-green glow around it. He was sure that other people had seen the UFO because anyone looking up in the sky that night would have noticed it.

About three months earlier, on January 11, 1999, another UFO was sighted in Washington, D.C. According to one witness, "My six-year-old brother pointed it out to myself, my mom, and her boy friend."

The previous month, on December 7, 1998, around 8:30 p.m., another UFO was sighted in the controlled airspace over Washington, D.C. According to the witness, "I was on my way home from work in the city of Washington, D.C., as a police officer. At that time, I saw a bright ball of light in the sky. It was pretty high. The sky was fairly clear that night, so you could see a good distance. As I drove, I kept watching the ball-shaped light which was very bright and stood out.

"Other aircraft could be seen at lower altitude. But after about 20 to 30 minutes I saw a jet approach at high speed to intercept, and the UFO went ballistic and was gone. I spent several years in the military and have seen just about every type of craft in the US inventory, both rotary and fixed wing, but I never saw a craft move so fast.

"The jet didn't have a chance. Please do not release my contact information. I do not want anyone at my job to think I was a nut. That's a bad thing for a cop. This same UFO was seen by a co-worker a few days before that. He is a non-believer, but told me about it. It was in the same spot and at the same time. I'm not sure what is going on here?"

The previous night, on December 6, 1998, another close encounter occurred in Washington, D.C. According to one of the witnesses, "We spotted a spherical, green UFO flying over the city as we were coming home from a nearby restaurant. The color and energy around the UFO looked similar to fireworks at night, but it was clearly something out of this world."

About two months earlier, on October 15, 1998, another close encounter occurred in Washington, D.C. According to one witness, "The UFO looked like a cross between a triangle, a chevron, an arrowhead, and a diamond shape. It was a clear, starry night. The UFO was very quiet and emitted a low-humming sound."

About three months earlier, on July 24, 1998, around 2:30 p.m., another alien incursion took place in Washington, D.C. This event made me wonder how many other tourists had accidentally captured images of UFOs while taking pictures at the Capitol building. That afternoon, a typical American family on vacation in DC was visiting the city's many museums.

After that, the family walked to the National Mall. While standing in front of the Capitol building the mother asked her kids to hold still and smile while she took their picture. At that time, she unintentionally took a picture of a UFO in the sky. Her daughter had made a funny face so the mother took a second picture. However, the UFO was not in the second picture even though everything else was. The clouds were the same, and the people in the background were there but in a slightly different position. There were just a few seconds between the two pictures.

It was only after arriving home and developing the film that the family realized they had inadvertently captured the image of a cigar-shaped UFO at the Capitol building. Naturally, they were very interested in finding out what the strange object in the picture really was, but they didn't know who to call. Unfortunately, that photograph has not been published.

About two months earlier, on May 22, 1998, at approximately 8:30

p.m., another alien incursion transpired in Brentwood, Maryland, which is located on the border of Washington, D.C. That night, a local resident was at her home near Rhode Island Avenue looking out her bedroom window toward Washington, D.C., when she sighted a UFO. The alien craft appeared to be the size of a star, but it seemed brighter and was flashing in a manner that made her question if it really was a star.

Grabbing her phone, she called a friend, who lived eight miles away, in Washington, D.C. The UFO was fairly low on the horizon, about treetop level, so she was certain her friend would be able to see it. However, it turned out the friend could not see it, due to some trees.

The witness then walked outside to get a better view. She recalled that, "The UFO looked like a circle with a dome on top." She was unable to make out any particular details, because the entire UFO had a brilliant-white glow that was not constant in its intensity. She observed the UFO for 45 minutes while describing the event to her friend over the phone. She said later that, "I got the strange feeling that somehow the UFO knew I was looking at it."

The previous month, in April of 1998, at about 2:00 a.m., a man was driving home after working in Washington, D.C. According to the witness, "I was about two miles south of downtown DC when I saw a spherical, glowing UFO that was moving in front of me.

"It was up in the sky moving south and then it made went up with great speed and disappeared behind some kind of blackness in the night sky. I recall it was a clear, cold night, and I had just got off work. Perhaps this orb had the ability to move inter-dimensionally. It just vanished into nothing. Perhaps it docked with another stealth UFO or crossed into another dimension."

A few months earlier, on January 13, 1998, a Washington, D.C., resident witnessed a bright flash from a UFO that suddenly dropped to the ground. No other information was provided.

The previous year, on July 28, 1997, at approximately 1:00 p.m., another alien incursion occurred in Washington, D.C. At that time, a UFO was accidentally captured on video by a young tourist. The boy's parents reported that while standing in front of the White House, their son captured something very strange with his video camera. The UFO only appeared in seven frames of a standard 30 frame per second VHS tape.

Apparently, the UFO had moved so fast, it was not seen at the time. As a result, the family didn't realize what they had caught on video until they were at home viewing their vacation tapes. Soon after that, the boy's parents had the video tape digitally analyzed. It was determined that the UFO had a solid form and reflected sunlight as if it were metallic.

Earlier that month, on July 5, 1997, Colonel Philip Corso was interviewed by Michael Lindemann of *CNI News*. Corso had been Chief of the U.S. Army's Foreign Technology Division and was a member of President Eisenhower's National Security Council. He later went on to work for Senator Strom Thurmond after retiring from the army in 1963.

At one point in their interview, Lindemann asked Corso about the possibility that the U.S. military and even the German military had acquired and exploited extraterrestrial technology prior to the Roswell crash?

Corso was well informed on the subject because he had worked with General Trudeau on *Project Paperclip*. He stated, "There were UFO crashes elsewhere, and the Germans gathered material, too. They were working on it. But they didn't solve the propulsion system. They did a lot of experiments on flying saucers. They had one craft that went up to 12,000 feet. But what we both missed out on was the guidance system. During our research, we began to realize that the aliens we captured were part of the guidance system."

Corso's last comment reminded me of what David Adair and Nassim Haramein had said about one's consciousness being able to merge with the artificial intelligence onboard alien space craft.

One night earlier, on July 4, 1997, around 11:00 p.m., another bizarre close encounter occurred in Washington, D.C., on the National Mall. That night, a young couple was enjoying a warm, summer's night when they suddenly witnessed a small, spherical UFO scanning the area.

About a month and a half earlier, on May 27, 1997, around 3:30 p.m., UFOs were sighted moving rapidly through the restricted airspace of Washington, D.C., and the Pentagon. According to one witness, "As I was driving home, I looked up and was extremely surprised to see two rapidly-moving, disk-shaped UFOs. They were a metallic, dull-grey color and were extremely smooth moving and fast."

About a month and a half earlier, on April 3, 1997, at approximately 8:15 p.m., another alien incursion transpired in Washington, D.C. That night, a federal employee and two friends witnessed a dark, crescent-shaped UFO flying over the capital city.

According to one of the witnesses, "The UFO was very strange. It had no lights and made no sound, but you could clearly see it outlined against the stars. We were looking at a comet that night when we saw the UFO. Although it was really big, I had a better view of it. But I really couldn't tell how big it was because it appeared to be above the clouds. I've watched jets fly in and out of Andrews Air Force Base, and I know how big they are. The UFO had to be bigger than any of those. The shape reminded me of a B-2, but much more curved; like a boomerang."

The previous year, in the summer of 1996, another close encounter occurred in Washington, D.C. While driving over a bridge at night, a DC resident was surprised to see a dull-white, solid beam of light that projected itself in a perfectly horizontally line from the "Freedom" statue on top of the Capitol Dome. The strange beam of light went south into the horizon as far as he could see.

About a year and a half earlier, on October 15 and 16, 1995, more alien incursions occurred in Washington, D.C. At that time, a vender had parked his SUV and set up his tables with the other merchants near the National Mall.

There were many people walking around the area, shopping, eating and just taking in the scenery. In his free time, the vender used his camcorder to film and talk with people in the area. At some point, he looked up into the clear night sky and noticed it was full of stars. That's when he noticed one particular "star" that was moving slightly back and forth. He figured his eyes were just tired and were playing tricks on him. However, after taking another look, he knew he wasn't just seeing things.

He pointed towards the object and alerted people nearby. Some of the other people then looked up and pointed in the opposite direction at another star that was making little circular motions. Focusing carefully on the sky, he realized there were actually dozens of other stars that were making subtle movements. He tried to capture the event on video, but the light was too low. However, he was able to record the voices of the people's reaction to the event. He watched the strange "dancing stars" in the sky for about 10 minutes after which he packed up his supplies and went to sleep. The next day, he was too busy working to look at the sky.

However, his friends reportedly saw UFOs flying overhead nearby which they described as "silver, metallic disks."

The previous month, on September 23, 1995, a local DC resident, who was a self-avowed UFO skeptic, was outside talking with a friend when they witnessed a UFO pass within 150 feet of their position. It was a life-changing event for both of the witnesses.

The previous month, on August 21, 1995, around 3:00 a.m., another alien incursion transpired in Washington, D.C. At that time, a local teenage resident was woken up by a bright light coming through his bedroom window. When he got up and looked outside, he saw a triangular-shaped UFO hovering across the street. He quickly woke up his brother and showed him the UFO, but they soon became terrified by the glowing, alien spacecraft and hid under the covers. They noted that the light from the UFO illuminated their room for about 15 minutes.

About two months earlier, on June 28, 1995, a group of 19 Senators and Congressmen reportedly were shown a preview of a historic, military film of an extraterrestrial autopsy at their request. The event allegedly took place at a secure location in the U.S. Capitol.

Thirteen days earlier, on June 15, 1995, a Washington, D.C., resident witnessed a red-glowing UFO that was lighting up low lying clouds as it moved silently through the sky. After a few moments, the UFO moved out of the clouds, and the witness could see there were actually about a dozen red UFOs moving together in a loose formation.

About one month earlier, on May 6, 1995, an interesting revelation was broadcast sometime after midnight during a popular talk radio show in Washington D.C. One of the guests that night was a woman named Donna Tietze, a former NASA employee in Houston, Texas.

When asked about her job, she said, "I worked at NASA during the *Apollo* missions. I left NASA around the time the space shuttles began flying. I worked in Building 8, in the photo lab. I had a secret clearance, so I thought I could go anywhere in the building. One day, I went into an area that was restricted.

"That was where they developed pictures taken from satellites and all of the missions; the *Apollo* missions and other flight missions. I went in there and talked to one of the photographers and developers that was busy putting together a mosaic of a lot of photos.

"I was trying to learn new methods and new things about the whole organization. While I was looking at the pictures, he directed my attention to one area. I looked and noticed there was a round, oval-shaped, very-white, circular dot. The image was on black and white photography. When I asked him if that was a spot on the emulsion, he said, 'All I can tell you is that spots on the emulsion do not leave circular shadows.'

"I looked again and noticed that there was a shadow under this white dot. I also noticed that the trees were casting shadows in the same direction as the shadow of this UFO because it was higher than the trees, but not too much higher than the trees. The UFO was close to the ground and it was spherical, but slightly elongated.

"I then asked him if it was an image of a UFO. He said, 'I can't tell you.' I then asked him what he was going to do with this piece of information. He said, 'We have to airbrush these things out before we sell these photographs to the public.' I realized at that point that there was a procedure set up to take care of this type of information from the public."

Earlier that year, on a spring morning in 1995, two US Capitol Police officers had a close encounter while on duty. One of the officers was a total skeptic prior to the event.

Earlier that year, on February 15, 1995, a frightened Washington, D.C., resident witnessed sparks falling from a hovering UFO.

About four months earlier, in October of 1994, around 10:40 p.m., a UFO hovered over the Potomac River, near the Pentagon, for about 10 minutes and then flew straight up and out of sight in an instant. One witness reported that it looked like a big helicopter without the tail, but bigger. It had windows all around. He could not tell which end was the front of the craft.

The previous month, on September 15, 1994, another Washington, D.C., resident witnessed a very-fast moving, spherical UFO that ionized the air with its powerful, field-propulsion system which caused it to glow. This is a common trait of UFO technology.

About two years earlier, on July 11, 1993, at approximately 11:00 a.m., another alien incursion took place in Washington, D.C. That morning, while driving through the capital, dozens of people witnessed a silver, metallic, domed, circular UFO that hovered for about 10 minutes just above the trees. The craft was about the size of a football field in diameter.

It hovered close to the treetops then sped away instantly and silently.

According to one of the witnesses, "It looked shiny like aluminum foil, but was so shiny it almost looked liquid. The treetops were reflected in it. It hovered very close to me as I drove down Rhode Island Avenue, NE. The traffic was bumper to bumper on a clear, sunny, Saturday morning.

"I first saw it when it approached from high up in the sky. I recall wondering why I could see a star in the clear-blue sky and then the 'star' got bigger as it grew closer and closer. It traveled along the traffic route of cars. This was a two lane section of road. The passengers in the car next to me saw it, too. I kept trying to drive slowly along and look up at the same time. I noticed the passenger in the car next to me was pushing on the driver's shoulder and pointing up. We all began to move forward a little and look up at this dome-shaped, shiny, silver, huge object that was following along with the traffic.

"I recall that I began to get the creeps, like it was looking at me! I began to pray while driving. At one point, I was almost afraid to look right at it was so very close; just over the trees. This area of the road was tree lined, and I kept getting glimpses of it as my car passed along under the canopy of the trees. At one point, I began thinking, 'Go away,' and immediately after that, the object began to slowly lift higher and reduce its speed. It stayed very still for a moment and then began to lift higher and move off steeply up and to my left. I watched so intently that I almost slammed into the back of the car in front of me. When I looked for it again, it was miles away and was becoming a tiny, shining, silver dot in the sky again.

"I began to honk my horn to the driver in the lane next to me whose passenger had also seen this thing and was gesturing wildly in their car. We both pulled over at a convenience store. The man, the driver, went into the store. It was really hot and sunny that day. The woman stayed out front with me, and we both discussed what we had just seen. She said her husband was upset and wanted a soda. We both excitedly exchanged our reactions about when we first noticed the craft and how it had to have been a UFO.

"Just then, her husband came out of the store and was still visibly shaken. He said he didn't know what the 'bleep' that was and he just wanted to get the 'bleep' home as fast as possible and not talk about it. Next Monday morning, on *The Bernie McCain Show* at *Radio WOL*, he did a segment on how many people had called the station to report seeing that UFO in many areas of Maryland and all over the Washington, D.C., neighborhoods. Mr. McCain had been out of town, but was called at his home in Philadelphia, on Saturday afternoon, by various friends that were all reporting the same incident.

"He said that when he arrived to the station on Monday morning, the phone messages about the mass UFO sighting were piled up on his desk, and the secretary said the message line had gone down from so many phone calls. I've told my husband and a few other people about it, but no one believes me. I am a wife, a mother, a grandmother, a good citizen, and a semi-retired Middle School English teacher. I am a Christian woman who is 50 years young, a non-drinker and non-drug user, I don't need glasses, and I have never been known to engage in stunts of any kind to seek attention. I don't know what that object in the sky was, but I have never seen metal like that before or since."

Another alien incursion occurred around the same time, in the early 1990's, at approximately 6:00 p.m., at the same location: Rhode Island Avenue NE, in Washington, D.C. According to a local resident, "I saw an unidentified flying object over my neighborhood. It was flying high at first. It then came down a little lower and was hovering over the trees for a while. I had just gotten off the bus, and I noticed there was a lot less traffic than normal when I crossed the street. The UFO had a round, saucer shape. The body was black with red and green lights. I watched it for a few moments then ran up to my apartment and quickly went upstairs to try and see it better, but it had disappeared."

Ten years prior to UFOs being photographed landing on Capitol Hill, a series of alien incursions occurred on the National Mall, on April 13, 1992, at approximately 5:45 p.m., in Washington, D.C. At that time, dozens of tourists visiting the Washington Monument began pointing at a UFO in the sky above the man-made obelisk. Photographs were reportedly taken, but were never published.

Some people looked for a moment and then turned away as though they did not want to see the UFO that was hovering above them. Apparently, this was something they simply could not understand or accept.

However, most of the people there, and in the surrounding area, stood transfixed by the sight of the large, bright, disk-shaped UFO that moved silently westward at approximately 30,000 feet over the heart of Washington, D.C. Following that large UFO were 10 smaller UFOs which were shining brightly as they passed over the Washington Monument complex near the White House.

A British family on holiday in DC that day later filed a detailed report regarding the event. According to the father, he first noticed a very-large, disk-shaped UFO in the sky. He estimated it was visually about one quarter the diameter of the full moon. He then noticed a formation of other, smaller UFOs that were much lower in the sky and were flying quickly to the west.

He could clearly see this was not a fleet of airplanes. At one point, the formation of UFOs stopped in mid-air, then reversed course and continued westward. At that time, they suddenly brightened and turned orange before vanishing into thin air!

He noted that this event did not create any excitement among the crowd of people gathered that afternoon. Most of them were acting as though it was just another day on the National Mall. However, the father recalled there was one young boy in the crowd that had asked him what the first disk-shaped craft was. When the father replied that it was a UFO, the boy appeared puzzled.

On the way back to their car, the British family saw two more UFOs passing over the Potomac River. It was coming from the Capitol building toward the Pentagon. According to the father, the UFOs drifted silently through the sky and were changing shape. He noted that a smaller UFO followed a larger UFO that would occasionally emit a bright flash of light which may have been a reflection of the late afternoon sun.

The previous year, on February 11, 1991, more residents in Washington, D.C., encountered a UFO. According to one witness, he and his wife saw a, "Powerful strobe light from the bottom of a bell-shaped UFO that was less than 500 feet in altitude. It lit up my bathroom and back yard as it passed over the area."

The previous month, on January 21, 1991, another close encounter occurred in Washington, D.C. One resident reported, "That night, I took my girlfriend to a movie. Later, when we arrived at her house, she was searching for her house keys, so I took a moment to look up at the sky and witnessed what I initially thought was a shooting star. But then, much to my surprise, the single glowing object separated into six or eight star-like objects.

"The group of UFOs then assumed a V shape before forming a tight cluster. By then, my girl friend turned around to see what I was looking at. When I pointed out the formation of UFOs, she asked what it was. I said I didn't know, and we went in the house and called the DC police, but they just made me feel like I was crazy, so I dropped it. However, what I saw was real."

One year earlier, on January 31, 1990, at approximately 6:00 p.m., a DC resident witnessed a glowing UFO moving slowly across the sky like an airplane, but it was a little bit faster and disappeared silently, slowly over the tree line.

Four days earlier, on January 27, 1990, in Washington, D.C., a network news editor witnessed a blue-white UFO that was visually about three or four times the size of grapefruit and was moving at treetop level. He described it as an, "Incandescent bright light at the center; like a magnesium flare. It looked like a ball of fire."

About three months earlier, according to a member of the *Nation of Islam*, Minister Louis Farrakhan stated in an October 24, 1989 press conference, that God would show a sign of the truth regarding the reality of UFOs. The following day, October 25, 1989, a UFO was seen over Washington, D.C. To some, that UFO was a sign from God. The UFO sighting was reportedly shown on television in Washington, D.C., for the three days that followed the minister's press conference. However, if it exists, I have been unable to locate a copy of that show.

Nine days earlier, on October 16, 1989, a large, cigar-shaped UFO had been sighted over Washington, D.C. According to one of the witnesses, "My daughter and I were driving on Interstate 95 which takes you past the Jefferson Memorial. We were on a bridge, stuck in stop-and-go traffic. My daughter, who was nine-years old at the time, said, 'look at that plane up there.' I looked up, but I didn't see a plane. I was in U.S. Navy at the time and worked on aircraft. What I saw in the sky was a very-large, silver, cigar-shaped flying object that was moving very slowly from my right to left above a hill, directly in front of us.

"It didn't move fast, but it was a steady speed. It moved above the hill until it got right in front of us. It stopped for a few seconds, then shot straight up in the air and was gone. I recall yelling 'wow!' I mean anybody that looked up would have seen it. The bridge was packed with cars."

About six months earlier, in May of 1989, at approximately 5:45 p.m., another alien incursion occurred in the District of Columbia. That evening, two local residents witnessed a group of UFOs.

According to one of the witnesses, "I was standing outside in a parking lot. When I turned around and looked up, at first I thought I was seeing a meteor shower or a star falling. As I looked closer, I saw three then four lights moving around in the sky. They then become stationary and were just hovering.

"When they resumed movement, they began circling around each other and another much larger object. They moved around each other forward to back, top to bottom and in a circular pattern. Then, a couple of more of them became visible, like they had appeared from the distance, and two or three of the closer moving lights disappeared into and reappeared out of this much larger spherical object.

"The larger, spherical object was never as bright as these smaller moving lights. It was outlined in black, but was clearly visible when the smaller lights hovered around it. I went back to my parent's house and got my father so he could look and see them for himself. This was also a sanity check for me. They were still there hovering and moving, and my father saw them too.

"While we were watching them, the whole procession began to move north. We got into my car and followed them in the sky for about a mile or two. Then, after we had parked and were out of the car, all of them disappeared. It was like they became invisible?"

The previous year, in October of 1988, at approximately 11:00 p.m., another alien incursion transpired in Washington, D.C. That night, while looking at the stars in a perfectly clear sky, a retired U.S. Marine officer saw three disc-shaped UFOs suddenly appear out of nowhere (they most likely had just come out of a wormhole/stargate in the sky). The spacecraft were flat on both sides and glowed bright yellow. The witness noted that for some reason the UFOs flew on edge with the flat side forward. He could not tell what size they were because they appeared to be outside of the earth's atmosphere, in space.

He said, "The UFOs were very-high up and traveled across the part of the sky I was looking at. Even though they were far away, I could easily see them because they were glowing so brightly. I have never seen anything move that fast. I could tell they were being controlled by someone because they moved in a triangular formation on the same course. They did not make any sound during the eight seconds I saw them before they disappeared back into space. I have worked as a jet engine mechanic while in the Marines, and I know it is not possible for anything to fly that fast: at least 2,000 mph."

Early that year, in January of 1988, around 2:00 a.m., two female college students in Washington, D.C., had just left a party, and were driving through an unfamiliar area of the city, when they suddenly came upon what appeared to be a six-car pileup in the middle of the intersection.

Although the women saw six wrecked vehicles, there were no people in sight, no emergency vehicles, no flashing lights or police? The two young ladies felt uneasy and drove slowly by the scene. They eventually noticed that, for some reason, they had arrived home much later than expected.

The women were emotionally upset by this strange episode, so they decided to try using hypnosis to find any hidden information. Apparently, one of the women was abducted by aliens while the other woman remained in a state of suspended animation in the vehicle.

Several short-gray humanoids took one of the women into a hovering object, medically examined her and then returned her back to the vehicle. She was then told that she would only remember a six-car pileup.

A few months earlier, in October of 1987, a report surfaced regarding the pending production of a video tape featuring an official interview with an ET. Since some ETs communicate telepathically, a military officer would serve as an interpreter. Reportedly, several newsmen were invited to Washington, D.C., to personally film a captured ET being interviewed by the U.S. military and then distribute the film to the public. However, because of the instability in the stock market at that time it was felt the timing was not right. In any case, it certainly seemed like an odd method to inform the public about extraterrestrials, but it would be in keeping with the actions of a panicked but powerful, military-media-industrial complex.

About four months earlier, on June 8, 1987, around 8:20 p.m., a UFO was sighted over DC that had an appearance and performance beyond the capability of known earthly aircraft. The UFO was only about 100 feet from three witnesses. It was visible for more than four minutes. A loud sound was heard.

During the previous decade, in the late 1970s, another alien incursion took place near Washington, D.C. It is a historical fact that airline pilots encounter UFOs on a fairly regular basis. However, there is a strict policy that active duty pilots, if they want to keep their jobs, cannot discuss the matter publicly. However, sometimes the information gets out anyway.

For example, one evening at an international airport, a car rental driver picked up an airline pilot captain. As they were driving, he asked the pilot if he had ever seen anything like a UFO. The pilot remained silent for a few moments before relating a very interesting story.

In the late 1970s, during the Carter administration, he was flying out of Washington, D.C. Onboard the aircraft were regular passengers as well as the Secretary of Transportation and his staff. As the jet was leaving DC, three green-glowing spheres appeared in front of them. He said that the UFOs appeared to be about 50 feet or more in diameter and were flying in formation. At that time, the pilots not only had visual contact, but the UFOs were also being tracked by ground radar. The pilot explained that because the UFOs were in front of their jet, none of the passengers could see what was going on.

Knowing this, the pilot then called the Secretary of Transportation to the cockpit to witness the UFOs. He thought the Secretary would want to know what was happening. At the time, the pilot believed this would be the biggest news story of the century. These were clearly not experimental military craft.

The pilot noted that the three spherical UFOs were identical and had oval-shaped windows or what appeared to be windows around the top third of the craft. He said that everyone in the cockpit at that time, including the Secretary of Transportation, agreed that the UFOs appeared to be some kind of spacecraft from another world. These same green spheres were photographed over Capitol Hill in July of 2002.

On the evening of July 4, 1977, two UFOs, that visually appeared to be the size of a star, were observed by four witnesses for 30 minutes near the Pentagon.

About four months earlier, on March 11, 1977, around 10:00 p.m., A UFO was sighted for six seconds hovering near the Pentagon. The UFO was about 150-feet wide and was observed in clear weather by a witness who was an experienced observer.

The previous month, on February 14, 1977, around 7:00 p.m., a UFO was sighted over DC by an experienced witness for over three minutes. He was located at Mount Ranier, Maryland, looking toward Washington, D.C.

About four months earlier, on October 14, 1976, at 8:16 p.m., UFOs were sighted passing over the Pentagon area by a witness using binoculars. One of the UFOs was visibly the size of the moon. The UFOs were observed in clear weather as they passed slowly over the area.

About six months earlier, on April 9, 1976, at 7:35 p.m., a meteor-like UFO was witnessed for 12 seconds by a married couple walking near the Pentagon. The UFO reportedly looked like the size of a star in a clear sky as it passed over the area.

About five months earlier, on November 20, 1975, a multitude of highly luminous, spherical UFOs were spotted in DC and the surrounding area.

The previous day, on November 19, 1975, around sunset, an *Eastern Airlines* jumbo jet was preparing to land at Washington National Airport. The veteran pilot, with more than 10,000 flight hours to his credit, had descended from 24,000 to 15,000 feet, when he caught sight of several cylindrical-shaped UFOs crossing from east to west in front of his plane at a distance of five miles. The weather was perfectly clear and visibility was unlimited. Because of the speed and trajectory that the UFOs traveled, the pilot was unable to point them out to his copilot.

That same month, in November of 1975, around 9:50 a.m., another UFO was sighted in the restricted airspace over Washington, D.C. The UFO appeared to be a thin, glowing-white, oval disc. It closely paced an airliner on landing approach to National Airport. The UFO then made a sudden, 90-degree turn and left the area at a high rate of speed. The UFO was observed for more than one minute.

That same year, in the late summer of 1975, another alien incursion occurred at approximately 7:00 p.m., in Manassas, Virginia. That night, after their high school graduation, a young man and his girlfriend were driving on a very-busy highway when a silver-grey UFO suddenly passed over head.

The UFO appeared to be extremely large and was very low in the sky. The high school students just sat there in awe. They had not consumed any alcohol or taken any drugs at the time. They found it strange that the UFO seemed to just float across the sky without making a sound. The weather conditions were clear on that balmy, summer evening. The driver of the car noted that the UFO was heading toward Washington, D.C., about 10 miles to the east. The UFO moved very slowly and silently, as though it was gliding at about 200 feet. As it passed overhead, the craft literally covered the entire four-lane highway.

The previous year, on October 17, 1974, around 6:55 p.m., another alien incursion took place in Washington, D.C. At that time, a local resident witnessed a UFO as it passed over the city.

Four months earlier, on June 6, 1974, at approximately 8:30 p.m., another alien incursion occurred in Washington, D.C. This event made me wonder who was really in control of America's airspace: us or them. That night, a group of local residents were entertaining guests outside on the third-floor balcony of their apartment when they saw a brilliant light approaching in the sky.

At first glance, it appeared to be a bright landing light of a jetliner flying low in the air slowly toward the Washington Monument. However, some of the witnesses immediately noticed that the object seemed too bright and too large to be an aircraft landing light. It remained in the same general position for about 15 to 20 seconds and then suddenly turned.

At that time, it looked as though it was coming toward the witnesses, but was in fact passing slightly to the east of the White House. This made all the witnesses openly question what sort of aircraft would be permitted to operate in prohibited/restricted airspace so close to the president's mansion.

Although it was overcast that evening, they could see that the UFO veered toward them at one point and then silently accelerated as it began to move across the city at a very high rate of speed: faster than any fighter jet could fly.

As the UFO quickly passed over their location, the witnesses could see it was a glowing, orange-red, disk-shaped craft. At that moment, all the witnesses became very excited and were shocked. Some of them were so frightened they jumped face down on the floor because they thought the UFO was going to crash into their building or the low hills behind them.

Just before it flew away, the witnesses could see the UFO was circular, disk-shaped or spherical. Later, they realized that it had made no noise at all. According to one of the witnesses, it was the most dramatic thing he had ever seen in the sky. It was such an amazing event that he couldn't wait to hear the official explanation. However, in the following days, there were no reports of it in the newspapers.

He noted that, in some ways, the lack of reporting of the UFO was actually more bizarre and terrifying than the phenomena itself. He simply could not understand how the incredibly-strange sight of a UFO flying low over the nation's capital would not be noticed and reported, or at least speculated on, by anyone in the media. It was a valid question that still deserved an explanation decades later.

That same summer, in 1974, on at least five consecutive Sunday mornings in Washington, D.C., a group of six local teenagers would meet and walk to Fort Stevens which is on a hill overlooking the playground and football field.

According to one of the witnesses, "Each time, at exactly 2:00 a.m., a blue, spherical UFO about the size of a beach ball would swoop down out of the sky and hover over the park no more than 150 yards away.

"Then, it would dart away and hover over a nearby building for a few moments before swooping over to another rooftop and hovering again. It repeated this activity four times before swooping down low over our heads and then we would run away screaming."

The previous year, on November 16, 1973, at approximately 5:00 a.m., another alien incursion transpired in Washington, D.C. At that time, a local resident witnessed a glowing UFO making odd maneuvers in the sky as it passed over the Washington Monument.

One month earlier, on October 30, 1973, another alien incursion took place in Washington, D.C. At that time, a local resident took a picture of a UFO as it passed over the city. The image was not made available to the public.

The previous year, sometime in 1972, more UFOs were sighted in the DC area by local residents who lived near Andrews Air Force Base which is a nuclear military facility.

That same year, sometime in early 1972, the media issued a story about an alien being that had been captured inside the Pentagon. The next day, the networks changed their story and reported that the person was not an alien, but had unusual abilities.

The previous year, on July 3, 1971, around 10:10 p.m., a UFO travelling near the Pentagon was observed in detail using a telescope. The UFO appeared larger than a star and was observed by one experienced witness for a few minutes.

About four months earlier, on March 2, 1971, another "star-like" UFO was sighted in the controlled airspace over Washington, D.C.

About four months earlier, on November 30, 1969, another UFO was sighted in the restricted airspace over Andrews Air Force Base.

Earlier that same year, in mid-1969, around 7:30 p.m., a disc-shaped UFO that was visually five times the size of the moon was observed in clear weather by a married couple. The UFO was sighted hovering over an electric power plant near the Pentagon for five minutes. Animal reactions to the object were reported.

That same summer, on July 21, 1969, at 9:31 p.m., a "star-like" UFO was sighted in the restricted airspace of Washington, D.C. The UFO had an appearance and aerobatic performance beyond the capability of known earthly aircraft. It was observed in clear weather by one experienced male witness for over one minute.

One year earlier, on July 10, 1968, around 11:00 p.m., at Quantico Marine Base, in Virginia, a cigar-shaped UFO was sighted. The craft was approximately 30-feet long and was glowing white with two yellow port holes and a flashing-green light below. It was later estimated that the UFO was in the area for about two hours. According to one of the military participants in this close encounter, "The voice I heard in the Control Tower identified himself as a U.S. Marine Corps Captain who was the Duty Officer. He said there were four or five other observers in the tower with him.

"At some point during the event, the UFO departed and was tracked by Washington FAA Center as it proceeded up the Potomac River (toward DC). It climbed to an altitude of approximately 1,000 feet at a speed of about 100 knots.

"It was tracked by the Center to a position directly over the White House where observers saw it turn upward at a high angle of attack and flash out of sight. The UFO was later reported (according to Washington Center) by a passenger airlines out of DC en route to NYC. The UFO tracked the airliner for a few seconds, and then turned and flashed out of sight."

Three months earlier, on April 12, 1968, around 11:40 p.m., two glowing, "fire balls" were sighted performing odd aerial maneuvers in the restricted airspace of Washington, D.C., by two male experienced witnesses for six seconds.

One month earlier, on March 12, 1968, another alien incursion transpired at approximately 11:40 p.m., in Washington, D.C. That night, two glowing UFOs were sighted performing odd aerial maneuvers in the restricted airspace of the capital city.

The previous month, in February of 1968, another alien incursion transpired in Washington, D.C. Allegedly, a local resident met a human/ alien that offered to give him a ride in a disc-shaped UFO which had landed in the suburbs. Although he declined, upon returning home, the DC resident realized four hours of time was missing.

The previous month, in January of 1968, another alien incursion transpired in Washington, D.C. At that time, a UFO was sighted passing through the restricted airspace of the capital city. The UFO was observed by one male witness for five hours. Occupants of the craft were allegedly seen. Traces of the UFO landing were found on the ground.

One month earlier, on December 16, 1967, at 3:00 p.m., another alien incursion transpired in Washington, D.C. That afternoon, a local resident witnessed a disc-shaped UFO in the restricted airspace of the capital. Telepathic phenomena were said to have occurred, and the witness was briefly abducted by aliens and then released. Later, he was allegedly contacted by men wearing black suits. Other residents reported seeing a "monster" in the area at dawn.

About two months earlier, on October 21, 22 and 23 of 1967, UFOs were sighted in the restricted airspace over Washington, D.C. The Air Force later claimed these events were just a military exercise.

The previous month, on September 18, 1967, another glowing UFO was sighted in the restricted airspace of Washington, D.C.

Four days earlier, on September 14, 1967, around 2:20 a.m., another alien incursion transpired in Washington, D.C. That morning, a glowing UFO was sighted passing through the restricted airspace of the capital city. The UFO was observed by one witness for ten minutes.

Two days earlier, on September 12, 1967, around 12:35 a.m., another UFO was observed over the Pentagon by one witness for 36 seconds.

The previous month, on August 23, 1967, another alien incursion transpired in Washington, D.C. That night, a glowing UFO was sighted making radical maneuvers in the sky as it passed through the restricted airspace of the city. At the time, the witnesses were located in Georgetown which is near the White House.

The previous day, on August 22, 1967, around 9:00 p.m., another alien incursion transpired in Washington, D.C. That night, a glowing UFO was sighted passing through the restricted airspace of the capital city. The UFO was observed by several witnesses for over 15 minutes.

The previous month, on July 17, 1967, around 1:00 a.m., another alien incursion transpired in Washington, D.C. That morning, a glowing UFO was sighted passing through the restricted airspace of the city by one witness for about ten minutes.

The previous month, on July 9, 1967, another alien incursion transpired in Washington, D.C. At that time, a local resident had a close encounter of the first kind with UFO as it passed low over the capital city. The UFO was observed by one witness that was an experienced observer. She noted the UFO had an appearance and performance beyond the capability of any known earthly aircraft.

The previous month, on June 5, 1967, around 9:55 p.m., one UFO was observed for over 20 minutes near the Pentagon by a local resident.

About two months earlier, on April 3, 1967, around 8:30 p.m., another alien incursion transpired in Washington, D.C. That night, three glowing UFOs were sighted passing through the restricted airspace of DC for about six seconds. One of the witnesses was a computer programmer at NASA Goddard Space Flight Center.

The previous month, in March of 1967, around 9:00 p.m., at Cheltenham Naval Base, in Maryland, two red, glowing octagonal-shaped UFOs blinked off and on alternately. Were observed by a group of experienced military witnesses. One the UFOs were seen to change color. There were no radar returns, but other witnesses in Washington, D.C., observed the UFOs as they zigzagged through the air before they departed by rapidly flying straight up and out of sight.

The previous month, on February 19, 1967, another UFO was sighted at night in the restricted airspace over Washington, D.C.

About three months earlier, on November 13, 1966, around 9:30 p.m., two UFOs were sighted in the restricted airspace over Washington, D.C. The UFOs were observed for more than three minutes by one witness.

Two days earlier, on November 11, 1966, around 9:30 p.m., another alien incursion transpired in Washington, D.C. That night, two glowing UFOs were sighted passing through the restricted airspace of the capital city.

The previous month, on October 28, 29, 30, and 31 of 1966, more alien incursions took place in Washington, D.C. At that time, "meteor-like" UFOs were observed at night passing through the restricted airspace.

Earlier that month, on October 11, 1966, around 7:10 p.m., a UFO was sighted over the Potomac River near the Pentagon. At the time, a strange noise was heard.

About two months earlier, on August 1, 1966, around 9:55 p.m., a UFO was sighted for at least ten minutes over Washington, D.C. The UFO had an appearance and performance beyond the capability of any known earthly aircraft. The disc-shaped UFO was reportedly only three-inches across and was observed by one male witness who reported the event to the DC Police Department.

Later that same night, about 10:55 p.m., in Washington, D.C., a physicist was driving north on the DC Beltway. He had just passed Andrews Air Force Base when, out of his open left window, he saw a bright light descend and hover briefly before moving rapidly to the east. Minutes later, the astonished scientist witnessed a cigar-shaped UFO descend over a house.

This time, the UFO was much closer, and it appeared to be as large as the house. The scientist slowed his car and looked at the object about 200 feet away for about 10 seconds and could see details of the UFO. It had a peaked top with a red light. The bottom was rounded with more red lights and a large, yellow light that was revolving slightly off-center.

The scientists recalled, "I could see clearly the top of the body which was a dark, non-shining material with no sharp edges. The most striking part was the eye-shaped object, off-center, to the right with two distinct, yellow regions. The lower region was revolving, blinking or scanning the area."

As the scientist turned his attention to the highway again, he noted that no other cars were in sight. When he glanced back again, he saw that the UFO was moving south at a very-high speed and at a low elevation. It disappeared in seconds.

The previous night, on July 31, 1966, another alien incursion occurred in Maryland. During a routine patrol, Prince George's County police witnessed a group of glowing UFOs maneuvering erratically across the sky near Washington, D.C.

Ten days earlier, on July 21, 1966, another UFO was sighted at night in the restricted airspace over Washington, D.C. Electromagnetic effects were noted.

About two months earlier, on May 13, 1966, around 12:45 p.m., two UFOs were observed for more than six minutes by two people at a Washington, D.C., airport.

About two months earlier, on March 23, 1966, a glowing UFO was sighted passing through the restricted airspace of Washington, D.C., at night. The UFO was observed by six witnesses.

Two days later, the Michigan Congressman and Minority Leader of the House of Representatives, Gerald Ford, became outraged with the Air Force's investigation of UFOs. Congressman Ford's office had reportedly been deluged with letters, telegrams and phone calls from anxious constituents who demanded that the official investigation itself be investigated.

On March 25, 1966, Congressman Ford issued a press release stating that he was calling for a full Congressional UFO inquiry. A few days later, another press release appeared along with a copy of a letter Ford had sent to the Chairman of the House Science and Astronautics Committee, and the House Armed Services Committee, stating that he wanted a Congressional inquiry to convene quickly.

As a result, on April 5, 1966, Congress held their first and only open hearing on UFOs. While the hearing failed to accomplish as much as it might have, it did produce an Air Force promise that arrangements would be made for an impartial, civilian investigation. Unfortunately, that never happened.

The previous year, on September 24, 1965, a glowing UFO was sighted passing through the restricted airspace of Washington, D.C.

The previous month, in August of 1965, another alien incursion occurred in Washington, D.C. That night, a glowing UFO was sighted passing through the restricted airspace of the capital.

The previous month, on July 31, 1965, another alien incursion took place in Washington, D.C. At that time, a glowing UFO was sighted passing through the restricted airspace of the capital.

Ten days earlier, on July 21, 1965, another alien incursion took place in Washington, D.C. At that time, a glowing UFO was sighted passing through the restricted airspace of the capital.

The previous month, on June 26, 1965, another alien incursion transpired at Washington National Airport. At that time, a brightly glowing UFO was sighted passing through the restricted airspace of the capital and it disrupted electronic equipment.

The previous month, on May 25, 1965, another alien incursion occurred in Washington, D.C. That night, a glowing UFO was sighted maneuvering in the restricted airspace of the capital.

The previous month, on April 29, 1965, another alien incursion transpired in Washington, D.C. That night, a glowing UFO was sighted performing maneuvers in the restricted airspace of the capital.

The previous month, on March 23, 1965, another alien incursion took place in Washington, D.C. That night, a glowing UFO was sighted passing through the restricted airspace of the capital.

Earlier that month, on March 6, 1965, another alien incursion took place in Washington, D.C. That night, a glowing UFO was sighted passing through the restricted airspace of the capital.

The previous month, on February 28, 1965, another dramatic alien incursion transpired, in the District of Columbia. That day, a UFO was captured on 8mm movie film by a U.S. government official named Madeline Rotterfor. An optical physicist that examined the film suggested that the apparent distortion seen around the UFO could have been caused by a powerful anti-gravitational field.

One week earlier, on February 21, 1965, another alien incursion occurred in Washington, D.C. At that time, a "star-like" UFO was observed and photographed performing strange maneuvers over the restricted airspace of the capital area. The UFO moved in a straight line across the sky and also performed strange maneuvers. Unfortunately, these photographs were not published.

The previous month, On January 25, 1965, around 12:45 p.m., a disc-shaped UFO was sighted passing over the Glover Park neighborhood in Washington, D.C. That afternoon, students at the Stoddert School were recessed for lunch. After lunch, five third-grade boys were playing a game of soccer in the yard.

At that time, one of the boys looked up and saw a UFO that was shaped like "an airplane without wings." The other boys realized that the UFO was lower than any commercial aircraft and looked like nothing they had ever seen before.

While they were observing the UFO passing over head, much to the amazement and delight of the boys, the energy field around the alien craft grew brighter and changed colors from silver, to orange, to red, and then green.

When the school lunch bell rang, the boys had to hurry back to class, but they were still excited about the UFO they had just seen. They told their teacher about it, but she replied that it was just a bunch of nonsense. When they went home, the boys told their parents, but they were skeptical or dismissive.

However, one father believed his son and his friends. He asked the boys to go to separate rooms and draw what they had seen at lunch. Then, he questioned them each about the event. The father was not sure what to think until the next day when he heard news reports on the radio about the UFO that had been sighted over DC. He said it gave him "the creeps thinking about it."

The previous day, on January 24, 1965, another UFO was sighted in the restricted airspace of Washington, D.C.

Thirteen days earlier, on January 11, 1965, around 4:10 p.m., another alien incursion took place in Washington, D.C. That afternoon, 12 to 15 white, disc-shaped UFOs were observed maneuvering erratically through the restricted airspace of the capital with military jets in hot pursuit. According to retired Marine Major Donald Keyhoe, Air Force jets pursued several UFOs over the city that day. I found it interesting that from December 1964 to January 1965 UFO sightings increased around Washington, D.C., which caused the CIA to seek information from Keyhoe's UFO intelligence group NICAP.

The attempted military intercept of UFOs over DC was confirmed by an army lieutenant-colonel and a group of army communications specialists, who said, "If our jets had been near any of the UFO landing sites, they may have swarmed down and attempted to keep it from getting away. But records of previous attempts by our military to capture UFOs indicated it would be a tough job." It was an amazing admission that UFOs had apparently landed somewhere in or near Washington, D.C., in 1965.

Eight days earlier, on January 3, 1965, another alien incursion took place in Washington, D.C. At that time, a local resident reportedly had a close encounter with a UFO. Also, around sunset of the same day, an *Electra* airliner had a near-collision with a UFO which avoided hitting the plane at the last moment.

Two days earlier, on January 1, 1965, another alien incursion occurred in Washington, D.C. At that time, a local resident reportedly had a close encounter with a UFO.

A few days earlier, on December 29, 1964, another alien incursion transpired in Washington, D.C. At that time, three UFOs were tracked on radar as they performed incredible, high-speed maneuvers in the restricted airspace of the capital.

About two months earlier, in September 1964, around 7:00 p.m., another alien incursion transpired in Washington, D.C. That evening, a disc-shaped UFO was sighted passing through the restricted airspace of the capital.

About two months earlier, on July 19, 1964, a UFO was sighted over an Air Force Base in Washington, D.C.

Six days earlier, on July 13, 1964, another spherical UFO was sighted in the restricted airspace of Washington, D.C.

Three days earlier, on July 10, 1964, another spherical UFO was sighted in the restricted airspace of Washington, D.C.

The previous month, on June 16, 1964, another UFO was sighted in the restricted airspace of Washington, D.C.

The previous month, on May 30, 1964, another alien incursion transpired in Washington, D.C. That night, a glowing UFO was sighted passing through the restricted airspace of the capital area.

Six days earlier, on May 24, 1964, another UFO was sighted in the restricted airspace of Washington, D.C.

About two months earlier, on March 28, 1964, at approximately 3:20 p.m., another alien incursion transpired in Washington, D.C. That afternoon, a UFO was observed by Mr. and Mrs. Steckling who had just left a department store near the White House when they sighted a silvery UFO that had what appeared to be three ball-shaped appendages underneath. The UFO was approximately 12,000 feet high and was flying very quickly. It paused for a few moments before darting out of sight in seconds.

The previous year, another alien incursion occurred on December 12, 1963, in Washington, D.C. At that time, a UFO was sighted passing through the restricted airspace of the capital area.

One night earlier, on December 11, 1963, another UFO was sighted in the restricted airspace of Washington, D.C.

About five months earlier On July 22, 1963, a glowing UFO was sighted in the controlled airspace near the Pentagon.

The previous month, on June 13, 1963, another UFO was sighted in the restricted airspace of Washington, D.C.

That same month, June of 1963, at approximately 7:30 p.m., another alien incursion transpired in Washington, D.C. At that time, local residents witnessed an orange, disk-shaped UFO that was visually about the size of a football field. One of the witnesses was outside playing with her friends when she noticed the large, orange-glowing UFO hovering over their heads. None of the astonished children could understand how something that big could be completely silent. The UFO was in the area for about 15 minutes before slowly disappearing from sight.

About four months earlier, on February 6, 1963, another alien incursion took place in Washington, D.C. At that time, a local resident had a close encounter with a UFO that was passing through the restricted airspace of the capital.

The previous night, on February 5, 1963, another alien incursion occurred over Washington, D.C. At that time, a private pilot and a journalist witnessed a pulsating, yellow-white UFO maneuver around their plane.

Two nights earlier, on February 3, 1963, around 4:00 p.m., a UFO was sighted over Washington, D.C. While walking near the White House on 16th street, a government employee witnessed a glowing, 100 foot wide UFO passing slowly over the tree tops. The witness noticed that the underside of the craft had the appearance of a giant cat's eye that was simply amazing to behold. The close encounter changed the woman's life. *She said it felt as though something had been downloaded into her mind.*

Six months earlier, on August 3, 1962, at 6:17 p.m., a UFO was sighted passing low in front of the Washington Monument. It is worth noting that this monument marks the center of prohibited airspace for the DC area.

Two months earlier, on June 28, 1962, another alien incursion occurred in Washington, D.C. At that time, a number of glowing UFOs were sighted performing odd maneuvers in the restricted airspace of the capital.

Nine days earlier, on June 19, 1962, another alien incursion occurred in Washington, D.C. At that time, a glowing UFO was sighted performing radical turns in the restricted airspace of the capital.

About seven months earlier, on December 13, 1961, at approximately 5:05 p.m., another alien incursion occurred in Washington, D.C. That evening, a retired naval pilot, and two other men, witnessed a sharply-defined, grey, diamond-shaped UFO with a bright tip that had a brownish-orange glow centered beneath it. The witnesses noted that the UFO was totally silent, and its light pulsated rapidly. It was sighted flying straight and level for a few minutes in the controlled airspace of the capital area.

The previous month, on November 7, 1961, another UFO was sighted passing through the restricted airspace of Washington, D.C.

The previous month, on October 6, 1961 a mysterious UFO over the Pentagon was sighted and reported by military witnesses.

The previous month, on September 22, 1961, another alien incursion transpired around 7:00 a.m., in Washington, D.C. That morning, a UFO was sighted passing through the restricted airspace of the capital.

About two months earlier, on July 11, 1961, a spherical UFO was sighted in the restricted airspace over Washington, D.C., by a military officer.

The previous month, on June 19, 1961, several cigar-shaped UFOs were sighted in the restricted airspace over Washington, D.C. A radio technician observed the UFOs with optical instruments. The story was reported in the local newspapers.

The previous day, on June 18, 1961, another alien incursion took place in Washington, D.C. At that time, a glowing, silent UFO was sighted making strange maneuvers over the restricted airspace of the capital.

Earlier that month, on June 1, 1961, another spherical UFO was sighted in the restricted airspace over Washington, D.C.

The previous month, on May 24, 1961, another spherical UFO was sighted in the restricted airspace over Washington, D.C.

Seven days earlier, on May 17, 1961, another spherical UFO was sighted in the restricted airspace over Washington, D.C.

About three months earlier, on February 24, 1961, another UFO was sighted in the restricted airspace over Washington, D.C.

Earlier that month, on February 4, 1961, another UFO was sighted in the restricted airspace over Washington, D.C., by a military officer.

That same year, sometime in 1961, another alien incursion occurred around 5:05 p.m., in Washington, D.C. That afternoon, three people witnessed a sharply-defined, diamond-shaped UFO that had a brownish-orange glow beneath its center in a diamond shape. The light was one-third the total size of the UFO. The alien craft pulsated rapidly and made no sound. The sighting lasted three minutes.

The previous year, on September 11, 1960, another UFO was sighted in the restricted airspace over Washington, D.C., and may have caused a conventional plane to crash.

Seven months earlier, on February 13, 1960, another UFO was sighted in the restricted airspace over Washington, D.C., and may have caused a conventional airplane to crash.

One month earlier, on January 4, 1960, a UFO was sighted in the restricted airspace over Washington, D.C., and may have caused a conventional airplane to crash.

Sometime in the early 1960s, an interesting conversation took place one afternoon at a family gathering in Washington, D.C. According to one of the family members, her brother had served in a special branch of the armed forces. He had worked in what he described as "missile guidance systems." At the party, after having a few drinks, he stated that the military was fully aware of the existence of UFOs.

He said that the U.S. Army not only revealed the existence of UFOs to him, they had specifically trained himself and the others in his crew how to recognize their peculiar movements and characteristics on radar from other aircraft.

Apparently, the military did this because they did not want an accidental nuclear exchange as a result of UFOs being potentially confused with missile launches from the People's Republic of China or the Soviet Union. However, the military never revealed to the soldiers anything more than the fact that UFOs were really here.

CHAPTER THIRTEEN

UFOs Routinely Penetrate DC Airspace

With so many alien incursions of American airspace occurring during the early years of the Cold War, official explanations of UFOs grew increasingly bizarre and less credible. Clearly, no one knew where the alien aerospace craft and their occupants originated from, but one thing was certain they kept coming to DC.

There were intense peaks of UFO activity in 1952 and 1957 that forced the government and military to address the matter publicly. Despite the limited resources that were directed at this issue, the official position was for everyone to just remain calm. The press was told that although UFOs had repeatedly penetrated controlled U.S. air space, they represented no threat to national security: or did they?

Another alien incursion of restricted airspace took place over Washington, D.C., sometime in the late 1950s. The son of one of the witnesses recalled that his father was an airline pilot for *Trans World Airlines* with thousands of hours of flight time. His father had also been a pilot for the Air Force during the Korean War and had earned a degree in mechanical engineer. He also had extensive interests in science and technology.

One day, while flying a commercial aircraft from Chicago to Dulles Airport near DC, the boy's father was acting first officer and had the controls as they prepared to land. This was decades before 9/11 and the new flight restrictions. The aircraft flew over the area near the White House at about 15,000 feet in a holding pattern for landing. At that time, the first officer sighted a UFO off to the side of the airplane.

He noted that the alien craft was about 50-feet long. It was a metallic, cigar-shaped craft with an internal passage running down the axis of it like a tube. The first officer then called the flight engineer, and the captain, to come observe the UFO. All of them witnessed the same unexplainable craft.

The UFO then shot upward at an incredible speed and passed quite close to their airplane as it disappeared into sky. The UFO did not appear on either the Civilian Air Traffic Control radar or the local Air Force Base radar and was not emitting a transponder signal or responding to radio requests as are required by federal law.

In December of 1959, another alien incursion transpired in Washington, D.C. At that time, a local resident reportedly had a close encounter with extraterrestrial beings. No details were given.

About two months earlier, on October 7, 1959, a UFO was encountered between Washington, D.C., and Atlanta, Georgia, by *Eastern Airlines* flight 541. The pilot, stewardess and a passenger noted that the UFO was a cigar-shaped object with portholes on its entire length.

Two months earlier, on August 3, 1959, a UFO was sighted over the District of Columbia.

The previous day, on August 2, 1959, a UFO was sighted passing through the restricted airspace of Washington, D.C.

The previous month, on July 6, 1959, another alien incursion of restricted airspace transpired around 4:00 p.m., in Washington, D.C. That afternoon, a local resident was reportedly abducted by aliens in a space craft. No details of the event were given.

Two hours earlier, on the same day, another alien incursion of restricted airspace took place in Washington, D.C. The bizarre event was reportedly witnessed from a secret government office concealed on the top story of a garage at 5th and K Street.

At that time, military intelligence officers were conducting a secret investigation of UFOs and their occupants. The officers were interested in establishing a dialogue with extraterrestrials. As an experiment, they tried all means available including speaking to the ETs through individuals that had allegedly had the ability to enter a trance state.

That afternoon, verbal communications were reportedly established, but the intelligence officers wanted to have physical proof that the ETs actually existed. When the ETs asked what type of proof they wanted, the military officers requested to see one of their space craft. The ETs then asked when they wanted this sighting to occur. The officers replied that they wanted to see a space craft right away. The officers were then told to go to the window and look outside.

When the intelligence officers went to the window, they witnessed a UFO moving low through the sky over DC a short distance from their office. The astonished officers described the UFO as a glowing, saucer-shaped craft that was brighter around the perimeter than in the center.

The confusion that followed abruptly ended the telepathic communication with the alleged extraterrestrial entities. Attempts to verify the UFO with Washington Center radar were unsuccessful. No unidentified targets were returning radar echoes from that part of the sky at that time.

Oddly enough, the secret office where the DC sighting occurred was run by the National Photographic Interpretation Center. For many years it was the most highly classified photo lab in the country where film taken by U-2's, SR-71's and spy satellites were analyzed.

The previous month, on June 4, 1959, another alien incursion transpired at 3:02 a.m., in Washington, D.C. That morning, a glowing UFO was sighted performing odd maneuvers in the restricted airspace of the capital.

A few months earlier, on March 7, 1959, around 9:30 a.m., another alien incursion occurred in the District of Columbia. That morning, a female reverend noticed a strange man in a white helmet standing behind a hedge. As she went to greet him, she noticed that the man was dressed in a white, one-piece suit that covered him from head to toe. The white helmet was part of the suit and looked like a hood.

Then, the reverend became frightened and yelled, and the strange man moved away very rapidly; apparently "floating" over the ground. A local man, who witnessed the alien's face from 15 feet away, reported that there were two black holes where the eyes should have been.

The previous month, on February 5, 1959, at approximately 2:00 a.m., another alien incursion was captured on film in Washington, D.C. That morning, a black and white aerial photograph of a glowing UFO was taken over the Capitol building.

The previous year, in 1958, Congressman William H. Ayres stated that, "Congressional investigations are still being held on the problem of UFOs, and the problem is one in which there is quite a bit of interest. Since most of the material presented to the Committees is classified, the hearings are never published."

That same year, on December 1, 1958, another alien incursion transpired in Washington, D.C. At that time, a photograph was taken of a UFO passing through the restricted airspace of the capital.

Earlier that month, on October 7, 1958, at 6:02 p.m., another alien incursion took place in the District of Columbia. The witness was John R. Townsend, then Special Assistant for Research and Engineering to the Assistant Secretary of Defense. That evening, Mr. Townsend sighted a large, stationary, sharply-outlined, Saturn-shaped, aluminum-colored UFO in a clear sky for about 10 seconds.

The hovering UFO then started rising rapidly at an estimated speed of 1,000 mph and disappeared over the horizon. As it receded into the distance, the UFO gave the impression it was growing smaller until it was unable to be seen. Townsend estimated that the UFO moved off at a speed of 36,000 miles-per-hour!

About one week earlier, on September 29, 1958, around 9:25 a.m., another alien incursion transpired in Washington, D.C. That morning, a UFO was sighted passing through the restricted airspace of the capital.

Earlier that month, on September 1, 1958, another alien incursion occurred in Washington, D.C. At that time, motion picture film was taken of a UFO passing through the restricted airspace of the capital. The film was not made available to the public.

About four months earlier, in May of 1958, another alien incursion allegedly transpired around 6:00 p.m., in Mount Zion, Maryland, just north-west of Washington, D.C. That night, a UFO reportedly crashed or was shot down near a Nike Ajax missile battery. One of the witnesses to the event was serving in the military at the time. He recalled that *The New York Times* was made aware of the UFO crash. Word of the event soon reached *The Washington Post* and *The Washington Star*.

Shortly before the Air Force arrived to clean up the crash site, the badly damaged UFO somehow managed to take off, leaving debris all over the corn field. The next night, around 11:00 p.m., the Gaithersburg, Maryland Missile Battery encountered several UFOs hovering 50 to 100 feet above them. They turned on the radar and saw the blips produced by the UFOs just above the ground clutter. The UFOs then took off at an incredible speed, but were then seen on radar several miles away in just one sweep of the radar. This meant that the UFOs had traveled at an average speed of 17,000 miles per hour.

The previous year, in 1957, Admiral Delmar Fahrney stated publicly that, "Reliable reports indicate there are UFOs coming into our atmosphere at very-high speeds, and they are controlled by thinking intelligences."

That same year, on November 7, 1957, around 6:30 p.m., another alien incursion occurred in Washington, D.C. That evening, a UFO was sighted passing through the restricted airspace of the capital.

The previous month, on October 20, 1957, at approximately 5:25 a.m., another alien incursion took place in Washington, D.C. That morning, a glowing UFO was sighted performing strange maneuvers in the restricted airspace of the capital.

The previous month, on September 26, 1957, around 12:10 a.m., another alien incursion occurred in Washington, D.C. That morning, a UFO was sighted passing through the restricted airspace of the capital.

The previous month, on August 2, 1957, another alien incursion occurred in Washington, D.C. At that time, UFOs were sighted in the restricted airspace of the capital and then a power failure occurred in the area.

The previous month, on July 9, 1957, around 2:00 p.m., another alien incursion occurred in Washington, D.C. At that time, while standing on the corner of 5th and K Street, a local resident allegedly had a face-to-face encounter with extraterrestrial beings. It is important to note that this was the same location that military intelligence officers reportedly saw a UFO while attempting to communicate with ETs in July of 1959.

Two months earlier, on May 2, 1957, at approximately 3:00 a.m., another alien incursion occurred in Washington, D.C. That morning, a glowing UFO was sighted passing silently through the restricted airspace of the capital.

The previous month, in April of 1957, at 12:47 a.m., another alien incursion took place in Washington, D.C. That morning, two glowing UFOs were sighted passing through the restricted airspace of the capital.

The previous year, at approximately 11:10 a.m., on November 28, 1956, another alien incursion transpired in Washington, D.C. That morning, a glowing UFO was sighted passing through the restricted airspace of the capital.

About two months earlier, on September 4, 1956, at approximately 1:45 a.m., another alien incursion took place in Washington, D.C. That morning, a UFO was sighted passing through the restricted airspace of the capital while performing strange maneuvers.

The east coast of America was not the only hot spot for violations of restricted airspace by UFOs that year. I found that top secret documents obtained from the U.S. military gave an insight into an astonishing series of alien incursions over East Anglia, England, in 1956.

After receiving numerous calls reporting bright UFOs darting across the sky, military jets from the Royal Air Force base at Lakenheath spent more than seven hours trying to shoot down the glowing space craft that were picked up on army radar screens.

This was not an isolated event. In the 1950s, the British and Americans were actively engaged in intercepting and firing on UFOs sighted over sensitive military bases. Many of the fighter pilots suffered extreme stress from their close encounters. Despite the military's best efforts, no UFOs were shot down at that time that we know of.

The classified documents regarding these events were obtained under the U.S. Freedom of Information Act by UFO researcher Dave Clarke. One U.S. Air Force intelligence report described how 12 to 15 UFOs were picked up on radar screens on August 13, 1956.

The UFOs were tracked for more than 50 miles. One UFO was apparently flying at 4,000 mph. The document stated that the radar operators reporting the sightings knew that their equipment was functioning well and had not caused false radar returns.

The radar logs also described unusual visual sightings of brilliant-white UFOs darting across the skies. At times, the UFOs flew in formation and performed sharp turns. One document described how a UFO was tracked on radar for 26 miles before it hovered for five minutes and then flew off.

A cable was sent from U.S. Air Force Headquarters in Washington, D.C., to the British Royal Air Force warning of the "considerable interest and concern" caused by the ongoing UFO sightings and demanded an immediate inquiry.

Three days earlier, on August 10, 1956, at approximately 5:10 a.m., another alien incursion transpired in Washington, D.C. That morning, a UFO was sighted in the restricted airspace of the capital performing strange maneuvers.

One month earlier, in July of 1956, another alien incursion occurred in Washington, D.C. At that time, three UFOs were sighted passing through the restricted airspace of the capital.

The previous month, in June of 1956, a major four-day symposium on UFOs was held in Washington, D.C. It was unquestionably the most important UFO affair of the 1950s and was attended by leading military men, government officials and industrialists.

Men like William Lear (inventor of the *Lear Jet*) and assorted generals, admirals and former CIA heads freely discussed the UFO problem with the press. One of the results of the meetings was the founding of the *National Investigation Committee on Aerial Phenomena* (NICAP) by physicist Townsend Brown; a pioneer in electrostatic field propulsion.

That same month, on June 28, 1956, around 2:10 a.m., another alien incursion transpired in Washington, D.C. That morning, two UFOs were sighted passing through the restricted airspace of the capital.

Two weeks earlier, on June 14, 1956, at approximately 12:20 a.m., another alien incursion occurred in Washington, D.C. At that time, two glowing UFOs were sighted maneuvering in the restricted airspace over the city.

The previous month, on May 14, 1956, around 6:15 p.m., another alien incursion took place in Washington, D.C. That evening, two disc-shaped UFOs were sighted on the ground. No other details were given, but it is significant that the UFOs apparently landed.

Two months earlier, on March 20, 1956, another alien incursion transpired in Washington, D.C. At that time, three glowing UFOs were sighted passing through the restricted airspace of the capital.

Four days earlier, on March 16, 1956, another alien incursion occurred in Washington, D.C. At that time, three glowing UFOs were sighted passing through the restricted airspace of the capital.

Eleven days earlier, on March 5, 1956, at approximately 12:20 a.m., another alien incursion took place in Washington, D.C. That morning, a glowing UFO was sighted in the restricted airspace of the capital.

The previous year, on October 13, 1955, around 9:00 p.m., another alien incursion transpired in Washington, D.C. That night, a glowing UFO was sighted passing through the restricted airspace of the capital.

Six days earlier, on October 7, 1955, at approximately 9:00 p.m., another alien incursion took place in Washington, D.C. That night, a glowing UFO was sighted passing through the restricted airspace of the capital.

That same year, in 1955, the CIA Director, Allen Dulles, stated that, "Maximum security exists concerning the subject of UFOs." No doubt the CIA was very concerned about ongoing alien incursions like the one that took place on September 7, 1955, at approximately 6:30 a.m., in Washington, D.C. That morning, two photographers witnessed a glowing, disc-shaped UFO passing through the restricted airspace of the capital. One of the witnesses worked for the Army Map Service.

That same year, in 1955, the head of the Senate Armed Services Committee, Senator Richard Russell, made a public statement regarding his sighting of a UFO. He said, "I have discussed this matter with the affected agencies of the government, and they are of the opinion that it is not wise to publicize the matter at this time."

That same year, on August 23, 1955, around 10:45 a.m., another alien incursion occurred near the Pentagon. That morning, a local man using a 400x telescope witnessed six or more orange UFOs that were flying individually and in geometric formations. The UFOs were also seen circling and stopping in mid-air.

The previous month, on July 26, 1955, another alien incursion transpired in the restricted airspace of Washington, D.C. At that time, a brightly-glowing, round UFO with a trail of light about five times the length of the UFO approached Washington National Airport. The UFO then stopped, oscillated and then moved off at high speed. Ceiling lights at the airport went out when the UFO approached, but became operational once the UFO left the area.

Earlier that same month, on July 6, 1955, at approximately 10:30 p.m., another alien incursion occurred in Washington, D.C. That night, a dark UFO was sighted passing in front of the moon by local residents.

The previous month, on June 26, 1955, another alien incursion took place in Washington, D.C., at the Washington National Airport. That night, ceiling lights went out as a round-shaped UFO approached. When the UFO became targeted in a powerful searchlight, the light suddenly lost power.

One day earlier, on June 25, 1955, another alien incursion occurred in the restricted airspace of Washington, D.C. That evening, local residents witnessed a glowing UFO passing very low over the city. Physical effects were reported from the close encounter.

The previous year, on September 6, 1954, at approximately 11:30 p.m., another alien incursion occurred in Washington, D.C. That night, a glowing UFO was sighted passing through the restricted airspace of the capital.

The previous month, on August 17, 1954, around 12:50 p.m., another alien incursion transpired in Washington, D.C. That afternoon, a glowing, disc-shaped UFO was sighted passing through the restricted airspace of the capital.

Thirteen days earlier, on August 4, 1954, at approximately 5:10 a.m., another alien incursion occurred in Washington, D.C. That morning, a glowing UFO was sighted performing incredible aerial maneuvers in the restricted airspace of the capital.

A few days earlier, on July 29, 1954, around 2:35 a.m., another alien incursion transpired in Washington, D.C. That morning, a glowing UFO was sighted passing through the restricted airspace of the capital.

Ten days earlier, on July 19, 1954, another alien incursion transpired over Washington D.C. At that time, a *Pan Am* DC-4 was buzzed by up to six disc-shaped UFOs. The pilot reported that the alien craft were shooting across the sky at crazy angles, above and below his aircraft, until they vanished out of sight.

Nearly one week later, a *Capital Airlines* DC-4 was directed by air traffic control to observe a UFO they were picking up on their radar screen over Washington, D.C. At that time, the flight crew encountered several bright UFOs hovering in the air. The UFOs then flew out of sight as the DC-4 approached. According the flight captain, "In all my years of flying I've seen a lot of falling or shooting stars, but these objects moved faster than anything I've ever seen. They couldn't have been aircraft. They were moving too fast."

Later that day, the same UFOs put the military on high alert when they entered the restricted air space above the White House. Commercial aircraft in the area reported mysterious, orange, green and red lights that kept crossing in front of their flight path.

The previous month, on June 25, 1954, at 11:47 p.m., another alien incursion occurred in Washington, D.C. That night, a glowing UFO was sighted passing through the restricted airspace of the capital.

That same month, a series of alien incursions transpired on June 12, 13, 14, 1954, in Baltimore and Washington, D.C. At that time, UFOs were witnessed violating restricted airspace by radar and by eye witnesses on the ground.

In June of 1954, a giant UFO was sighted at a very-high altitude. It remained in the area for two hours while maneuvering between Washington, D.C., and Baltimore, Maryland.

The previous month, on May 16, 1954, around 3:15 p.m., another alien incursion took place in Washington, D.C. That afternoon, a glowing, disc-shaped UFO was sighted passing through the restricted airspace of the capital.

Three days earlier, on May 13, 1954, another alien incursion transpired in Washington, D.C. At that time, several large, glowing UFOs maneuvered over Washington National Airport for three hours. The UFOs were observed visually, and on radar, violating restricted airspace.

Two days earlier, on May 11, 1954, around 10:45 p.m., another alien incursion took place in Washington, D.C. At that time, three Air Force military police stationed at Washington National Airport witnessed two bright UFOs moving straight and level over the area. The UFOs were sighted on three separate occasions that night. The UFOs were seen to make 90-degree turns and fade away as they left. Each of the three sightings lasted about 45 seconds.

Four days earlier, on May 7, 1954, another alien incursion occurred in Washington, D.C. At that time, UFOs were sighted penetrating restricted airspace by eyewitnesses on the ground.

The previous day, on May 6, 1954, another alien incursion transpired in Washington, D.C. At that time, naval radar tracked an enormous UFO circling 90,000 feet above DC. The UFO was also sighted visually.

The previous day, on May 5, 1954, another alien incursion occurred in Washington, D.C. At that time, two huge UFOs maneuvered at high altitude over the DC area. Fighter pilots sent to intercept were relieved that their jets were unable to fly high enough to engage the massive, powerful UFOs.

About four months earlier, on January 29, 1954, another alien incursion transpired around 12:10 a.m., in Washington, D.C. That morning, a glowing UFO was sighted passing through the restricted airspace of the capital.

Sometime that decade, during summer in the early 1950s, at approximately 8:00 p.m., another alien incursion occurred in Washington, D.C. The witnesses were 12 to 14 years old at the time. They were playing outside on the porch which looked out over the Potomac River and the DC skyline where aircraft routinely approached the Washington National Airport on their landing route.

At that time, they witnessed a round UFO come down out of the sky towards a plane that was coming in for a landing. They noted that the strange, glowing, spherical UFO flew around the incoming aircraft. It then flew in a large circle before quickly flying off in the same direction it had come from and then disappeared in a split second. The witnesses estimated that the alien incursion had lasted about two to three minutes.

They were so excited by what they had witnessed they began telling people in the neighborhood and calling friends and relatives on the phone. The next day, the children looked in the local papers and found only one small article about the UFO sighting. The newspaper claimed it was just a meteor that was out of its orbit. All four of the children had never heard of a meteor coming out of the sky, making a circle in the sky, and then shooting back up into space again.

That same year, one day in 1953, another alien incursion occurred. At that time, a retired U.S. Air Force lieutenant colonel, witnessed seven UFOs flying over Washington, D.C.

Later that same year, on October 10, 1953, at approximately 2:35 a.m., another alien incursion transpired in Washington, D.C. That morning, a UFO was sighted moving erratically through the restricted airspace of the capital. Also, earlier that same morning, while flying over the Baltimore area, an *American Airlines* DC-6 had a near-collision with a dark UFO that emitted a blinding white beam of light.

A few months earlier, on July 25, 1953, at 7:09 a.m., another alien incursion occurred in Washington, D.C. That morning, a glowing UFO was sighted passing through the restricted airspace of the capital.

About five months earlier, on February 23, 1953, at approximately 9:30 p.m., another alien incursion took place in Washington, D.C. That night, a glowing UFO was sighted passing through the restricted airspace of the capital.

Earlier that month, on February 9, 1953, around 10:30 p.m., another alien incursion transpired in Washington, D.C. That night, a red-glowing UFO was sighted passing through the restricted airspace of the capital. It flew low over the city before climbing rapidly into space.

The same night, another alien incursion took place in North Carolina. Alerted by a naval signal tower at Norfolk, Virginia, a Marine Corps fighter pilot chased a silver UFO which had been sighted earlier, from the ground, while over Washington, D.C.

After flying in his F-9F Panther for half an hour without seeing anything unusual, the military pilot was returning to base. While flying over the base at about 20,000 feet, he witnessed the red lights of the UFO below him. What caused him to notice the UFO was that it moved from a position below his aircraft to 10,000 feet vertically above him in a matter of seconds.

He then turned and chased the UFO at a little over 500 mph, but was unable to gain on it. The fighter pilot estimated the UFO was about 10 miles from him during the three-to-four-minute chase. At that distance, it visually appeared about one-quarter-inch wide and about three-inches long.

He noted that the UFO was the color of white heat, and it had a red glow behind it. It had two red lights on the left hand side that were bounding and flashing off the end; encircling an arc. At one point, he seemed to briefly gain on the object, but it suddenly dropped down from his altitude and rapidly disappeared toward the Atlantic Ocean.

About three months earlier, on November 30, 1952, at approximately 12:30 a.m., and again at 6:30 a.m., more alien incursions occurred in Washington, D.C. That morning, radar operators and military officers at Washington National Airport reported tracking UFOs.

Fifteen days earlier, on November 15, 1952, at approximately 2:40

a.m., another alien incursion occurred in Washington, D.C. That morning, a silent, glowing UFO was sighted in the restricted airspace over the capital.

Five days earlier, on November 10, 1952, around 9:50 p.m., another alien incursion took place in Washington, D.C. That night, a glowing UFO was sighted passing silently through the restricted airspace of the capital.

About two months earlier, on September 20, 1952, another alien incursion transpired in Washington, D.C. At that time, a silent, glowing UFO was sighted passing through restricted airspace over the capital.

Eighteen days earlier, on September 12, 1952, at approximately 9:30 p.m., another alien incursion took place in Allen, Maryland. That night, while using binoculars, members of a Ground Observer Corps sighted a UFO. They noted that the UFO emitted a white light with a red trim and some type of streamers. The craft was observed for 35 minutes and was later sighted passing directly over the U.S. Capitol in Washington, D.C.

That same year, in 1952, a CIA memo stated that, "In view of the wide interest within the Agency, outside knowledge of Agency interest in UFOs carries the risk of making the problem even more serious in the public's mind than it already is."

The previous month, on August 15, 1952, around 9:35 p.m., another alien incursion transpired in Washington, D.C. That night, a glowing UFO was sighted passing through restricted airspace.

Two days earlier, on August 13, 1952, at approximately 8:00 p.m., another alien incursion transpired in Washington, D.C. That night, 68 UFOs were tracked on radar performing incredible maneuvers in the restricted airspace of the capital.

The previous week, on August 5 and 6, 1952, more alien incursions took place in Washington, D.C. At that time, two UFOs were sighted on radar performing incredible aerial maneuvers in the restricted airspace of the capital.

The previous month, on July 29, 1952, at approximately 2:30 p.m., a series of alien incursions occurred at Langley Air Force Base, in Virginia. That afternoon, an air traffic controller officer witnessed a UFO traveling at an estimated 2,600 mph. It was flying below 5,000 feet and was headed toward the air base for about two minutes before turning away.

About twenty minutes later, around 2:50 p.m., three radar operators at Langley tracked a UFO radar target moving away rapidly and then stopping for two minutes before moving again extremely fast. The incursion lasted approximately four minutes.

That same day, July 29, 1952, as many as 12 UFOs at a time were tracked by CAA radar moving in a 15-mile-wide formation, in the District of Columbia. An Eastern Airlines pilot that was asked to visually check on the radar targets reported seeing nothing in the sky. CAA officials later said the targets disappeared from the radar screen when the plane was in their area, then came back in behind the plane after it left. At about the same time, an Air Force pilot sighted three round, white UFOs 10 miles southeast of Andrews Air Force Base, in Maryland. Later, at approximately 1:30 a.m., as many as nine UFOs were tracked on radar in the DC area. The UFOs performed impossible maneuvers in the sky before departing.

Ironically, later that same day, the Air Force held a press conference at the Pentagon during which all the recent UFO sightings in and around DC were attributed to temperature inversion layers that had caused "radar mirages." Additionally, the strange lights people were seeing and photographing and even chasing in military jets were claimed to be just typical ground lights reflected in the sky under freak atmospheric conditions. Knowing that the press and public would be relentless in their questions, the Air Force announced a new scientific program to evaluate UFO sightings.

The media aggressively covered the historical events in Washington, D.C. In fact, the day of the Pentagon press conference, *The Cedar Rapids Gazette* headline read "Saucers Swarm Over Capital."

In the summer of 1952, former Washington National air traffic controller, Howard Cocklin, stated that, "I saw it on the radar screen and out the window. It was an unidentified, whitish-blue object: not just a light. It was a solid form of a saucer-shaped craft. I have never seen anything like that saucer; not before or since. It just went away. Where did it go?"

That same summer, on July 28, 1952, in the evening, another close encounter of the first kind reportedly occurred in Washington, D.C. That same day, the daily news papers reported a United Press story from Washington, D.C., that stated the Air Defense Command had ordered its jet pilots to pursue and, if necessary, "shoot down" UFOs sighted anywhere in the country. Apparently those orders were followed to the letter. Allegedly, a UFO was shot at by a military jet causing pieces of it to fall to earth where they were later recovered and analyzed. The sensational information had come, in part, from a Canadian scientist named Wilbert Smith.

In July of 1962, just months before Smith died, he confided to a friend that he had been visited by Canadian government officials as well as American government officials many times regarding UFOs. Reportedly, these were upper-echelon people with attaché cases that were chained and locked to their wrists. They brought samples of alien hardware and metal that had been recovered which they wanted him to analyze.

Smith claimed that United States military intelligence agencies literally had tons of recovered hardware from crashed UFOs. They also had huge archives of photographs and movies of UFOs. They apparently admitted this to Smith when he was the director of research for *Project Magnet* from 1950 to 1954.

According to Smith, there were many UFO sightings over Washington, D.C., in 1952. He was told that during that time, an Air Force jet managed to shoot a piece off of a small, two-foot wide, disc-shaped UFO which was found two hours later. The piece of exotic metal had a white glow to it. After two weeks, the metal had diminished to a brown texture.

The piece of the UFO had a very-distinct edge. It was curved and had been shot off the edge of a small, disc-shaped UFO. One portion of the aluminum was as hard as quartz. It could only be broken down for analysis by grinding, but the composition seemed similar to standard kitchen pots.

There was some confusion whether or not there were one or two pieces of UFO debris recovered from the DC incident. However, at least one piece was recovered by naval commander Alvin Moore, an intelligence officer with the CIA, and was later taken to Smith.

Smith claimed that Vice Admiral Knowles told him that this specific piece of metal had been shot off a UFO by a military aircraft and was seen to fall in the yard of a farmer across the Potomac River in Virginia, just outside the city of Washington. Upon searching the area, several metallic pieces of the UFO were reportedly found.

The piece that Smith allegedly analyzed was a chunk of brownish, shapeless, metal-like structure. It was not more than two inches in diameter. The edge was rounded in cross section, perhaps a quarter inch thick, and was considerably thicker at the center.

The outer surface was smooth, but not polished. At the broken sections, there were obviously iron particles and even some evidence of rust. The weight was somewhat lighter than solid iron, but not much. Mr. Smith stated that a chemical test had been made of the piece and that iron had been found in it, but little else could be identified.

In a November 1961 interview, Smith said, "I visited with Admiral Knowles, and I had with me a piece of metal that had been shot off a small flying saucer near Washington, D.C., in July of 1952. I showed it to the Admiral. It was a piece of metal about twice as big as your thumb which had been loaned to me for a very short time by the U.S. Air Force. The only difference in the metal of UFOs is that they are much harder than our materials."

Regarding the UFO that was shot at near DC, Smith said, "The pilot was chasing a small, glowing disk that was about two feet in diameter. After being shot, a small chunk flew off the UFO and the pilot saw it glowing all the way to the ground. He radioed in his report, and a ground party hurried to the scene.

"The thing was still glowing when they found it an hour later. The entire piece weighed about a pound. The segment that was loaned to me was about one third of that. There was iron rust, but the thing was in reality a matrix of magnesium orthosilicate. Embedded in the matrix of that metal were thousands of 15 micron (0.00059 inch) spheres."

In the summer of 1952, there were many alien incursions of the restricted airspace over Washington, D.C. One event that occurred at dawn, on July 27, 1952, was highly significant. At that time, Air Force personnel and other trained personnel at Washington National Airport witnessed a large, round UFO reflecting sunlight.

It was seen hovering over the U.S. Capitol building. After about a minute, the UFO wavered briefly then shot straight up into the sky and disappeared from sight. It was clear that despite the military's best efforts, the restricted airspace over Washington, D.C., could not be secured when it came to UFOs.

That same day, July 27, an Air Force *Project Blue Book* officer and a naval electronics officer arrived at Washington National Airport Center. At that time, the officer and other radar operators witnessed seven solid UFO targets on radar.

The naval electronics expert checked on temperature inversions, but they were minor and could not explain what was going on. He then advised his Air Force Command Post, and requested an interception mission. By the time the F-94 jets arrived from Delaware, no unidentified targets remained, and no visual contacts were made.

Earlier that night, UFO targets were seen on the radar at Washington National Airport which is located just south east of the Capitol building. That night, civilian pilots witnessed glowing-white UFOs on four occasions. The witnesses included a *United Airlines* pilot that had a close encounter near Herndon, Virginia and two CAA pilots that sighted UFOs over Maryland. Also, a *National Airlines* pilot, while flying at 1,700 feet near Andrews Air Force Base, saw a UFO "flying directly over their airliner."

Later that morning, Air Force crews of two F-94's and ground observers witnessed four disc-shaped, silver-bluish, glowing UFOs flying in a V-formation. The UFOs all suddenly shot straight up and disappeared at 5,000 feet. The UFOs were tracked by naval ground radar at Norfolk and by airborne radar.

Later that night, at 9:54 p.m., Andrews Air Force Base surveillance radar tracked 10 to 12 UFOs violating the restricted airspace of Washington, D.C., at will. A few minutes later, at 9:57 p.m., Washington National Airport saw the same group of UFOs on their radar.

In fact, from 9:15 p.m. until morning, 8 to 12 UFOs had registered on ARTC radar at the Washington National Airport. One of the UFOs that appeared at 9:30 p.m. was reported as a big target. At that time, the Air Force Command Post was notified of UFO radar targets. As a result, two F-94 jet interceptors were scrambled from New Castle Air Force Base, in Delaware, to investigate.

Later, after his hair raising close encounter, one of the F-94 pilots reported that, "Based on my experience in fighter tactics, it is my opinion that the UFO was controlled by something having visual contact with us. The power and acceleration of that UFO were beyond the capability of any known U.S. aircraft."

A few hours later, on July 26, 1952, at approximately 12:20 a.m., F-94 jet interceptors were again scrambled from New Castle Air Force Base, in Delaware, to investigate Washington, D.C., radar reports of UFOs. One F-94 pilot made visual contact and appeared to be gaining on a target. Both the F-94 and the UFO were observed on radar and "appeared to be traveling at the same approximate speed." When the F-94 pilot tried to overtake the UFO, it disappeared visually and on radar. The pilot remarked about the "incredible speed of the object."

Later that same day, at about 2:30 p.m., radar operators at Langley Air Force Base, in Virginia, sighted a UFO on their radar for a couple of minutes. The UFO moved at speeds of up to 2,600 mph before disappearing from radar.

At about 2:50 p.m., the same radar operators picked up another UFO that suddenly stopped and hovered for a couple of minutes before leaving the area.

Around 7:30 p.m., an Air Force lieutenant at Andrews Air Force Base sighted a dark, disc-shaped UFO moving slowly northeast with an "oscillating, rolling motion." The UFO was last seen entering some clouds.

From 8:00 p.m., until sometime after midnight in the Washington, D.C., area, credible people such as radar operators, F-94 fighter pilots, and airline pilots all witnessed UFOs. At that time, many UFOs were tracked by radar moving at various speeds over the area. Motion picture film and still photos were taken of UFOs as they slowly passed over the capital area. The photos and film were later confiscated and classified by the military (in 1995 and 2005, two of those films were leaked to the public and can be viewed in the photo section of unicusmagazine.com).

Another of the F-94 pilots that was involved in the alien incursions that occurred in Washington, D.C., stated that on the night of July 26, 1952, he had taken off from Dover Air Force Base, in Delaware, and headed for DC. He was ordered to remain below 10,000 feet. He recalled that, "We quickly figured out that we were not going to catch or get near this UFO. We tried for a few minutes to acquire the UFO. We tried very hard. We gave it our best effort. That night, we had the state of the art electronic equipment, but the UFO we were trying to catch was too elusive.

"At times, it moved at supersonic speeds and other times very slowly. Its ability to change direction was so quick, and so erratic, that there was no way a manned, jet aircraft could stay with the UFO as it turned, climbed or descended like that. We just couldn't catch it, or lock on with our radar."

There were many pilots involved in the defense of DC airspace that suffered in various ways from their extraterrestrial encounters. Another F-94 pilot that had flown one of the first intercept missions reported that, "The next day, back at the base, some strange things happened. I started getting interviewed by high ranking officers. They took my radar officer and I into separate rooms and debriefed us. Then, they threatened us. They did certain things that really surprised me. After a few days, they told us in no uncertain terms not to say a word about this to anybody. They even threatened me with a court martial.

"The interrogation phase happened right after our attempted intercept of UFOs. We were called in several times. Each time, it seemed to get a little heavier and a bit more serious. Sometimes, I felt like maybe they didn't believe me, but they had my radar operator, and they had other crews that had been on the same type of incident.

"We were always truthful with them. Eventually, we were ordered to forget about it. They told us it officially didn't happen and not to ever talk about it to anybody. After that, we just didn't talk about it. But I knew there were some other pilots, from other air bases, that had also scrambled to intercept UFOs on that particular mission in DC."

That same month, on July 24, 1952, another alien incursion transpired in Washington, D.C. That night, two UFOs were picked up on radar performing incredible aerial maneuvers in the restricted airspace of the capital.

Four days earlier, on July 20, 1952, around 1:00 a.m., another series of alien incursions took place. At that time, a *Capital Airlines* DC-4, taking off from Washington National Airport, was called by the control tower to check on unidentified radar targets in the area. Once airborne, the pilots and crew witnessed three UFOs. Minutes later, three more UFOs were sighted near Martinsburg, West Virginia. The pilots reported that "the UFOs looked like falling stars without tails which moved rapidly up, down, and horizontally and could hover."

Later that morning, around 3:00 a.m., another *Capital Airlines* flight crew, approaching Washington National Airport to land, reported a UFO following them from Herndon, Virginia, to within four miles of Washington National airport which was confirmed on radar.

Chief CAA air traffic controller Harry Barnes later said that, "The pilot's subsequent description of the movement of the objects coincided with the position of our radar targets at all times while in our range. For six hours, there were at least ten UFOs moving above Washington, D.C. They were not ordinary aircraft."

Also during that time, at Andrews Air Force base, in Maryland, five witnesses observed three reddish-orange UFOs moving erratically.

Later that night/morning, additional UFOs appeared on radar at Washington National Airport in DC. Then, at 1:05 a.m., five witnesses at Andrews Air Force Base sighted three reddish-orange UFOs moving erratically.

Earlier, Air Force radar operators at Andrews Air Force Base, in Maryland, tracked 10 UFOs for 15 to 20 minutes. The UFOs approached a runway, then scattered and made sharp turns and reversals of direction.

Between 4:30 a.m., and 6:30 a.m., additional UFOs were tracked on ARTC radar at Washington National Airport. It is clear from the historical record that all these alien incursions were not isolated events.

For example, the previous night, on July 19, 1952, from 11:40 p.m., to 6:00 a.m., Washington National Airport picked up numerous UFOs on radar, and visual sightings by ground observers, and pilots in the air. Just before midnight, CAA radar picked up a number of UFOs which varied in speed from 0 mph to about 800 mph in a manner inconsistent with conventional aircraft.

On that day, July 19, 1952, a number of experienced CAA radar operators observed UFOs on their radar screens. At one point, compatible returns were being received not only at the ARTC radar but also on the ARS radar in a separate location at Washington National Airport and on radar at Andrews Air Force base. It was significant that both ground and airborne observers sighted UFOs in locations matching those of the blips on the ground radar.

The previous day, on July 18, 1952, at approximately 2:00 a.m., another alien incursion occurred in Washington, D.C. At that time, a radio station chief engineer observed six or seven bright-orange, glowing, disc-shaped UFOs moving in single file. Then, in turn, each UFO veered sharply upward and disappeared from sight.

Five days earlier, on July 13, 1952, at approximately 4:00 a.m., another alien incursion took place. That morning, the crew of a National Airlines plane en route to Washington National Airport sighted a UFO about 60 miles outside of DC. At that time, they observed a UFO that looked like a glowing, blue-white ball of light hovering in the sky.

According to one of the crew members, "The UFO suddenly came up to 11,000 feet. It then maintained a parallel course, on the same level, at the same speed as us, until the pilot turned on all his landing lights. The UFO then departed from the vicinity at an estimated 1,000 mph. The weather was excellent for observation." The crew all agreed that the UFO "took off straight up and away." The UFO was tracked on radar by Washington National radar operators at that time.

Six days earlier, on July 7, 1952, another alien incursion transpired in Washington, D.C. At that time, a glowing UFO was sighted passing silently through the restricted airspace of the capital.

Six days earlier, on July 1, 1952, at approximately 7:25 a.m., another alien incursion occurred. That morning, two F-94's were scrambled to intercept a UFO that a Ground Observer Corps spotter sighted near Boston. At that time, two fighter jets were vectored into the general area. The F-94s searched the area, but officially did not see anything unusual.

According to a declassified report, that night two UFOs had come down across Boston, on a southwesterly heading, crossed Long Island and then hovered for a few minutes over the Army's secret laboratories at Fort Monmouth before proceeding toward Washington, D.C.

Soon after that event, the Air Force received an important telephone call from a physics professor at George Washington University who had just witnessed a dull-grey, smoky-colored UFO hovering over Washington, D.C., for about eight minutes. The professor reported that every once in a while, the UFO would move through an arc of about 15 degrees to the right or left, but it always returned to its original position.

While he was watching the UFO, he took a quarter out of his pocket and held it at arm's length to compare its size with the UFO. The UFO was visually about half the diameter of the quarter. When he first saw the UFO, it was about 30 to 40 degrees above the horizon, but during the eight minutes, it steadily dropped lower in the sky until the buildings in downtown Washington, D.C., blocked his view of the alien craft.

The professor was standing in the heart of DC when the event occurred. He first noticed the UFO when he saw hundreds of people along the streets looking up in the air and pointing. He estimated that at least 500 people were looking at it. Soon after that event, Washington newspapers printed a small article stating that hundreds of phone calls had been received by people reporting a strange UFO in the restricted airspace of the capital.

That same year, 1952, an FBI memo regarding UFOs stated, "Some military officials are seriously considering the possibility of incursions by interplanetary ships."

During a 21st century Washington, D.C., briefing to the media regarding official disclosure of the existence of UFOs and ETs, retired Colonel Ross Derickson recalled that, "While I was at the Atomic Energy Commission (AEC), in 1952, I had my first incident with UFOs, which was in mid-July, when they flew over Washington, D.C.

"At that time, I witnessed nine UFOs. I was a staff officer for the military liaison committee between the chairman of the AEC and the Secretary of Defense. I became acquainted with not only the Army, Navy and Air Force but civilian agencies. I developed other contacts with the CIA and the NSA.

"During that period of time, one of my functions was to accompany a security team which visited all of the nuclear facilities to check on the security of weapons. We were getting reports of UFOs [entering restricted] airspace over storage facilities, and that went on continuously.

"After those series of incursions, which went on through the entire '50s, I was assigned to the Unified Command under Admiral Felt during the 1960s. I was the officer in charge of the alternate command post involved with nuclear weapons operation planning. During that period of time, I maintained contacts with NORAD, with the SAC operations, and was involved with operational plans for the use of nuclear weapons. At that time, I also learned of a number of military incidents involving UFOs."

That same year, on June 21, 1952, another alien incursion transpired in Washington, D.C. At that time, local residents witnessed UFOs passing through the restricted airspace of the capital.

One day earlier, on the night of June 20, 1952, another alien incursion occurred in Washington, D.C. At that time, a glowing UFO was sighted passing through the restricted airspace of the capital.

Earlier that month, on the night of June 7, 1952, another alien incursion transpired, in Washington, D.C. At that time, a glowing UFO was sighted moving wildly through the restricted airspace of the capital.

The previous month, on May 23, 1952, at approximately 8:00 p.m., another alien incursion took place in Washington, D.C. That night, a formation of 50 glowing, silent UFOs were sighted on radar and by eye witnesses on the ground. The UFOs performed incredible maneuvers while passing through the restricted airspace of the capital.

The previous day, on May 22, 1952, between 1:00 a.m., and 2:00 a.m., another alien incursion took place in the District of Columbia. That night, a top ranking CIA official and several dinner guests, including a retired general, witnessed a silent, red-glowing UFO as it approached from the west at about 5,000 feet. Then, the UFO suddenly climbed almost vertically in the southeast and leveled off for a few seconds before going into a near vertical dive. It then leveled off again and disappeared to the east.

Six days earlier, on May 16, 1952, around 3:25 a.m., another alien incursion transpired in Washington, D.C. That morning, a glowing UFO was sighted by a local resident as it passed through the restricted airspace of the capital.

The previous day, on May 15, 1952, at approximately 10:25 p.m., another alien incursion occurred in Washington, D.C. That night, two lieutenants and their girlfriends witnessed a glowing, golden-red, oval-shaped UFO moving low and slow on a level path before departing at an incredible speed.

About one month earlier, on April 2, 1952, another alien incursion transpired in Washington, D.C. At that time, a local resident took a photo of a UFO passing through the restricted airspace of the capital.

About two months earlier, on February 13, 1952, at approximately 2:30 a.m., another alien incursion occurred over Washington, D.C. That morning, the flight crew of a C-47 was flying over the capital when they encountered a glowing UFO.

A few months earlier, on November 18, 1951, at approximately 3:20 a.m., another alien incursion took place in Washington, D.C. That night, the crew of *Capital Airlines* Flight 610 and an Andrews Air Force base senior air traffic controller witnessed a UFO that had multiple bright lights. The UFO followed the civilian aircraft for about 20 minutes before it turned and flew away.

That same year, in 1951, an F-51 pilot described his close encounter with a UFO to Air Force intelligence officers. The pilot recalled that the UFO was flat on the top and bottom. From a front view it appeared to have round edges that were slightly beveled. There were no vapor trails, or exhaust, or any visible means of propulsion. The UFO was sighted traveling at a tremendous speed. The pilot was considered by his associates to be highly reliable, of mature judgment, and a credible observer.

On September 28, 1951, the sci-fi movie *The Day the Earth Stood Still* appeared in movie theaters across America. Considering all the alien incursions that had occurred in the Washington, D.C., and the surrounding area prior to that time, it was clear that someone knew something extraordinary was going on and decided to write about it as fiction.

According to the script, after orbiting the Earth at 4,000 mph, a human-looking alien named Klaatu landed his UFO on the National Mall in Washington, D.C., in a circular clearing located between the Washington Monument and the White House called the Ellipse. After landing safely, Klaatu exited the UFO wearing a silver space suit and was accompanied by a large humanoid robot called Gort. They were met by soldiers and astonished citizens.

Unfortunately, when Klaatu offered the people of Earth a technological device as a gift, the soldiers thought it was a weapon and shot him. In response, the robot emitted an energy beam that caused all human weapons in the area to evaporate without harming the soldiers.

Klaatu was then taken to Walter Reed Army Hospital, where he quickly recovered. At that time, he was visited by Mr. Harley, the Secretary to the President of the United States. Klaatu then tried to convince the humans to organize a meeting of world leaders so he could present an important message to humanity. However, Mr. Harley explained to Klaatu that the United Nations was a largely defunct and irrelevant organization. Frustrated, Klaatu claimed that his people had learned long ago to live without their leaders always fighting against each other.

Klaatu then escaped from the hospital and decided to meet a typical human family. He rented a room at a boarding house on Harvard Avenue and met a family and other guests. To hide his true identity, Klaatu told them that his name was "Carpenter," a name he found on a suit he had stolen from the hospital. Two of the residents of the boarding house were government employees with the Department of Commerce. One of them was a widow named Helen who had a son named Bobby.

The next morning, Klaatu/Carpenter listened carefully to the paranoid discussions among the boarding house residents regarding the alien and his UFO. The humans were convinced that the spaceship was the work of the Soviets, or Democrats, or some other enemy of America.

Helen had a boyfriend named Tom. When he planned a day getaway for himself and Helen, "Carpenter" offered to take care of Bobby for them. Bobby then gave Mr. Carpenter a tour of Washington, D.C., including Arlington National Cemetery where Carpenter was deeply troubled by the fact that "all these people were killed in wars."

They then visited the Lincoln Memorial, where Carpenter was impressed by the inscription of Abraham Lincoln's Gettysburg Address. At that time, he concluded that there may be someone intelligent people on Earth who would understand his message. He then asked Bobby who the greatest person on Earth was. Bobby informed him it was a leading American scientist that conveniently lived in Washington, D.C.

Carpenter then proposed that he and Bobby visit the scientist. However, when they arrived at his house, the scientist was not home. Carpenter then used his alien technology to open the locked door and leave a calling card in the form of a mathematical solution to a problem on the scientist's blackboard.

However, Carpenter's cover was soon blown and he was forced to reveal his identity to the scientist. Klaatu then tried to convince the scientist to organize a meeting among all the world's scientists who, in turn, would carry his messages to their leaders. The scientist then urged Klaatu to think of a back-up plan in case his message was rejected. Klaatu agreed to a demonstration as long as it was not destructive.

He returned to his UFO that night to program specific instructions into his highly-advanced computer to demonstrate the seriousness of his message. Klaatu had decided to remotely turn off electric devices all over the world including the ignition systems of all vehicles with some exceptions, such as hospitals and planes in flight. Hence the title of the movie; *The Day The Earth Stood Still*.

The day of the electrical blackout, Klaatu was trapped in an elevator with Helen. At that time, he explained the whole situation. Because of the power blackout, which lasted 30 minutes, Klaatu was considered a national security threat by the U.S. military. They decided that he must be taken dead or alive.

Soon, Helen understood Klaatu's real mission. Later, after the blackout was over, Tom confronted Helen with his recently acquired knowledge that "Mr. Carpenter" was actually the space man. Tom insisted that by betraying Klaatu, he could become rich and famous.

When Helen asked Tom about the impact that betraying Klaatu would have on the rest of the world, he said, "I'm not interested in the rest of the world." Repulsed by Tom's indifference, Helen rushed to help Klaatu. However, Klaatu was shot again, this time fatally.

Concerned about what actions Gort would take in the event of his death, Klaatu had taught Helen the command phrase "Gort, Klaatu barada nikto" to use in the event he was killed. During a dramatic face-to-face encounter, the huge robot nearly killed Helen before she could utter the alien words.

The robot then aborted his attack against Helen and carried her into the UFO. He then retrieved Klaatu's dead body, brought him inside the UFO, and revived him. However, even Klaatu's alien technology was only capable of reviving him long enough to deliver his message.

After Klaatu/Carpenter was revived, he stepped out of the UFO and spoke to the assembled scientists. He told them they could either decide to abandon global warfare, and join other interplanetary races of people and live in peace, or be destroyed by the powerful robot race of Gort. The mortally wounded alien and his interplanetary police robot then boarded their UFO and departed from Washington, D.C.

It is probably just a strange coincidence, but in real life, the most dramatic photograph of a fleet of UFOs in the night sky over Washington, D.C., was taken in front of the Carpenters Union building located Senate side of the Capitol, on July 16, 2002.

A few months before *The Day the Earth Stood Still* appeared in theaters, on June 27, 1950, at approximately 7:00 p.m., another alien incursion transpired in Washington, D.C. That evening, three glowing UFOs were sighted passing through the restricted airspace of the nation's capital.

Two days earlier, on June 25, 1950, around 9:25 a.m., another alien incursion took place in Washington, D.C. That morning, a silent, glowing UFO was sighted passing through the restricted airspace of the nation's capital.

The previous month, on May 29, 1950, at approximately 9:20 p.m., another alien incursion occurred near Mount Vernon, Virginia. That night, a captain with 10,000 flying hours, his copilot, a flight engineer, a steward-ess, and multiple passengers were on a DC-6 airliner headed southwest out of Washington, D.C.

They were en route to Nashville, flying at 7,500 feet and travelling at 250 mph when they encountered a spindle-shaped UFO that was esti-mated to have been 150-feet long. It was a metallic object that emitted an intense-blue light on the tail. The event began when the copilot sighted a bright blue light on a direct collision course with their DC-6 airliner. At that time, the captain executed emergency evasive maneuvers and turned 45 degrees to the right.

The UFO then passed the aircraft quickly to the left at a slightly higher altitude and crossed in front of part of a full moon to the south where its submarine-like silhouette was clearly seen. The flight captain then turned the aircraft back onto its original course which allowed the crew to get the UFO in view again.

The witnesses recalled that the UFO appeared to remain station-ary for about 30 seconds. The copilot then noticed that the UFO had circled around to their right side. The captain banked right again, while the UFO paced the airliner for about 20 to 30 seconds before climbing to the east at a 30-degree angle and disappearing at a fantastic speed.

About two months earlier, on April 9, 1950, another alien incursion transpired during broad daylight in Washington, D.C. According to one of the witnesses, "A retired naval officer and I, and two girlfriends, had just come out of the *Translux Theatre* in downtown DC. That's when I looked up and observed a metallic UFO hovering low over the city. It was silent and appeared to have a bright fire in the center. It was about as big as a mid-sized military aircraft.

"I instinctively yelled, 'Look, a flying saucer!' At that exact moment, it went up and way. The others only saw a bright light. I wish I had drawn it at the time. It was circular, but had a tambourine-like appearance with four spherical attachments on the sides."

Five days earlier, on April 4, 1950, during a White House Press Conference in Washington, D.C., President Harry Truman said, "I can assure you the flying saucers, given that they exist, are not constructed by any power on earth."

The previous month, on March 26, 1950, another alien incursion transpired over Washington, D.C. At that time, a former Air Force aircraft inspector/pilot flew his plane directly at a disc-shaped UFO. After the close encounter, the UFO then zoomed up into the overcast sky and disappeared.

In the 1950's, the first director of the CIA, Rear Admiral Roscoe Hillenkoetter, said, "I know that neither Russia nor the U.S. has any aircraft even approaching such high speeds and maneuvers. Behind the scenes, high ranking officers are soberly concerned about the UFOs, but through official secrecy and ridicule, many citizens are led to believe that they are nonsense."

CHAPTER FOURTEEN

Days of Discovery

During my investigation, I discovered that radiation was an important piece of the UFO puzzle. There were many well-documented reports of people and plants and other objects that had been burned by the energy emitted from UFOs. It was clear that UFOs employed a very powerful energy source.

I began looking at this aspect of the subject very carefully after learning that the DC photographer, Mr. Allen, had been burned by some type of radiation on July 16, 2002, while shooting a three-and-a-half minute film exposure of UFOs on the Senate side of the Capitol. It was a strange fact, but everything in the area that night was exposed to excessive amounts of radiation, and no one officially seemed to care.

Yet, I found some U.S. scientists had inadvertently discovered that UFOs emitted radiation decades ago, in the late 1940s. The scientific investigation that led to the discovery was first reported by an Air Force intelligence officer named Captain Edward J. Ruppelt.

According to Ruppelt, the UFO radiation investigation had begun accidentally in the fall of 1949, in the United States. At that time, a group of scientists set up their equipment to measure the small amount of background radiation that was always present in the atmosphere. They knew that background radiation never increased by any significant amount unless there was a cause.

Reportedly, two scientists were monitoring their equipment one day when the radiation reading suddenly spiked for a few seconds and then returned back to normal. The scientists noted that the unknown increase they recorded at that time was not sufficient to be dangerous, but it definitely was unusual. All indications pointed to an equipment malfunction as the most probable explanation. However, a diagnostic check of their equipment revealed no trouble.

Just as the two scientists were about to start a more detailed check, a third scientist came rushing into the lab. He excitedly told them that as he was pulling his car into the parking lot at the research lab, something in the sky had caught his eye. High in the clear blue sky, he had sighted three spherical, silvery UFOs traveling in a V formation.

He immediately noticed that the UFOs were traveling too fast to be conventional aircraft, so he quickly stopped his car and shut off the engine. The UFOs made no sound. All he could hear was the whirring of a generator in the nearby research lab. He stood staring at the sky for a few seconds until the UFOs had disappeared from sight. He then ran to the lab to tell the other scientist what he had witnessed.

After listening to his story, the other two scientists then told their colleague about the unusual radiation they had just detected. Moments later, the three scientists began to question if there was any connection between the two incidents. Had the UFOs caused the excessive radiation? Although it was rumored that those scientists did find a correlation, and then made their findings available to the military, the rumor stopped there.

However, captain Ruppelt was determined to get more details. Nearly one year after he had first heard the UFO radiation story, he received a phone call from a friend on the West Coast. At that time, the friend told Ruppelt he had recently been in contact with two people that had the whole story, and they were willing to meet Ruppelt in Los Angeles.

Two days later, he met the two people at the Roosevelt Hotel, in Hollywood. They talked for several hours. In the process, Ruppelt obtained details regarding the UFO radiation study from his informants who were physicists working for the Atomic Energy Commission that did not want any publicity. They told Ruppelt that the rumors regarding a UFO radiation study had been correct, but were incomplete. The scientists said that after the initial UFO sighting had taken place, word spread at the research lab that the next time the instruments registered abnormal amounts of radiation, some of the personnel were to go outside immediately and look for UFOs in the sky.

About three weeks after the first incident, while excessive radiation was registering on the instruments in the lab, a UFO was seen streaking across the sky. Again, the instruments were checked and found to be functioning normally.

According to the scientists, after the second UFO radiation event occurred, an investigation began at the laboratory. However, the scientists that made the visual observations weren't sure that what they sighted was a UFO or some type of experimental type of airplane.

One of the scientists thought it was possible that some type of radar equipment inside the odd-looking airplane, if that's what it was, might have affected the radiation-detection equipment. Arrangements were then made to fly all types of aircraft over the area with their radar in operation.

Predictably, nothing unusual happened. All possible types of airborne research equipment were tracked during similar flights in the hope that some special equipment not normally carried in aircraft would be found to have caused the jump in radiation. However, nothing out of the ordinary occurred during these tests either. Therefore, there must have been a UFO radiation connection.

Yet, for some reason, the scientists tentatively concluded that the abnormally high radiation readings were officially due to some freakish equipment malfunction and that the UFOs sighted visually were birds or airplanes. A report to this effect was made to military authorities. But since the conclusion stated that no "flying saucers" were involved, the data was not sent to the Air Force's *Project Blue Book*.

Shortly after the second UFO radiation episode, the research group finished its work. However, as the story of the UFO radiation study spread, it was widely discussed in scientific circles. As a result, the conclusion that it was just an equipment malfunction began to be more seriously questioned. Some of the scientists felt that further investigation of such phenomena was in order.

Ruppelt learned that these scientists, and the original investigators, began working together privately. They had decided to make a few more tests on their own time using radiation detection equipment that was specially designed, so the potential for a malfunction was minimal. The scientists had formed a group of like-minded people that were interested in the project. They gathered on evenings and weekends in an abandoned building on a small mountain peak where they had set up their equipment.

To insure privacy, and to avoid arousing undue interest among outsiders, the lead scientist and his colleagues told people that they had formed a "mineral club." The equipment that the group installed in the abandoned building was designed to run automatically. *Geiger* tubes were arranged in a pattern so that some idea as to the direction of the radiation source could be obtained.

To get data on visual sightings, the scientists had to rely on the UFO grapevine which existed at every major laboratory in the country. Late in the summer of 1950, they were in business. For the next three months, the independent scientific group kept their radiation equipment operating 24 hours a day, but the tapes showed nothing except the usual background activity. The flying saucer grapevine reported sightings in the general area of the tests, but none were close to the instruments located on the mountain top.

However, early one day in December, the scientists received a report of a silvery, circular UFO near their instrument shack. The UFO had been sighted by several people. When the scientists checked the equipment in the shack, they found that several of the *Geiger* tubes had been triggered at 10:17 a.m. The registered radiation increase was about 100 times greater than the normal background activity. Three more times during the next two months, the equipment recorded abnormal radiation on occasions when visual sightings of UFOs were reported. One of the visual sightings was also verified by radar.

After these incidents, the scientists kept their instruments in operation until June 1951, but nothing more was recorded. They also noted that during this period, while the radiation level remained normal, the visual sightings of UFOs in the area dropped off, too. The scientists then decided to concentrate on determining the significance of the data they had obtained.

The scientists, and their research group, made a detailed study of their findings. They had friends working on many research projects throughout the United States and managed to visit with them while on business trips. They investigated the possibility of unusual sunspot activity, but sunspots had been normal during the brief periods of high radiation. As confirmation that sunspots were not the cause, their record tapes showed no burst of radiation when sunspot activity had been abnormal.

The scientists checked every possible research project that might have produced some stray radiation for their instruments to pick up, but they found nothing. They checked and rechecked their instruments, but could find no factor that might have caused false readings. They even showed other scientists their findings hoping that these outsiders might be able to put their fingers on errors that had been overlooked. After spending a year analyzing their data, the scientists still had no answer other than the UFO sightings and the high radiation had taken place more or less simultaneously.

In time, as more scientists became aware of the initial study, they started radiation detection groups of their own. In fact, while working in a large laboratory on the East Coast, an Air Force colonel told the UFO radiation story to some of his friends, and they decided to look personally into the situation.

As a result, that laboratory made an extensive survey of the surrounding area. An elaborate system of radiation-detection equipment was set up for a radius of 100 miles around the lab. In addition, the defenses of the area included a radar network.

With the help of the colonel, the research group got permission to check the records of the radiation survey station and to look over the logs of the radar stations. They found instances where, during the same period of time that radiation in the area had been much higher than normal, radar had picked up a UFO.

One evening, just before sunset, in July of 1951, two scientists from the colonel's group were driving home from the laboratory. As they sped along the highway, they noticed two cars stopped up ahead with people standing beside the road looking up at something in the sky.

The two scientists stopped, got out of their car and scanned the sky. Low on the eastern horizon, they saw a bright, circular UFO moving slowly north. They watched it for a while, took a few notes, and then quickly drove back to the lab.

At the lab, they were informed that radar had picked up an unidentified target near the spot where the scientists in the car had seen the

UFO, and it had been traveling north. A fighter jet had been scrambled, but when it got into the proper area, the radar target was off the scope. The pilot briefly sighted something that looked like the reported UFO, but before he could check further, he had to turn into the sun to get on an interception course, and he lost the object.

Several days passed before the radiation reports from all stations could be collected. When the reports did come in, they showed that stations east of the laboratory, on an approximate line with the radar track, had shown the highest increase in radiation. Stations west of the lab showed nothing.

The potential significance of this well-documented incident motivated the colonel's group to extend and refine their activities. Their plan was to build a radiation detection instrument in an empty wing tank and mount it on an F-47. That way, when a UFO was reported, they would fly a search pattern in the area and try to establish whether or not a certain sector of the sky was more radioactive than other sectors. Also, they proposed building a highly-directional, radiation detector for the F-47 and attempt to actually track a UFO. The year was 1951.

The design of such equipment was started, but many delays occurred. Before the colonel's group could get any of the equipment built, some of the members left the lab for other jobs. The colonel who started the operation was also transferred elsewhere. Although the project at that lab was finished, all the people involved had kept it quiet in order to avoid ridicule. In the end, the UFO radiation study was officially labeled as "inconclusive evidence."

On December 24, 1949, at approximately 6:00 p.m., an F-51 fighter jet took off from Andrews Air Force Base and attempted to intercept a domed, disc-shaped UFO, but was unsuccessful. According to the public record, a fighter jet was launched to intercept the UFO that was violating controlled air space in DC. However, for unknown reasons, the jet crashed and the UFO quickly flew off. The UFO was observed by multiple military witnesses over the base for more than one minute. It would not be the last time a military jet was sent to intercept a UFO over DC.

About four months earlier, in August of 1949, around 2:30 p.m., a UFO was observed near the Pentagon by one witness for over three minutes.

The previous month, on July 4, 1949, a U.S. Air Force intelligence officer's wife took two pictures of a group of UFOs as they passed low over the Pentagon. According to the now retired military officer, "We were out for the Fourth of July celebration that day on the National Mall. Later, as we drove passed the Pentagon, we saw the cars in front of us slowing down and people were looking out their windows. My two-year-old daughter was in the back seat, and my wife Mary was sitting beside me.

"I remember Mary gasping for air as if she had spotted a ghost. That scared me, so I slowed down and asked her what was the matter. She said, 'Look!' When I looked in the direction she was pointing, I was absolutely amazed at what I saw. There were several unidentified objects flying over the grounds of the Pentagon.

"We had not seen many aircraft at all that Fourth of July, so even if they had been earthly aircraft I would have been surprised, but these were not from Earth! They were shaped differently than anything I had ever seen flying in the area. They had the ability to slow down and speed up like no aircraft the Air Force had, then or now.

"I quickly told Mary to get my camera out of her purse where she had been carrying it during our picnic earlier that day. That camera took great color pictures. As I continued to drive slowly, Mary took two pictures.

"Soon after that, the strange flying objects disappeared as quickly as they appeared. I believe I am the only person to have a picture of those objects. Most people I talked to later, who were in DC that day, said they didn't see them.

"I can only wonder what the people in the cars on the road with us that day that did see the UFOs were thinking. They were probably wishing they had their cameras. There are only two photos of these objects in existence. I have one, and the Air Force has the other.

"I never told anyone about this until now [2006]. I kept one photo for myself, but handed the other photo over to the team that I worked with at the Pentagon. I never heard another word about what we saw and photographed that day. It was as if no one wanted to acknowledge what was captured on that color film.

"I often joked with my wife that the aliens had come to celebrate

America's Independence Day. My daughter was too young to remember anything, but my wife and I will never forget what we saw that Fourth of July, in 1949."

About two months earlier, in May of 1949, according to a military photographer, an alien body recovered from the crashed UFO in Roswell, in July of 1947, was autopsied scientifically in a medical theatre in Washington, D.C., in the presence of leading scientists from the U.S., England, and France.

The previous month, on April 7, 1949, the U.S. Air Force once again attempted to intercept a UFO over Washington, D.C. There were no other details given regarding the incident.

About six months earlier, on November 18, 1948, another alien incursion occurred from 9:45 p.m., to 10:03 p.m., at Andrews Air Force Base, in Maryland. It was the first officially reported military intercept of a UFO in the restricted airspace around Washington, D.C.

That night, an Air Force Reserves second lieutenant sighted a glowing-white UFO circling over Andrews Air Force Base. When visual contact was made with the UFO, it started taking evasive action, and the T-6 pilot then turned his wing and tail navigation lights off. The UFO then quickly flew up and over his jet. The pilot then attempted to fly closer to the UFO by making a series of very-tight, 360-degree turns with his flaps down while making a steady climb. However, the UFO was able to turn quicker and tighter than the military aircraft.

Another amazing feature was the quick variation of the UFOs airspeed. It could jump from 80 mph to 600 mph almost instantly. The pilot remained in visual contact with the UFO for about 10 minutes. During that time, the UFO was positioned between the lights of Washington, D.C., and the T-6 jet. The pilot noted that he could only see a "glowing-white, oval-shaped UFO with no wings and no exhaust flame."

At one point, the pilot pulled his jet up sharply and flew underneath the UFO. He came within 300 to 400 feet and then turned his landing lights on it. He saw that it had a very-dull, grey glow to it and was oblong in shape. The UFO then performed a very-tight turn and headed for the Atlantic Ocean at about 500 to 600 mph.

The pilot reported that, "At about 9:45 p.m., I noticed a UFO moving over Andrews Air Force base. It appeared to be a continuously-glowing, white light. I thought it was an aircraft with only one landing light, so I moved closer because I wanted to get into the landing pattern. I was well above landing traffic altitude at this time.

"As I neared the UFO, I noticed it was not another airplane. Just then, it began to take violent, evasive action, so I tried to close on it. I first made contact at 2,700 feet over the field. I switched my navigation lights on and off, but got no answer, so I went in closer. Then, the UFO quickly flew up and over my airplane.

"I then tried to close again, but the UFO turned. I then tried to turn inside of its turn and, at the same time, get the UFO between the moon and my aircraft. I never did manage to get into a position where the UFO was silhouetted against the moon.

"While climbing, I made three-to-four passes at the UFO in order to identify it. While diving at approximately 240 mph, the UFO would climb vertically and then drop below me from behind and continue to circle.

"I chased the UFO up and down and around for about 10 minutes. Then, as a last resort, I made a pass and turned on my landing lights. Just before the UFO made a final, tight turn and headed for the Atlantic Ocean, I saw that it was a dark-grey, oval-shaped craft; smaller than my T-6. The UFO had no wings and no tail surfaces. I couldn't tell if the light was on the UFO or if the whole UFO was glowing."

Other witnesses of the event included a crew chief and a master sergeant who had been standing on the flight line and had witnessed the entire incident. Also, a staff sergeant saw the UFO make two low passes over the base.

About four months earlier, on July 24, 1948, at approximately 2:40 a.m., a "meteor-like," glowing UFO was sighted passing silently through the restricted airspace of Washington, D.C.

About three months earlier, on April 30, 1948, around 10:15 a.m., the pilot of a naval aircraft from Anacostia Naval Air Station in Washington, D.C., sighted a yellow-glowing, spherical UFO. The craft was 25 to 40 feet in diameter and was at an altitude of about 4,500 feet. It was heading due north at a constant altitude about 1,000 feet below the military aircraft. The UFO flew slowly through the air at approximately 100 mph in the opposite direction of the wind and crossed through the no-fly zone of the nation's capital.

That same year, in late 1948, a series of incursions by extremely-bright, green-glowing spheres occurred in Washington, D.C. It is important to note that these bright-green UFOs were identical in their size and shape to the green, spherical UFOs photographed in Washington, D.C., in July of 2002.

In 1948, most of the incursions by green spheres took place over the southwestern United States where a lot of military research and development was taking place, specifically in New Mexico. The many incursions by the spherical, green-glowing UFOs worried some people in the government specifically because they were being sighted over sensitive, research installations.

It was the early days of the Cold War, and some experts had concluded that the bright-green UFOs were actually man-made, foreign, spy devices. In any case, the green UFO spheres were seen by so many reputable people that everyone agreed they were real. As a result, secret conferences were convened at Los Alamos, and in Washington, D.C., by the Air Force's Scientific Advisory Board.

The previous year, on July 7, 1947, around 11:00 p.m., an Air Force Lieutenant Colonel witnessed a UFO about the size of a small airplane in restricted airspace near the Pentagon. The UFO emitted a strange, glowing, white light. It was travelling at less than 500 feet above the ground at about 1,350 mph. On that same night, eight spherical, glowing UFOs were observed by another military witness in Washington, D.C.

The previous night, on July 6, 1947, around 8:40 p.m., another alien incursion transpired in Washington, D.C. That night, a local resident witnessed a glowing UFO passing through the restricted airspace of the capital.

The previous night, on July 5, 1947, at approximately 11:30 a.m., another alien incursion occurred in Washington, D.C. That morning, people were unloading groceries from their cars while some of the neighborhood kids were playing a game they called "wire-ball" which involved throwing a tennis ball at the power-line wires.

As one of the boys was getting ready to throw the ball, he saw something flash in the sky. Then, he noticed a round, flat, shiny-metal UFO and excitedly pointed at the sky. He and his friends then counted a total of six UFOs that were very high in the sky and were headed in the same direction in no apparent formation.

The children noted that the UFOs would occasionally turn over slowly and could travel while on edge. They also noted that the UFOs would occasionally shoot off to the right or left, but would maintain their general course. The kids were so excited and yelling that people came out of their homes and looked up. However, the children soon learned that they didn't dare speak of the event to anyone that wasn't there that day. If they did, they were immediately dubbed "the crazy kid that saw the little green men from Mars."

The previous day, on July 4th, 1947, at 4:10 a.m., a blazing ball of fire was seen hovering near a woman's home in the District of Columbia for a few minutes.

The previous day, on July 3, 1947, at 9:30 p.m., another alien incursion transpired in Washington, D.C. At that time, three glowing UFOs were sighted passing through the restricted airspace of the nation's capital for several minutes by two women living in NE Washington, D.C. The UFOs reportedly made "a jet-like noise." Earlier, at 7:00 p.m., One of the women had sighted a single, bright-gold, disc-shaped UFO that moved very fast and straight though the sky. In a few seconds, it had disappeared over the horizon.

That same day, there were a cluster of three UFO sightings between Baltimore, Maryland and Washington, D.C.

The previous year, in March of 1946, another alien incursion took place around 2:20 p.m., in Washington, D.C. That afternoon, a local resident witnessed a UFO pass within 600 feet of his position.

That same year, in mid-1946, at approximately 2:30 p.m., a disc-shaped UFO was sighted near the Pentagon. The UFO had the appearance and performance beyond the capability of any known earthly aircraft. The UFO was observed for a few minutes by at least one witness.

About two years earlier, on June 22, 1944, another alien incursion occurred. A UFO was allegedly shot down by the U.S. military as it flew over the island of Oahu, Hawaii. One female alien was captured and flown to Washington, D.C. No other details were given.

Four months earlier, on February 22, 1944, in Washington, D.C., President Franklin D. Roosevelt reportedly wrote a Top Secret memo on White House stationary for "The Special Committee on Non Terrestrial

Science and Technology." Both the title and the content clearly alluded to extraterrestrial life, the former using the word "non terrestrial" and the latter talked about "coming to grips with the reality that our planet is not the only one harboring intelligent life in the universe."

One month earlier, on January 1, 1944, another alien incursion allegedly took place in a wilderness area outside Washington, D.C. Strange as it may sound, U.S. fighter planes flying over West Virginia, or the Western Maryland mountains, reportedly shot down a UFO.

The fighter pilots noted that although their bullets had punched holes in the disc-shaped UFO, each hole had somehow slowly closed back up. This process went on until there were so many bullets hitting the UFO it wasn't able to recover. At that time, parachute-like devices ejected and then the UFO was lost in the clouds before hitting a mountain.

Special crash recovery teams were dispatched from Bolling Air Base and Andrews Air Base in DC. Apparently, civilian and military personnel located the remains of the UFO. At the crash site, there was a gigantic hole in the side of the mountain near the top. The recovery teams also found that large trees had been neatly cut in two as the UFO plowed into the mountain. Although no survivors were found, no dead bodies were found either. The UFO had reportedly exploded upon impact.

Many of the thousands of pieces from the craft were field tested. The studies lasted three weeks in complete secrecy. All the UFO pieces not taken away were buried in a large hole. All the men were ordered not to talk about the event and could not take any of the material from the craft. The metal had many strange qualities such as being as lightweight as aluminum foil.

The previous year, one day in 1943, another alien incursion took place. At that time, a Washington, D.C., policeman reported seeing two UFOs passing through the restricted airspace of the capital.

One year earlier, on October 29, 1942, another alien incursion occurred. While taking aerial photographs of Washington D.C., an image of a UFO streaking over the Pentagon was accidentally captured on film. It had the same shape as one of the UFOs photographed at the Pentagon in 1949.

CHAPTER FIFTEEN

Close Encounter Under the Capitol

While researching historic UFO events in Washington, D.C., I came across an interesting letter alleging that dead aliens, and a wrecked UFO, had been secretly stored under the Capitol building sometime before or during the 1930s. The letter was written in December of 1999, but was not made public until 2002: the same year UFOs landed on Capitol Hill.

Coincidentally, in 2002 an ambitious addition to the Capitol had begun. The very expensive construction project involved the creation of a massive, three-story "Visitors Complex" underground in front of the existing Capitol building.

It is also worth noting that towards the end of 2002, very-old, dusty, molded, payroll ledgers from the first historic years of the Senate were discovered by accident in the sub-basement of the Capitol. This discovery was relevant because it indicated that many items had been stored under the Capitol building since its construction that had been overlooked.

Keep that in mind regarding the aforementioned letter that was written to East Coast UFO researchers by the daughters of Reverend Turner Hamilton Holt; a cousin of Cordell Hull who was the Secretary of State under Franklin Roosevelt.

In the letter, the daughters shared a secret that had been in their family for decades. They claimed their father, the reverend, had been shown something shocking under the Capitol in Washington, D.C., by his cousin the Secretary of State, in the 1930s.

When he first told his daughters what he had seen under the Capitol, he was a young, intelligent man of sound mind and body. He apparently wanted to tell his story to someone because he didn't want the information to be lost.

Reverend Holt carefully explained to his daughters that one day, while in Washington, D.C., his cousin Cordell swore him to secrecy. Cordell then took his cousin to a sub-basement in the U.S. Capitol building and showed him an amazing sight. At that time, the reverend saw four large, glass jars filled with fluid that contained beings of an unknown origin. Nearby, there was a wrecked, circular aircraft of some kind.

The reverend instructed his daughters to make the information known publicly some day, after he and his cousin Cordell were dead, because he felt it was very important. He also mentioned that his cousin Cordell had said "they" were afraid this would create panic if the public found out about it.

If that were true, and "they" were so worried about disclosure, Cordell Hull had absolutely no reason to show these creatures and their dismantled UFO to his cousin, a respected reverend, unless he was deeply troubled by the facts.

Hull knew the Capitol complex well because he had begun working there in 1907 when he was first elected to the U.S. House of Representatives. He was then re-elected to six more terms and served as a U.S. Senator from 1931 to 1937. He was also chairman of the Democratic National Committee and became Secretary of State under President Franklin D. Roosevelt. He served in that position from 1933, until 1944, when he resigned due to ill health. He was also offered the Vice Presidency, but declined. In 1945, Hull won the Nobel Peace Prize.

Reverend Holt and Senator Hull were cousins and friends. Holt was not a nut. He had attained a doctorate degree in theology from Ashland Theological Seminary, and was a well respected minister, a community leader, and had written a book entitled *Life's Convictions*.

It was interesting to note that both of his daughters claimed they had been independently told about the alien creatures under the Capitol by their father. One of the daughters recalled that her father described the alien aircraft as being a "silver, metallic vehicle" that had been partially taken apart. He noted the material was a color he had not seen before. For lack of a better word, he called it "silver." Reverend Holt was not a man that was known for lying or even exaggerating. The daughters felt that by telling this story, they were following their father's wishes.

When UFO investigators contacted the curator at the U.S. Capitol building, not surprisingly, they were told that no one had ever heard about alien creatures being stored under the Capitol. However, they were able to confirm there was an area of the sub-basement that was divided into storage rooms back in the 1930s and that the building had been structurally changed over the years, especially in 2002.

After retiring from government service, Cordell Hull wrote his memoirs, but did not include any mention of the alleged alien creatures and a UFO hidden under the Capitol. Actually, his omission made perfect sense as that would have been a highly-classified secret if true.

It is a matter of record that Hull was also deeply involved in the international affairs of secret societies. He understood the nature of the real enemy and had been trained by men who knew how the world operated. In World War II, Hull was aware that the enemy was not Germany itself. It was the covert, financial cabal of the *Thule Society* that reportedly controlled Hitler.

When America's new intelligence agency, the OSS, was formed and placed outside the State Department's control, Hull created a secret intelligence and covert operations unit within the State Department. That unit was called Consular Operations or ConsOps. Members of that original unit had sought out the German survivors of the conspiracy to assassinate Hitler. The survivors and their families were then smuggled out of Europe, before the end of the war, and brought into the United States.

Another interesting fact was that the planning of the United Nations could be traced to the State Department's ConsOps which had been created by Cordell Hull, in 1943. All of the members of that secret committee, with the exception of Hull, were members of the Council on Foreign Relations (CFR).

They met with Hull regularly to plan, select, and guide the labors of the State Department's ConsOps. It was, in effect, the coordinating agency for all of the State Department's postwar planning. Those CFR officials were also responsible for the final shape of the United Nations.

Hull was clearly an international power broker. In 1943, he served as a United States delegate to the Moscow Conference. Under *Operation Paperclip*, Hull was instrumental in having Nazi rocket scientist Werner von Braun, and his team, form the foundation of America's post-war aerospace program. This led to the creation of NASA which was ultimately responsible for America's long-term exploration of space.

However, Hull was most noted for being one of the architects and most ardent supporters of the United Nations. He was the main figure pushing the State Department to write the United Nations Charter. That charter was signed on June 26, 1945, in San Francisco, by the 50 original member countries. It entered into force on October 24, 1945, after being ratified by the five founding members. However, Hull had resigned the position of Secretary of State, in November of 1944, because of failing health.

President Roosevelt said upon Hull's departure that, "He was the one person in the world who has done the most to make this great plan for peace through the United Nations an effective fact." Hull was honored with the *Nobel Peace Prize*, in November of 1945, in recognition of his efforts for peace and understanding in the Western Hemisphere. On international and possibly interplanetary affairs, Hull was very well informed.

I realize that the story of aliens and a crashed UFO being hidden under the U.S. Capitol sounded extremely odd, but why would anyone fabricate such an amazing account? I also know that although many people believe UFOs or aliens had not been sighted and or photographed in the 1930s, they were wrong.

For example, an alien incursion occurred on July 15, 1939, at 5:04 p.m., in Belton, South Carolina. That evening, a local resident witnessed a dark-red, glowing UFO passing about 30 degrees above the horizon. The UFO left no trail and made no sound whatsoever.

That same month, in July of 1939, a bizarre alien encounter took place one day in rural Alabama. At that time, FBI agents were investigating unusual reports regarding a fortuneteller who had acquired military secrets. Upon arriving at the designated residence, the agents found a woman sitting on the front porch.

The men approached the bottom steps of the porch and identified themselves as FBI agents. They told the woman that they were there to ask her some questions. She smiled and agreed to answer their questions truthfully, but warned them that although she was not a fortuneteller she could read their minds. She said she had been reading minds for a very-long time.

When asked where she was born, she replied, "Another world."

She was then asked what she was doing on Earth. She explained that she was guarding something that did not concern humans. Thinking the woman was hiding her true identity, the agents informed her that they were going to have to take her in for further questioning. However, the mysterious woman insisted that she had no intentions of going anywhere with them.

The lead FBI agent then ordered one of his men to escort "the lady from another world" to the car. However, as the agent walked up the steps of the porch he suddenly began trembling and fell to the ground. The woman remained seated and in a deadly serious tone of voice told the agents that if they made any further attempts to approach her, none of them would leave alive. They quickly agreed to her terms, and the agent on the ground got up and was unharmed.

Before leaving, the agents were very inquisitive about the woman's strange statements and asked her to provide proof that she was indeed from another world. She thought for a moment, and then instructed them to have their superiors pick an area of 100 square miles of the earth's surface. They were to then put markers around it and make sure no airplanes flew over the area.

After the agents returned to their headquarters, and reluctantly reported their strange encounter, their superiors surprisingly agreed to do exactly what the strange woman had instructed. Weeks later, the agents drove into the uninhabited area that had been selected for the demonstration of "proof." An inspection of the area revealed that it was now completely devoid of life. The agents that filed the report were ordered to forget the whole thing and to never contact the strange woman from another world again.

That same decade, in the late 1930s, another alien incursion transpired at approximately 9:00 p.m., in West Virginia. At that time, a local man had just left the church after services. It was a long walk to his home down a dark, country road. Often, especially after church services or revivals, groups of people would be walking together on the road to their respective homes, but that night the man was walking alone.

Not far from the church, as the man reached the top of a hill, he began to feel uncomfortable. He wasn't afraid or spooked by anything he could actually see, but a powerful feeling had come over him. He looked around as he continued walking, but did not see or hear anything unusual.

Less than five minutes later, he had reached the bottom of the hill when something caused him to turn around and look behind him. That's when he found himself face-to-face with a large ball of white light suspended very low in the sky nearby. One thing he knew for certain, it wasn't the moon.

He recalled that, "The faster I walked, the faster the [UFO] picked up speed." He noted that as the UFO followed him, it never attempted to overcome him or out-distance him. Instead, it tagged along behind him on the long dark road for approximately another mile.

When he reached a fork in the road, he noticed that the white ball of light had suddenly disappeared. He said, "I looked one second, and it was there. The next, it was gone." He could not tell whether it had sped away or just blinked out.

Around the same time, in 1938, another alien incursion occurred one afternoon near Saint Louis, Missouri. At that time, a local woman witnessed a UFO parked on the ground and many alien entities rushing around it. She recalled that when the aliens re-entered the UFO it left at an incredible rate of speed.

What is truly amazing is that, at first glance, one of the entities appeared to be a young girl. However, she was actually a fragile combination of human and alien. She had large, black eyes with no whites around them. She looked physically different as her eyes were more rounded than the little, grey, humanoid aliens. She had a pointed chin, a high forehead and very-fine, thin hair.

The local woman also noticed one other alien entity that appeared different from the rest. There was a normal-looking, adult, human female that accompanied the hybrid human/alien girl! The adult, human-looking alien was described as a six-foot tall, white-skinned female with brown hair and brown eyes who was wearing some sort of form-fitting, one-piece uniform. This historic report is stunning when compared with Jerry Wills' life story in Chapter Nine of this book.

That same year, in 1938, another close encounter took place near Stewart, British Columbia. While searching for a missing trapper, in a remote glacial area near the Alaskan border, constable Larry Requa entered a cave and discovered five alien-looking skeletons that had larger than normal skulls. One of the strange skeletons was reportedly still wearing a metal medallion that had star symbols on its surface.

All of the aliens were facing a stone altar. Constable Requa got the impression that the aliens had been stranded on earth and died. He noted that the cave had unusual characteristics. It had a vertical configuration, and the walls were extremely smooth as though someone had used a mechanical device to create the tunnels that led from the cave. Rumor had it that as of July, 2000 the alien skeletons were still in the cave.

In mid-November of 1938, another extraterrestrial encounter took place one night in Cape Cod, Massachusetts. At that time, a local woman was preparing to cross the street when something strange caught her eye. She noticed a large creature moving in the shadows.

The creature suddenly jumped directly towards her as if it were on springs and spread its large, cape-like, black wings. The woman froze and was too startled to scream. The dark, menacing presence hovered over her for a moment and then vanished. She described the alien creature as all black, with eyes like balls of fire. It was at least eight-feet tall. The woman also noted that the alien made a terrifying, buzzing sound like a monstrous insect.

That same month, in the same location, another close encounter occurred one night, in Cape Cod, Massachusetts. At that time, a local-man's dog had cornered a strange creature in the yard. When the man went outside with his shotgun, he was confronted by a tall, black monster that had what looked like long, silver ears.

Thinking it was some kind of wild animal, he shot at it. However, it didn't react like any wild animal. It reportedly laughed and then jumped over the eight-foot fence and out of the yard. Around the same time, a local boy was coming home from the library when a tall, black figure jumped out at him from nowhere and "spit blue flames in his face."

While researching UFO and ET reports from the 1930s, I began to wonder if the many, real-life close encounters that had taken place on the East Coast could have caused thousands of American's to believe the Earth was being invaded by "Martians."

From 8:00 p.m., to 9:00 p.m., on Sunday, October 30, 1938, The Columbia Broadcasting System had aired Orson Welles' Radio adaptation of H. G. Wells' novel, *War of the Worlds*. It was the first science fiction story of interplanetary warfare involving Earth. Oddly enough, the fictional invasion had started on the U.S. East Coast, in New Jersey.

Before H.G. Wells' story, UFO sci-fi stories featured only peaceful alien beings visiting earth. In contrast, H.G. Wells' aggressive aliens had arrived with powerful weapons, and they were ready to take over the Earth as their new home. These fictional aliens from Mars were so powerful that humans were incapable of stopping them. However, in the end, a lowly Earth bacterium finally killed them off. As an indirect result of the novel's political overtones, some people began to believe that any and all alien visitations had to be a full-scale alien invasion that would lead to the extermination of mankind.

During the *War of the Worlds* radio broadcast, some people were frightened to the point that they cried, prayed, tried to rescue loved ones, and called for ambulances and police. There was an unprecedented public panic. Many people perceived the broadcast as reality because, at the time, radio was their most reliable source of news, and everything on the show that night was portrayed so realistically.

For example, some of the specific street names and places described were known to be real for many people. However, from this intense public reaction, I presume that at that time in history most Americans believed that extraterrestrial life existed, and that aliens were capable of traveling to earth by UFOs to invade our planet. Generally speaking, due to our own hostile nature and deadly world wars, we humans on Earth have a paranoid perspective of our interplanetary neighbors.

However, that does not mean there are no alien adversaries to be concerned about. For example, that same year, in the fall of 1938, another alien encounter took place one night in Cape Cod, Massachusetts. At that time, local residents sighted a mysterious attacker. The alien being was described as standing over seven-feet tall, with ferocious-looking eyes and pointed ears. He reportedly could "breathe blue flames" into his victim's face and had "incredible leaping abilities."

Around the same time, in the fall of 1938, another alien encounter transpired in Donnell Heights, Maryland. At that time, local residents complained to police that a tall, thin prowler dressed in black was terrorizing them. He easily eluded capture by the police. Witnesses swore that he possessed extraordinary leaping abilities and could run and jump like a gazelle. One witness who saw the prowler's face described it as "horrifying."

Earlier that year, in the summer of 1938, another alien encounter occurred at twilight in Silver City, New Mexico. At that time, four children reportedly witnessed a man wearing a grey suit floating in the sky over them at treetop level. One of the girls recalled that, "He seemed to be wearing a belt which was wide and had points sticking out of it." He also wore a "Flash Gordon" type of cap and a wide cape.

The flying humanoid drifted silently across the sky above the speechless children who stood and stared up at him until he finally disappeared from sight into the distance. Although the report was made by children, I found similar, recent reports of flying men in America. There were some clear photographs and videos taken of these airborne alien entities in the skies over Mexico and Southern California in the 21st century.

In the summer of 1938, another alien incursion took place one night in Somerville, Massachusetts. At that time, a man witnessed a UFO approach from the east. At first, he thought it was a blimp moving silently through the sky. However, he didn't observe a gondola, or propeller, that was typical of a blimp.

Through one of the several portholes, on the side of the strange craft, he could see the silhouette of a person sitting and apparently watching him, and he could also see more beings moving behind the other portholes. He had a strong urge to wave and felt as though they were old friends.

The previous year, in 1937, another alien encounter took place one afternoon in Saginaw, Michigan. At that time, a local fisherman was shocked to see a scaly, humanoid creature climb out of the water onto a riverbank, lean against a tree, and then jump back into the water. The witness later suffered a nervous breakdown from his close encounter.

That same year, in the summer of 1937, another alien incursion allegedly occurred in the town of Czernica which was a territory of Germany at the time. One day, local residents reportedly witnessed a multi-colored, glowing, disk-shaped UFO crash into a field. The area was cordoned off by SS troops, and the UFO was then transported to a military base where it was held under ultra-tight security.

The UFO was about 22-feet wide and 12-feet high. The craft had a large dome on top and was encircled by a narrow outer rim, and a smaller flat dome on the bottom with a flat lower section. The very top of the dome was also flat. The craft had six oval-shaped structures resembling portholes that were not transparent. These devices radiated a type of light near the base of the upper dome. On the under surface of the outer rim were 12 lights. When the UFO was powered down, the color of the disk was a dull, metallic grey.

The entrance to the disk-shaped UFO was located on the top of the upper dome. Inside the circular cabin were three small seats, and there were control panels around the dome where the three alien beings were found. One alien was dead, the other two were alive. One of the living aliens died soon after the crash. The second living alien remained in custody for about a month and a half before it died.

The origin of the aliens, and their crashed craft, was allegedly a binary star system we call 61 Cygni which is a binary star system located about 11.4 light-years from our Sun in the south central part of the Constellation Cygnus. It was interesting to note that the Nazis were reportedly told by the surviving alien that they (the Gray ETs) had built underground bases in the polar region of the Canadian Northern Territories; the same region where alien skeletons had been accidentally found in a cave.

The aliens from the crashed UFO in Germany were small, dwarf-like creatures that stood three feet or less in height. They had large, hairless, pear-shaped heads. They had small, frail bodies with long, narrow hands that had only four fingers. They had grey skin and large, dark, almond-shaped eyes.

The Nazis were apparently afraid to move the disk any great distant, because they thought it might explode during transport, so a research laboratory was constructed nearby. In time, the disk was moved to a more secure location underground, in a mine where they excavated uranium ore. That complex reportedly had an extensive network of underground hangars connected by tunnels.

The UFO, the dead alien bodies, and the remaining living extraterrestrial were moved into this complex. The only surviving alien apparently supplied the Germans with some type of information, but was desperately asking the Nazi's medical doctors for help. Unfortunately, they could not help the alien because of its extremely different biological design.

Apparently, no substantial technical data was provided by the alien that could help the Nazi scientists to comprehend its technology, despite their desperate attempt to obtain such data. However, the alien was able to inform the Germans that their UFO had crashed because of a technical malfunction.

Adolph Hitler and other individuals such as Werner Von Braun and Hermann Goring were said to have inspected the crashed disk, and the alien bodies. Hitler reportedly consulted with Nazi scientists in an attempt to use the UFO as a super weapon.

Among the scientists allegedly involved in investigating the crashed disc were physicist Max Von Laue, Otto Hahn, who discovered nuclear fusion, and Werner Heisenberg, who formulated the "Uncertainty Principle" of quantum physics.

Although the alien technology was extremely difficult to understand, the UFO allegedly inspired some Nazi scientists to construct different models of disc-shaped aircraft that were powered by conventional means.

The capture and back engineering of this extraterrestrial spacecraft could have been one of the factors that motivated Hitler to expand his conquest during World War II; hoping to use the craft as a weapon and eventually conquer the world. However, toward the end of the war in 1945, upon receiving word of the approaching Soviet troops, the underground complex housing the UFO was demolished. In the process, the spacecraft and the alien bodies were buried in one of the underground tunnels. The entrance was sealed with many huge rocks.

The previous year, in 1936, another alien encounter took place at a gold mine in Great Falls, Maryland, Late that night, a security guard was performing his rounds when he witnessed a bizarre-looking, alien creature crawling through one of the mine shafts. The being was described as a man-like creature with fiery eyes and a 10-foot-long tail. The astonished security guard cautiously observed the creature as it crawled out of the mine and disappeared into the forest.

That same year, in November of 1936, another alien incursion occurred one night in Eklutna, Alaska. At that time, two local men witnessed a cigar-shaped UFO. One of the men recalled that it was a very-cold,

Saturday night when he and a co-worker decided to try and hitch a ride to Anchorage to see a movie. As the two men walked down the road, the sky was pitch black. The stars glistened like jewels, and the air was still.

The men walked along at a brisk pace to keep warm. They had covered four or five miles with no sign of any vehicles on the road. But as the men entered an open area, they heard a strange, whining sound approaching. When they turned around, they saw an intense, bluish light coming their way. At first they were happy, because they thought it was a truck coming toward them that had one headlight burned out. However, they soon realized that the light was not on the road. It was in the air!

This was startling to say the least. The men were dumbfounded, and it took them a few seconds to react. The strange-blue light was flying rather slowly toward their position at about 35 to 40 mph. Moments later; the men jumped on the ground and flattened themselves in the snow as the UFO passed overhead.

After it passed over them, the men stood up and kept watching the strange, glowing craft. They recalled that the UFO was cigar shaped and glowed brightly. As they watched it fly low over the steep terrain in the distance, they both thought it would crash into the mountain. But just before it hit anything, the UFO flew smoothly up and over and down the other side of the mountain. Both of the men looked at each other and asked, "What the Hell was that?"

Earlier that same year, in July of 1936, another alien incursion occurred one day in Palm Springs, California. At that time, a local resident witnessed three helmeted, humanoid figures without wings flying over the area.

The previous year, in 1935, another alien encounter took place one day in Genesco, Illinois. At that time, a young man working on a farm had gone out to fix a water pump when he suddenly heard a strange noise. Looking up, he saw a bizarre, alien entity watching him. The creature had a head like an eagle with shiny, red eyes and it was wearing a military-style jump suit. The being stared directly at the witness for about 45 seconds then suddenly ran down the road and disappeared from sight.

Two years earlier, in 1933, another alien encounter transpired one summer afternoon near Cudworth, Saskatchewan. A woman was standing alone in a field, beside a pond, on a farm where she lived. Suddenly, on the opposite side of the pond, she observed a number of little green men that were about four-feet tall and had appeared from nowhere. All the strange looking beings wore silver jumpsuits.

That same year, in the summer of 1933, another alien encounter took place near Nipawin, Saskatchewan. Following a week of strange lights being sighted in the sky, three local residents decided to investigate for themselves. Around midnight, they drove out toward Lake Tobin. They drove as far as they could in their pickup truck.

They then walked toward a strange light that was on the ground in a boggy area, less than a quarter mile away. As they approached the light, they saw a large, oval-shaped UFO sitting on legs. The craft had a dome shape on the top, and it gave off a bright-orange glow that lit up the area.

There was an open hatch, and they saw about a dozen humanoid figures less than five-feet tall that were climbing up and down a ladder and making repairs to their ship. The aliens reportedly wore silvery suits and helmets that covered their face like a ski mask.

The three witnesses watched for about half an hour and then left. Several days later, they located the landing site during the day and found four clear, landing gear marks around a circle of scorched earth.

Earlier that same year, on April 18, 1933, another alien incursion occurred at approximately 7:00 p.m., at the New York World's Fair. That night, during an evening exhibition, a strange-looking UFO suddenly appeared and hovered for 20 minutes lighting up the sky over the crowd. One of the witnesses later reported that many people saw the UFO and pointed up in the air. It made no noise and suddenly darted off straight up and disappeared into the star-lit, cloudless sky.

Around that same time, in the early 1930s, another alien encounter occurred. It was truly incredible because a picture was taken. I first saw the photograph in question posted on the Internet. It was reportedly taken in a forest clearing. It shows a small, alien figure walking in the foreground. The bizarre image was captured by a man living in Alaska.

The little, alien entity was seen when the man was on his way to a lake. Apparently, after spotting the alien, the local man chased it until he got close enough to take a picture. It was four months before the photograph was developed because he lived in such a remote, sparsely-populated area.

Around that same time, in the early 1930s, another alien encounter took place in the small town of Glenwood, Washington. At that time, a local resident was walking to a neighbor's house to help them work in the fields. When the young man came to a ridge, he suddenly noticed there were no sounds at all!

Then, a shadow came over him blocking the sun out entirely! He looked up into the sky and saw a huge, rectangular UFO flying above him. The young man noted that the bottom of the strange craft reflected the ground like a mirror. As the UFO slowed down over him, three small, glowing spheres flew out of an opening near the bottom. The flying spheres came straight toward the terrified witness.

He was so scared he had a hard time moving. However, he quickly turned around and started to run away. At that time, he noticed that he was unable to move very fast. Although his feet were moving, he felt like he was being pulled backwards. Suddenly, the three little spheres shot passed his head and around a tree and up and out of sight. Immediately after that, he could move at a normal speed again. And that's exactly what he did! He didn't stop running until he was safe in the root cellar under his house.

He estimated the UFO was at least one-mile long and a half-a-mile wide by its position to the mountains and by the shadow that it cast. He eventually found about a dozen other people that had seen the same large UFO. He also heard local stories of other people being chased by the same little, glowing spheres; in some cases for miles! He recalled that at one point, nobody wanted to leave their house, because they were afraid of being chased by the flying spheres.

Around that same time, in the spring of 1932 or 1933, another close encounter took place one evening. At that time, a large family was living in a small, rural town located in the Appalachian foothills. There were very-few cars in those days, so most people walked to and from a town or church. They often walked for miles along hilly paths or long stretches of isolated dirt roadways: night or day.

One evening, a local woman in her forties was returning home from the town a couple of miles away. She was walking alone on the road. Near dusk, she found herself on a particularly isolated stretch of road near a spot the locals called "Water Tank Hill." It was known in those days for its "ghost lights." Evidently, these ghostly lights were seen by various people who described them as "red, glowing fireballs" which would zigzag or bob along the hill and adjacent ridges. As mysteriously as they would appear, they would disappear and then reappear again in cycles.

The woman had just started down a gentle slope in the road when suddenly, something shot out just in front and above her in the sky from a ridge near the infamous Water Tank Hill. It startled her so badly that she actually "froze in mid-step." The next thought to cross her mind was that she must be looking at one of the "ghost lights." She said it looked like a "red, glowing, ball of light."

However, she quickly realized it had to be something other than a ghost light, and that frightened her even more because she had no explanation at all for what she was seeing. As the red, spherical, UFO hovered silently in the air, she saw protrusions from the object. She recalled that, "It looked like antennas or legs sticking out from it."

Therefore, in her mind, "it" was a machine and not a ghost, and this object defied any concept of any machine she knew about. When asked if "it" could have been an airplane, the woman shook her head emphatically no.

She went on to say that once she saw these strange protrusions on the UFO, she ran like "a scared rabbit" the rest of the way home. She didn't know if the UFO followed her or not, because she was too afraid to look up. Once she got inside the house, she bolted the door and wouldn't look outside.

This was a rare thing for a person to do in those days. Most people usually left their doors unlocked at all hours. She was not a person who was easily frightened, but what she saw that spring night unnerved her for some time. A similar event had occurred at the same location in the late 1930s.

In 1933, another alien incursion took place in Chrysville, Pennsylvania. At that time, a local man observed a faint, violet-colored, glowing UFO that had landed in a field. Walking over to it, he found an oval-shaped craft about nine-feet wide and six-feet tall with a circular opening that was similar to a vault door. Pushing it, he found the room filled with a violet light. He observed many instruments and noticed the smell of ammonia. He did not see any occupants.

That same year, in 1933, another example of UFO-related radiation burns occurred in Queensland, Australia. At that time, a very-small, disc-shaped UFO was seen hovering behind a house by a young boy. Thinking it was a toy, the small UFO was grabbed and then quickly released by the boy who suffered itching and blistering on his hands as a result of touching the craft.

That same year, in 1933, another close encounter occurred. An aboriginal woman was allegedly abducted by a UFO in the isolated region of Discovery Well which is a desolate area located at the northern edge of the Great Sandy Desert, in Western Australia.

The aboriginal woman claimed her tribe had been frightened off from Discovery Well when a "large, shiny egg" suddenly came down out of the sky. In broad daylight, the strange UFO flew low over them and landed. Then, several beings, described as strange-looking, grey-skinned humanoids, came out of the UFO.

The woman said she was then "stunned" by an object carried by one of the alien beings. She was then carried aboard their craft. The interior of the UFO was glowing. She was strapped to a shining table and apparently "experimented with." When the woman told local ranchers of her experience they just laughed.

Two years earlier, on February 15, 1931, another alien incursion occurred in the early afternoon, in Holyoke, Colorado. At that time, a young, local rancher was riding his horse while checking on cattle after a snowstorm. As he rode over a small hill and down to a draw about 25-to-30-feet deep, he looked up and saw an aluminum-colored, oval-shaped UFO in the air. It had a door that was transparent like glass that opened. Then, someone appeared in the doorway that looked human, but not as tall as a normal human.

The alien reportedly looked down at the rancher. The rancher noted that the alien was wearing a dark uniform. The rancher's horse was spooked by the UFO and stumbled quite a bit, so the rancher looked down for a moment, and when he looked up again the UFO had vanished.

The previous year, on June 1, 1930, another alien incursion took place at approximately 2:00 a.m. in Freeville, New York. Early that morning, on a remote dark road, a local motorist and his passenger witnessed a very-large, triangular UFO for about 20 minutes. The weather was clear and the night sky was perfect for star gazing. There was very little artificial light in the area. At first, the driver of the car noticed a bright star with tiny flashes around it. Then, about 100 feet away, he noticed another bright star flashing. And again, at a third point, there was another bright star flashing. Together they formed a triangle.

The driver noted that between the star-like lights there was total darkness, and no stars could be seen. As the witnesses watched, they noted that the UFO was about 2,000 feet up in the sky and was moving very slowly to the east. Decades later, upstate New York would become famous for its sightings of large, triangular UFOs passing silently through the night in the Hudson Valley.

In the 1930s, another close encounter ended up being fatal for the alien. At that time, in Mandurah, Australia, a small humanoid alien showed up at a farm asking for water. The being was shot dead by a terrified farmer.

Yet another alien encounter occurred one evening in 1930, in the same area of Australia. The event was first reported in 1982 after a 67-year-old woman saw a picture of Steven Spielberg's fictional alien from the movie *ET*. The alien image in the photograph had helped her recall an experience she had at age 15 while living near the wetlands at Mandurah, Australia.

One night in 1930, around 8:00 p.m., the teenage girl was reading with her parents by the light of a hurricane lamp with the door partly open. Suddenly, a "little pink creature walked in." She recalled it was about 24 inches in height with large ears. It had big, bulbous eyes, small hands, large feet, a slit of a mouth, no hair, and was covered with a film that made it look shiny as if it was wet or oily.

The girl and her mother were terrified, and the father went white as a sheet. Being a religious man, he believed it was the work of the devil. He gathered his courage and caught the creature in a net. The daughter noted that it made a very strange "EE, EE" sound as her father carried it outside. She never saw it again and went to bed feeling very scared that night.

She didn't think about her alien encounter again until many decades later when she saw a picture of the Hollywood *ET*. In comparison, the alien she witnessed in real life looked very different. She said, "Only its eyes were the same as the fictional creature. It had a normal body but smaller; like a child's body." She did not see any reproductive organs on the creature. She said it reminded her of an elf.

Perhaps that was why on June 27, 1982, Ronald Reagan made one of his most unusual remarks ever regarding aliens when he hosted Steven Spielberg at the White House for a private screening of the soon-to-be-released movie *ET: The Extraterrestrial*. The movie featured a young alien that is accidentally stranded on Earth and wants to return home. However, U.S. government agents try to capture and study him.

Along with the Reagans, 35 other people were invited to the special screening. The event started with a reception in the Blue Room where the Reagans met with their guests. From there, the group moved to the Red Room where the Presidential party had dinner. At 8:22 p.m., in the White House Theater, the movie ET began.

The movie emotionally moved the Reagans. Spielberg later recalled that, "Nancy Reagan was crying towards the end, and the President looked like a 10-year-old kid." Following the screening, President Reagan reportedly leaned over, clapped Spielberg on the shoulder, and quietly commented, "You know, there aren't six people in this room who know how true this really is." Unfortunately, the sudden surge of people approaching Spielberg prevented him from pursuing the strange comment made by the 40th President of the United States.

CHAPTER SIXTEEN

Historic Close Encounters

During my research and reporting of this subject, I found that some people believe all UFOs are actually built by clandestine groups of humans. And yes, as I reported earlier in this book, some UFOs have been built by humans in modern times. But the historical records of UFO sightings and extraterrestrial encounters indicate we have been visited by intelligent beings from other worlds for a long time. In fact, a series of alien incursions by UFOs was reported in 1929, less than two decades after the Wright Brothers helped mankind take its first baby steps toward powered flight.

For example, one night in 1929, in Fermeneuve, Canada, a local resident was returning home when he witnessed a UFO that landed. It had a glowing, yellow light which made his horse very nervous. When he got within 19 feet of the UFO, he saw four or five dwarfish figures running around. He noted that they had childlike voices. After a few moments, he saw the dark UFO take off with a machine-like sound and a rush of air. He estimated the UFO was 30-feet wide and 15-feet high.

That same year, in 1929, in Canada, at least five people witnessed a huge ball of light giving off fiery colors. The object slowly landed. Later, it gradually vanished after illuminating the whole countryside for 30 minutes.

That same year, in 1929, another alien incursion took place in the North Atlantic. The third mate of a ship reported that while 400 miles off the coast of Virginia he sighted a UFO traveling at an estimated 100 mph toward Bermuda. The UFO gave him the impression that it was a large, passenger craft, but an investigation failed to show any airship or airplane in the area at that time.

That same year, on July 5, 1929, at approximately 2:00 p.m., an alien incursion occurred near Burns, Oregon. That afternoon, a mother and her daughter were in the mountains driving through a narrow pass in the rocks when a UFO flew very slowly over the top of their car, so they stopped. Then, the UFO stopped, and the mother noticed that in the middle of the UFO were windows. In one of the windows were two alien beings that looked like average humans. They were pointing with their arms and hands toward the car below.

The daughter became very excited and jumped out of the car. She noted that the UFO was two shades of brown and that it hovered for about 40 seconds. At that time, it emitted a soft hum, but did not move at all. As it was leaving, the UFO moved very slowly, and the girl saw one of the alien beings walk to another window. She estimated the UFO was at least 300-feet long. Then, in a blink, it was gone. She recalled her mother telling her to never say anything about their encounter, because people would think they were crazy.

Two years earlier, in 1927, an alien incursion took place in Romania. At that time, a cylindrical-shaped UFO flew over a village at an altitude of about 900 feet. It was grey and flew silently. It was estimated to be 60-feet long and about 12-feet wide.

That same year, in 1927, an alien incursion occurred in Sausalito, California. Writer Ella Young reported that while sitting outside the Madrona Hotel, she witnessed a cigar-shaped UFO shoot out of a cloud beyond the bay and move across the sky toward Mount Tamalpais. It was not shaped like any airship she knew. She reported that, "It was long and slender with a yellow color and was traveling at great speed. It seemed to progress by alternately contracting and elongating its body."

That same year, in 1927, an alien incursion transpired one afternoon in Scottsbluff, Nebraska. At that time, pilot Barney Oldfield encountered what he later described as weird things that looked like "flying manhole covers."

The previous year, on February 14, 1926, in the afternoon, another close encounter took place in Washington, D.C. It was the first potential account of an alien abduction in the nation's capital. According to the abductee/witness, "I was 12-years old then and was walking home from school when I noticed a light in the sky. It looked like nothing I had ever seen before or since. It [the UFO] was in the shape of an isosceles triangle and was spinning as if rolling. It had one light on each point of the triangle.

"The color of the UFO was reddish black, but there were lights all over the middle of it. It was flying at least 1,000 mph, and as quickly as it came, it vanished beyond the horizon without making a sound! Throughout that experience, and even afterwards, I was shocked and very confused. Most of my memory after seeing the UFO is missing. I do recall getting home at 11:00 p.m. that night, and my parents were worried sick."

That same year, in 1926, an alien incursion occurred in Asia. While on expedition through Mongolia, explorer Nicholas Roerich, and members of his caravan, witnessed a huge, oval-shaped UFO flying high in the clear blue sky. It had a shiny surface that reflected the sun on one side, and it moved at great speed from one horizon to the other.

The previous year, in 1925, an alien incursion took place one night in Chevy Chase, Maryland, which is on the border of the District of Columbia. At that time, a mysterious fireball "exploded" just outside the city limits. However, no remains of a meteor were found.

That same year, in 1925, an alien incursion transpired in Moora, Australia. At that time, two teenage girls encountered a disc-shaped, shimmering UFO that was resting on four legs in a field. The young girls ran off in fear.

That same year, on December 28, 1925, an alien incursion occurred at approximately 6:00 p.m. near Atkinson, Illinois. That evening, a young boy and his uncle witnessed a disc-shaped UFO in the sky above their farmland. The stars were beginning to come out as the young boy and his uncle were doing their choirs. While taking a break, the boy looked up and noticed two stars that were brighter than the others. This caught his attention, so he studied them for a moment.

As he did so, he realized that one of the stars was moving away from the other. A few moments later, a UFO was suddenly above him, and the whole area became as bright as day. He looked around and could see everything clearly.

He described the UFO as being bright as daylight and that it was just a short distance above him. He could see a dark shape in the light that was about 10 feet in diameter. He noted that the dark shape was enveloped in some sort of a glowing atmosphere.

The UFO hovered for a few moments and then its light dimmed as it glided over the field about 25 feet in the air. As it flew toward some buildings on the ranch, it had to ascend slightly to clear a tall barn. It soon faded from view.

The previous year, in 1924, an alien incursion took place in Ireland. Two boys watched for several minutes as an illuminated UFO, several feet long, flew through the air a few feet off the ground at approximately 10 mph. It passed over a hedge and crossed a field before encountering a railroad track. The UFO then turned sharply and began moving along the length of the track until it was out of sight.

The previous year, in 1923, an alien incursion occurred in Quetta, Pakistan. At that time, a UFO "exploded" in mid-air over the city. Flaming debris rained down from the sky, destroying a few buildings. The fire lasted for hours, leaving only melted metal and "thin wires."

The previous year, in 1922, an alien incursion took place in Poland. At that time, many people witnessed a silvery UFO. It had two hemispheres divided by a rotating ring. The UFO "shot a beam of light" and then ascended with a loud noise and departed.

That same year, in 1922, an alien incursion occurred in Davenport, Iowa. At that time, twin eight-year-old girls witnessed a disc-shaped UFO in the sky near their town.

That same year, in 1922, an alien incursion transpired in Hubbell, Nebraska. That night, a local hunter was following strange animal tracks when he heard a high-pitched sound and saw a circular UFO blocking out the starlight overhead. The UFO then became brilliantly lighted and landed in a hollow. Soon afterward, a creature over eight-feet tall was seen flying from the direction where the UFO had landed. It left tracks in the snow.

That same year, in 1922, an alien incursion occurred in Wales, England. At that time, two local men witnessed a UFO fall into the ocean so slowly they thought it was an airplane that had crashed and was sinking. A boat was sent out to investigate, but nothing was found.

The previous year, in 1921, an alien incursion occurred in Killingly, Connecticut. At that time, a brightly-illuminated, circular UFO was sighted above a cloud at night.

The previous year, in 1920, an alien incursion took place near

Mount Pleasant, Iowa. At that time, local fishermen witnessed a blue-glowing, egg-shaped UFO land.

That same year, on June 15, 1920, an alien incursion occurred in Mussell County, Montana. At that time, local residents reported seeing UFOs that looked like someone was carrying a bright lantern.

The previous year, in 1919, an alien incursion took place in Wiltshire, England. At that time, two British soldiers witnessed several orange-glowing, spherical UFOs hovering over Salisbury Plain.

The previous year, in 1918, an alien incursion occurred in Australia. At that time, a luminous, cross-shaped UFO was sighted hovering over Lismore, New South Wales.

That same year, in 1918, an alien incursion took place in Waco, Texas. At that time, several soldiers at Rich Field witnessed a 100 to 150 foot long, cigar-shaped UFO. One of the men recalled that, "It flew directly overhead and was no more than 500-feet high, so we got an excellent view of it. It had no motors or rigging. It was noiseless and had a sort of flame color. I could observe no windows. We all experienced the weirdest feeling of our lives that day and sat in our tent puzzling over it for some time."

The previous year, in 1917, early one spring morning, a dramatic alien incursion took place in Belgium. Strange as it may sound, fighter ace Baron Manfred von Richthofen, also known as the bloody "Red Baron," allegedly became the first human in modern history to shoot down a UFO! The aerial alien encounter clearly illustrated that UFOs are considered legitimate military targets.

The event was witnessed by another former German fighter ace named Peter Waitzrik. He watched in astonishment as the Red Baron shot down a UFO that had undulating, orange, lights. Waitzrik reported that he stared in disbelief at what happened next. Two bruised and battered, alien occupants of the downed space craft climbed from their ship and ran off into the woods.

When Waitzrik first related his story publicly, he was an energetic, 105 year old, retired, airline pilot. When interviewed, he recalled that, "The Baron and I gave a full report on the incident back at headquarters, and they told us not to ever mention it again. Except for my wife and grand kids, I never told a soul. However, it's been over 80 years, so what difference could it possibly make now?

"The Red Baron and I were flying an early-morning mission over western Belgium in the spring when a UFO suddenly appeared in a clear-blue sky directly ahead of our *Fokker* tri-planes. We were terrified because we'd never seen anything like it before. The U.S. had just entered the war, so we assumed it was something they'd sent up. The Baron immediately opened fire, and the UFO went down like a rock; shearing off tree limbs as it crashed in the woods.

"Then, two little baldheaded guys climbed out and ran away. I assumed the glittering, silver spaceship was some sort of enemy invention until the flying saucer scare began in the late 1940s. It convinced me that the Baron had shot down a UFO.

"The craft he shot down was about 136 feet in diameter and looked just like those saucer-shaped spaceships that everybody's been seeing for the last 50 years. There's no doubt in my mind now that it was not a U.S. reconnaissance plane the Baron shot down. It was some kind of spacecraft from another planet, and those little guys that ran off into the woods weren't Americans, they were space aliens of some kind."

That same year, in 1917, a dramatic alien incursion transpired in Fatima, Portugal. At that time, local residents witnessed flying disks that looked like "aircraft of light." Also observed were double-supersonic detonations, odd lights, electro-static charges, star-like objects, and a mysterious white substance that fell from one of the UFOs but disappeared when it made contact with the ground. It is important to note that the glowing spheres and disc-shaped UFOs were witnessed by a crowd of somewhere between 50,000 to 100,000 people!

It was reported that, at one point, a silver disc appeared in the sky, and the rain stopped, and the clouds rolled back. Then, the sun dimmed, and everything took on a grey, opaque appearance. The disc then dove in an erratic, zigzag pattern at the crowd, stopped just above their heads and then slowly maneuvered back into the sky. As it faded from view, the sun brightened and began to shine normally again. A local reporter took a photo of the disc, but it was never made public.

That same year, in 1917, an alien incursion occurred in Salida, Colorado. At that time, a minister, and his family, used a telescope to observe a silver-colored UFO that they described as "a wagon wheel flying through the sky."

That same year, in October of 1917, an alien incursion took place in Youngstown, Pennsylvania. At that time, a local teenage boy was walking along the railroad tracks when he witnessed a saucer-shaped UFO with a platform and rows of lights. It was sitting in a field about 90 feet away.

He cautiously watched the UFO for a couple of minutes before it took off with a high-pitched sound, rising gradually into the air. He estimated it was the size of an average car. The top of the UFO was dome-shaped. The teenager also noted that the UFO had elongated windows through which moving figures could be seen.

The previous year, in 1916, an alien incursion occurred in Ireland. At that time, a brightly-glowing UFO was sighted hovering in the sky. It was visible for 15 minutes before flying to the northwest and hovering for 45 minutes. It eventually vanished.

The previous year, in 1915, an alien incursion took place in Canada. The event was reported in newspapers as "the phantom invasion." At that time, mysterious spacecraft invaded the skies over the capital of Canada.

That same year, in 1915, a mass abduction occurred during World War I, in Turkey. At that time, the entire First, Fourth Norfolk regiment of the British Army disappeared in an attempt to take Hill 60 at Suvla Bay, near Gallipoli. In front of 22 witnesses, a regiment of over 800 men marched into a strange formation of lenticular clouds hovering over Hill 60 and were never seen again. The regiment was thought to have been captured and was officially listed as missing. After the war, Britain demanded the return of the regiment, but the Turks denied any knowledge of the regiment's existence. No trace of the soldiers was ever found.

The previous year, on December 22, 1914, an alien incursion took place in Europe. A British soldier stationed on the front lines during World War I witnessed a zeppelin-like object that rose straight towards the clouds: not like a normal airship, but straight up. After rising up vertically, it suddenly flew forward at approximately 200 mph. It then turned around and darted backwards and then suddenly rose again; disappearing into the clouds. The object was also witnessed by two sergeant majors.

That same year, in 1914, an alien incursion occurred in Canada.

At that time, eight people witnessed a UFO floating on the waters of Georgian Bay. The witnesses noted alien entities on the exterior of the UFO that were operating a hose they had placed into the water. When the aliens noticed they were being observed by humans, they all quickly returned inside. However, one alien was still standing on the outside of the UFO when the craft took off.

That same year, in 1914, an alien incursion took place in Norway. At that time, a glowing UFO was observed over a large area. Many reliable people, including a sheriff, sighted the strangely-illuminated, alien craft. The sheriff watched it with binoculars. It was also observed through binoculars from a small steamboat. At the time, the sky was dark and completely overcast. Suddenly, a luminous point of light, like a very-large star, appeared to the east. The light was white, but then shifted its color to red and blue. The UFO flew silently and slowly at various elevations before it left at great speed.

That same year, in 1914, an alien incursion occurred in Benton Harbor, Michigan. At that time, three glowing UFOs flew low over the town.

The previous year, in 1913, an alien incursion took place in Toronto, Canada. At that time, several office workers witnessed a fleet of UFOs flying overhead in groups. The UFOs returned later that day in a scattered formation.

That same year, in June of 1913, an alien incursion occurred in Lansing, Michigan. An article in the Lansing State Journal reported that, "So swiftly did the strange craft travel that it was not more than three minutes before it flew across the entire sky. The craft carried no lights of any kind and was too elongated for an ordinary balloon. It flew at a great height, and when it passed to the northwest of the city it had reached an even higher altitude." A large crowd of people at the local racetrack also witnessed the event.

That same year, in 1913, an alien incursion took place over Milwaukee and Sheboygan, Wisconsin. At that time, a large, cigar-shaped UFO was witnessed flying slowly overhead. It flashed a bright light over the streets and buildings before flying back out over Lake Michigan; an area where UFOs would repeatedly be sighted in the future.

The previous year, in 1912, an alien incursion occurred in Lockport, Illinois. At that time, witnesses observed a UFO that flew slowly in front of the full moon for about three minutes. The UFO was rectangular with flat ends and was about two-thirds the diameter of the full moon in length.

The previous year, in 1911, an alien incursion took place in New York, New York. At that time, a "mystery airship" was sighted flying slowly under the Brooklyn Bridge.

The previous year, in 1910, an alien incursion occurred in France. At that time, a rare photograph was taken of a strange UFO that hovered over the tree tops beyond a line of spectators at a race track.

That same year, in 1910, an alien incursion transpired in New Zealand. At that time, several witnesses, including a priest, a mayor, and a policeman saw a cigar-shaped UFO hovering 90 feet off the ground. The witnesses noted that a man appeared at a door on the UFO and was heard shouting something in an unknown language. The door then closed, and the UFO quickly accelerated and was soon out of sight.

That same year, in 1910, an alien incursion occurred off the coast of Normandy. At that time, the crew of a French fishing boat saw "a large, black, bird-like object" fall from the sky into the sea. The astonished fishermen noted that the UFO briefly bounced back into the air before it fell once more into the ocean and disappeared.

That same year, in 1910, an alien incursion took place over Alabama and Tennessee. At that time, a large, cigar-shaped UFO hovered over the area while shining a bright light down on local residents.

That same year, in 1910, an alien incursion occurred in Arkansas. At that time, two local children witnessed a bright UFO hovering just above the trees about 50 yards from their position. They noted that the UFO had no windows, was silver-colored, and was shaped like a Zeppelin but not quite as big. As the strange craft slowly began to fly away, it suddenly vanished before the astonished children's eyes. Naturally, no one believed the children when they reported the event.

That same year, in June 1, 1910, an alien incursion took place in Wills Point, Texas. That afternoon, a 12-year-old girl witnessed a cigar-shaped UFO moving silently across the sky in front of her house. She noted that the UFO travelled at a rapid pace. She said it was very large and grey with no wings.

That same year, in 1910, a series of alien incursions occurred in England. At that time, mysterious airships were seen, mostly at night, around many areas of Britain. The strange craft were described as being oblong with a powerful searchlight. Witnesses also noted that these craft were capable of propelling themselves through the air silently at great speed. One of the UFOs was witnessed by two police officers in different parts of the same city at 5:10 a.m. Both officers noted that the UFO had a long body with a light attached. As it passed overhead at great speed, it made a steady buzz like a high-powered engine.

That same year, in 1910, an alien incursion took place in the Persian Gulf. At that time, UFOs described as "rotating wheels which could go under water" were sighted by a Danish ship captain.

That same year, in 1910, an alien incursion occurred in Wales, England. At that time, a local man was walking along a road near the mountains when he came upon a large, tube-shaped UFO sitting in a field. Aboard were two men wearing fur coats that were talking excitedly in a language the witness could not understand. The grass at the site was found to be flattened after the UFO flew away.

That same year, in 1910, an alien incursion took place in Worcester, Massachusetts. At that time, local residents witnessed a dark UFO that gave off brilliant rays of light. The witnesses noted that the strange flying machine was so high in the sky that its form could not be distinguished. The UFO flew around Worcester and then moved west to Marlborough where it was also observed. It then returned to Worcester where it hovered for a time over an insurance building before leaving the area.

That same year, on August 1, 1910, an alien incursion occurred in Gore, New Zealand. Early that morning, a local resident reported seeing a bright-yellow, glowing UFO that shot up into the sky.

The previous day, on July 31, 1910, at approximately 4:55 p.m., an alien incursion took place in Fairfax, New Zealand. That afternoon, a local resident witnessed a UFO in the sky. He described it as a dark object that quickly flew over the top of the hills in the east and then rapidly climbed up towards the west. He noted that the UFO was cigar shaped with a box-like structure in the center underneath.

That same day, on July 31, 1910, an alien incursion occurred in Greenvale, New Zealand. Early that morning, while feeding the horses, a local farmhand heard a strange whirring sound that frightened the animals. When he looked up, he saw a UFO overhead that was about 150-feet long. It was well lit and was moving so fast that by the time he woke his friends up, the lights of the UFO were fading in the distance.

Three days earlier, on July 28, 1910, an alien incursion occurred around 2:00 a.m. in Dunedin, New Zealand. At that time, a UFO flew low over the city. One local resident reported that he was awakened by a horrible noise. He said, "The noise was like a ship dragging its anchor. I got out of bed and went around to the front and saw something floating in the sky. It was a great, black thing with a searchlight attached."

The previous day, on July 27, 1910, an alien incursion took place at approximately 10:00 a.m. in Lambourne, New Zealand. That morning, while working near the mouth of a river, two local men witnessed a large, boat-shaped UFO moving high in the sky.

Two days earlier, on July 25, 1910, an alien incursion occurred around 8:30 p.m. in Kaitangata, New Zealand. That night, a mysterious UFO appeared at the beach. It was viewed through a very-powerful "night glass" (a telescope that can see objects in the dark) by two local men. The UFO appeared to be a large, dark superstructure with a powerful headlight and two smaller lights at the side. When first sighted, it was flying low over the roof tops. But it then glided higher in the air and flew north, then swooped to the west, and then moved to the east before finally disappearing over the horizon. However, about 10:30 p.m., the strange UFO returned briefly. This time, it disappeared as it flew out to sea.

Two days earlier, on July 23, 1910, an alien incursion took place in Kelso, New Zealand. That afternoon, a small group of schoolchildren and some local residents witnessed a UFO that flew down and bobbed around in the sky over the school for a few minutes.

Four days earlier, on July 19, 1910, an alien incursion occurred in Oamaru, New Zealand. At that time, three residents witnessed a "flickering light" flying around in the sky.

Two months earlier, on May 28, 1910, an alien incursion occurred in Solon, Maine. That night, a local resident witnessed a comet-looking UFO that made a zigzag pattern in the sky.

The previous year, on July 24, 1909, an alien incursion occurred at Kaka Point, in New Zealand. That night, half-a-dozen boys were playing on the beach when they witnessed a huge, illuminated UFO moving in the sky. The UFO appeared as if it was going to land nearby. The boys noted that the light from the UFO was reflected off the tin roof of a nearby beach house. The boys thought that the UFO had been attracted by their lantern on the beach. However, instead of landing, the UFO then flew very low around the rocks at the point and soon disappeared. The boys estimated the UFO was at least as big as a house.

The previous month, on June 16, 1909, an alien incursion took place at 4:10 a.m. in Dong Hoi, Vietnam. That morning, a UFO with an elongated shape that was flat at both ends flew over the city casting a powerful light. Local fishermen reported that the phenomenon lasted about 10 minutes. The UFO was last seen entering the water about four miles off the coast.

The previous year, in 1908, an alien incursion occurred in Sofia, Bulgaria. That afternoon, a very-bright, spherical UFO flew slowly above the town square.

That same year, in 1908, an alien incursion took place in Denmark. At that time, many people around the country reported sighting a bright airship in the sky.

That same year, in 1908, an alien incursion occurred off the coast of Delaware. At that time, a British ship was sailing to Philadelphia when it was surrounded by a dense, "glowing cloud" which mysteriously magnetized everything on board. The compass was observed to swing wildly. When sailors tried to move some chains on the bridge, they found that they were stuck to the metal floor. Suddenly, the "glowing cloud" rose up and was seen hovering above the ocean for some time.

That same year, in 1908, an alien incursion took place in Bridgewater, Massachusetts. At that time, a black, spherical UFO with a brilliant spotlight was seen hovering and moving over the area.

That same year, in 1908, an alien incursion occurred between 7:00 p.m., and 9:00 p.m. in Kent, Washington. For two nights in a row, a reddish, cigar-shaped UFO, two or three times as bright as Jupiter, flew over the area.

That same year, in 1908, an alien incursion took place in Cherbourg, France. At that time, local residents witnessed an oval, reddish UFO that hung in the sky.

That same year, in 1908, an alien incursion occurred in Bucovina, Rumania. That evening, a retired doctor witnessed a brightly-glowing, elongated, disc-shaped UFO that appeared larger than the full moon.

That same year, in 1908, an alien incursion took place at about 1:30 a.m. in Silshee, California. That morning, a local resident witnessed a bright light in the sky heading toward him. As the alien craft passed overhead, the man could see the form of an "airship" in the light. The strange light was also seen by the postmaster in a nearby town.

The previous year, in 1907, an alien incursion took place in Burlington, Vermont. At that time, a torpedo-shaped UFO silently "exploded" over the downtown area. The event was witnessed by many local residents including a bishop and a governor. It appeared to be another example of alien "Star Gate" technology.

The previous year, on November 11, 1906, an alien incursion was captured on film at an astronomical observatory in Wien, Austria. The photographic plate was taken with a *Bruce* telescope with an exposure time of three hours. Although the UFO was very dim, it had a periodic flash.

That same year, in 1906, a dramatic alien incursion occurred in the North Atlantic off the coast of Newfoundland. That day, deck hands onboard a ship witnessed what they initially assumed were three meteors falling into the ocean directly ahead of their ship. The UFOs fell out of the sky into the water, one after another, at a distance of about five miles. Although it was daylight, the UFOs left a red streak in the air from zenith to the horizon. Simultaneously, all the men on the ship began shouting. Then, one of the men sighted a huge UFO falling through the sky in a zig-zag manner less than a mile away. The man noted that he could distinctly hear the hissing of water as the UFO entered the ocean.

The UFO fell into the ocean with a rocking motion leaving a broad, red streak in its wake. The men estimated the UFO must have weighed several tons and appeared to be approximately 10 to 15 feet in diameter. The UFO was disc-shaped, which probably accounted for its peculiar rocking motion. When the metallic UFO struck the water, spray and steam rose to a height of at least 40 feet and, for a few moments, the surface of the ocean looked like the mouth of a crater.

Two years earlier, in 1904, an alien incursion occurred in Korea. At that time, local residents witnessed three bright-red UFOs that appeared beneath the clouds. The UFOs then changed elevation and flew above the broken clouds and moved off into space. The largest UFO was estimated to have been visually about six times as large as the sun. It was egg-shaped and flew with the larger end forward. The second UFO was visually about twice the size of the sun, and the third UFO was visually about the size of the sun. Their close approach to the earth was a remarkable event for the local residents. The UFOs were sighted in the area for at least two minutes and were carefully observed by three people whose accounts all agreed as to the details.

That same year, in 1904, an alien incursion took place in Rolling Prairie, Indiana. At that time, a local mother and her two sons witnessed two whitish-blue, glowing UFOs about 1,200 feet from their position. The UFOs hovered approximately nine feet above the ground for a while before disappearing over a hill.

The previous year, in 1903, an alien incursion occurred around 11:00 p.m., in Argenteuil, France. That night, local residents witnessed a red-glowing UFO that traveled about four miles in 20 minutes. The UFO was seen through field glasses and did not appear to be a balloon.

On December 17, 1903, Wilbur and Orvil Wright successfully flew their powered aircraft in North Carolina, USA.

The previous year, in 1902, a New Zealand farmer named Richard Pearse single-handedly designed and built his own engine and flying machine in his barn. He made his first successful flight in March of 1902.

That same year, in 1902, an alien incursion took place in Devon, England. At that time, a British colonel witnessed numerous brightly-colored UFOs that looked to him like little suns, or shiny-toy balloons, flying through the air.

That same year, in 1902, an alien incursion occurred in the Gulf of Guinea, in Africa. At that time, three passengers and a second officer on a ship witnessed a huge, dark UFO with strange lights directly ahead. The UFO was last observed sinking slowly into the water. It was estimated to have been 600-feet long.

The previous year, on August 14 1901, around dawn, Gustave Whitehead took to the air in a bird-like monoplane near Bridgeport, Connecticut. The inventor flew his vehicle a distance of approximately a half mile.

Two years earlier, on November 1, 1899, an alien incursion took place around 7:00 p.m. in Dordogne, France. At that time, a UFO that looked "like an enormous star" was seen moving in the sky. At times, the UFO glowed white, then red, and sometimes blue. It moved swiftly from side to side like a kite.

That same year, in 1899, an alien incursion took place in Luzarch-es, France. At that time, a local resident observed a spherical, luminous UFO rise above the horizon and then visually shrink in size as it flew into the distance over a period of 15 minutes.

That same year, in 1899, an alien incursion occurred in South Africa. The South African government was inundated with UFO reports. Apparently, phantom airships equipped with powerful searchlights had mysteriously appeared in the skies and frightened many people in the area.

That same year, in 1899, an alien incursion took place in Prescott, Arizona. That day, a local doctor observed a luminous UFO in the sky that "traveled with the moon all day" until it disappeared around 2:00 p.m. A similar glowing object in the sky had been observed the day before in the town of Tonto, Arizona.

That same year, in 1899, an alien incursion occurred from 10:00 a.m., to 4:00 p.m. in El Paso, Texas. On that day, a luminous object was seen in the sky. The glowing object could not have been Venus because it was only seen for part of the day, and it did not appear again.

The previous year, in 1898, an alien incursion took place in Lille, France. At that time, an astronomer looking through his telescope sighted a rectangular-shaped, red-and-black UFO with a violet band of light on one side. It was not in the position of any known planet. It remained stationary for 10 minutes, then "cast out sparks and disappeared."

The previous year, on April 15, 1897, an alien incursion occurred in Howard, South Dakota. At that time, a UFO descended from the sky and briefly followed a locomotive as it traveled slowly down the tracks.

That same day, on April 15, 1897, around 9:00 a.m., an alien incursion took place in Washington, D.C. That morning, astonished residents witnessed a UFO passing overhead. The mysterious, technologically-advanced "airship," with powerful lights, flew above the Potomac and gradually disappeared from view over the hills of Virginia to the southeast. It had an unusual appearance and performance. It was observed for a few minutes as it passed overhead.

The UFO was reportedly sighted by the officers and soldiers stationed at Fort Myer. It was also witnessed by the attaches of the Analostan Boat Club and by hundreds of other reputable citizens, who were willing to take an oath as to what they had witnessed. Most of them reported that the UFO looked like "an oblong balloon with a slight pitch in the direction it was going."

People who were fortunate enough to have field glasses reported it was a double-barreled arrangement, shaped like a catamaran, hanging vertically, rocking from side to side and often shifting position as if it was drifting in the atmosphere.

Sometimes, one of the ends would be pointed toward the observers and then they would see it full broadside. No smoke, or smokestack, or wings, or other means of propulsion could be detected. It appeared there were two cylinder-like objects that were coupled together. It was suggested at the U.S. Department of Agricultural that the UFO was actually a kite sent up by the weather bureau for the purpose of meteorological experiments, but the people who saw the UFO insisted that this was not possible.

Although the UFO left the area that morning, it returned to Washington, D.C., later that evening. It reportedly approached the Washington Monument at an altitude of 600 feet, then flew toward Georgetown and disappeared around 11:00 p.m.

Three days earlier, on April 12, 1897, an alien incursion took place in Girard, Illinois. At that time, a large crowd of miners witnessed a UFO land. The night operator of the local railroad stated that he came sufficiently close to the strange craft to see a man emerge from it and make repairs. The UFO was elongated like a ship with a roof and a double canopy. It was last seen flying off to the north.

That same day, April 12, 1897, an alien incursion occurred in Nilwood, Illinois. At that time, three local residents witnessed a UFO land on their property. Before the three witnesses could reach it, the cigar-shaped craft with a dome rose into the air and slowly flew off into the distance.

Eleven days earlier, on April 1, 1897, an alien incursion took place in Everest, Kansas. At that time, the entire town witnessed a UFO passing under the clouds. Some of the witnesses noted that the UFO came down out of the sky slowly and then flew away very fast. They also reported that when the UFO was directly over the town, it swept the area with a powerful light.

It was then seen to rise up at a fantastic speed until it was barely discernible. It then came down and swooped low over the witnesses. At one point, it remained stationary for five minutes at the edge of a low cloud which became illuminated. At that time, everyone could clearly see the silhouette of the alien airship.

That same month, in April of 1897, an alien incursion occurred at approximately 10:30 p.m. in LeRoy, Kansas. A wealthy, prominent farmer reported that strange people inside an airship had attacked his cattle. At that time, the farmer, his son, and their farmhand grabbed axes and ran from the house to the cow lot where a cigar-shaped UFO, about 300-feet long, floated some 30 feet above his cattle.

The UFO had a carriage underneath which was brightly lit with numerous windows. Inside were six strange-looking beings speaking in a foreign language. These beings suddenly became aware of the farmers and aimed a powerful beam of light at them. The UFO then increased its power and rose higher into the air taking with it a two-year-old heifer which was roped around the neck by a cable made of a half-inch thick, red material.

The next day, a neighbor found the stolen cow's skin, legs and head in his field. He was mystified at how the remains got where they were because there were no tracks in the soft soil. The farmer later signed a sworn statement regarding the event. The affidavit was also signed by ten local, leading citizens.

That same month, in April of 1897, a fatal alien incursion occurred in Aurora, Texas. Early one morning, local residents were astonished by the sudden appearance of a UFO that was traveling slowly and very low to the ground as it passed over the public square. When it reached the north part of town, it collided with the tower of a windmill and broke into pieces with a terrific explosion, scattering debris over several acres, wrecking the windmill and water tank.

The alien pilot of the ship was allegedly the only one aboard, and while his remains were badly disfigured, it was later determined that he was not from this world. Papers found on his person were written in some unknown hieroglyphics that could not be deciphered.

The UFO was too badly damaged to form any conclusion as to its construction or motive power. It was built of an unknown metal that resembled a mixture of aluminum and silver. It was estimated to have weighed several tons. Many of the local townspeople viewed the wreckage and collected pieces of strange metal from the debris. They even gave the UFO pilot a funeral. He was reportedly buried in a grave in a small town north of Aurora.

Three months earlier, on January 24, 1897, an alien incursion occurred in Hastings, Nebraska. That morning, a UFO was sighted in the sky. It circled the town for a few minutes and then zoomed away to the north.

That same year, in 1897, an alien incursion occurred in Winnipeg, Canada. At that time, a mysterious airship flew over Winnipeg, the capital of Manitoba province, in full view of many citizens for at least 15 minutes. The strange, alien craft approached from the west, following the river. After passing over a hospital, the UFO veered sharply to the north and was soon out of sight.

That same year, in 1897, an alien incursion took place in Homan, Arkansas. A local resident was hunting when he heard the noise of what sounded like a steam engine in the woods nearby. He then followed the noise and found a UFO landed in a clearing. The hunter then approached and spoke with one of the occupants who wore dark glasses. The hunter reported that there were three or four occupants in the craft. He was amazed when the craft quickly rose up and flew away.

That same year, in 1897, an alien incursion occurred in Hot Springs, Arkansas. At that time, two policemen were riding on horseback when they witnessed a bright light in the sky. The astonished policemen then watched the light float down to the ground about nine miles away. They had only ridden a short way toward the UFO when their horses refused to continue. Soon after, two strange men were seen carrying lights toward them. Behind them, a UFO could be seen in the clearing. The officers estimated that the strange craft was at least 60-feet long.

That same year, in 1897, an alien incursion took place in McKinney Bayou, Arkansas. At that time, a local judge was surveying a tract of land when he witnessed a peculiar-looking UFO anchored to the ground. He later recalled that, "It was manned by three men who spoke a foreign language. But judging from their looks, one would take them to be Japanese."

That same year, in 1897, an alien incursion took place in Gas City, Indiana. At that time, a UFO landed on the property of a local man, terrifying the farmers and causing the horses and cattle to stampede. Then, six occupants of the UFO came out of the craft and appeared to make some repairs. Before a crowd of people could approach, the UFO rose into the air rapidly and flew away.

That same year, in 1897, an alien incursion occurred in Downs Township, Illinois. While working in his field, a local farmer witnessed a UFO land near his location. At that time, six people emerged from the strange craft and spoke to him for a few minutes before flying away.

That same year, in 1897, an alien incursion took place in Linn Grove, Iowa. At that time, a large UFO was seen travelling slowly toward the north. The UFO landed and soon after that five local men located the craft. They found two strange beings aboard the craft that tried to conceal themselves. The witnesses were surprised at how long the alien beings hair was. Moments later, the UFO rose into the air and flew off to the north.

That same year, in 1897, an alien incursion transpired in Waterloo, Iowa. At that time, a large UFO was observed at dawn. The alien craft was about 40-feet long and was shaped like a giant cigar.

That same year, in 1897, an alien incursion took place in Williamston, Michigan. At that time, at least a dozen farmers witnessed a UFO maneuvering in the sky for an hour before it landed. Then, a strange man about six-feet tall exited the craft. He was almost naked and was suffering from the heat. He indicated to the farmers that he was the pilot of the craft. One of the witnesses noted that the alien pilot's speech was musical, but too loud, as though he was always yelling. One farmer then walked up to the UFO pilot and was struck by the alien with a defensive blow that broke the farmer's hip.

That same year, in 1897, an alien incursion occurred in Kansas City, Missouri. At that time, 10,000 residents witnessed a large, black,

UFO that hovered for a while and was flashing green, blue and white lights. The UFO then flew rapidly straight up into space.

That same year, in 1897, an alien incursion took place in Perry Springs, Missouri. At that time, a passenger train on the *Wabash* line was followed by a low-flying UFO for 15 minutes. All the passengers on the train witnessed the alien craft, which had a powerful, red-and-white light. After about 15 minutes, the UFO flew ahead of the train and disappeared rapidly into the distance.

That same year, in 1897, an alien incursion occurred in Omaha, Nebraska. At that time, the majority of the city's population witnessed a UFO moving across the sky. It looked like a huge light that flew slowly northwest at a low altitude.

That same year, in 1897, an alien incursion took place in Howard, South Dakota. At that time, a UFO came down out of the sky and then continued on close to the ground as it followed a train. The event was reported by the engineer of the train.

That same year, in 1897, an alien incursion took place in Hillsboro, Texas. At that time, a local lawyer was surprised to see a bright UFO in the sky. His horse was so scared by the strange sight, it nearly toppled the carriage. When the UFOs main light was turned off, a number of smaller lights became visible on the underside of the dark object. The UFO soon left the area, but when the lawyer was on his way back home, one hour later, he saw the UFO rising in the sky once again. It reached the altitude of the cloud ceiling and flew away at a fantastic speed with periodic flashes of light.

That same year, in 1897, an alien incursion occurred in Josserand, Texas. At that time, a local resident was awakened by a machine-like noise. Looking outside, he saw a heavy, lighted UFO land in his wheat field. He quickly got dressed and walked outside toward the UFO. He was soon met by two men who asked permission to draw water from his well. He then had a discussion with the rest of the crew from the strange machine. Although he was told how the UFO worked, he could not comprehend their explanation.

That same year, in 1897, an alien incursion took place in Merkel, Texas. At that time, residents returning from church were shocked to observe a heavy object being dragged along the ground by a rope that was attached to a UFO. The object attached to the rope then got caught in a railroad track. The UFO was too high to be seen clearly, but a bright light was observed. After about 10 minutes, an alien being crawled down the rope and cut one end free and then went back aboard the craft which flew away. Witnesses noted that the being from the UFO was small and was wearing a light-blue uniform

That same year, in 1897, an alien incursion occurred in Rockland, Texas. At that time, a local man witnessed a UFO circling 15 feet above the ground. The UFO was elongated with various protrusions and blinding lights. The UFO went dark when it landed. The witness was then met by the alien pilot of the UFO who told him his purpose was peaceful and requested some common hardware items to repair his space craft.

The previous year, on November 26, 1896, an alien incursion occurred in Lorin, California. At that time, residents witnessed a UFO that looked like a large, black cigar with a fish-like tail that flew at tremendous speed. The UFO turned quickly and disappeared in the direction of San Francisco. The body of the strange craft was at least 100-feet long, and attached to that was a triangular tail. The surface of the UFO looked as if it were made of aluminum which exposure to wind and weather had turned dark.

One day earlier, on November 25, 1896, an alien incursion took place in Sacramento, California. At that time, a glowing UFO was seen flying rapidly across the sky. However, as it neared the southern boundary of the city, it turned directly toward the west and, after passing the city, went south. The UFO was visible for over 20 minutes.

The previous year, in 1895, an alien incursion took place in Oxford, England. At that time, a disk-shaped UFO was seen rising above some trees and disappearing into the east

Two years earlier, in 1893, an alien incursion occurred in the North China Sea. At that time, officers on a ship witnessed unusual lights flying in the sky. The lights appeared sometimes in a large formation while other times they spread out in unusual geometric patterns. One of the witnesses recalled that the UFOs resembled Chinese lanterns. The next night, the strange lights reappeared, but with a reddish glow and small amounts of smoke.

The previous year, in 1892, an alien incursion took place in the

Netherlands. At that time, an astronomer observing the moon through his telescope sighted a large, black, disk-shaped UFO as it moved across his field of view.

That same year, in 1892, a series of alien incursions occurred in Poland. At that time, a phantom airship began appearing. The UFO often appeared at night and was usually equipped with powerful searchlights.

The previous year, in September of 1891, an alien incursion took place at about 2:00 a.m. in Crawfordsville, Indiana. That night, two men were working outside when a glowing UFO flew overhead. The men described the craft as being about 20-feet long, and eight-feet wide. They watched the UFO moving in the sky for a few moments before it flew off.

Three years earlier, in 1888, an alien incursion occurred in Ragusa, Italy. At that time, many luminous UFOs were seen moving through the sky in a straight line for about one hour.

The previous year, on November 12, 1887, an alien incursion took place around midnight in Cape Race, Nova Scotia. At that time, a huge, glowing, spherical UFO was sighted by a fishing vessel. The bright UFO slowly emerged from the ocean and then rose in the air to an altitude of about 60 feet. The strange, glowing sphere then flew against the wind and briefly stopped near the fishing vessel. The UFO then quickly flew away and disappeared in the distance. The close encounter lasted about five minutes.

The previous year, on October 24, 1886, a dramatic alien incursion occurred in Venezuela. That night, a family of nine people was awakened by a loud, humming noise and a dazzling light that illuminated the interior of their house for a few moments. The occupants were terrified and believed that the end of the world had come. They then got on their knees and began to pray, but soon after, began vomiting violently.

To make matters worse, the people also experienced swelling in the upper part of their bodies, particularly around their face and lips. The harmful effects of the unidentified light were similar, if not identical, to radiation poisoning.

It should be noted that the brilliant light was not accompanied by a sensation of heat, although there was a smoky appearance and a peculiar smell. The next morning, the swelling had subsided, but large black blotches now appeared on the face and body of the family members.

Oddly, no pain was experienced until the ninth day when the victim's skin peeled off and the blotches transformed into dangerous, raw sores. The hair on their heads nearest to the intense light completely fell out. All the family members were seriously injured in the same way.

Another strange effect of the UFO radiation was that the trees around the house showed no signs of injury until nine days later. At that time, the trees suddenly withered almost simultaneously as the development of sores upon the bodies of the residents of the house. All of the family members ended up in a local hospital. Their appearance was described as truly horrible.

The previous year, on November 1, 1885, at about 9:30 p.m., an alien incursion took place in Constantinople, Turkey. That night, local residents witnessed an elongated, disc-shaped UFO that was giving off a powerful glow. The UFO seemed to float in the air. It visually appeared to be four or five times larger than the full moon.

It flew slowly and cast a light on the area below that was about ten-times brighter than a large electric bulb. At dawn the next morning, a brilliant UFO that was glowing blue and then green was sighted traveling at a height of 15 feet. The UFO made a series of turns around a pier. Its blinding luminosity lit the streets and the inside of the houses below.

Two years earlier, in 1883, an alien incursion took place in Segeberg, Germany. At that time, a teacher and some of her students witnessed two fiery, spherical UFOs that were visually twice the size of the full moon. The large, glowing, spherical UFOs were observed moving together in a clear sky.

That same year, in 1883, an alien incursion occurred in Zacatecas, Mexico. At that time, an astronomer working at the local observatory witnessed over 100 circular UFOs pass in front of the sun. The astronomer managed to take a photograph of one of the unidentified objects. It was the first known picture of a UFO.

One year earlier, in 1882, an alien incursion took place over Europe. At that time, a huge, saucer-shaped UFO was witnessed by numerous people in England, and other parts of Europe, during the night. It was seen to travel in the sky at an approximate altitude of 130 miles in an east-west direction. A number of eminent scientists witnessed the object and published a report of their conclusions. The report stated that the

UFO appeared to have a well-defined, disc-like shape. The flight of the object, though swift, appeared to be orderly and controlled.

The previous year, in 1881, an alien incursion occurred in Georgia, North America. At that time, a local farmer witnessed a UFO that terrified his farmhands and some visitors. The UFO was first sighted in a cornfield. It was estimated to have been about four feet in diameter and flew about 100 feet in elevation. The body of the UFO was perfectly black with a fire in the center that emitted a strong, sulfur smell.

At one point, the UFO then divided itself into three parts that flew rapidly over the field, twisting up the corn stalks by the roots and carrying them up. These three small UFOs were then seen to come together with a loud cracking sound, and a burning light, and then the UFO shot straight up into the heavens.

Before it left the area, three young ladies moved closer to observe the UFO and encountered a shower of burning sand, and they quickly ran back to the house. The farmer was completely baffled that even though the UFO contained what looked like fire, it did not appear to burn the corn below. However, the sulfur-smelling exhaust sickened and burned anyone who was close enough to get a breath of it.

The previous year, in 1880, an alien encounter took place in Aldershot, England. At that time, a strange being dressed in tight-fitting clothes and a shining helmet flew over the heads of two sentries who fired their rifles at the being without result. The flying being then stunned the sentries with a beam of light they described as "blue fire."

That same year, in 1880, an alien incursion occurred in France. At that time, a member of the French Academy observed a glittering, white-gold, cigar-shaped UFO in the sky that had pointed ends.

That same year, in 1880, around midnight, an alien incursion took place in the Persian Gulf. At that time, a ship's captain, and several other members of the crew, witnessed two glowing, circular UFOs that were estimated to have been 1,500 feet in diameter. The UFOs appeared underwater on each side of the ship. The close encounter lasted 20 minutes.

That same year, in 1880, an alien incursion occurred in Lamy, New Mexico. At that time, four men were surprised to hear voices in the sky coming from a strange-looking, balloon-shaped UFO that flew over them. The men later recalled that the UFO was shaped like a fish and seemed to be guided by a large, fan-like device. There were about ten alien beings aboard. Their language was not understood. The object flew low over the area before it rose up into the sky and rapidly disappeared toward the east.

That same year, in 1880, an alien incursion took place in Venezuela. At that time, a 14-year-old boy witnessed a luminous, spherical UFO descend from the sky and hover near him. Although he felt somehow "drawn" to it, he chose to run away and not look back.

The previous year, in 1879, an alien incursion occurred in the Persian Gulf. At that time, the crew of a ship witnessed two luminous UFOs that were about 130 feet across. The UFOs were seen traveling above the water before diving underneath it.

One year earlier, in 1878, an alien incursion took place in Texas. At that time, a farmer witnessed a dark, fast-moving, saucer-shaped UFO high in the sky. It continued on its way and was soon out of sight. A local newspaper reported that the farmer was a gentleman of undoubted veracity.

The previous year, in 1877, an alien incursion occurred in Venice, France. At that time, local residents witnessed a cigar-shaped UFO that discharged many smaller, glowing spheres that were extremely luminous. The peculiar-looking fleet of UFOs then flew slowly toward the north for approximately one hour.

Two years earlier, in 1875, an alien incursion took place in Prague, Czechoslovakia. According to a local professor, "The craft was of such a strange nature that I do not know what to say about it. It emitted a blinding-white light and flew slowly across the face of the moon, but remained visible afterwards."

The previous year, in 1874, an alien incursion occurred in Oaxaca, Mexico. At that time, local residents witnessed a huge, gently-swaying, trumpet-shaped UFO that was estimated to be 425-feet long. It hovered in the sky for six minutes before departing.

The previous year, in 1873, an alien incursion took place in broad daylight in Bonham, Texas. At that time, a huge, cigar-shaped UFO swooped low over the town on two occasions. It then disappeared quickly to the east.

The previous year, in 1872, an alien incursion occurred in Banbury, England. At that time, a UFO shaped "like a haystack" flew through the sky, sometimes high, sometimes very low. The UFO emitted fire and dense smoke. It produced the same effect as a tornado; knocking down some trees and stone walls before it suddenly vanished.

The previous year, in 1871, an alien incursion took place at the Meudon Observatory, in France. At that time, an astronomer sighted a number of spherical UFOs that resembled those witnessed years earlier at Nuremberg and Basel. Among the spherical UFOs was a circular craft that appeared to descend from the sky "like a disk falling through water."

The previous year, in 1870, an alien incursion occurred in the Atlantic Ocean. At that time, a UFO was sighted from a ship. The UFO appeared to be a light-grey, disc-shaped craft that flew against the wind.

The previous year, in 1869, a dramatic alien incursion took place in Ashland, Tennessee. At that time, a flaming, cylindrical-shaped UFO passed over the neighboring woods kicking up small branches and leaves of trees. At first, the UFO traveled slowly, at approximately five miles-per-hour, but soon gained speed. It then passed directly over a team of horses singeing their manes and tails to the roots. The UFO then flew towards a house taking a stack of hay with it. The UFO seemed to increase its heat and speed as it passed over a house and instantly caught all the shingles on the roof on fire. The UFO then flew over a wheat field setting fire to all the hay stacks that happened to be in its path.

After leaving the field, the UFO flew over a stretch of woods which extended to the river. The green leaves on the trees were burned to a cinder for a distance of 20 yards in a straight line due to the intense radiation coming from the UFO. When the UFO reached the river, it suddenly turned and followed the water raising a tall column of steam that went up to the clouds about half-a-mile high. At least 200 people witnessed the strange phenomena.

The previous year, in 1868, an alien incursion occurred in Copiago, Chile. At that time, a strange UFO flew low over the town. It had bright lights and made metallic, engine noises.

That same year, in 1868, an alien incursion took place in Oxford, England. At that time, astronomers at a local observatory sighted a luminous UFO that moved quickly across the sky. Then, it stopped and changed course to the west and then flew to the south where it hovered approximately four minutes before flying off into the distance.

Eight years earlier, on August 8, 1860, an alien incursion took place near Cherokee, North Carolina. That night, a curious light in the sky was sighted by local residents. One of the witnesses recalled that, "A large comet passed so near that we could plainly feel the heat. In a few minutes, after it passed, there were two loud cracks; one immediately after the other." The strange, powerful sound then rolled across the sky for several minutes. The event reportedly terrified some of the local women.

One month earlier, on July 13, 1860, an alien incursion took place at approximately 9:45 p.m. in Wilmington, Delaware. That night, local residents witnessed a pale-blue, glowing, 200-foot long, cloud-like UFO moving slowly and silently through the sky. Three smaller, bright-red, glowing spherical UFOs followed at a uniform distance behind the first UFO.

That same year, in 1860, an alien incursion occurred in Shreveport, Louisiana. At that time, local residents witnessed a strange light in a clear sky. The UFO appeared to be about 900 feet in length. Its color was that of a red-hot stove. Beautiful rays of light ascended from the center of the UFO to a considerable height presenting a stunning and sublime appearance. The witnesses watched the radiant UFO for about an hour.

Ten years earlier, in October of 1850, the first recorded alien incursion in Washington, D.C., took place. That night, a glowing UFO was observed by a perplexed local man standing in front of a building He watched in amazement as the extraordinary space craft passed slowly and silently through the sky over his neighborhood.

Three years earlier, in 1847, an alien incursion occurred in London, England. At that time, a spherical UFO was sighted rising vertically through the clouds.

The previous year, in 1846, an alien incursion took place on the eastern seaboard of America. At that time, a "luminous, flying disc" was sighted over a large area of the East Coast.

The previous year, in 1845, an alien incursion occurred in Naples, Italy. That night, astronomers working at an observatory sighted several luminous, disc-shaped UFOs in the sky which left trails of light as they traveled.

Two years earlier, in 1843, an alien incursion took place in Warwick, England. At that time, a cloud-like UFO passed over the area. Witnesses also reported seeing three alien beings in the sky.

The previous year, in 1842, an alien incursion occurred in Russia. At that time, small, perfectly-hexagonal, metallic objects fell out of the sky after a "strange cloud" appeared.

Two years earlier, in 1840, a series of alien encounters began in southern New Jersey and the surrounding area. An ugly, flying alien nicknamed "the Jersey Devil" was blamed for killing livestock at night. Joseph Bonaparte, the eldest brother of Napoleon Bonaparte, is said to have seen the Jersey Devil while hunting on his New Jersey estate. Commodore Stephen Decatur claimed to have fired upon the strange creature while testing ammunition on a New Jersey firing range. He and his audience were dumbfounded to watch the Jersey Devil continue its flight apparently unharmed.

Four years earlier, in 1836, an alien incursion took place in the coastal town of Cherbourg, in France. At that time, local residents witnessed a UFO they described as a "gleaming aerial vessel" that was seen moving very low in the sky.

Three years earlier, in 1833, an alien incursion occurred in Canada. At that time, a large, square, luminous UFO was seen hovering over Niagara Falls for more than an hour.

Two years earlier, in 1831, an alien incursion took place in Thuringia, Germany. At that time, a brilliant, luminous, disc-shaped UFO was seen moving in the night sky.

Five years earlier, in 1826, an alien incursion occurred in the English Channel. At that time, sailors sighted a grey, torpedo-shaped UFO flying overhead.

The previous year, in 1825, an alien incursion took place in Poland, Ohio. At that time, a brilliant UFO was visible in the sky for more than an hour.

Five years earlier, in 1820, an alien incursion occurred in Embrun, France. At that time, a formation of UFOs was sighted passing over the town. A local resident recalled that, "Numerous observers have seen, during an eclipse of the moon, strange illuminated objects in the sky moving in straight lines. They were equally spaced and remained in line when they made turns. Their movements were made with military precision."

The previous year, in 1819, an alien incursion took place in Amhurst, Massachusetts. At that time, a silvery-white, brightly-glowing, spherical UFO was seen passing through the sky. It was accompanied by a violent explosion. A gelatinous substance was reportedly found later.

Three years earlier, in 1816, an alien incursion occurred in Edinburgh, Scotland. At that time, many local residents witnessed a large, luminous, crescent-shaped UFO passing over the city.

Four years earlier, in 1812, an alien incursion took place in Bucovina, Romania. Around mid-day, residents witnessed a UFO that looked like "a large star with many rays of light." The strange, star-like UFO appeared again that night and was seen traveling in many directions.

Four years earlier, in 1808, an alien incursion occurred in Piedmont, France. At that time, a formation of luminous, disc-shaped UFOs was observed traveling through the sky.

Five years earlier, in 1803, an alien incursion took place in Barsdorf, Germany. At that time, local residents witnessed a UFO that looked like a shooting star which grew larger and brighter as it fell to earth. A strange buzzing noise was heard as the UFO flew close to the ground before "landing and bursting into flames." The next day, a jelly-like mass was found on the snow.

Four years earlier, in 1799, an alien incursion occurred in England. At that time, a brightly-glowing, spherical UFO passed through the sky. Some witnesses described it as a "large, red, pillar of fire" that was seen in the sky flying south. The UFO was preceded by "flashes of extremely vivid electrical activity." In the same area, other UFOs were also seen leaving luminous trails that year. One witness recalled sighting a "beautiful ball of blazing white light with red sparks flying off it" that flew silently across the sky.

Three years earlier, in 1796, an alien incursion took place in Germany. At that time, a brightly-glowing UFO that was visually the size of the moon was seen passing through the sky. Moments later, a large detonation was heard, and a dark-bituminous substance fell to earth.

Three years earlier, in 1793, an alien incursion occurred in Northumberland, England. At that time, a brightly-glowing, oval-shaped UFO was observed in the sky over the city for approximately five minutes.

Three years earlier, in 1790, an alien incursion took place in Alencon, France. At that time, a local police inspector witnessed a large, red, spherical UFO as it flew low over a farm. Reportedly, when the UFO landed, a man came out and spoke in a language no one understood. The UFO then "exploded" without making a sound and disappeared. The enigmatic event was witnessed by many local townspeople and was well documented. It was another possible example of alien "Star Gate" technology.

Three years earlier, in 1787, an alien incursion occurred in Edinburgh, Scotland. At that time, local residents witnessed a brightly-glowing UFO that looked like the sun as it traveled horizontally across the sky. It dropped its elevation a little, then rose up again and disappeared in a flash of light behind a cloud.

The previous year, in 1786, an alien incursion took place in England. At that time, a brightly-glowing, spherical UFO was seen hovering in the sky for approximately 40 minutes during a hurricane-force wind.

Three years earlier, in 1783, an alien incursion took place in England. On that day, during a royal celebration, a luminous UFO appeared from beneath a cloud and soon became brilliantly lit before coming to a halt. According to an English astronomer's account of the incident, "This strange sphere seemed at first to be pale blue in color, but its luminosity increased, and it soon set off again towards the east." Even though the sun was shining, the UFO was reported to have lit up everything on the ground and eventually disappeared with a terrific "explosion."

That same year, in 1783, an alien incursion occurred in Greenwich, England. At that time, a UFO was observed in the sky that "gave birth to eight satellites." All nine of the UFOs then disappeared slowly towards the southeast.

That same year, in 1783, an alien incursion took place in Sudbrooke, England. That night, several people witnessed a luminous UFO hovering in the sky. The UFO emitted steady flashes of "lightning," which lasted about 30 seconds. The UFO then separated into eight pieces. All the UFOs then traveled swiftly straight up before disappearing across the horizon in an arc.

Six years earlier, in 1777, an alien incursion occurred in France. At that time, a French astronomer sighted numerous dark, spherical UFOs in the sky.

Fifteen years earlier, in 1762, an alien incursion occurred in Lausanne, Switzerland. At that time, a huge, spindle-shaped UFO was seen crossing the sun by two different astronomical observatories.

Four years earlier, in 1758, an alien incursion took place near Cambridge, England. At that time, a dazzling UFO, as bright as day, was witnessed descending over Britain at an estimated 30 miles-per-second. According to one witness, "The light seemed to descend obliquely towards the earth and then rose again with renewed splendor."

Six years earlier, in 1752, an alien incursion occurred in Augermanland, Sweden. At that time, many small, luminous, spherical UFOs were sighted coming out of a large, bright, cylindrical UFO.

Seventy six years earlier, in March of 1676, in England, Sir Edmond Halley, the astronomer who discovered *Haley's* comet, saw a, "Vast body visually bigger than the moon." He estimated it was 40 miles above him. He also stated that it made a noise, "Like the rattling of a great cart over stones." After estimating the distance it traveled in a matter of minutes, he came to the conclusion that it moved faster than 9,600 miles per hour.

Eight years earlier, in November 1668, in New England, colonial minister Cotton Mather witnessed a star-like point of light passing over the face of the moon while using a telescope.

Five years earlier, in 1663, in Russia, a fiery ball of light stopped over a lake. The noisy object gave off blue smoke, and two beams of light projected ahead of it. Fishermen on the lake were burned by the intense heat. The object disappeared and returned again about one hour later. It was observed by many groups of witnesses.

Nineteen years earlier, in 1644, an alien incursion took place over Boston, Massachusetts. At that time, two bright UFOs were seen in the night sky.

Five years earlier, in March of 1639, another dramatic alien incursion, and possible alien abduction, occurred over the Boston area. That night, three local men boarded a small boat and set out for a trip down the Muddy River. They had been moving downstream for about a mile when the men suddenly sighted a huge, brightly-glowing UFO hovering in the sky.

They recalled that the UFO "flamed up" as it hovered and appeared to be about "three yards square." As the bewildered men watched the UFO, it changed its shape and flew "swift as an arrow" toward the town of Charlton.

The illuminated UFO then flew back and forth in the sky for two or three hours. When the UFO finally disappeared, the men were shocked to find that their boat had somehow been carried against the tide back to the place where they had first started their trip.

According to the Massachusetts colony's governor, many other credible people saw the same UFO at about the same place in the sky that night. Some of the witnesses said the strange light in the sky was occasionally seen shooting out flames and sparks.

In August of 1608, many citizens in the South of France witnessed UFOs over the coastal town of Nice. There were three strange, luminous vessels which revolved at high speed above the city. The three machines stopped near a fortress and descended to just above the ocean where they caused the water to boil and emit a red-orange vapor. Numerous citizens saw two humanoid beings with large heads and large luminous eyes, dressed in a red suit with silver scales, connected to the flying machine by tubes. The aliens were reportedly busy for several hours doing some sort of work.

In 1606, in Japan, a whirling ball of fire was seen hovering over a castle.

In 1577, in Germany, people witnessed, "Objects that came out of the clouds resembling large, tall and wide hats. They landed in great numbers and shown a variety of colors."

On August 7, 1566, in Switzerland, many dark spheres were sighted across the sky above the city of Basle. That day, at dawn, over several hours, many frightened citizens saw the black spheres involved in a formidable aerial battle over their city. According to one report, "We saw many large, black balls which moved at high speed in the air towards the sun, then made half-turns, banging one against the others as if they were fighting a battle. A great number of them became red and flaming. After a while, the flames were consumed and died out."

On April 14, 1561, in Nuremberg, Germany, at dawn, local residents were reportedly terrified by UFOs. The *Nuremberg Gazette* reported that there was a "dreadful apparition" with "cylindrical shapes from which emerged black, red, orange and blue-white spheres that darted about."

Some people reported that the spheres were only about three inches in length, and there were four of them moving together in a square formation. Between these balls, some people saw a number of red crosses. They also reported seeing two large pipes. There were large and small pipes, and attached to that were four or more clusters of three balls. At some point, all the UFOs started fighting against each other.

The events lasted about one hour and had such repercussions that a local artist, Hans Glaser, made a woodcut of it. His artwork showed two immense, black cylinders launching many blue and black spheres, blood red crosses, and flying discs that seemed to fight a battle in the sky. It also indicated that some of these spheres and objects may have crashed outside the city.

In 1529, in Prussia, two burning suns were seen and then a great burning beam landed suddenly. It took off again into the sky, where it became circular in shape.

In 1517, in Romania, a large, blue-glowing disk appeared and remained in the sky for some time.

On October 11, 1492, at about 10:00 p.m., in an area of the Atlantic Ocean now called the Bermuda Triangle, Christopher Columbus witnessed a glowing UFO come out of the water. It vanished and reappeared several times during the night, moving up and down "in sudden and passing gleams." He hurriedly summoned Pedro Gutierrez who also saw the light. After a short time, it vanished only to reappear several times during the night; each time dancing up and down.

In 1463, in Europe, Hermann Schabben painted a picture of a UFO that he had witnessed in the sky.

On November 1, 1461, in France, local residents reported seeing, "A fiery thing like an iron rod of good length, and as large as one half of the moon. It was in the sky for less than a quarter of an hour." This UFO was also described as being "shaped like a ship from which fire was seen flowing."

On September 12, 1271, in Japan, a UFO appeared in the sky just as a Buddhist priest was sentenced to be executed. The UFO resembled a very-bright, full moon, and it illuminated the earth below. The local people considered the UFO to be a bad omen and cancelled the priest's execution.

In 1254, in England, "When the moon was eight days old, a sky ship appeared. It was big, and gracious, and had beautiful, glowing colors."

On September 24, 1235, in Japan, General Yoritsume, and his army, witnessed strange lights in the sky for several hours. The UFOs were described as looking like "stars moving in the wind."

In 1211, in England, "During a Sunday mass, the congregation saw an anchor descend and catch on a tombstone in the churchyard. The churchgoers rushed outside to see a strange ship in the sky with people on board. One occupant of the vessel leaped over the side, but did not fall: as if swimming in water. He made his way through the air toward the anchor. The people on the ground tried to capture him. The man then hurried up to the ship. His companions cut the anchor rope, and the ship then sailed out of sight. The local blacksmith made ornaments from the abandoned anchor to decorate the church lectern."

In 1207, in England, "An aerial ship caught its anchor on a pile of stones. An occupant came down from the ship and managed to free it, however, he was asphyxiated by the atmosphere."

In 1200, in England, "A silvery, flat, shiny, disc-like object appeared near the abbey and frightened everyone near it."

In 1180, in Japan, ancient documents describe, "An unusual shining object seen in the night as a flying earthenware vessel. The object, which had been heading northeast from a mountain in Kii province changed its direction and vanished below the horizon, leaving a luminous trail."

In 1133, in Japan, "A large, silvery disk is reported to have come out of the sky and pass close to the ground."

In 1113, in England, "A group of churchmen were at the coastal town of Christchuch when they were astonished to see 'a dragon' come out of the sea, breathing fire out of its nostrils."

In 1078, in England, "A wild fire appeared in the sky such as no man before remembered seeing and moreover it did harm in many places."

In 1034, in Europe, "A cigar-shaped, fiery object was seen soaring through the sky in a straight course from south to east and then veering toward the setting sun."

In 1015, in Japan, "Two objects in the sky were seen giving birth to smaller, luminous spheres."

In August of 1027, in Egypt, "A number of star-like objects were seen to fly over Cairo and the Nile Delta."

In 927, in France, "The whole eastern part of France saw fiery armies appearing in the sky. Similar phenomena happened several times under King Pepin the Short, under King Charlemagne, and under King Louis I. These sovereign's administrative acts enacted penalties against creatures that travel on aerial ships."

In 919, in Hungary, "An object that looked like a flaming torch was seen in the sky together with spheres which flew over giving out a brighter light than the stars."

In 842, in France, "Multicolored armies were seen in the sky. These sightings of infernal armies were nocturnal."

In 840, in France, "As he was coming out of the Cathedral, an Archbishop saw a mob stoning three men and a woman alleged to have been seen coming from an aerial ship."

In 810, in Germany, the secretary and biographer of King Charlemagne reported that, "A large sphere descended like lightning from the sky. It traveled from east to west and was so bright it made the king's horse rear up so that he fell and injured himself severely."

In 796, in England, "Small globes were seen flying about the Sun."

In 776, in Germany, "As the Saxons were laying siege to the castle of King Charlemagne, flying shields that were reddish in color appeared in the sky and rained down fire on the attacking army."

In 763, in Ireland, "Ships were seen in the air."

In 748, in England, "Ships were seen in the air with their men."

In 747, in China, "Huge, flame-breathing dragons were reported being seen in skies, accompanied by men in airships."

In 746, in England, "Dragons were seen in the heavens."

In 674, in England, "In this year, a thin and tremulous cloud, a kind of rainbow, appeared proceeding from the east and turned into the color of blood."

In 671, in Japan, "A flaming object was seen flying over many villages and districts."

In 664, in England, "At a monastery, a great light appeared in the sky at night and shone over nuns who were singing in the burial ground. They reported that the light lifted up, moved to the other side of the monastery, and then ascended into the night sky. Priests said the light surpassed the brightness of day."

In 650, in India, "One night in the hot season, a man and his wife were sleeping on the roof of their summer house. As the couple slept, a demi-god was seated in his aerial car over head. His gaze suddenly fell upon the woman. The demi-god lowered the car and placed her asleep within. She was abducted and never seen again."

In 643, in Japan, "Five colored banners and umbrellas shone in the sky, and descending, hung over the temple to the sound of strange music."

In 642, in Japan, "On the ninth day of the seventh month, a guest star entered the moon."

In 640, in Japan, "On the seventh day of the second month of spring, a star entered the moon."

In 619, in Japan, "A bright object, like a human figure, was seen over the Gamo River."

In 584, in France, "Strange domes and golden globes raced across the sky."

In 457, in northern France, "A blazing thing like a globe was seen in the sky. Its size was immense, and on its beams hung a ball of fire like a dragon out of whose mouth came two beams of light; one of which stretched beyond France, and the other reached toward Ireland and ended in fire-like rays."

In 398, in the Byzantine Empire, "A thing that looked like a burning globe presenting a sword shown brilliantly in the sky over the city. It seemed almost to touch the earth from the zenith. Such a thing was never recorded to have been seen before by man."

In 393, in the Roman Empire, "Strange lights were seen in the sky. Suddenly, a bright globe appeared at midnight and shone brilliantly near [Venus]. This globe shone a little less brilliantly than the planet, and little by little, a great number of other glowing orbs drew near the first globe.

"The spectacle was like a swarm of bees flying around the beekeeper, and the light of these orbs was as if they were dashing violently against each other. They blended together into one awful flame and bodied forth to the eye as a horrible two-edged sword. The strange globe, which was first seen now appeared like the pommel to a handle, and all the little orbs, fused with the first, shone as brilliantly as the first globe."

In 312, "Constantine and his army witnessed a luminous cross in the heavens."

In 98 A.D., in Rome, "At sunset, a burning shield passed over the sky. It came sparkling from the west and passed over to the east."

In 93 A.D., in England, "Dragons were seen flying in the air."

In 80 A.D., in Scotland, "Wondrous flames were seen in the skies one winter night. Everywhere the air burned, and on many nights, when the weather was serene, a ship was seen in the air moving fast."

On May 21, 70 A.D., Josephus wrote, "A demonic phantom of incredible size appeared in the sky. That day, before sunset, there appeared in the air over the whole country chariots and armed troops coursing through the clouds and surrounding the cities."

In 60 A.D., in Scotland, "A ship was seen speeding across the night sky."

In 9 B.C., in Japan, "Nine moons were seen in the night sky over the community of Kyushu."

In 12 B.C., in Rome, "A comet-like object hovered for days over Rome and then melted into flashes resembling torches."

In 42 B.C., in Rome, "Something like a sort of weapon, or missile, rose with a great noise from the earth and soared into the sky."

In 48 B.C., in Rome, "Thunderbolts had fallen upon Pompey's camp. A fire had appeared in the air over Caesar's camp and had fallen upon Pompey's. Meanwhile, in Syria, two young men announced the result of the battle (in Thessaly) and then vanished."

In 66 B.C., in Rome, "A spark was seen to fall from a star and increase in size as it approached the earth. After becoming as large as the moon it diffused a sort of cloudy daylight and then returning to the sky changed into a torch."

In 73 B.C., in Northern Turkey, while Roman legions were engaged in battle near the Black Sea a huge, flaming object fell from the sky between the two armies. The UFO was said to have a shape like a wine jar and was the color of molten lead.

In 81 B.C., in Central Italy, "A gold-colored fireball fell from the sky to the ground, increased in size, seemed to move off the ground toward the east and was big enough to blot out the sun."

In 85 B.C., in the Roman Empire, "A burning shield scattering sparks ran across the sky."

In 90 B.C., in Rome, "A globe of fire, of golden color, appeared burning in the north with a terrific noise in the sky, then fell, gyrating to the earth. It then seemed to increase in size, rose from the earth, and ascended into the sky where it obscured the disc of the sun with its brilliance."

In 99 B.C., in Rome, "There fell things like a flaming torch in different places from the sky. Towards sunset, a round object like a globe, or round, or circular shield took its path in the sky from west to east."

In 122 B.C., in France, "Three Suns and three moons were seen in the sky."

163 B.C., in Southern Italy, "In Capua, the sun was seen by night. At Formice, two suns were seen by day. The sky was afire. In Cephallenia, a trumpet seemed to sound from the sky. There was a rain of earth. A windstorm demolished houses and laid crops flat in the field. By night an apparent sun shone at Pisaurum."

In 214 B.C., in Northern Italy, "At Hadria an altar was seen in the sky and about it the forms of men in white clothes."

In 218 B.C., in Rome, "Glowing lamps were seen in the sky at Praeneste. A flying shield was observed at Arpi, and in the Amiterno district, the sky was all on fire, and strange men in white garments appeared."

In 222 B.C., in Rome, "Three moons appeared at once."

In 329 B.C., in Central Asia, Alexander the Great is reported to have encountered "two great silver shields" flying in the sky. The two great, silver shields in the sky were "spitting fire around the rims" and diving repeatedly at his army as they were attempting a river crossing. The action so panicked his elephants, horses, and men they had to abandon the river crossing until the following day.

In 332 B.C., in Phoenicia, "During the siege of the trade capital of Phoenicia by the Greeks, a fleet of flying shields is described as having plunged from the sky and crashed upon the city walls."

In 400 B.C., in India, "Blazing discs burned and destroyed an entire city and its inhabitants before returning to the hand of Vishnu."

In 593 B.C., Ezekiel had a close encounter with a UFO and ETs on the Cheber River, in Chaldea which is located in the country now called Iraq.

In 1480 B.C., in Egypt, people witnessed, "A circle of fire that appeared in the sky. After some days, it became larger and shone with the brightness of the sun, extending to the very limits of the heavens."

In 1500 B.C., in Egypt, "Circles of fire are said to have hovered in the sky over the palace while fishes, winged creatures, and other objects, rained down from the sky."

In 2345 B.C., in China, "One day, ten suns appeared in the sky."

In 2500 B.C., in India, "There were aerial dogfights among gods that piloted flying machines called Vimanas."

3000 B.C., in China, "People from the sky descended to Earth on a bright star which was the shape of a saucer."

12000 B.C., in China, ETs apparently came to Earth from Sirius and were called Dropa by the local natives. The Dropa came down from the clouds in "air gliders" and were stranded here. These alien beings left behind strange stone disks with information etched on them. Some of the Dropa reportedly married into local tribes, thus passing on their DNA.

Conclusion

The nation's capital is a relatively small geographic area that allegedly has the most secure airspace in America, or at least that is what we are lead to believe. Although it is unclear why UFOs have visited the East Coast of America more than any other region on Earth, one thing is certain; hundreds of these alien incursions have occurred in Washington, D.C.

The conclusions I have reached during my investigation so far are:

UFOs emit a measurable amount of radiation from a power source that is nuclear or greater. Clearly, the U.S. military has been aware of this fact for decades.

With that controlled energy source, some UFOs are able to warp space (and possibly time) to create what we refer to as a "worm hole" or "Star Gate." However, in the process, immense amounts of radiant energy are released.

UFOs employ an advanced form of field propulsion that allows them to out maneuver all conventional aircraft and weapons systems currently built by humans on earth – including radar. This means that our current prohibitions and restrictions of American airspace are unenforceable when it comes to UFOs. Therefore, alien incursions by UFOs will continue especially in Washington.

In this book, I have closely examined what the citizens of Washington, D.C., and the surrounding area, have reported seeing in the sky from the present to the past. I have sited hundreds of examples of alien incursions of restricted airspace which without the proper authorization, a flight plan, a transponder, or a radio make them legitimate targets for the U.S. military to shoot down on sight. I also interviewed a variety of experts on the implications of UFOs and alien life forms visiting earth to show that this subject impacts a wide range of social issues.

I realize that some people might wonder why they should care about UFOs repeatedly violating U.S. airspace. Well, even though the media has not reported it, in the five years following 9/11 thousands of aerial anomalies have appeared on the radar installations that monitor the restricted and prohibited air space around the nation's capital. The ongoing situation has caused the U.S. military to scramble fighter jets and helicopters hundreds of times every year. Each one of these incidents is considered a serious threat to national security.

It is a matter of record that deadly force can be used to intercept any unauthorized or unidentified craft in restricted/prohibited airspace. A dramatic example of this occurred during the terrorist hijacking of Flight 93 on 9/11. On that day, military jets were ordered to fire on any aircraft that was flying without a transponder or radio.

The official story is that three F-16 fighters were scrambled at 9:24 a.m., and were airborne over Washington, D.C., by 9:40 a.m. Those fighter pilots saw the Pentagon on fire, and at that time the Capitol building was considered a potential target as well. By then, the President had authorized the military to shoot down any unidentified aircraft. The Secret Service had advised the fighter pilots to protect the White House at all costs.

Flight 93 was the only aircraft left in the sky flying off course that fateful morning, and it was heading toward DC with its transponder off. Flight 93 reportedly crashed only 125 miles from DC, in Pennsylvania. Some have argued that it was shot down.

Not being a pilot, I was unaware of all the rules and regulations imposed on air traffic in America. But, as I studied this subject, I could imagine what driving a car would be like if I had to install an operational transponder, file a drive plan and constantly stay in radio contact with other drivers and radar control tower operators while attempting to get to my destination.

I interviewed various aviators about their experiences and was informed that nearly all of the airspace in America is restricted by degrees.

According to the Federal Aviation Administration, all of the sky over the United States, from less than one inch off the ground to outer space, is considered "controlled" American airspace. That airspace is divided into several levels ranging from the least restrictive to the most restrictive or prohibited.

Special use airspace included prohibited areas like the Capitol (designated as P56-A), restricted areas, warning areas, military operations areas, alert areas, and controlled firing areas. In these areas, aeronautical activity is limited usually because of military use or national security concerns.

There are also airport advisory areas, military training routes, and areas where temporary flight restrictions, or prohibitions, apply. For example, temporary flight restrictions are often established over large forest fires to help keep aircraft from straying into hazardous conditions. Smaller, temporary flight restrictions are often issued for presidential movements and some large sporting events, etc.

On August 4, 2005, the *Associated Press* reported that the federal government planned to permanently restrict a large airspace over the Washington, D.C., area. Federal officials also announced they were seeking to make it a criminal offense if a private pilot knowingly entered the new security zone that extended from Maryland to Virginia.

The Federal Aviation Administration told the *Associated Press* that the 9/11 attack on the Pentagon indicated a need for constant vigilance in aviation security. Although there is no current information to suggest that terrorists planned to use airplanes to attack the nation's capital in the future, new security measures were implemented anyway. These security measures included improved radar coverage, anti-aircraft missiles, and a system that used lasers to warn pilots away from restricted airspace.

However, government officials were still concerned that pilots had violated the new security zones hundreds of times since they temporarily restricted airspace over the capital, just before the start of the Iraq war in 2003. In many cases, fighter jets which were authorized to shoot down any unidentified aircraft, had escorted the offending pilots to the nearest airport. And if a pilot was foolish enough not to comply, they would be blown out of the sky with deadly force.

The restricted airspace over the DC area includes an outer ring with a radius of about 30 to 45 miles at an altitude of 18,000 feet. That zone extends east beyond Baltimore, west beyond Dulles International Airport in Virginia, north to Gaithersburg, Maryland and about 30 miles south of Washington, D.C. A plane that flies into that outer zone is required to first file a flight plan, emit a special signal so air traffic controllers can follow it and maintain radio contact with the ground at all times.

An inner zone extends about 15 miles in all directions from the Washington Monument (P56-A) which is the exact area where UFOs were photographed three times in 2002. Most aircraft are strictly prohibited from flying into that area. The Federal Aviation Administration's proposal seeks to allow the government to impose criminal penalties such as fines, and up to one year in prison, for anyone who knowingly or willingly entered the outer zone. Apparently, even though civilian pilots have flown into the outer zone more than 1,600 times from 2003 to 2004, only a few were fined. Pilots that flew into the outer ring would only be fined up to $5,000. Federal lawmakers have proposed raising that penalty and making it mandatory. One proposal sought to revoke the license of a pilot up to five years if they violated the inner security ring (P56-A). They would also be subject to pay up to $100,000 in fines.

Because of this serious state of affairs, on July 21, 2005 a special oversight committee met in Washington, D.C., on the subject of controlling restricted/prohibited airspace. The stated goal of the committee was a detailed assessment of the management and coordination of America's national air defense.

During the meeting, committee Chairman Tom Davis said, "While we are all aware that restricted airspace exists across the National Capital Region, restricted and prohibited airspace is also scattered throughout the United States.

"It includes such obvious places as Camp David, and Crawford, Texas, to military bases. There can also be temporary flight restrictions put in place during certain sporting events, depending on the President's location. It is the responsibility of pilots to be aware of these areas.

"To give you a sense of what we are talking about, we have two maps on display. One map shows all the restricted and prohibited areas in the United States, including military bases. If you look at the coastal areas of the U.S., you can see there is an uninterrupted Air Defense Identification Zone (ADIZ) which encompasses the entire U.S. water border.

"There is also an ADIZ surrounding Alaska and Hawaii. These zones are in place for defensive purposes, and they establish requirements for incoming international flights, including providing an established flight plan before entering the ADIZ.

"The other map shows the restricted airspace over the National Capital Region. In total, the Washington, D.C., restricted air space is approximately 3,000 square miles. The map shows two rings around the region. The inside ring is the Flight Restricted Zone (FRZ) which extends 15 miles around Ronald Reagan National Airport.

"Included within the FRZ is the prohibited airspace over the White House, the National Mall, the U.S. Capitol and the Naval Observatory [P56-A and B.] The outside ring is the ADIZ; a 30-mile radius around Reagan National airport, which spans out to Dulles International airport, Baltimore Washington International airport, and Andrews Air Force Base. At the top left of the map, you can see the bottom of a circle. This is the three mile prohibited airspace for Camp David in Thurmont, Maryland, which would be expanded when the President is at Camp David.

"The situation is quite complicated when we take into account the many departments and agencies involved. That is why we are here today, to better understand how these entities are working to manage and coordinate their efforts to protect and defend the United States' restricted and prohibited airspace.

"One of the best steps taken in this effort was the creation of the National Capital Region Coordination Center (NCRCC). Housed in Herndon, Virginia, the NCRCC is an interagency group that monitors restricted and prohibited airspace 24 hours a day, every day, in and around Washington, D.C. It is the only area of the country with such a center.

"The Department of Defense, the FAA, the Secret Service, Customs and Border Protection, the Department of Homeland Security and the U.S. Capitol Police, along with Transportation Security Administration which acts as the executive agency, are represented at the NCRCC full time. During major events, or surge operations, the Federal Bureau of Investigations, United States Park Police, the Coast Guard, and local law enforcement including Washington, D.C., Police are also NCRCC participants.

"Each agency or department at the NCRCC is responsible for its own mission and jurisdiction as it relates to airspace security. However, the participants work together in identifying aircraft that have violated or may violate prohibited airspace. While the response to each possible aircraft violation is decided by each government entity independently of the others, the information is immediately shared by all participants at the NCRCC. That is our understanding of how it works. However, I know the Government Accountability Office has some concerns about how well the coordination and information sharing actually functions.

"According to NCRCC statistics, from January 27, 2003 to July 17, 2005 there were 3,495 airspace incursions in the National Capital Region. An airspace incursion can include a variety of incidents including penetrations of prohibited airspace. Of the 3,495 incursions, 655 resulted in the decision to launch or divert government assets to intercept an aircraft.

"As many of you know, occasionally these airspace violations lead the Capitol Police, and or the Secret Service, to evacuate the Capitol complex and the White House. While none of us are particularly fond of the evacuations, I think it is important to note that only three times out of 3,495 incursions has that happened.

"Despite the good work of the NCRCC, there are still questions to be asked regarding the government's efforts to secure United States' airspace. In July of 2005, the Government Accounting Office (GAO) released an unclassified version of their report on the interagency management of restricted airspace. The GAO has asked some important questions such as:

How is air defense working without a single government agency taking the lead?

How do we adequately determine a threat to restricted and prohibited airspace when agencies and departments have different definitions of what constitutes a threat?

How will the Department Of Defense, the Federal Aviation Administration, and the Department of Homeland Security continue to work to improve information sharing?

"I believe these are all valid questions that merit discussion, and these agencies will have a chance to respond to the GAO's concerns. In the Washington, D.C., area, we have three commercial airports, countless general aviation airports, and we are pleased to welcome general aviation back to Reagan National. All of this aviation, combined with the flight restrictions, shows that protecting America's airspace, particularly around the nation's capital, is a challenge.

"As the committee responsible for oversight of the federal government, and the District of Columbia, it is our obligation to ensure these agencies are working seamlessly together. A fast, coordinated response is absolutely vital if we are ever again faced with aircraft that have hostile intent."

Intrigued by the above information, I did some research and found that the NCRCC was part of another newly formed federal agency called the Domestic Event Network (DEN) which had been created soon after 9/11. The DEN was designed to function as a nationwide, open-phone line managed by the Federal Aviation Administration from their headquarters in Washington, D.C.

Moreover, the DEN was intended to provide for open and improved communications and common situational awareness for federal agencies with jurisdiction over the security of U.S. airspace. Participants could link to the DEN to give and receive information.

Agencies that participated in the DEN included the National Transportation Safety Board, the Department of Defense, the Federal Aviation Administration (FAA), FAA Field Offices, the National Capitol Police, Immigration and Customs Enforcement, the Secret Service, the Federal Bureau of Investigation and other agencies as necessary.

It is important to note that all these agencies were spending millions of tax dollars each year to supposedly secure the restricted and prohibited airspace over America. This made me wonder, how many federal agencies would it take to secure approximately 3,000 square miles of airspace around Washington, D.C.? According to my math, the answer was an unlucky 13, and they were all apparently unable to stop UFOs from routinely penetrating the controlled airspace over the capital.

After learning which agencies were actually in charge of the restricted and prohibited airspace around the DC area, I decided to call the Capitol Police and ask them a few questions. When the Capitol Police Public Relations officer answered the phone, I identified myself as a freelance journalist that was investigating an incident that occurred at the Capitol on July 16, 2002.

When the officer asked me what this was pertaining to, I explained that I had received photographic evidence indicating that someone actually landed an unidentified vehicle on the Capitol building around 12:30 a.m., on July 16, 2002. After a long pause, he asked me what type of vehicle I was referring to.

When I told him that I could not identify the vehicle in question, it was obvious that he was getting frustrated with me. He then asked what the story was specifically about, so that he could understand my needs and better help me.

I took a deep breath and explained that a professional photographer living and working in Washington, D.C., had sent me some pictures taken at the Capitol. The photographer had been filming in Senate Park between 12:30 p.m. and 1:00 a.m. on July 16, 2002 when he captured images of anomalous objects flying over the Capitol. One of them had briefly landed on the roof of the Capitol.

After a moment of silence, the officer asked what kind of information I was looking for. I told him I wanted to know if the Capitol Police kept logs of anomalous events, because in the photographs it didn't appear that any security personnel were responding to the potential threat.

After a few more moments of silence, the officer told me that any police records they kept were not normally made available to the public. He stressed that he was not saying that anything did or didn't happen on the night in question.

I then explained that I just wanted to give someone in charge of Capitol security the opportunity to officially comment about the event caught on film. I then asked him if someone landed an airborne vehicle on the Capitol building at night, would security personnel respond.

Rather than answer my question, he asked me if we were talking about something the size of a toy or a full-sized aircraft with a person inside of it. I told him that the vehicle in question was about the size of a large SUV, but it was clearly not any kind of known aircraft.

My last statement only brought more silence from the officer. After a few moments, he offered to dig a little deeper to see if he could get any information for me. He then asked me what I specifically wanted to know about and promised to get back to me with some answers. I took that opportunity to ask the following:

>Do members of the Senate or the House work late at night in the Capitol?

>Are Capitol Police on patrol during the entire evening?

>Do security cameras tape events around the Capitol and its perimeter 24 hours a day?

Early one morning, a few days later, I received a phone call from the same public relations officer. His tone was mechanical, and he spoke as if he was reading from a script. The answers he gave me had obviously been cleared by his supervisors. In response to my questions he said:

>Members of the Senate and House will work after hours as long as it takes to get the job done.

>Capitol Police patrol the building and grounds continuously.

>Security cameras are always monitoring the interior and exterior of the Capitol building and its surrounding perimeter.

After spending hundreds of hours investigating this case, I was convinced that an extraterrestrial event of epic proportions had occurred in Washington, D.C., on July 16, 2002. I realized that it was quite possible that some members of the House, the Senate, and military officers, were in the Capitol building working late on that Tuesday night.

It is a matter of public record that many distinguished members of Congress take intelligence briefings in secure rooms on the top floor of the Capitol building. Those briefing rooms are located directly below the roof where a UFO landed on July 16, 2002.

Another interesting bit of information I found regarding the Capitol was reported by UFO researcher Tom Horn. He had interviewed Colonel Jesse Marcel Jr. who was the son of Major Jesse Marcel: the intelligence officer involved in cleaning up the Rosewell UFO debris field in July of 1947.

Regarding the pieces of the alien craft his father had brought home late one night in July of 1947, colonel Marcel said, "What I saw was not of this earth. Though it was material, I held it in my hands, and the pieces were as light as a feather."

Colonel Marcel then went on to describe a strange event that occurred in 1991 while he was in Washington, D.C. When he arrived at his motel, there was a message waiting for him on the phone in his room from an individual that must remain anonymous. This person requested to meet with Marcel the following afternoon, in a specific room, at the Capitol building.

Although Marcel felt uneasy, he agreed to the clandestine meeting. When he arrived, he was ushered into the office of this individual. This person wanted to talk to Marcel about the Roswell UFO crash event. He then asked Marcel if he would be more comfortable having a conversation "in a secure room." When Marcel explained that he wouldn't discuss anything he hadn't said before, the government employee once again suggested that they use a secure room. He said, "Well, maybe I want to tell you something you don't already know."

After leaving the office, they proceeded downstairs to a secure room where allegedly no listening devices existed. Marcel described the area as, "The dungeons of the Capitol building." This meant they were somewhere in the sub-basement of the Capitol: the same area that dead aliens and a dismantled UFO were reportedly stored in the past.

When the two men sat down at a table, Marcel noticed a book about alien abductions, UFO technology and Roswell. The government insider tapped on the book with his finger and said, "This is not fiction." He continued talking for a while and then asked Marcel if he knew where the material recovered from the Roswell ranch was being kept. Marcel found the question curious and replied, "No. Don't you?"

The man's answer was so strange Marcel then asked, "If extra-terrestrial activity is real, and you guys know it, when is the government planning official disclosure of what really happened at Roswell?"

The anonymous individual thought for a moment then said, "If it was up to me, we would be doing it now."

Oddly enough, on September 18, 2006, just before 8:00 a.m., a 20-year-old man from the District of Columbia stole a car and drove at high speed to the Capitol. When he arrived in front of the Capitol, he drove the stolen car through a construction barrier. He then jumped out of the car and ran up the steps of the Capitol and found his way inside through an unlocked, third-story door. He then ran downstairs into the Capitol sub-basement where he was captured. At that time, he suffered a seizure and was taken to a local hospital.

The police reported that the man later told them he was "being chased by the devil," or "the demons." Although it is a matter of interpretation, it is quite possible that the young man encountered a UFO or an alien. He was obviously scared out of his mind and was trying to get to a safe location. However, in my opinion, the U.S. Capitol is the last place a person should go to get away from demonic or alien beings.

In fact, exactly two weeks earlier, on September 4, 2006, a UFO was videotaped hovering over the Capitol. The image of the strange, glowing, disc-shaped craft was inadvertently broadcast for a few seconds by Channel 5, *FOX News* in Washington, D.C., during their 10:00 p.m. broadcast. The story they reported was that the Senate was back in session to discuss minimum wage. The producers at *FOX* had no idea that the UFO hovering over the Capitol was the real story.

According to a national *Roper* poll taken in August of 2002 (just one month after UFOs were photographed landing on Capitol Hill) 72 percent of Americans believe that the government had not told them everything it knows about UFOs. The poll also found that 68 percent of the U.S. population felt that their government knows more about ETs than they will admit.

I found it interesting that slightly more men than women believe such information should be shared with the public. The poll also found that 80 percent of people 18 to 24 years old felt that UFO information should be released and that 75 percent of people 25 to 34 years old and

73 percent of those 35 to 49 years old agreed that this information should be released. Apparently, the younger a person is, the stronger their belief that the government should share information about UFOs and ETs with the public.

A total of 53 percent of the respondents said that their level of trust in the government had remained stable over the past five years, while 29 percent said that they trusted the government less than they did five years ago. A 55 percent majority of the respondents said that the government was not sharing enough information with the public in general.

It is interesting to note that on average, 60 percent of the people surveyed felt that the U.S. government should not withhold information about UFO sightings. Incredibly, 58 percent of the people polled believed that the government should report encounters with extraterrestrial life when national security is not an issue.

The statistics indicated that a majority of Americans were ready, willing, and able to cope with the reality of UFOs and ETs visiting earth. One can only hope that our world leaders will recognize that it is time to publicly address this important issue especially as it relates to Washington, D.C.

To discover the rest of the shocking, bizarre, hidden history of UFOs and ETs in Washington I urge you to read my second book on this extremely-sensitive subject, *Covert Encounters in Washington, D.C.*

UFO SIGHTINGS IN WASHINGTON, D.C.

1850
1897
1930s
1942
1943
March, 1946
July 3, 5, 6, 1947
April 30, 1948
July 24, 1948
November 18, 1948
April 9, 1950
June 25, 27, 1950
November 18, 1951
February 13, 1952
April 2, 1952
May 15, 23, 1952
June 7, 20, 21,1952
July 1, 7, 18, 19, 20, 26, 27, 28, 1952
Sometime in July, 1952
August 5, 6, 13, 15, 1952
September 20, 1952
November 10, 15, 30, 1952
February 9, 23, 1953
July 25, 1953
October 10, 1953
January 29, 1954
May 5, 6, 7, 1954
May 11, 13, 16, 1954
June 12, 13, 14, 25, 1954
July 19, 26, 29, 1954
August 4, 17, 1954
September 6, 1954
June 25, 26, 1955
July 6, 1955
September 7, 1955
October 7, 13, 1955
March 5, 16, 20, 1956
May 14, 1956
June 14, 28, 1956
August 10, 1956
September 4, 1956
November 28, 1956
April of 1957
May 2, 1957
July 9, 1957
August 2, 1957
September 26, 1957
October 20, 1957
November 7, 1957
September 29, 1958
December 1, 1958
February 5, 1959

June 4, 1959
July 6, 1959
August 2, 1959
Sometime in 1961
June 18, 1961
September 22, 1961
December 13, 1961
June 19, 28, 1962
February 5, 6, 1963
June of 1963
December 12, 1963
March 28, 1964
May 30, 1964
September 1964
December 29, 1964
January 3, 11, 25, 1965
February 21, 1965
March 6, 23, 1965
March 1965
April 29, 1965
May 25, 1965
June 26, 1965
July 21, 31, 1965
August of 1965
August 1, 1966
October 28, 1966
November 11, 1966
April 3, 1967
July 9, 17, 1967
August 22, 23, 1967
September 14, 1967
December 16, 1967
January of 1968
February of 1968
March 12, 1968
July 21, 1969
October 30, 1973
November 16, 1973
October 17, 1974
October of 1988
April 13, 1992
Early 1990's
July 11, 1993
August 21, 1995
October 15, 16, 1995
April 3, 1997
July 28, 1997
May 22, 1998
July 24, 1998
April 14, 1999
June 6, 1999
August 14, 1999
January 1, 2000

March 3, 2000
Sometime in 2000
September 29, 2000
May 11, 12, 2001
September of 2001
November of 2001
December 14, 2001
July 4, 16, 20, 26, 30, 31, 2002
August 16, 2002
September of 2002
September 8, 2002
November 11, 19, 2002
December 16, 2002
January 27, 2003
March 8, 2003
July 22, 2003
March of 2004
March of 2004
March 13, 2004
April 15, 2004
May 21, 2004
May of 2004
July 17, 2004
August 31, 2004
September 28, 29, 2004
October 31, 2004
November 30, 2004
December 7, 8, 9, 2004
February 12, 23, 2005
April 27, 2005
May 2, 2005
May 22, 2005
June 14, 2005
July 14, 27, 2005
October 26, 2005
December 6, 2005
January 1, 2006
Early 2006
February 15, 2006
March 15, 2006
April 5, 15, 2006
April of 2006
May 4, 17, 26, 2006
July 24, 2006
September 4, 2006

Index

Made in the USA
Middletown, DE
24 September 2023

39244337R00216